Kaplan Publishing are constantly finding new difference to your studies and our exciting o offer something different to students looking

This book comes with free MyKaplan online study anytime, anywhere. **This free online resource is not sold separately and is included in the price of the book.**

Having purchased this book, you have access to the following online study materials:

CONTENT	ACCA (including FBT, FMA, FFA)		FIA (excluding FBT, FMA, FFA)	
	Text	Kit	Text	Kit
Electronic version of the book	✓	✓	✓	✓
Knowledge checks with instant answers		✓		✓
Material updates	✓	✓	✓	✓
Latest official ACCA exam questions*		✓		
Timed questions with an online tutor debrief using video icon***		✓		
Consolidation Test including questions and answers	✓		✓	

* Excludes BT, MA, FA, FBT, FMA, FFA; for all other papers includes a selection of questions, as released by ACCA

*** Excludes BT, MA, FA, LW, FBT, FMA and FFA

How to access your online resources

Kaplan Financial students will already have a MyKaplan account and these extra resources will be available to you online. You do not need to register again, as this process was completed when you enrolled. If you are having problems accessing online materials, please ask your course administrator.

If you are not studying with Kaplan and did not purchase your book via a Kaplan website, to unlock your extra online resources please go to www.mykaplan.co.uk/addabook (even if you have set up an account and registered books previously). You will then need to enter the ISBN number (on the title page and back cover) and the unique pass key number contained in the scratch panel below to gain access. You will also be required to enter additional information during this process to set up or confirm your account details.

If you purchased through the Kaplan Publishing website you will automatically receive an e-mail invitation to MyKaplan. Please register your details using this email to gain access to your content. If you do not receive the e-mail or book content, please contact Kaplan Publishing.

Your Code and Information

This code can only be used once for the registration of one book online. This registration and your online content will expire when the final sittings for the examinations covered by this book have taken place. Please allow one hour from the time you submit your book details for us to process your request.

Please scratch the film to access your unique code.

Please be aware that this code is case-sensitive and you will need to include the dashes within the passcode, but not when entering the ISBN.

ACCA Diploma in Financial and Management Accounting (RQF Level 2)

FA1

Recording Financial Transactions

STUDY TEXT

KAPLAN PUBLISHING'S STATEMENT OF PRINCIPLES

LINGUISTIC DIVERSITY, EQUALITY AND INCLUSION

We are committed to diversity, equality and inclusion and strive to deliver content that all users can relate to.

We are here to make a difference to the success of every learner.

Clarity, accessibility and ease of use for our learners are key to our approach.

We will use contemporary examples that are rich, engaging and representative of a diverse workplace.

We will include a representative mix of race and gender at the various levels of seniority within the businesses in our examples to support all our learners in aspiring to achieve their potential within their chosen careers.

Roles played by characters in our examples will demonstrate richness and diversity by the use of different names, backgrounds, ethnicity and gender, with a mix of sexuality, relationships and beliefs where these are relevant to the syllabus.

It must always be obvious who is being referred to in each stage of any example so that we do not detract from clarity and ease of use for each of our learners.

We will actively seek feedback from our learners on our approach and keep our policy under continuous review. If you would like to provide any feedback on our linguistic approach, please use this form (you will need to enter the link below into your browser).

https://docs.google.com/forms/d/1Vc4mltBPrfViy8AhfyKcJMHQKBmLaLPoa_WPqFNf4Ml/edit

We will seek to devise simple measures that can be used by independent assessors to randomly check our success in the implementation of our Linguistic Equality, Diversity and Inclusion Policy.

British Library Cataloguing-in-Publication Data

A catalogue record for this book is available from the British Library.

Published by:

Kaplan Publishing UK
Unit 2 The Business Centre
Molly Millars Lane
Wokingham
RG41 2QZ

ISBN: 978-1-83996-102-1

© Kaplan Financial Limited, 2022

Printed and bound in Great Britain.

Acknowledgments

These materials are reviewed by the ACCA examining team. The objective of the review is to ensure that the material properly covers the syllabus and study guide outcomes, used by the examining team in setting the exams, in the appropriate breadth and depth. The review does not ensure that every eventuality, combination or application of examinable topics is addressed by the ACCA Approved Content. Nor does the review comprise a detailed technical check of a the content as the Approved Content Provider has its own quality assurance processes in place in this respect.

We are grateful to the Association of Chartered Certified Accountants for permission to reproduce past examination questions. The answers have been prepared by Kaplan Publishing.

All rights reserved. No part of this publication may be reproduced, stored in a retrieval system, or transmitted, in any form or by any means, electronic, mechanical, photocopying, recording or otherwise, without the prior written permission of Kaplan Publishing.

The text in this material and any others made available by any Kaplan Group company does not amount to advice on a particular matter and should not be taken as such. No reliance should be placed on the content as the basis for any investment or other decision or in connection with any advice given to third parties. Please consult your appropriate professional adviser as necessary. Kaplan Publishing Limited and all other Kaplan group companies expressly disclaim all liability to any person in respect of any losses or other claims, whether direct, indirect, incidental, consequential or otherwise arising in relation to the use of such materials.

CONTENTS

	Page
Introduction	P.5
Syllabus and study guide	P.7
The examination	P.11
Study skills and revision guidance	P.13

Chapter

1	Business transactions	1
2	Types of business documentation	13
3	Double entry bookkeeping	37
4	Banking: payments and receipts	73
5	Sales and sales records	105
6	Recording sales	135
7	Purchases and purchase records	157
8	Recording purchases	181
9	Recording receipts and payments	191
10	Maintaining petty cash records	213
11	Payroll	233
12	Bank reconciliations	263
13	Control accounts	281
14	The trial balance	307
Answers to activities and exam-style questions		331
Index		385

Quality and accuracy are of the utmost importance to us so if you spot an error in any of our products, please send an email to mykaplanreporting@kaplan.com with full details.

Our Quality Co-ordinator will work with our technical team to verify the error and take action to ensure it is corrected in future editions.

INTRODUCTION

This is the new edition of the Foundations in Accountancy study text for FA1, *Recording Financial Transactions,* approved by the ACCA and fully updated and revised according to the examiner's comments.

Tailored to fully cover the syllabus, this study text has been written specifically for Foundations level students. A clear and comprehensive style, numerous examples and highlighted key terms help you to acquire the information easily. Plenty of activities and self-test questions enable you to practise what you have learnt.

At the end of most of the chapters you will find multiple-choice questions. These are exam-style questions and will give you a very good idea of the way you will be tested.

ACCA SUPPORT

For additional support with your studies please also refer to the ACCA Global website.

SYLLABUS AND STUDY GUIDE

Position of this examination syllabus in the overall syllabus

No prior knowledge is required before commencing study for FA1. The syllabus content for FA1 provides the basic techniques required to enable candidates to prepare financial statements for various enterprises at a later stage. Candidates will, therefore, need a sound knowledge of the methods and techniques introduced in this examination syllabus to ensure they can employ them in later studies and examinations. The methods used in this syllabus are extended in FA2, *Maintaining Financial Records,* and further developed in FA, *Financial Accounting.*

Syllabus

A TYPES OF BUSINESS TRANSACTION AND DOCUMENTATION

1 Types of business transaction

(a) Understand a range of business transactions including:

  (i) Sales
  (ii) Purchases
  (iii) Receipts
  (iv) Payments
  (v) Petty cash
  (vi) Payroll **Ch's 2 – 5**

(b) Understand the various types of discount including where applicable the effect that trade discounts have on sales tax **Ch's 5 & 9**

(c) Describe the processing and security procedures relating to the use of:

  (i) Cash
  (ii) Cheques
  (iii) Credit and debit cards
  (iv) Debit cards for receipts and payments and electronic payment methods. **Ch's 2 & 4**

2 Types of business documentation

(a) Outline the purpose and content of a range of business documents to include but not limited to:

  (i) Invoice
  (ii) Credit note
  (iii) Remittance advice **Ch's 2 & 5**

(b) Prepare the financial documents to be sent to credit customers including:

  (i) Sales invoices
  (ii) Credit notes
  (iii) Statements of account. **Ch's 2 & 5**

(c) Prepare remittance advices to accompany payments to suppliers. **Ch. 2**

(d) Prepare a petty cash voucher including the sales tax element of an expense when presented with an inclusive amount. **Ch's 2 & 10**

3 Process of recording business transactions within the accounting system

(a) Identify the characteristics of accounting data and the sources of accounting data records, showing understanding of how the accounting data and records meet the business' requirements. **Ch's 1 & 2**

(b) Understand how users can locate, display and check accounting data records to meet user requirements and understand how data entry errors are dealt with. **Ch's 1 & 2**

(c) Outline the tools and techniques used to process accounting transactions and period-end routines and consider how errors are identified and dealt with. **Ch. 14 (and throughout)**

(d) Consider the risks to data security, data protection procedures and the storage of data. **Ch. 2**

(e) Understand the principles of coding in entering accounting transactions, including

  (i) describing the need for a coding system for financial transactions within a double entry bookkeeping system
  (ii) describe the use of a coding system within a filing system. **Ch. 3**

(f) Code sales invoices, supplier invoices and credit notes ready for entry into the books of prime entry. **Ch's 3, 5 & 7**

(g) Describe the accounting documents and management reports produced by computerised accounting systems and understand the link between the accounting system and other systems in the business. **Ch's 3, 6 & 9**

B DUALITY OF TRANSACTIONS AND THE DOUBLE ENTRY SYSTEM

1 Books of prime entry

(a) Outline the purpose and content of the books of prime entry including their format. **Ch. 3**

(b) Explain how transactions are entered in the books of prime entry. **Ch's 3 & 5**

(c) Outline how the books of prime entry integrate with the double entry bookkeeping system. **Ch's 5 & 7**

(d) Enter transactions including the sales tax effect where applicable into the books of prime entry. **Ch's 5 & 7**

2 Double entry system

(a) Define the accounting equation. **Ch. 3**

(b) Understand and apply the accounting equation. **Ch. 3**

(c) Understand how the accounting equation relates to the double entry bookkeeping system. **Ch. 3**

(d) Process financial transactions from the books of prime entry into the double entry bookkeeping system **Ch's 5 - 11**

3 The journal **Ch's 3, 13 & 14**

(a) Understand the use of the journal including the reasons for, content and format of the journal.

(b) Prepare journal entries directly from transactions, books of prime entry as applicable or to correct errors.

4 Elements of the financial statements **Ch. 3**

(a) Define and distinguish between the elements of the financial statements.

(b) Identify the content of a statement of financial position and statement of profit or loss and other comprehensive income.

C BANK SYSTEM AND TRANSACTIONS

1 The banking process **Ch. 4**

(a) Explain the differences between the services offered by banks and banking institutions.

(b) Describe how the banking clearing system works.

(c) Identify and compare different forms of payment.

(d) Outline the processing and security procedures relating the use of cash, cheques, credit cards, debit cards for receipts and payments and electronic payment methods.

2 Documentation **Ch. 2**

(a) Explain why it is important for an organisation to have a formal document retention policy.

(b) Identify the different categories of documents that may be stored as part of a document retention policy.

D PAYROLL **Ch. 11**

1 Process payroll transactions within the accounting system

(a) Prepare and enter the journal entries in the general ledger to process payroll transactions including:

   (i) Calculation of gross wages for employees paid by the hour, paid by output and salaried workers

   (ii) Accounting for payroll costs and deductions

   (iii) The employers' responsibilities for taxes, state benefit contributions and other deductions

(b) Identify the different payment methods in a payroll system, e.g. cash, cheques, automated payment.

(c) Explain why authorisation of payroll transactions and security of payroll information is important in an organisation.

E LEDGER ACCOUNTS

1 Prepare ledger accounts

(a) Enter transactions from the books of prime entry into the ledgers. **Ch's 5 - 11**

(b) Record journal entries in the ledger accounts. **Ch's 3, 13 & 14**

(c) Balance and close off ledger accounts. **Ch's 3, 13 & 14**

F CASH AND BANK

1 Maintaining a cash book Ch. 9

(a) Record transactions within the cashbook, including any sales tax effect where applicable.

(b) Prepare the total, balance and cross cast cash book columns.

(c) Identify and deal with discrepancies.

2 Maintaining a petty cash book Ch. 10

(a) Enter and analyse petty cash transactions in the petty cash book including any sales tax effect where applicable.

(b) Balance off the petty cash book using imprest and non imprest systems.

(c) Reconcile the petty cash book with cash in hand.

(d) Prepare and account for petty cash reimbursement.

G SALES AND CREDIT TRANSACTIONS

1 Recording sales Ch. 5

(a) Record sales transactions taking into account:

　(i) various types of discount

　(ii) sales tax

　(iii) the impact on the sales tax ledger account where applicable

(b) Prepare the financial documents to be sent to credit customers.

2 Customer account balances and control accounts

(a) Understand the purpose of an aged receivable analysis. Ch. 6

(b) Produce statements of account to be sent to credit customers. Ch. 6

(c) Explain the need to deal with discrepancies quickly and professionally. Ch. 6

(d) Prepare the receivables control account or receivables ledgers by accounting for:

　(i) sales

　(ii) sales returns

　(iii) payments from customers including checking the accuracy and validity of receipts against relevant supporting information

　(iv) discounts

　(v) irrecoverable debt and allowances for irrecoverable debts including any effect of sales tax where applicable.

Ch's 6 & 13

H PURCHASES AND CREDIT TRANSACTIONS

1 Recording purchases Ch. 7

(a) Record purchase transactions taking into account:

　(i) various types of discount

　(ii) sales tax

　(iii) the impact of the sales tax ledger account where applicable

(b) Enter supplier invoices and credit notes into the appropriate book of prime entry.

2 Supplier balances and reconciliations

(a) Prepare the payables control account or payables ledgers by accounting for:

　(i) purchases

　(ii) purchase returns

　(iii) payments to suppliers including checking the accuracy and validity of the payment against relevant supporting information

　(iv) discounts **Ch's 8 & 13**

I RECONCILIATION Ch's 12 & 13

1 Purpose of control accounts and reconciliation

(a) Describe the purpose of control accounts as a checking devise to aid management and help identify bookkeeping errors.

(b) Explain why it is important to reconcile control accounts regularly and deal with discrepancies quickly and professionally.

2 Reconcile the cash book

(a) Reconcile a bank statement with the cash book.

3 Reconcile the receivables control account

(a) Reconcile the balance on the receivables control account with the list of balances.

4 Reconcile the payables control account

(a) Reconcile the balance on the payables control account with the list of balances.

J PREPARING THE TRIAL BALANCE   Ch. 14

1 Prepare the trial balance

(a) Prepare ledger balances, clearly showing the balances carried down and brought down as appropriate.

(b) Extract an initial trial balance.

2 Correcting errors

(a) Identify types of error in a bookkeeping system that are disclosed by extracting a trial balance.

(b) Identify types of error in a bookkeeping system that are not disclosed by extracting a trial balance.

(c) Use the journal to correct errors disclosed by the trial balance.

(d) Use the journal to correct errors not disclosed by the trial balances.

(e) Identify when a suspense account is required and clear the suspense account using the journal.

(f) Redraft the trial balance following correction of all errors.

THE EXAMINATION

Format of the examination

	Number of marks
50 multiple-choice questions (2 marks each)	100

Time allowed: 2 hours

This is a computer-based examination.

Computer-based examinations

- Be sure you understand how to use the **software** before you start the exam. If in doubt, ask the assessment centre staff to explain it to you.

- Questions are **displayed on the screen** and answers are entered using keyboard and mouse. At the end of the examination, you are given a certificate showing the result you have achieved.

- **Multiple choice questions** may ask for numerical answers, but could also involve paragraphs of text which require you to select a narrative, rather than numerical, answer. This could be, for example, requiring you to select the correct definition from several possible answers.

- **Don't panic** if you realise you've answered a question incorrectly – you can always go back and change your answer.

Answering the questions

Multiple-choice questions – read the questions carefully and work through any calculations required. This examination comprises a mixture of narrative and computational questions.

If you don't know the answer, eliminate those options you know are incorrect and see if the answer becomes more obvious. Remember that only one answer to a multiple-choice question can be right!

If you get stuck with a question skip it and return to it later. Answer every question – if you do not know the answer, you do not lose anything by guessing. Towards the end of the examination spend the last five minutes reading through your answers and making any corrections.

Equally divide the time you spend on questions. In a two-hour examination that has 50 questions you have about 2.4 minutes per a question.

Do not treat multiple-choice questions as an easy option. **Do not skip any part of the syllabus** and make sure that you have *learnt* definitions, *know* key words and their meanings and importance, and *understand* the names and meanings of rules, concepts and theories.

STUDY SKILLS AND REVISION GUIDANCE

Preparing to study

SET YOUR OBJECTIVES

Before starting to study decide what you want to achieve – the type of pass you wish to obtain.

This will decide the level of commitment and time you need to dedicate to your studies.

DEVISE A STUDY PLAN

Determine when you will study.

Split these times into study sessions.

Put the sessions onto a study plan making sure you cover the course, course assignments and revision.

Stick to your plan!

Effective study techniques

Use the **SQR3** method

Survey the chapter – look at the headings and read the introduction, summary and objectives. Get an overview of what the text deals with.

Question – during the survey, ask yourself the questions that you hope the chapter will answer for you.

Read through the chapter thoroughly, answering the questions and meeting the objectives. Attempt the exercises and activities, and work through all the examples.

Recall – at the end of the chapter, try to recall the main ideas of the chapter without referring to the text. Do this a few minutes after the reading stage.

Review – check that your recall notes are correct.

Use the **MURRED** method

Mood – set the right mood.

Understand – issues covered and make note of any uncertain bits.

Recall – stop and put what you have learned into your own words.

Review – go over the material you covered to consolidate the knowledge.

Expand – read relevant articles and newspapers.

Digest – go back and reconsider the information.

While studying…

Summarise the key points of the chapter.

Make linear notes – a list of headings, divided up with subheadings listing the key points. Use different colours to highlight key points and keep topic areas together.

Try mind-maps – put the main heading in the centre of the paper and encircle it. Then draw short lines radiating from this to the main sub-headings, which again have circles around them. Continue the process from the sub-headings to sub-sub-headings, etc.

Revision

The best approach to revision is to **revise the course as you work through it**.

Also try to leave **four to six weeks before the exam for final revision**.

Make sure you **cover the whole syllabus**.

Pay special attention to **those areas where your knowledge is weak**.

If you are stuck on a topic find somebody (a tutor) to explain it to you.

Read around the subject – read good newspapers and professional journals, especially ACCA's *Student Accountant* – this can give you an advantage in the exam.

Read through the text and your notes again. Maybe put key revision points onto index cards to look at when you have a few minutes to spare.

Practise exam-standard questions under timed conditions. Attempt all the different styles of questions you may be asked to answer in your exam.

Review any assignments you have completed and look at where you lost marks – put more work into those areas where you were weak.

Ensure you **know the structure of the exam** – how many questions and of what type they are.

Chapter 1

BUSINESS TRANSACTIONS

This chapter introduces the common types of business transaction. Later chapters will look at how transactions are recorded, how accounting records are controlled and how the accuracy of these is scrutinised.

CONTENTS

1. Types of business transaction
2. Cash and credit transactions
3. Terminology
4. Petty cash
5. Payroll
6. Keeping a record
7. Key personnel
8. Control over transactions
9. Timing of transactions

LEARNING OUTCOMES

At the end of this chapter, you should be able to:

- understand the main types of transaction that a business is likely to undertake
- distinguish between cash and credit transactions
- distinguish between transactions in goods and in services
- distinguish between receipts and payments and income and expenditure
- understand the need to document business transactions
- identify the key personnel involved in initiating, processing and completing transactions
- understand the need for effective control over transactions
- identify the timing of various transactions.

1 TYPES OF BUSINESS TRANSACTION

Every business sells goods or services to customers and gets paid for what it sells. Every business buys goods and services from suppliers, and pays for what it buys.

For example, retail businesses such as department stores and supermarkets have to buy goods for resale to shoppers, and a garage has to buy car parts and components to do repairs on customers' cars. Businesses buy stationery and computers for their office work.

Many businesses have employees, and have to pay for their labour.

All businesses incur expenses for various services, such as the supply of electricity, telephone services, property rental costs and local taxation (business rates).

2 CASH AND CREDIT TRANSACTIONS

Most business transactions for buying and selling goods or services are either cash transactions or credit transactions.

- With a **cash transaction**, the buyer pays for the item either upon exchange of goods/services or they pay in advance. For example, sales in a shop or supermarket are cash transactions, because the customer pays at the cash desk or check-out point.

- With a **credit transaction**, the buyer doesn't have to pay for the item on receipt, but is allowed some time (a 'credit period') before having to make the payment.

Example of a credit transaction

Velocity Book Publishers places an order with a printing company, Q Print, to print 5,000 copies of a new book they are publishing. Q Print agree to print the books and Velocity Book Publishers will be given up to 60 days to pay after the books have been printed. Q Print delivers the books into the warehouse of Velocity Book Publishers on 1 March, and submits a demand for payment (known as an invoice) for $15,000, payable on or before 1 May.

This is a credit transaction because Velocity Book Publishers does not have to pay for the purchased items when it orders the books, nor even when the books are received. Instead, it has been given time to pay after the goods have been received.

Most transactions between two businesses are credit transactions. In other words, businesses usually buy from other businesses and sell to other businesses on credit. The credit terms, such as how long the buyer has to pay, are agreed between the buyer and the supplier in advance.

	Cash	Credit
Sale	Goods or a service are provided and the customer pays immediately.	Goods or a service are provided and the customer pays later.
Purchase	Goods or a service are purchased and paid for immediately.	Goods or a service are purchased and paid for later.

ACTIVITY 1

A client is given a haircut by a self-employed hairdresser. The client pays for this with $20 cash.

1 What kind of transaction is this from the client's perspective?

- A The sale of goods by the hairdresser
- B The sale of a service by the client
- C The purchase of goods by the hairdresser
- D The purchase of a service by the client

2 What kind of transaction is this from the hairdresser's point of view?

- A A cash sale
- B A credit sale
- C A cash purchase
- D A credit purchase

For a suggested answer, see the 'Answers' section at the end of the book.

Every purchase from one person or firm's point of view is a sale from the view of the other party to the transaction. The purchaser makes payment and seller receives it in exchange for the goods or services supplied.

3 TERMINOLOGY

Precise terminology is important in bookkeeping and accounts. Key terms are given at the end of each chapter to highlight appropriate terminology. It is important to be clear on the following:

- **Sales** – the exchange of goods or services for money. Terms such as commission and fees are also used instead of sales for some services.

- **Purchases** – buying goods for resale or consumption.

- **Receipts** – money received, often but not exclusively, from cash sales.

- **Payments** – money paid out in cash or by cheque or other form of bank payment as described below.

- **Income** – a more general term than sales including also interest received, rent received from letting part of the business premises and so on.

- **Expenses** – indicates money spent for rent, electricity for lighting, telephone accounts and so on. This does not include purchases of goods for resale.

- **Expenditure** – includes purchases, expenses and money spent on buying anything else for the organisation.

FA1: RECORDING FINANCIAL TRANSACTIONS

3.1 METHODS OF PAYMENT

You need to know about the different methods of receiving payments from customers, or making payments to a supplier. Four common methods of receiving payments and making payments are used in many businesses:

- payments in 'cash', in other words, in notes and coins

- payments by debit and credit cards and electronic payment methods

- payments by cheque

- automated receipts and payments through the business bank accounts. Examples are standing orders and direct debits.

Receiving and making payments by each of these methods will be described in later chapters.

4 PETTY CASH

Most businesses prefer to make as few payments in notes and coins ('cash') as possible. It is more secure to pay by cheque or online because there is less risk of loss or theft. However, sometimes it is more convenient, or even necessary, to make payment in cash.

Examples of items that might be paid for by a business in cash might include the following:

- payment for small office expenses such as coffee, biscuits, stamps etc

- payment for taxi fares for business purposes

- payment for travel costs such as rail and bus for business purposes

- payment for flowers to send to an employee who is off sick.

A small amount in cash is held on business premises for such purposes. In a business that rarely makes cash transactions, such as a large engineering firm, this is convenient. In the type of business that regularly handles cash such as a restaurant, it is useful to keep a small amount of petty cash separate from income received from sales. This makes it easier to reconcile the cash received with the records of meals served and investigate any discrepancies than it would be if a number of employees were able to take cash from the sales income to spend on various expenses at any time.

5 PAYROLL

Many businesses have employees who are paid by the employer for the work they do. Most employers will have a set day on which employees should be paid, and it is the payroll department's responsibility to ensure that wages are paid on the correct due days.

Weekly paid employees (wage earners) will be paid at least once a week, normally on the same day each week. Commonly the pay day will be either Thursday or Friday if the working week is from Monday to Friday.

Monthly paid employees (salary earners) will be paid once a month, and there will be a formula for determining the pay day. For example, this may be:

- the last day of the calendar month
- the last Thursday or Friday of the calendar month
- the same date each month, such as the 26th.

Employees may be paid their wages in several ways:

- in cash
- by cheque
- by bank transfer
- through the Banks Automated Clearing System (BACS).

Making payments by these methods will be described in later chapters.

The payroll department also makes payments to outside agencies, such as tax and social services authorities and pension schemes.

ACTIVITY 2

1. Which of the following terms would be used to classify a payment for electricity to heat the business premises of a firm of plumbers?

    A   Expense

    B   Purchase

    C   Receipt

    D   Sales

2. Which of the following would be paid for by petty cash?

    A   Car repairs on the business owner's private vehicle

    B   Packet of envelopes at local store

    C   Paying a supplier for goods bought on credit

    D   Wages and salaries

3. Which of the following transactions are associated with payroll?

    A   Income from cash sale of computer used to calculate salaries

    B   Postage and stationery, office expenses

    C   Taxes on employee income, pension scheme payments, wages

    D   Credit purchase of safety equipment for delivery staff

For a suggested answer, see the 'Answers' section at the end of the book.

6 KEEPING A RECORD

A business keeps detailed records of its sales, purchases, receipts and payments. There are several reasons for keeping records.

- A business needs to keep track of how much it owes to its suppliers and how much it is owed by credit customers.

- Records of sales and purchases are useful in the event of a query or dispute with a customer or supplier.

- Keeping records of transactions means that checks can be carried out to make sure that they have been processed honestly, and that there have been no mistakes or fraud.

- Keeping records of sales, purchases and other expenses allows a business to monitor how well it is performing, and whether it is making a profit or a loss.

Similar reasons apply to keeping petty cash records. Payroll records must also be maintained to ensure that employees are properly rewarded for their work and to ensure that correct deductions are made.

Transactions are recorded in accounts. The system of recording transactions is therefore called the accounting system or the bookkeeping system. The system organises transactions into sets of structured ledger accounts. Accounting records will be explained in later chapters.

To maintain records, it is important to maintain documents providing evidence of transactions. Chapter 2 looks at these documents in some depth.

7 KEY PERSONNEL

In most businesses it is likely that a number of different people will be involved in different types of business transaction.

For example, in a department store, the sales will be made by the shop floor assistants. The purchases of goods for resale will be made by the departmental buyers. The general expenses will be paid by the accounts department, the wages by the payroll department and any purchases of equipment will probably be made by the store manager.

In a large organisation the number of people involved in business transactions may be in the thousands so it is important to have a system on control over the amount they spend or authorise to prevent the organisation getting into difficulties. Senior management authorise the larger items of expenditure because they have greater knowledge of the business policy and precise financial position of the organisation.

8 CONTROL OVER TRANSACTIONS

If so many people in an organisation are involved in so many different types of transaction then it is important that these transactions are properly controlled. This has two aspects.

- Only properly authorised employees can enter into transactions. For example only properly trained sales assistants can make sales to customers and only the departmental buyer can enter into a transaction to buy goods for the store.

- Transactions are carried out in the correct manner and following the correct procedures. For example, each time a shop assistant makes a sale the amount of the sale must be entered into the till and the money received placed into the till.

When a transaction takes place in a business, the systems that a business operates should ensure the correct recording of the transaction.

For example when money is received for a cash sale this receipt must be recorded as part of the monies received in the day and also as a sale. The accounting systems should ensure that the cash received is rung up on the till and recorded on the till roll. This receipt should then also be recorded in the accounting entries as a sale.

However, on occasions, errors may be made when transactions are recorded. A transaction, or one element of it, may fail to be recorded altogether or it may be recorded at the wrong amount.

Businesses will therefore usually have a variety of internal checks or controls in order to pick up any errors that have been made so that they can be corrected.

8.1 EXAMPLES

The types of internal checks and controls include:

- reconciliations of cash in the till to the till roll records
- checking of the addition of cheque listings used to complete paying in slips
- reconciliations of actual amounts of petty cash to the petty cash records
- checking of accounting entries
- checking of cheque payment or petty cash authorisations, and
- reconciliations of cash records to bank statements received.

9 TIMING OF TRANSACTIONS

The timing and frequency of business transactions will vary. Some, such as sales, may take place on a daily basis, others, such as salaries, on a monthly basis. Items such as electricity and gas bills will tend to be paid on a quarterly basis. Purchases of equipment will probably not be particularly frequent.

Whenever transactions occur they should be promptly recorded in the accounts on the day that they occur. This is important to ensure that the business records are correct and up to date. It is also necessary for legal reasons in respect of sales and other taxes and, as you will see in your later studies, to ensure that the accounts provide a true and fair view of the business to management, owners and others.

ACTIVITY 3

The manager of the Research and Development Unit of a large chemical company has been given control of the investigation of the potential healing properties of a naturally occurring compound found in the Amazonian rainforest.

1   State why the manager will need to ensure careful records are maintained of the receipts and payments associated with this project.

2   Explain why the manager will need to set up a system of authorisation and control for expenditure.

3   Explain why timing is important when dealing with financial transactions under such a project.

For a suggested answer, see the 'Answers' section at the end of the book.

CONCLUSION

All forms of business are set up to provide some form of goods or services to their customers or to benefit the public (i.e. charitable work). In order to facilitate the provision of such goods and services they will need to engage in a series of transactions. These transactions need to be recorded in the bookkeeping system so that the individuals that control the business can print off reports to help them understand the performance and position of the business. This information, if of a good quality, will help them run the business in a more effective and efficient manner.

Cash and credit transactions are used in the sale and purchase of goods and services and in the receipt of income and payment of expenditure.

Small, day-to-day transactions are commonly paid in cash. Larger transactions tend to be paid for by cheque or other payment made from the business bank account, for example; online transfers. Such expenditure is authorised at different levels in the business and within a system of financial control.

Payments to employees are also controlled and authorised and made regularly and in a timely manner, as are all other payments.

KEY TERMS

Account – A record of similar financial transactions in a business.

Expenses – Money spent for rent, electricity for lighting, telephone accounts and so on. This does not include purchases of goods for resale.

Income – A more general term than sales including also interest received, rent received from letting part of the business premises and so on.

Ledger – A set of related accounts.

Payroll – List of employees and the wages or salaries due to each.

Petty cash – A small amount of cash held for the payment of expenses.

Purchases – Buying goods for resale.

Receipt – Written statement of an amount of money that has been paid/received.

Sales – The exchange of goods or services for money. Terms such as commission and fees are also used instead of sales for some services.

Till roll – Printed listing of all payments received through a till/point of sale desk in a retail outlet.

SELF TEST QUESTIONS

Paragraph

1	Explain the difference between a customer and a supplier.	1
2	What is a cash transaction?	2
3	What is a credit transaction?	2
4	Give examples of purchases and expenses.	3
5	When would petty cash be used?	4
6	Name three payments made by the payroll department.	5
7	Give two reasons why a business keeps a record of business transactions.	6
8	Senior personnel authorise major expenditure in a business. Why?	7
9	Give a reason for maintaining a system of internal check or control.	8
10	Why is it important for a business to pay expenses, such as wages, on time?	9

FA1: RECORDING FINANCIAL TRANSACTIONS

EXAM-STYLE QUESTIONS

1 A business buys goods on credit. When will this require the accounting records to be updated?

    A   Only when the goods are received

    B   Only when the goods are paid for

    C   When the goods are received and again when they are paid for

    D   When the goods are received, again when they are paid for and when the goods are resold

2 Which of the following describes the receipts generated by an Internet Service Provider?

    A   Income from sale of goods

    B   Income from giving a service

    C   Payments for employees

    D   Payments for share capital

3 How would you describe petty cash?

    A   Cash for some small everyday expenses

    B   An overdraft arranged by the bank

    C   Spare cash invested in a separate bank account

    D   Money in the current account

4 A stationery business sold computer supplies to a customer for payment in one month. Which of the following are true in respect of this transaction?

    (i)   It is a cash transaction

    (ii) The expenditure must be authorised by the stationery business

    (iii) A record of the transaction must be kept in case of future query by the stationery business

    (iv) The stationery business will need to ensure that it receives payment in one month

    A   (i) only

    B   (ii) and (iii)

    C   (iii) and (iv)

    D   All of the above

5   Which section of a grocery business pays salaries?

    A   Accounts department

    B   Payroll

    C   Sales

    D   Store manager

For suggested answers, see the 'Answers' section at the end of the book.

Chapter 2

TYPES OF BUSINESS DOCUMENTATION

In the first chapter you looked at the different transactions that take place in business. As you saw, these need to be evidenced and recorded. This chapter looks at the documents which underlie those business transactions. It covers the syllabus content on types of business documentation.

CONTENTS

1. Documents for business transactions
2. Processing a cash transaction
3. Credit transaction procedures
4. Processing a credit transaction: a credit sale
5. Processing a credit transaction: a credit purchase
6. Statements of account
7. Returns, credit and debit notes
8. Petty cash claim
9. Document retention policies
10. Data protection

LEARNING OUTCOMES

At the end of this chapter, you should be able to:

- distinguish between different types of business documentation
- outline the purpose and contents of a range of business documents
- describe the documentation and the flow of documentation for different transactions including internet transactions
- identify the personnel involved in preparing and authorising documents.

1 DOCUMENTS FOR BUSINESS TRANSACTIONS

When a business sells or buys, each stage in the transaction is documented. Some businesses use electronic documents in their computer systems and that electronic information can be sent from the computer of suppliers to customers without the need for paper. Nevertheless, many transaction documents are still produced in a paper form.

We need to produce documents for business transactions for several reasons.

- As evidence of the transaction and its details. For example, suppose that Charu buys some flower pots from Gopi, which Gopi delivers. Charu might complain to Gopi that 250 flower pots had been ordered but only 200 were delivered, and that the agreed price was $1.50 per pot, whereas Gopi was now asking for $1.75 for each pot. If the order has been documented, the dispute can be resolved by checking the order details.

- As evidence of the stage that the transaction has reached. Documents are produced at different stages in a transaction. You might have had some experience of this yourself. Suppose you buy a new set of chairs for your house from a local store. The sales assistant will take down details of your order in the store, and ask you to sign it as evidence that you have placed the order. The document you sign is called a sales order. Some weeks later, the chairs might be delivered to your house by a delivery van, and you will be given a document by the van driver, which you might have to sign as evidence that you have received the goods. This document is called a delivery note. Sometimes you may receive a letter first containing an advice note which will advise you that the delivery will be made on a specific day and will list the items to be delivered. When you order the chairs, or after they have been delivered, you will be required to pay. The store will confirm the payment to you when the payment occurs, by giving you a receipt. A receipt is a document providing evidence that you have paid.

- For checking and confirming. In business, it is difficult to keep track of every business transaction. Documents can be used to check details and confirm that everything is correct. For example, a business might receive an invoice from a supplier demanding payment for goods that the supplier has delivered. Before the business makes the payment, someone should check that everything is in order, and that the goods were ordered and have been delivered properly (as the supplier has claimed) and that the amount asked for in payment is correct. This checking process is carried out by looking at the relevant documents.

- For recording the transaction details. Accounting for business transactions is explained in later chapters. Briefly, details of all the sales and purchase transactions of a business are recorded in its 'accounts' or 'books'. To keep accounting records, a business needs a record of the transaction details. These details come from the documents relating to each transaction.

You need to know: **what** the main business documents are and what details they contain; **why** they are needed; **who** produces and authorises them; and **when** they are needed.

Depending on the way in which orders are made transactions are processed in different ways and with different documentation.

2 PROCESSING A CASH TRANSACTION

Cash transactions are fairly straightforward. The buyer orders goods or services and pays for them immediately or on delivery. The seller delivers the goods or provides the service, and often gives the customer a **receipt** as evidence of payment.

You have been the buyer yourself in many cash transactions, but let's look at a number of different cash transactions from the viewpoint of the seller.

Example 1: Over-the-counter sale

Sales in a shop are 'over the counter'. The customer selects the goods required, takes them to a sales desk or check-out point, pays for them, and takes them away. The seller gives the customer a **receipt**, as evidence of the transaction and the payment. If the customer than wants to return the goods, because there is something wrong with them, the seller can ask to see the receipt, to check that the customer did actually buy the items recently in the shop. Sales are also recorded automatically by the seller's cash register, and at the end of the day, a **till roll** might be produced by the cash register, listing all the items sold through the check-out point during the day.

Example 2: Verbal order

Another type of transaction involving a face-to-face verbal order is where the goods or services are not available immediately. Instead, the customer orders them for future delivery. In many cases, the customer might be asked to pay a deposit with the order, and make the rest of the payment ('pay the balance') when the goods or services are delivered.

Suppose for example that you go to a car dealer to buy a new car. The salesperson will show you a demonstration model, and talk to you about all the optional extras you can buy with the car. The salesperson will then take down the details of your order on a **sales order form**, which you will sign. This form will include the name and address of seller and purchaser together with the full details of the order and agreed costs. You will probably have to pay a deposit, which could be, say, 10% of the purchase price. The car dealer uses this order form to process your order, by asking the manufacturer to supply a car to your specification. You will be given a copy of the sales order form as evidence of your order, and as a receipt for your deposit. (Alternatively, you might be given a separate receipt for the deposit.) When the car is delivered to the car dealer, you will be sent an **invoice**, stating the full purchase price and the deposit you have already paid, and asking you to pay the rest of the purchase price. When you have paid, you will go to the car showroom and receive a **receipt** for your payment, and then you can drive away.

Sometimes the extent of an order is not completely clear. For example, if your heating or air conditioning system breaks down you would call an engineer to fix the problem. Usually the engineer will examine the equipment and then provide you with a **quotation**. This will contain details of the work needed including a list of replacement parts and labour and an indication of the amount the repair will cost. Sometimes the quotation will be preceded with an **estimate** which may be provided verbally at the time the engineer calls. The **quotation** is a more formal document, which may be relied on by the prospective purchaser and which is provided in writing to confirm agreement of the estimate.

Example 3: Telephone order

The procedures for taking orders by telephone can vary, but might be as follows.

Suppose that you want to buy a book and telephone the company with your order. The details of your order will be taken, and entered on a **sales order form**. A sales order form might be a paper document, but nowadays it is usual to enter the order details by keyboard into a computer system which displays an order form on screen. Payment details will also be taken.

The sales order is then used to create a **dispatch note**, which is an instruction to the warehouse to send the book to the address you have given. A copy of the dispatch note will be attached to the package containing your book, and this copy is called a **delivery note**. When you receive the book, you will also receive the delivery note, as evidence that the item has been delivered to you. (Some businesses use two copies of a delivery note, which the customer is asked to sign. One copy is then kept by the supplier, as evidence that the customer has actually taken delivery of the goods.)

You will also be given a receipt, as documentary evidence that you have paid for the book. The receipt could either be a separate document, or included within the delivery note.

Example 4: Written order

A common example of a written order in a cash transaction is buying goods from a mail order firm, using an order form in the firm's catalogue.

Suppose for example that you have a sales catalogue from Postal Fashions, a mail order firm that sells items of clothing. You might place an order for some shirts by filling in the form, indicating which shirts you want and how many, and signing it. This order form might be called a **purchase order**. You would send the form, together with your cheque payment or credit card details, to Postal Fashions. The firm would copy the order details on to a **dispatch note**. (In practice, order details are usually keyed into a computer system from the order form, and the system then produces a dispatch note and delivery note automatically.)

The shirts would then be posted to you with a **delivery note**, which will probably also include a statement that you have paid for the items in full. In other words, in this type of transaction, the delivery note also acts as a receipt.

Example 5: Internet order

Increasingly, customers are using the Internet to make orders. A common way of selling on the Internet is for a business to have a website that allows customers to select the goods or services they want to buy, by placing them in an electronic 'shopping basket'. Usually, the customer enters credit card or debit card details with the order, to pay for the purchased items. If the customers wish to purchase books, they enter their requirements on an electronic **order form** which may involve simply ticking a box or specifying the quantity they wish to purchase. They will then be taken through a secure internet buying system which results in a paid invoice and/or a **receipt** which can be printed out at the end of the transaction. A copy may also be emailed to the purchaser. The books are then despatched with a **delivery note**.

ACTIVITY 1

What do you think is the difference between a sales order form and a purchase order form?

For a suggested answer, see the 'Answers' section at the end of the book.

The cash transactions above are ones you will recognise as taking place between individuals and organisations. Businesses also buy from other organisations using cash. Purchases must be properly agreed and authorised within the purchaser business.

2.1 CHEQUE REQUISITION

Internal cheque requisition forms are completed by junior members of staff to be authorised by more senior management. They contain details of proposed purchases, including: the nature of the goods, their cost and the chosen supplier. The cheque requisition form is then sent to the cashier (or other authorised person having control of the business cheque book). A cheque is drawn up and provided for the purchase.

Many organisations maintain a system whereby a cheque requisition form is required for any abnormal expense, any item of capital expense and any payment request not supported by a relevant invoice.

Given below is an example cheque requisition form for payment of balance on the sales director's company credit card.

```
                    J Forrester
                Wholesales Supplies Ltd

                CHEQUE REQUISITION FORM

    Date:        17 July 20X7

    Please draw a cheque on the company's bank account as follows:

    Payable to:   Bankcard
    Amount:       $848-23
    Explanation:  Settlement of June 20X9 Company Barclaycard
                  (statement attached)
    Signature:    Sales Director
    Approved:     Managing Director
```

Note the following details:

- The requisition form should give enough detail of the payee (person to be paid, Bankcard in this case) and amount for the cheque to be drawn up.

- The explanation should explain precisely the reason for the payment.

- Although there is no invoice, any supporting documentation, such as the statement in this case, should be attached to the requisition form.

- The requisition should be signed by the person requesting it and approved or authorised by an appropriate senior person within the organisation.

3 CREDIT TRANSACTION PROCEDURES

The procedures for credit transactions are a little more complex than for cash transactions. Here, we shall focus on credit transactions where both the buyer and the seller are a business. We shall begin by looking at a credit transaction from the viewpoint of the seller. Then we shall look at the same type of transaction from the viewpoint of the buyer.

For any credit transaction, both parties to the transaction, buyer and seller, must agree what the **credit terms** should be.

- For regular customers, a supplier will agree credit terms for **the amount of time the customer will be given to pay**, and in addition will set a **credit limit** for the customer. A credit limit is the maximum amount that the customer will be permitted to owe, taking all unpaid purchases together. For example, suppose that Dilip's Deli is a food store that buys frozen pizzas on credit from a supplier, Tuscan Pizzas. Tuscan Pizzas might agree to allow Dilip's Deli 60 days to pay for deliveries of its pizzas, but set a credit limit of $2,000 on the account. This means that Dilip's Deli must pay for deliveries within 60 days and in addition, the total amount it owes to Tuscan Pizzas at any time cannot exceed $2,000.

- For 'one off' credit transactions, the buyer and seller will agree credit terms for the individual order. These will consist simply of how much time the customer will be given to pay for the items purchased.

- The credit terms are agreed by the credit controller or a senior manager in the selling organisation. Transactions above agreed limits and other transactions on credit need to be separately authorised.

4 PROCESSING A CREDIT TRANSACTION: A CREDIT SALE

Businesses usually like to receive an order in writing for a credit transaction. It helps to have a written order in the event of any subsequent dispute with the customer. Even when a customer makes the order by telephone, the supplier usually asks the customer to confirm the order in writing.

Since the customer initiates the written order, the order document is a **purchase order**.

On receipt of the order, a member of the sales team or order processing team must check the order details, to make sure that they are valid and correct. At this stage, it might be necessary to check that the customer has enough credit left, and that the order would not breach the customer's credit limit.

If the order is for the purchase of goods that the supplier already has in stock, the supplier will produce a dispatch note for the warehouse and a **delivery note**. (In practice, it is likely that the order details will be keyed into a computer system, which then produces a dispatch note and delivery note automatically.)

The goods are then delivered to the customer, who signs the delivery note. A copy of the delivery note comes back to the supplier, as evidence that the customer has taken possession of the goods. The delivery note is matched with the purchase order.

TYPES OF BUSINESS DOCUMENTATION : CHAPTER 2

The purchase order details are also used to produce an invoice. For the seller, it is called a **sales invoice**. One copy goes to the customer. One or more copies are kept by the supplier. An invoice can be used, when the customer eventually pays, to check that the payment is correct. The invoice might even be stamped 'PAID' to show that the customer no longer owes the money. (In practice, invoice details are usually held on computer, and when a customer pays, the computer record is used to check that the payment is correct, and is updated to record the fact that the customer has now paid.)

When a customer pays, the payment might be accompanied by a **remittance advice**. This is a document containing details of the payment, including the sales invoice number. A remittance advice can be valuable in helping the supplier to recognise what the payment is for, and which invoice or invoices is/are being paid.

4.1 THE SALES INVOICE

Invoices are particularly important source documents used in recording credit sales and purchases.

An example of a sales invoice is shown below with a description of its contents. The contents will be explained in more depth in a later chapter.

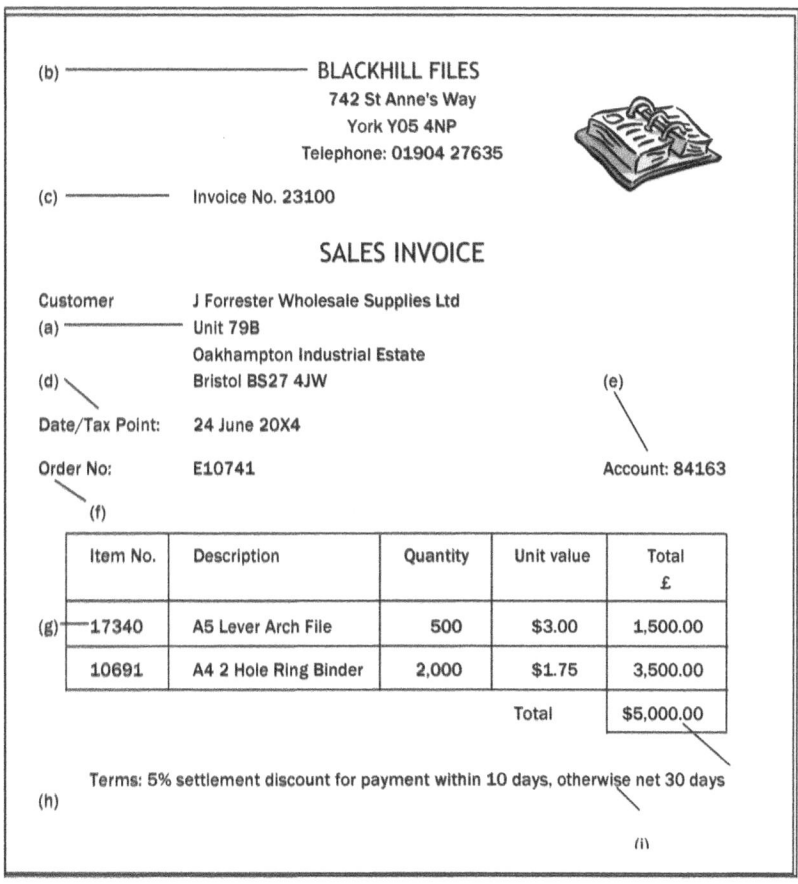

(a) Customer name and address

(b) Name of your business, business address and telephone number

(c) Invoice number

(d) Invoice date

(e) Customer account reference

(f) Order number

(g) Quantity and description and price

(h) Final total value

(i) Settlement terms – these state when the invoice should be paid

5 PROCESSING A CREDIT TRANSACTION: A CREDIT PURCHASE

It is important that purchases are properly authorised. If they are not, anyone could order whatever goods they want. For example, a junior office clerk might decide to order a new computer from a supplier because the clerk wants a machine that is faster and more powerful than the one they currently have.

5.1 PURCHASE REQUISITION

To get a purchase authorised, it is usual to fill in a form known as a **purchase requisition**. The form is prepared by the person wanting the goods, and is then signed by another person who has the authority to agree to the order being made. (In much the same way, if someone wants to obtain an item that is held in the firm's own stores, he or she might have to prepare a **stores requisition**, and get it signed by an authorised person.)

The authorised purchase requisition is now given to a person whose job is to place the order with a supplier. Larger businesses may have a purchasing department, with buyers whose job is to place orders with suppliers on the best terms available. In smaller organisations, orders might be authorised and placed by a senior manager.

5.2 PURCHASE ORDER

A **purchase order** is prepared and sent to the chosen supplier, once the details have been discussed with the supplier, and the sales price and credit terms agreed. Purchase orders should have a unique identity number (the purchase order number).

An example of a purchase order is shown below together with a description of its contents.

TYPES OF BUSINESS DOCUMENTATION : CHAPTER 2

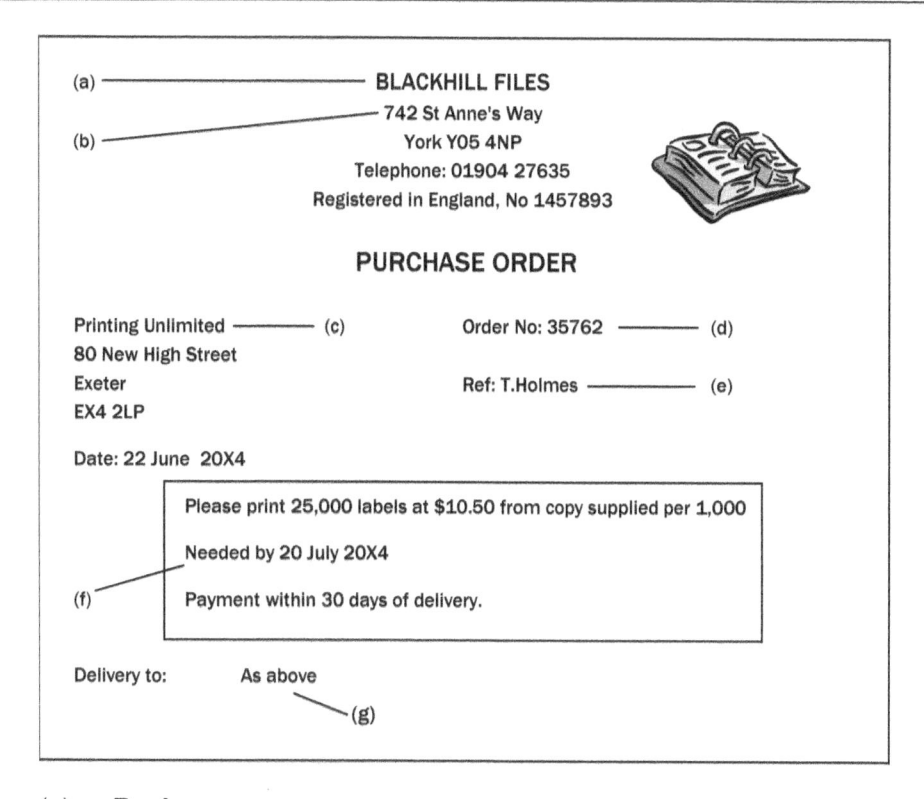

```
(a) ─────────────  BLACKHILL FILES
                    742 St Anne's Way
(b) ─────────────   York YO5 4NP
                   Telephone: 01904 27635
                  Registered in England, No 1457893

                      PURCHASE ORDER

Printing Unlimited ──── (c)      Order No: 35762 ──── (d)
80 New High Street
Exeter                           Ref: T.Holmes ──── (e)
EX4 2LP

Date: 22 June 20X4

        ┌──────────────────────────────────────────────────┐
        │ Please print 25,000 labels at $10.50 from copy supplied per 1,000 │
        │                                                  │
        │ Needed by 20 July 20X4                           │
(f) ────│                                                  │
        │ Payment within 30 days of delivery.              │
        └──────────────────────────────────────────────────┘

Delivery to:    As above
                    ──── (g)
```

(a) **Business name**

This is the business name of the buyer.

(b) **Registered office and company registration number**

Most countries have legal requirements relating to disclosure of specified information. For example, in the United Kingdom, whenever a limited company uses its name on business letters or on documents, such as this purchase order, it must state its registered office and registration number. This disclosure is voluntary on invoices and credit notes. Note that individual countries may have slightly different requirements.

(c)/(g) **Supplier name and address**

This is where the purchase order is sent.

(d) **Purchase order number**

Each purchase order has a unique identification number.

(e) **Business contact**

This information allows a supplier to contact a particular individual in the event of a query.

(f) **Delivery date**

It is important to specify the delivery date on a purchase order as it is possible that a supplier might not be able to send the goods when they are needed.

The purchase order is sent to the supplier, but a copy is kept by the buyer. Until the goods are delivered, this copy might be held in the purchasing department.

5.3 DELIVERY NOTE AND GOODS RECEIVED NOTE

When the goods are delivered, the supplier provides a **delivery note**. The employee taking the delivery, who might be a member of the stores staff, should immediately check the delivery note details against the physical items that have been delivered. For example, if the delivery note states that 40 boxes of photocopier paper have been delivered, the boxes should be counted to make sure there are 40, and not just 39.

Delivery notes are not in a standard format, because each supplier has a different design of form, often in different paper sizes and colours. It is therefore quite common for the details of a delivery to be copied from the delivery note on to a **goods received note**. Extra details can be added on to a goods received note, such as the stock identity numbers of the items delivered.

The next step is to check that the items delivered were actually what were ordered. This is done by comparing the details on the goods received note with the purchase order. If the supplier has supplied the wrong items, or the wrong quantity, the problem should be identified and resolved as soon as possible after the delivery has been made – and certainly before the goods are paid for.

5.4 PURCHASE INVOICE

The supplier sends an invoice when the goods are delivered, or soon after. It is called a **purchase invoice**. The invoice goes to the accounts department.

A purchase invoice is similar to a sales invoice, except that it is an invoice received from a supplier instead of an invoice sent to a customer. In fact, for the supplier of the goods or services, it is a sales invoice. This means that a purchase invoice is likely to have the words 'sales invoice' printed on it.

A business receives invoices from many different suppliers, and so purchase invoices come in different sizes and the information they contain is set out differently by each supplier.

An example of a purchase invoice is shown below.

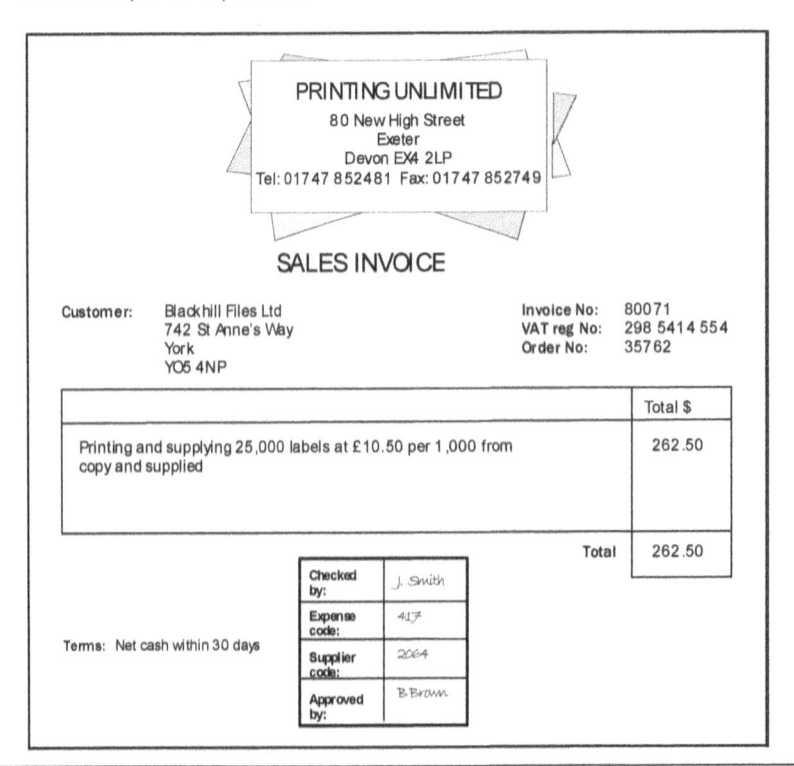

```
              PRINTING UNLIMITED
                80 New High Street
                      Exeter
                  Devon EX4 2LP
         Tel: 01747 852481  Fax: 01747 852749

                  SALES INVOICE

Customer:   Blackhill Files Ltd       Invoice No:  80071
            742 St Anne's Way         VAT reg No:  298 5414 554
            York                      Order No:    35762
            YO5 4NP
```

	Total $
Printing and supplying 25,000 labels at £10.50 per 1,000 from copy and supplied	262.50
Total	262.50

Checked by:	J. Smith	
Expense code:	417	
Terms: Net cash within 30 days	Supplier code:	2064
Approved by:	B. Brown	

A purchase invoice is missing some items of information that the buyer needs to add. This additional information is added when the invoice has been received and when it is checked. In many cases, the information is added by stamping a grid-like box on to the invoice, or putting a stick-on label on the invoice. The box or label is used to add items of information such as:

- the signature or initials of the person who has checked the invoice, for example by checking the details against the purchase order and goods received note

- a code identifying the nature of the expense

- possibly, a code identifying the supplier

- the signature or initials of the person who approves the invoice for payment.

ACTIVITY 2

A purchase invoice for a business that buys goods from a supplier is the sales invoice from the supplier. A business receives purchase invoices from its suppliers, and it keeps a copy of sales invoices that it sends to customers.

If you were shown a batch of sales invoices for your business and a batch of purchase invoices, how might they look different?

For a suggested answer, see the 'Answers' section at the end of the book.

5.5 PAYMENT AND REMITTANCE ADVICE

Someone in the accounts department checks the details on the invoice against the purchase order. To do this, the purchase order and the invoice have to be matched together. If the purchase invoice shows the buyer's purchase order number, the task of matching the documents is made much easier and quicker.

If the invoice details appear correct, the invoice should be submitted for authorisation by a responsible person, possibly a senior manager. Usually, authorisation is given by means of adding a signature to the invoice.

The details of the authorised invoice are then recorded in the accounting system, and payment is made when the agreed credit period comes to an end.

When paying an invoice, some businesses send a remittance advice with their payment. A remittance advice is a document giving details of the invoice that is being paid (or possibly, of several invoices that are all being paid at the same time), including the supplier's invoice number. If any prompt payment discount has been deducted from the invoice amount in making the payment, this will also be detailed on the remittance advice. This will help the supplier to identify what the payment is for.

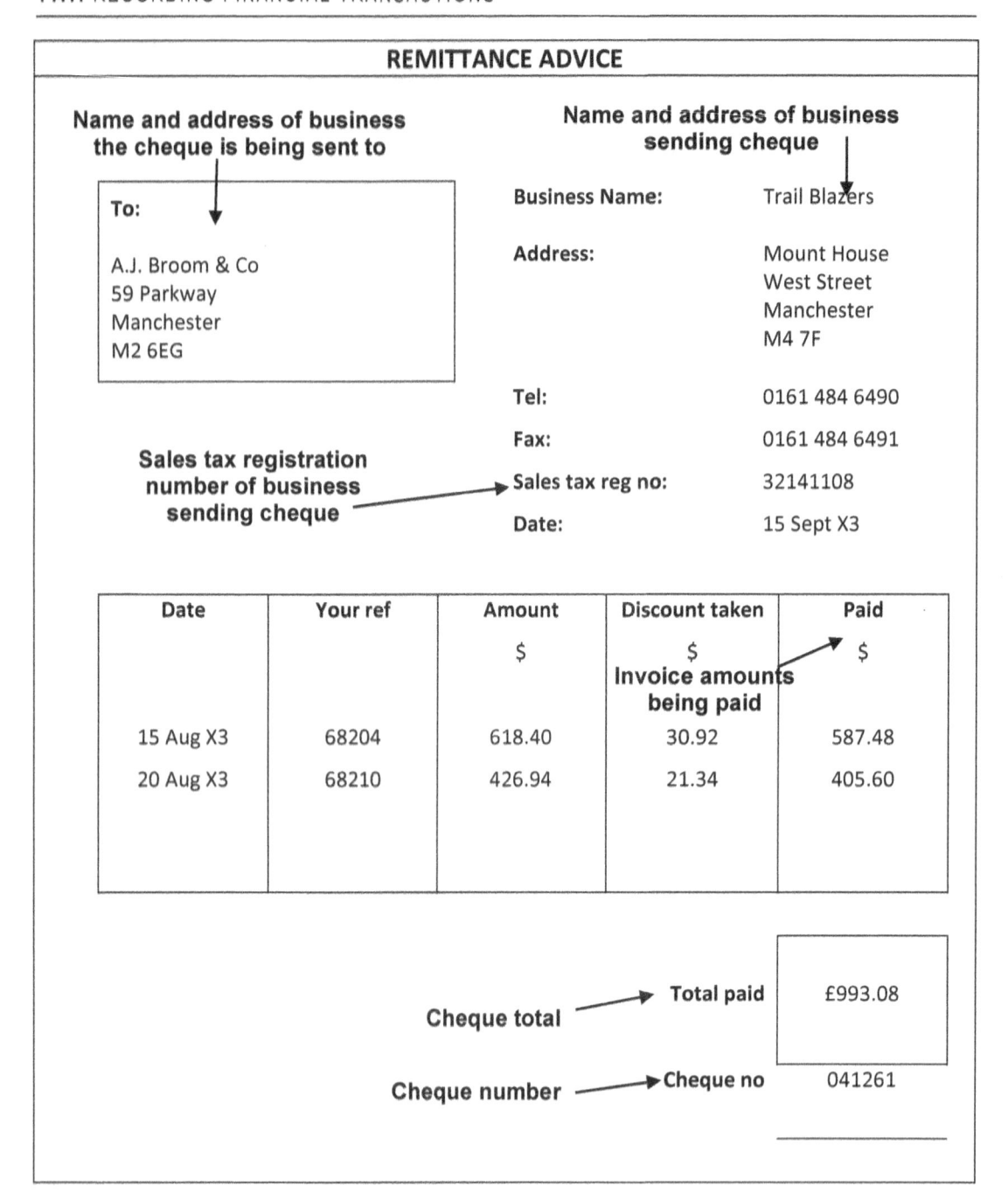

REMITTANCE ADVICE

Name and address of business the cheque is being sent to

To:

A.J. Broom & Co
59 Parkway
Manchester
M2 6EG

Name and address of business sending cheque

Business Name:	Trail Blazers
Address:	Mount House
	West Street
	Manchester
	M4 7F
Tel:	0161 484 6490
Fax:	0161 484 6491
Sales tax reg no:	32141108
Date:	15 Sept X3

Sales tax registration number of business sending cheque → Sales tax reg no

Date	Your ref	Amount $	Discount taken $	Paid $
			Invoice amounts being paid	
15 Aug X3	68204	618.40	30.92	587.48
20 Aug X3	68210	426.94	21.34	405.60

Cheque total → Total paid — £993.08

Cheque number → Cheque no — 041261

TYPES OF BUSINESS DOCUMENTATION : CHAPTER 2

ACTIVITY 3

Explain the purpose of the following sales documents, and list them in the order in which they are produced:

- sales invoice
- delivery note
- remittance advice
- sales order.

Also, explain the purpose of the following purchase documents, and list them in the order in which they are produced:

- goods received note
- purchase order
- purchase invoice.

For a suggested answer, see the 'Answers' section at the end of the book.

6 STATEMENTS OF ACCOUNT

Instead of sending out a remittance advice to customers with each invoice, a business might choose to send out a statement of account to each customer at regular intervals, typically every month.

A statement of account shows how much the customer still owes. It might show the total amount owed by the customer at the date of the previous statement of account, the new invoices sent to the customer since then, the amounts the customer has paid, and so the total that the customer currently owes.

An example of a statement of account is shown below. This has been sent by a business called Disks and Labels Ltd to its customer, J Forrester Wholesale Supplies Ltd.

DISKS AND LABELS LTD

76 Wood End Road
Newcastle Upon Tyne
NE4 9AJ
Tel: 0141 839 4444

J Forrester Wholesale Supplies Ltd
Unit 79b
Oakhampton Industrial Estate
Bristol BS27 4JW

VAT Reg No. 341 5079 584

Date: 5 June 20X3

STATEMENT OF ACCOUNT

Date	Description	$	$	Balance owing ($)
14 May	Balance B/f			1,729.46
26 May	Invoice 314/X5	397.42		2,126.88
29 May	Invoice 386/X5	927.04		3,053.92
3 June	Cheque rec'd		1,729.46	1,324.46
4 June	Invoice 019/X5	1,062.96		2,387.42
			Amount now due	2,387.42

A customer might return the statement of account with the next payment. If so, the statement of account might be used in a similar way to a remittance advice.

When the customer receives the monthly statement of account, the customer will reconcile it against the record held of the previous transactions. Any discrepancies are queried. Because the statement is produced by a supplier it acts as a useful external check of the internal records of the customer.

Statements of account represent the ledger account of the customer in the supplier's books of account.

7 RETURNS, CREDIT AND DEBIT NOTES

7.1 SALES RETURNS AND CREDIT NOTES TO CUSTOMERS

It is quite common in business for a customer to return goods to a supplier, because some of the goods are faulty, or not what the customer ordered. Sometimes, goods are sold to a retailer on a 'sale or return' basis, which means that if the retailer doesn't resell the goods, they can be sent back to the supplier.

Suppose for example that a book publisher sells 100 copies of a book on credit to a book distributor at a price of $15 for each book. The publisher will send an invoice to the distributor for $1,500. Some weeks later, the distributor might send back 20 of the books because they are not needed and there is a sale or return agreement. The amount owed by the distributor is now just $1,200, not $1,500.

It might seem logical to suppose that the publisher will issue a new invoice for $1,200 to replace the original invoice for $1,500. However, if the book distributor is a regular customer of the publisher (an 'account customer'), this isn't what happens. Instead of issuing a new invoice to replace the old invoice:

- the original invoice for $1,500 remains

- the publisher issues a document called a credit note. In this example, the credit note will be for $300 (20 books at $15 each). A credit note could be described as a negative invoice. It is a statement that the supplier (here, the book publisher) is reducing the amount owed by the customer. Here, the effect of the credit note is to reduce the amount owing on the book distributor's 'account' by $300, so the net amount the distributor owes is just $1,200 ($1,500 − $300).

- A credit note looks like a sales invoice. An example of a credit note is shown below. This has been issued by a supplier of office stationery, to an account customer who has returned some items of stationery that had been purchased but had been damaged in transit.

BLACKHILL FILES
742 St Anne's Way
York Y05 4NP
Telephone: 01904 27635

Credit note No: C456

CREDIT NOTE

Customer   J Forrester Wholesale Supplies Ltd
Unit 79B
Oakhampton Industrial Estate
Bristol BS27 4JW

Date/Tax Point: 24 June 20X4
Order No: E10741   Account: 84163

Item No.	Description	Quantity	Unit value	Total $
17340	A5 Lever Arch File	50	$3.00	150.00
10691	A4 2 Hole Ring Binder	100	$1.75	175.00
			Total	$325.00

Reason for return: Damaged in transit

7.2 CREDIT NOTE FOR PURCHASE RETURNS

Credit notes arise with purchases as well as sales, and for the same reasons. If the buyer is dissatisfied with the goods, and the seller agrees to take them back, the seller will issue a credit note for the items returned. The amount owed to the seller is then the amount of the original invoice less the value of the credit note.

7.3 DEBIT NOTE

A debit note is a document raised by a customer and issued to a supplier to request a credit note for goods returned because, for example, they were faulty.

ACTIVITY 4

1   Which document is used to correct an overcharge in an original invoice?

    A   Credit note

    B   Debit note

    C   Dispatch note

    D   Goods received note

2   Which document provides a summary of the credit transactions between a customer and supplier during the previous month?

    A   Advice note

    B   Internal cheque requisition

    C   Invoice

    D   Statement of account

For a suggested answer, see the 'Answers' section at the end of the book.

8 PETTY CASH CLAIM

The petty cash system within a business also has its own documents.

The initial record of any petty cash claim is a petty cash voucher. Blank petty cash vouchers are obtainable from stationery suppliers in pads, and each voucher is torn off the pad when it is used. An example of a blank voucher is shown below.

```
+-------------------------------------------------+
| Petty Cash Voucher       No. _____         |
|                                                 |
| Date  _____                                |
|-------------------------------------------------|
|                              AMOUNT             |
| For what required            $        ¢         |
|                           +--------+--------+   |
|                           |        |        |   |
|                           |        |        |   |
|                           |        |        |   |
|                           +--------+--------+   |
|                                                 |
| Signature   _____                 |
|                                                 |
| Authorised  _____                 |
+-------------------------------------------------+
```

Notes on filling in a voucher

- Petty cash vouchers should be given a unique identification number. For control purposes, they should be numbered sequentially by the person in charge of petty cash.

- Each voucher should be dated (with the date it is filled in and authorised).
- The details of the expenditure and the amount should be entered. If there is a receipt, this should be attached by a staple or paper clip.
- The person claiming the petty cash should sign the voucher.
- The person authorising the claim should also sign the voucher.

8.1 SUPPORTING DOCUMENTATION

To make sure that a petty cash claim is for a valid business expense then each claim must normally be supported by documentation proving that the expense is genuine. Before the petty cash claim is authorised, this supporting documentation must be checked.

Most types of petty cash claim are for straightforward office expenses such as the purchase of coffee, biscuits, stamps, bus and taxi fares, and so on.

In these cases, a simple receipt is sufficient evidence of the payment for the expense. For bus fares, the ticket itself might be used as the evidence.

However, if the payment includes sales tax (such as 'value added tax' or 'VAT'), a proper receipt showing the supplier's name and the sales tax registration number is required. Most till roll receipts do show this information.

In each case the supporting documentation should be attached to the petty cash claim.

Many of the examples throughout the text use VAT as an example of the sales tax that might be included within relevant documents.

9 DOCUMENT RETENTION POLICIES

The documents used to process a transaction are not thrown away, but are held on file for some years. For sales transactions, the customer's order, the delivery note and the sales invoice might all be stapled together and filed. Similarly, for purchase transactions, a copy of the purchase order, delivery note, goods received note and purchase invoice might be stapled together and filed.

The documents should be filed in a way that will make it possible to find them if they are needed at some time in the future, for example, in case of a dispute between the customer and the supplier documents could be produced that confirm goods had been supplied and what price had been charged for them. In addition, retention of business documents enables a business to prepare accounting information and to prepare annual financial statements.

There are good commercial reasons for retaining documents and there are also some legal requirements. Some countries also have legal requirements for business documents to be retained for a minimum number of years (usually three or six years). Some business tax and sales tax laws, for example, require that documents are retained for a number of years in case of enquiry and investigation.

Documents can take up a considerable amount of room so businesses often store images of old documents on microfiche or on a digital medium long after the original documents have been destroyed. Computerisation allows digital information to be stored on discs, tapes and so on almost permanently.

Any important records should be securely stored safely away from fire, water and other risks that could damage the information. Duplicate files are generally maintained for computerised data at locations away from the main business premises.

Documents that should be part of a retention policy include the following:

- records of cash received and paid – cash book and petty cash book records
- amounts owed to the business, such as trade receivables records
- amounts owed by the business, such as trade payables records
- records of the inventory count at the year-end
- records of assets used in the business e.g. items of plant and equipment.

ACTIVITY 5

Suppose that, for filing purposes, a business staples together:

- the customer's order, the delivery note and a copy of the sales invoice for all sales transactions
- a copy of the purchase order, delivery note, goods received note and purchase invoice for all purchase transactions.

In what order do you think these documents should be filed, for ease of future reference?

For a suggested answer, see the 'Answers' section at the end of the book.

10 DATA PROTECTION

A completely different aspect of business transactions is the need for a business to keep records and information about people. The law attempts to provide some protection for individuals:

- to prevent businesses holding data about them, when there isn't a legitimate reason for doing so
- to require businesses to make sure that the data is not inaccurate
- to allow individuals the right to inspect any personal data about them that is held by someone else.

The data protection rules affect businesses. This is because businesses hold personal data records, for example about their customers and employees, mostly on their computer systems. Businesses find personal data useful for marketing and other purposes.

Personal data is data about a specific individual. It could include not just name and address, but age and date of birth, education details, annual salary, family details, and so on. Personal data about a customer might include not just how much the customer owes, but how much was purchased in the past and details of those purchases. In other words, a personal data record could include a history of the customer's purchasing history.

As an example of relevant legislation businesses in the UK that hold files of personal data about individuals are required to comply with the Data Protection Act 2018 which introduced the General data Protection Regulations (GDPR).

First, they must register with the Data Protection Commissioner as a user of personal data. As a user of personal data, a business must comply with certain data protection principles. These include the following.

- Information in personal data files must be obtained and processed lawfully and fairly.

- Personal data should be held only for specified lawful purposes.

- Personal data should not be used or disclosed in any way except for these purposes.

- The amount of personal data held should be sufficient and relevant for its purpose, but should not be excessive.

- Personal data should be accurate and, where necessary, should be kept up-to-date.

- Personal data should not be held for longer than is necessary.

- An individual is entitled to know that a data user is holding personal data about him or her. The individual has the right to look at this data and, where appropriate, to insist that it should be corrected or deleted.

If the personal data about an individual is inaccurate, or if there has been an unauthorised disclosure of the information by the data user to someone else, the individual has a right of legal action against the data user.

Processing personal data is not permitted except under certain conditions, such as:

- with the consent of the individual

- as part of a contractual arrangement between the data user and the individual

- for legal reasons.

Some personal data does not come within the scope of the Act, such as:

- personal data about employees for payroll purposes

- personal data about customers and suppliers for the purpose of maintaining accounting records.

Countries other than the UK also have laws on data protection or privacy which are less or more stringent.

Risks to data security and storage include the following issues:

- accidental loss or corruption of data due to poor business practices and procedures

- deliberate loss or destruction of data due to criminal or other inappropriate behaviour

- unauthorised access to data leading to misuse of data for an improper purpose.

The risks to data security and storage may be managed in a number of ways, including:

- recruitment of appropriate staff who act with honesty and integrity

- training of staff so that they understand the risks associated with data security and storage and how to effectively manage those risks

- good business practices regarding data management, processing and updating.

- effective segregation of duties between employees to minimise the risks of undetected errors and similar problems

- physical controls regarding management of risk of damage to data from fire, smoke and other hazards.

ACTIVITY 6

You work in the accounts office of your company and receive a telephone call from someone who says that they are the bank manager of North Bank in the local High Street. The bank has been approached by a customer of your company, for a loan to pay off the debt they still owe your company. The bank manager asks how much the customer owes, and would also like to check the marital or relationship status of your customer.

What is the legal position?

For a suggested answer, see the 'Answers' section at the end of the book.

CONCLUSION

In this chapter you have looked at a variety of documents used in business as evidence of transactions. You will appreciate that they differ depending on their purpose and are often issued in order to indicate different stages of, for example, the sales and purchasing as indicated below.

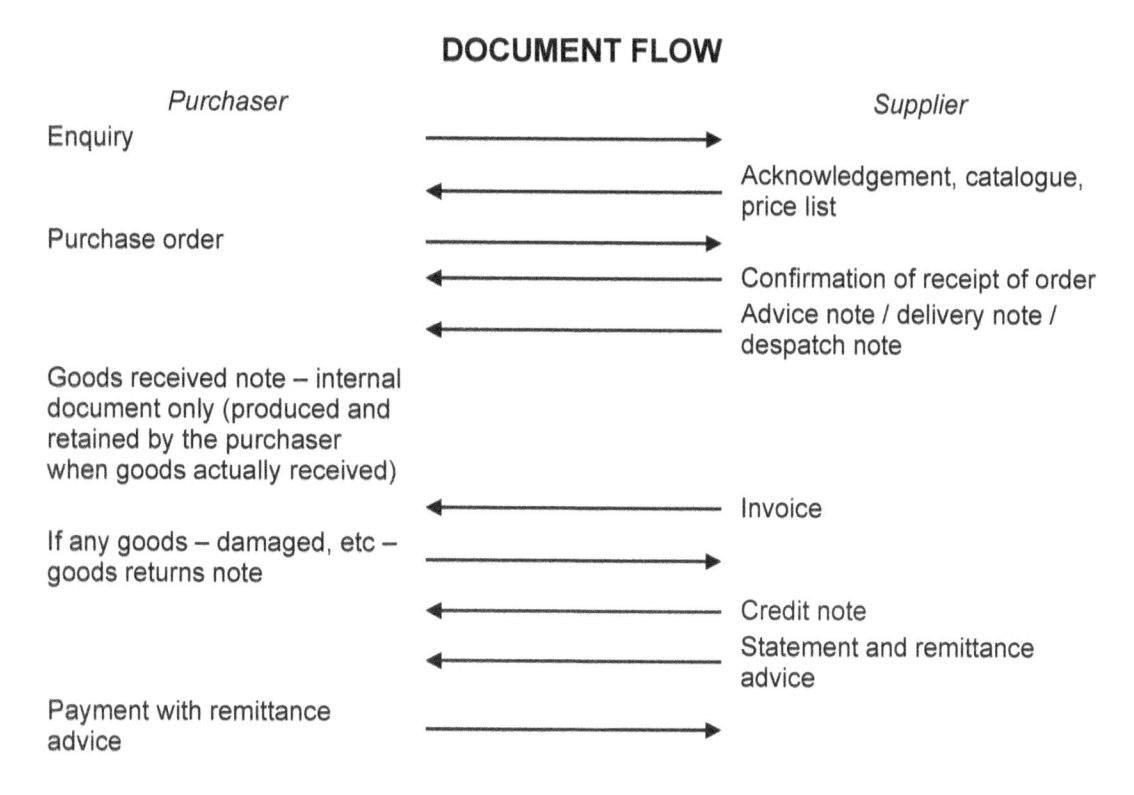

DOCUMENT FLOW

Purchaser		Supplier
Enquiry	→	
	←	Acknowledgement, catalogue, price list
Purchase order	→	
	←	Confirmation of receipt of order
	←	Advice note / delivery note / despatch note
Goods received note – internal document only (produced and retained by the purchaser when goods actually received)		
	←	Invoice
If any goods – damaged, etc – goods returns note	→	
	←	Credit note
	←	Statement and remittance advice
Payment with remittance advice	→	

Documents, particularly associated with making payments, must be properly authorised. Generally this takes the form of the signature of an authorised person.

Documents are used throughout a business to record transactions and the financial implications of those transactions. Key documents that are used in recording financial transactions are invoices, credit notes, receipts and petty cash vouchers. Statements and payslips are useful summaries which can be used as a check of transactions.

KEY TERMS

Advice note – Document issued to a customer or received from a supplier, advising that a delivery will be made on a specific day and listing the items to be delivered.

Credit note – Document issued to a customer or received from a supplier, indicating that the amount owed is being reduced for sales returns/purchase returns.

Debit note – A debit note is a document raised by a customer and issued to a supplier to request a credit note for goods returned because, for example, they were faulty.

Delivery note – Document sent with products delivered to a customer. One copy kept by the customer, one copy signed by the customer and retained by the supplier.

Internal cheque requisition – Form for use within a business, properly authorising payment to be made to a supplier.

Payslip – Document given to each employee giving details of pay and deductions from pay.

Petty cash voucher – Document kept in the petty cash giving details of money paid out and the reasons for the expense.

Price quotation – Document sent to a potential customer quoting price for some goods or a service. If signed and accepted by the customer, it becomes a purchase order from the customer.

Purchase invoice – Written request for payment from a supplier, giving details of items delivered.

Purchase order – Order from a customer on a form or document produced by the customer.

Purchase requisition – Request for an item to be purchased for the business. It should be authorised before being acted on.

Quotation – Indication of the costs of a specific contract or job. *See also* price quotation.

Personal data – Data about a specific individual.

Receipt – Written statement of an amount of money that has been paid/received.

Remittance advice – Document sent with payment, listing the items/invoices that are being paid.

Sales invoice – Written request to a credit customer for payment, giving details of items sold.

Sales order form – Order from a customer on a form produced by the seller.

Statement of account – A list of invoices, credit notes, settlement discounts received and payments made for a given period of time, sent by a supplier to a credit customer. The statement also shows the current amount owed by the customer.

Till roll – Printed listing of all payments received through a till/point of sale desk in a retail outlet.

SELF TEST QUESTIONS

Paragraph

1	What is an advice note?	1
2	Explain the purpose of a receipt.	1
3	What is the difference between an estimate and a quotation?	2
4	What is the difference between a dispatch note and a delivery note?	2
5	Give two examples of when a cheque requisition form would be used.	2
6	State the purpose of a credit limit.	3
7	Give four items that would appear in a sales invoice.	4
8	What is the difference between a purchase requisition and a purchase order?	5
9	What are the benefits of using a goods received note?	5
10	Describe a purchase invoice.	5
11	What is a debit note?	7
12	Draw up a petty cash voucher.	8
13	Why should a business have policies for the retention of documents?	9
14	What are the main data protection principles?	10

EXAM-STYLE QUESTIONS

1 The types of documentation that might accompany a complex transaction for a machine includes three of the following. Which is the odd one out?

   A Invoice for outstanding amount from manufacturer

   B Initial enquiry letter from manufacturer

   C Price quotation for machinery from manufacturer

   D Deposit remittance from purchaser

2 Which of the following does not contain an amount in money?

   A Delivery note

   B Quotation

   C Payslip

   D Receipt

FA1: RECORDING FINANCIAL TRANSACTIONS

3   Which of the following lists is in the correct chronological order?

   A   Sign petty cash voucher, spend money, obtain receipt, authorise voucher

   B   Quotation, purchase order, purchase invoice, cheque requisition

   C   Invoice, credit note, debit note, delivery note, remittance advice

   D   Receipt, purchase invoice, statement, despatch note

4   Which document is used by a supplier to correct an earlier overcharge?

   A   Advice note

   B   Credit note

   C   Debit note

   D   Invoice

5   From the following list of situations where an invoice has been sent, choose one that would **not** require a credit note to be raised:

   A   A customer has returned some or all of the goods because they are damaged or faulty.

   B   A customer has returned some or all of the goods because they are not the ones that were ordered.

   C   A customer has never received the goods although an invoice was sent out.

   D   Postage and packaging was omitted on the original invoice.

6   Which of the following describes a goods received note?

   A   It is a formal request, sent by a business to a supplier requesting the delivery of the goods specified on the purchase order.

   B   It is an internal check document that serves as a record of the quantity and condition of goods that have been delivered to the business.

   C   It is a discount that is offered to a customer if the invoice is paid by a certain date.

   D   It is a means of identifying a transaction as being of a particular type by allocating to it an appropriate reference number.

7   Which of the following documents would not be entered in the accounting records after it has been raised?

   A   A credit note

   B   A debit note

   C   A quotation

   D   A payslip

For suggested answers, see the 'Answers' section at the end of the book.

Chapter 3

DOUBLE ENTRY BOOKKEEPING

The purpose of this chapter is to introduce the double entry method of accounting or bookkeeping. It explains the principles on which the method is based, introduces the nominal ledger (general ledger) and explains how cash transactions are accounted for within the nominal ledger. The difference between capital and revenue expenditure is also explained which is an important principle in accounting.

CONTENTS

1. Elements of the financial statements
2. Capital, assets and liabilities
3. The accounting equation
4. Income, expenses and profit
5. The dual aspect of every transaction
6. Nature and function of double entry
7. Double entry bookkeeping: basic rules
8. Balancing an account
9. Capital expenditure and revenue expenditure
10. Books of prime entry
11. Computerised accounting

FA1: RECORDING FINANCIAL TRANSACTIONS

LEARNING OUTCOMES

At the end of this chapter, you should be able to:

- understand and apply the accounting equation
- explain the fundamental rules of double entry accounting and debits and credits
- identify and classify assets, liabilities, income and expenditure
- recognise the duality of transactions
- understand the nature and function of primary financial records
- identify the main types of ledger account
- understand the importance of coding transactions correctly
- record a complete series of basic transactions within a double entry system
- prepare journal entries and identify the uses of the journal
- balance off ledger accounts, recording closing balances
- distinguish between capital and revenue expenditure and identify examples of each
- understand the basic functions of a computerised accounting package.

1 ELEMENTS OF THE FINANCIAL STATEMENTS

As an introduction to this chapter, it is useful to begin with some definitions. The items defined will be explained in more detail within the chapter.

- **Asset** – an asset is a present economic resource which the business controls as a result of a past event. It is used to generate future economic benefits for a business. An asset could either be sold for cash or could help the business to generate sales income and profits. An example of an asset used to generate future economic benefits is plant and equipment used by a business to produce goods to sell to customers.

- **Liability** – a liability is a present obligation to transfer an economic resource as a result of a past event. This could be a bank loan or overdraft outstanding, or amounts owed to suppliers for goods received but not yet paid for.

- **Capital (or equity)** – capital (or equity) is the amount due to the owner of a business after liabilities have been paid.

- **Income** – income arises through increases in assets or decreases in liabilities that result in an increase in equity, other than changes relating to contributions from the business owners in the form of capital introduced. The principal source of income for a business is the amount generated from the sale of goods or services to customers during an accounting period. This is often referred to as sales income or sales revenue. Income is also regarded as an inflow or increase in economic benefits during an accounting period.

- **Expense** – expenses incurred are decreases in assets or increases in liabilities that result in decreases in equity, other than changes relating to withdrawals by the business owners in the form of drawings. Expenses are incurred by a business to enable it to make sales and generate income. Examples of expenses incurred by a business include telephone, stationery and postage costs, or heat, fuel and power charges for gas and electricity usage. In effect, expenses are resources used up during an accounting period to help the business generate revenue.

You need to understand and be able to explain the following terms. However, the compilation or preparation of these statements is beyond the syllabus requirements of this syllabus.

- **Statement of financial position** – this is a statement of assets and liabilities of the business compiled at a specific date. It consists of the assets, liabilities and capital of the business at that date. Assets may be classified as being either current assets or non-current assets. Liabilities can also be classified as being either current or non-current depending upon when they fall due to be paid.

- **Statement of profit or loss and other comprehensive income** – this statement summarises the income and expenses of a business for a period of time. The difference between income and expenses is the profit or loss made by the business during that accounting period. This statement is often abbreviated to 'the statement of profit or loss' and, for the purposes of your studies for this syllabus, it will be referred to as the '**statement of profit or loss**'.

Examples of the statement of financial position and statement of profit or loss and other comprehensive income are included for reference.

Statement of profit or loss for a business for the year ending 31 December 20X2

	$	$
Sales revenue		x
Less: sales returns		(x)
Cost of goods sold:		
Opening inventory	x	
Purchases	x	
Less: purchase returns	(x)	
	x	
Less: closing inventory	(x)	
		(x)
Gross profit		xx
Less: Expenses		
Electricity	x	
Rent	x	
Repairs	x	
Sundry expenses	x	
Loan interest	x	
Total expenses		(xx)
Net profit for the year		xxx

Statement of financial position of a business as at 31 December 20X2

Non-current assets

	$	$
Property	X	
Plant and equipment	X	
Van	X	
		XX
Current assets		
Inventory	X	
Receivables	X	
Cash at bank	X	
		XX
Total assets		**XXX**
Opening capital	X	
Add capital introduced	X	
Add net profit for the year	X	
Less drawings	(X)	
Closing capital		XX
Non-current liabilities		
Bank loan		XX
Current liabilities		
Payables	X	
Sales tax owing	X	
		XX
Total capital and liabilities		**XXX**

2 CAPITAL, ASSETS AND LIABILITIES

A business invests in equipment, motor vehicles, materials and other items. Items that a business controls, including money in the bank, are called assets. Examples of assets are:

- land and buildings owned by the business

- plant, machinery and equipment

- motor vehicles

- amounts owed by customers buying goods on credit ('receivables')

- inventory of materials or goods for resale

- money held in bank accounts or in petty cash.

The nature of assets varies from business to business. The assets of a farming business, for example, might include farm machinery, barns and livestock.

Due to the way modern trade is conducted businesses will undoubtedly, at some point, incur liabilities. These are financial amounts that the business owes due to either contractual or legal obligations.

Examples of liabilities are:

- money owed to suppliers for goods and services provided but not yet paid for ('trade payables')

- bank loans and overdrafts

- money owed to the tax authorities.

Liabilities are a means of financing a business. The liabilities are incurred to purchase the assets necessary to trade and to administer the operations of the business. Another method of financing a company is for the owners to invest their own funding into the business. Amounts invested by the owners are referred to as 'capital' or 'equity'. Most commonly the owners of a business inject share capital into a business, so called because in return for their investment they receive shares as evidence of ownership. Consequently they are commonly referred to as 'shareholders'.

At any given point in time, the financial position of a business can be described in terms of the current combination of its owner's capital, its assets and its liabilities. These are all presented on the **statement of financial position**, one of the primary summaries in the financial statements.

2.1 SEPARATE ENTITY CONCEPT

There are a number of different ways to set up a business and in each of these the legal positions of the business and its owners can vary considerably. For example; with sole traders and partnerships the owners and the business are legally to be one and the same, e.g. a window cleaner. In contrast, with a limited liability company the company and its owners (the 'shareholders') are considered separate legal entities.

The separate entity concept is that, from an accounting perspective, a business is treated as an entity in its own right, separate from its owner, no matter what the actual legal position happens to be.

Example 1

An individual, Hopper, set up in business by opening a coffee shop, named 'Hopper's Coffee'. From an accounting perspective:

- There is the business, Hopper's Coffee.

- Hopper's Coffee has an owner, who has invested capital in the business.

Accounting records are produced for the business, Hopper's Coffee. The accounts are the accounts of the business, not the accounts of its owner. For accounting purposes, the owner is regarded as a separate person, who has invested capital and might take out profits.

Suppose that Hopper invested $5,000 in the business to set it up, and paid this money into a business bank account. From the point of view of the business, Hopper's Coffee, it has $5,000 in cash, which is an asset of the business. It also has $5,000, which reflects the fact that the owner has invested in the business. The opening financial position of the business can therefore be stated as:

Assets: cash	$5,000	
Capital	$5,000	

FA1: RECORDING FINANCIAL TRANSACTIONS

3 THE ACCOUNTING EQUATION

At any point in time, the following relationship always exists between capital, assets and liabilities:

Capital = Assets – Liabilities

This is known as the accounting equation. Like any equation, it can be rearranged and presented, for example, as follows:

Assets = Liabilities + Capital, or Liabilities = Assets – Capital

Over time, the assets, liabilities and capital of a business change continually, but the relationship in the accounting equation is always true. This is because of the way in which assets, liabilities and capital are defined and also because of the way in which changes in the three elements are recorded. The reason this equality is maintained is that the assets controlled by the business had to be financed by someone, either the owner or lenders. Conversely, the input from the owner and lender has to be represented by an asset or assets to the same value.

In the example above, when Hopper sets up the business, the opening accounting equation is:

	ASSETS		=	LIABILITIES	+	CAPITAL
Cash	$5,000		=	$0	+	$5,000

The accounting equation still holds true with each accounting transaction of the business. Here are some examples.

Example 2

Hopper buys furniture (chairs and tables) for the shop for $1,500, paying the supplier out of the business bank account. The accounting equation after this transaction is:

	ASSETS		=	LIABILITIES	+	CAPITAL
		$				
Furniture	(+ $1,500)	1,500				
Cash	(– $1,500)	3,500				
		5,000	=	$0	+	$5,000

Example 3

Now Hopper spends a further $2,000 to buy coffee-making equipment and $800 on crockery and cutlery, paying cash out of the business bank account. The accounting equation after these transactions is:

	ASSETS		=	LIABILITIES	+	CAPITAL
		$				
Equipment	(+ $2,000)	2,000				
Furniture		1,500				
Tableware	(+ $800)	800				
Cash	(– $2,800)	700				
		5,000	=	$0	+	$5,000

Example 4

Hopper persuades the bank to lend $1,000 to develop the business. The bank loan is accounted for as a liability of the business, and the accounting equation is now as follows:

	ASSETS		=	LIABILITIES		+	CAPITAL
		$			$		
Equipment		2,000					
Furniture		1,500					
Tableware		800					
Cash	(+ $1,000)	1,700		Loan (+ $1,000)	1,000		
		6,000	=		1,000	+	$5,000

4 INCOME, EXPENSES AND PROFIT

Businesses exist to sell goods or services, from which they earn income. Income from selling goods or services is usually called sales revenue, turnover, or simply sales. There might be other sources of income too, such as interest earned on money in a bank deposit account.

To earn its income, a business incurs expenditure. Items of expenditure are called expenses. Examples of expenses include:

- the cost of salaries and wages for employees
- telephone charges and postage costs
- the rental cost on a building used by the business
- the interest cost on a bank loan.

A summary of the incomes, expenses and profits for the last financial year of a business is presented in the **statement of profit or loss**, one of the primary summaries in the financial statements.

The accounting equation can be expanded to show the effect of transactions in more detail. If capital changes, this will be matched by changes in assets and/or liabilities.

4.1 THE ACCOUNTING EQUATION EXPANDED

Every transaction has a dual effect upon the accounting equation. The accounting equation can be expanded to show the effect of transactions in more detail, to reflect income, expenses and drawings.

For example, a cash sale for $250 increases both cash and sales income by $250 as follows:

| Increase Cash | $250 |
| Increase Sales income | $250 (i.e. increase capital) |

Payment of a repairs expense amounting to $25 in cash reduces cash and increases expenses as follows:

| Increase Repairs expense | $25 (i.e. reduce capital) |
| Reduce Cash | $25 |

Withdrawal of cash drawings will, ultimately, reduce the proprietor's capital account balance. Many businesses record individual drawings transactions in a drawings account, and then transfer the total of drawings for the accounting period to the capital account. For example, a withdrawal of $150 cash by the proprietor would be recorded as follows:

Increase Drawings $150 (i.e. reduce capital)

Reduce Cash $150:

The accounting equation can therefore be expanded to reflect such transactions as follows:

Assets = Capital + Income − Expenses − Drawings + Liabilities

4.2 INVENTORY

An important item of expense for most business is the cost of purchased goods or materials. Retail businesses buy goods for resale. Manufacturing businesses buy raw materials and components that they turn into finished goods for sale to customers.

- Materials purchased for resale as part of the business' trade are recorded as **assets**, referred to as **inventory**. At this point they are not recorded as expenses. They are assets because the business will be able to use them in the future to generate income.

- When the goods are sold and income is recognised the asset is removed (because the business no longer physically has it). **The cost of the goods or materials is at this point recognised as an expense.** In this way the cost of the goods is **matched** to the income it earns so that the profit on the sale can be determined.

Example 5

Let's continue with the example of Hopper's Coffee. Suppose that Hopper's now buys coffee, tea, milk, sugar, biscuits and cakes for $700, and pays in cash from the business bank account. The accounting equation is now as follows:

				ASSETS		=	LIABILITIES		+	CAPITAL
		$					$			
Equipment		2,000								
Furniture		1,500								
Tableware		800								
Inventory	(+ $700)	700								
Cash	(− $700)	1,000					Loan	1,000		
		6,000	=				1,000	+	5,000	

4.3 PROFIT FROM TRADING

To take the above scenario a stage further, it is useful to look at the concept of profit. When a business makes a profit from trading, the profit becomes a part of the owner's capital, and so is added to capital.

Example 6

Suppose that in the first day of trading, Hopper uses up $650 of the inventory, and makes sales totalling $1,050. All sales are in cash. In other words, Hopper makes $400 profit on the day from trading. Profit becomes a part of the owner's capital, so the accounting equation at the end of the day will look like this:

ASSETS	$	=	LIABILITIES	$	+	CAPITAL		$
Equipment	2,000							
Furniture	1,500							
Tableware	800							
Inventory (− $650)	50					Original		5,000
Cash (+ $1,050)	2,050		Loan	1,000		Profit	(+ 400)	400
	6,400	=		1,000	+			5,400

5 THE DUAL ASPECT OF EVERY TRANSACTION

Looking at the examples above showing the accounting equation, you should notice that:

- All business transactions affect assets, liabilities, capital, income or expenses.

- For each business transaction, there are two sides, shown in the workings for the accounting equation by plus and minus signs. Something increases in value, and something else either reduces in value or increases in value by the same amount.

- Assets are the 'opposites' of liabilities and capital. An increase in an asset will either have a corresponding decrease in a different asset or an increase in either a liability or capital balance.

- Profit increases capital. Profit is equal to income minus expenses. Increasing income is the same as increasing capital and increasing an expense is the same as decreasing capital.

Examples 1 to 6 are summarised below. However, for Examples 5 and 6, the calculation of the profit has been ignored. The purchase of the coffee and other materials is shown as **'purchases'** rather than inventory in Example 5. The sales in the first day of trading are also shown as **'sales'** in Example 6, without calculating the profit.

Examples 5 and 6 are shown in this way because a business does not calculate its profit after every transaction or at the end of every trading day. Instead, it simply records purchases and sales, and leaves the calculation of profit until the end of the financial year.

	Example	Assets $	Liabilities $	Capital $	Income $	Expenses $
1	Start up	+ 5,000		+ 5,000		
2	Furniture Cash	+ 1,500 – 1,500				
3	Equipment Tableware Cash	+ 2,000 + 800 – 2,800				
4	Cash/bank loan	+ 1,000	+1,000			
5	**Purchases** (cash)	– 700				+ 700
6	**Sales** (cash)	+ 1,050			+ 1,050	

In a double entry accounting system, the dual aspect of every accounting transaction is recorded. 'Double entry' means that each transaction is recorded twice, to reflect its dual aspect.

ACTIVITY 1

1 Jackson pays for computer equipment by a cheque from the business bank overdraft. Which parts of the accounting equation are changed by this transaction?

　　A　Assets and liabilities

　　B　Assets and income

　　C　Liabilities and profit

　　D　Capital and income

2 Which concept underlies the principle of double entry bookkeeping in which every transaction is recorded twice?

　　A　Dual aspect

　　B　Cost of goods

　　C　Profit

　　D　Separate entity

For a suggested answer, see the 'Answers' section at the end of the book.

6 NATURE AND FUNCTION OF DOUBLE ENTRY

6.1 ACCOUNTS AND THE NOMINAL LEDGER *(GENERAL LEDGER)*

In a double entry accounting system (or 'bookkeeping' system), transactions are recorded in accounts. A business keeps accounts for each asset item and liability item, for each item of expense and each item of income, and for the owner's capital. These accounts are kept together in a ledger, called the **nominal ledger** *(general ledger)* **or main ledger**. (You will probably come across all three terms in your work.)

- **An account** is a record, built up over time, of all the transactions that have occurred relating to the particular asset, liability, item of income or item of expense. For example, the sales account is used to record details of sales by the business over a period of time, and a telephone expenses account is used to record details of all telephone bills and any other telephone-related expenses. Similarly, a motor vehicles account is used to record the buying and disposals of motor vehicles by the business.

- **A ledger** is a term that simply means a set of related accounts. The accounts for capital, assets, liabilities, income and expenses are related accounts because they make up the double entry system of accounting. They are therefore kept together in the same ledger, the nominal (general) ledger.

6.2 DEBITS AND CREDITS

Many businesses use computer software packages and have a computerised system of accounting. However, to gain an understanding of double entry accounting, it helps to begin by looking at a 'manual' set of accounts. 'Manual' simply means that the accounts are recorded on paper rather than on a computer.

Each account has two sides, a debit side and a credit side. By convention, the debit side is shown on the left and the credit side on the right. For practical purposes, it is both clearer and more convenient to think of the words debit and credit as meaning the left- and right-hand sides of the page respectively.

Account name (and code)			
Date and Reference	$	Date and Reference	$
DEBIT SIDE		CREDIT SIDE	

You might see that the account looks a bit like the letter T, which is why you might hear manual accounts drawn up in this way referred to as 'T-accounts'.

A recognised shorthand form is used for debit and credit:

Dr = Debit

Cr = Credit

7 DOUBLE ENTRY BOOKKEEPING: BASIC RULES

There are five types of account:

- asset
- liability
- capital
- income
- expense.

Every transaction will affect two accounts because of the dual aspect.

By convention, an increase in an asset or an expense is recorded on the debit (or left-hand) side of that item's account. Assets and expenses are the opposites of liabilities, capital and income, so an increase in a liability, capital or income balance is recorded on the credit (or right-hand) side.

It follows that decreases in assets or expenses are recorded on the credit side, while decreases in liabilities, capital or income are recorded on the debit side.

If more than two accounts are used to record a transaction, the total value of the debit entries and the total value of the credit entries for the transaction must still be equal.

The following rules of double entry accounting apply:

- An **asset** is recorded as a **debit** entry in an asset account.
- A **liability** is recorded as a **credit** entry in a liability account.
- Owner's **capital** is recorded by a **credit** entry in the capital account.
- **Income** is recorded as a **credit** entry in an income account, such as the sales account.
- **Expenses** are recorded as a **debit** entry in an expense account.

More specifically:

An increase in ...	is recorded as a ...	
	Debit	Credit
Asset	✓	
Expense	✓	
Liability		✓
Capital		✓
Income		✓

DOUBLE ENTRY BOOKKEEPING : CHAPTER 3

A decrease in ...	is recorded as a ...	
	Debit	Credit
Asset		✓
Expense		✓
Liability	✓	
Capital	✓	
Income	✓	

These are rules that you should learn. You can simplify this task by remembering that **an increase in an asset or expense is a debit**. It then follows that a decrease in either must be a credit. Liabilities, capital and income are the opposite.

To help you identify whether a debit or credit entry is required you can use the well-known mnemonics 'DEAD CLIC' or 'PEARLS.'

Debit	Credit
Expenses	**L**iability
Asset	**I**ncome
Drawings	**C**apital

Debit	Credit
Purchases	**R**evenue
Expenses	**L**iabilities
Assets	**S**hareholder's capital

Note: The above represents where items are placed when there is an increase, i.e. an increase in an asset is a debit. Decreases in these items are recorded on the opposite side, for example, a decrease in an asset value would be a credit and a decrease in a liability would be a debit.

This principle will be developed and illustrated in the remaining part of this chapter.

Example

These basic rules can be illustrated using the transactions already described for Hopper's Coffee and summarised in section 5. The date of each transaction is not shown here, but in practice transaction dates would be recorded in the accounts.

Transaction 1: Set up the business with $5,000 cash.

Here there is an increase in capital and assets. The asset is cash in the bank, which is recorded in an account called '**Bank**'.

Capital

	$		$
		Bank	5,000

Bank

	$		$
Capital	5,000		

Commonly there is a folio or reference column in the T-account. This provides a reference so that the transaction can be traced through the accounting records if required. The reference could be to a page number in the 'day book' where the transaction was first recorded (see Session 10).

The reference column is used to indicate the other account in the nominal ledger where the 'other side' of the double entry can be found. So here, there is a reference to 'Bank' or 'Cash' in the Capital account and a reference to the Capital account on the Bank or Cash account.

Transaction 2: Purchase furniture for $1,500 in cash.

Here, there is an increase in one asset (furniture) and a reduction in another (cash in the bank).

Furniture

	$		$
Bank	1,500		

Bank

	$		$
Capital	5,000	Furniture	1,500

In the Bank account, the **debit entry exceeds the credit entry** by $3,500 ($5,000 – $1,500). We therefore say that there is a **debit balance** on the account. The debit balance is $3,500, showing that the business has $3,500 cash in the bank.

Transaction 3: Purchase equipment for $2,000 cash and tableware for $800 cash.

Here we actually have two transactions, similar to the one above. They are recorded as follows:

Equipment

	$		$
Bank	2,000		

Tableware

	$		$
Bank	800		

Bank

	$		$
Capital	5,000	Furniture	1,500
		Equipment	2,000
		Tableware	800

The total value of the credit entries in the bank account is now $4,300. The debit entry exceeds the credit entries by $700, so there is a debit balance on this account of $700, indicating that the business still has $700 in its bank account.

Transaction 4: Bank loan of $1,000.

A bank loan creates a new liability, but also adds to cash in the bank (an asset). The balance on the Bank account now rises from $700 to $1,700, which is the amount by which total debit entries ($6,000) exceed total credit entries ($4,300).

Bank loan

	$		$
		Bank	1,000

Bank

	$		$
Capital	5,000	Furniture	1,500
Bank loan	1,000	Equipment	2,000
		Tableware	800

Transaction 5: Purchases of $700.

Purchases of materials are recorded in a purchases account, which is an expense account. Since the purchases are paid for in cash, there is a credit entry in the Bank account and a reduction in the bank balance to $1,000.

Purchases

	$		$
Bank	700		

Bank

	$		$
Capital	5,000	Furniture	1,500
Bank loan	1,000	Equipment	2,000
		Tableware	800
		Purchases	700

Note that purchases of materials or goods are recorded in the purchases account. Sales of materials or goods are recorded in a sales account. Only the start and end of year balance of goods or materials is recorded in an inventory account. There are no accounts called 'materials' or 'goods' and these terms should not be used in the bookkeeping system.

Transaction 6: Cash Sales of $1,050.

Sales are recorded in a sales account, which is an income account. Since the income is all in cash, there is a debit entry in the Bank account for the increase in the bank balance of $1,050.

Sales

	$		$
		Bank	1,050

Bank

	$		$
Capital	5,000	Furniture	1,500
Bank loan	1,000	Equipment	2,000
Sales	1,050	Tableware	800
		Purchases	700

Transaction 7: Rent payable of $200

Rent payable is a type of expense. It will therefore be recorded in an expense account, just like purchases, with a debit entry. Since the amount is paid in cash, there is also a credit entry in the bank account.

Rent payable

	$		$
Bank	200		

Bank

	$		$
Capital	5,000	Furniture	1,500
Bank loan	1,000	Equipment	2,000
Sales	1,050	Tableware	800
		Purchases	700
		Rent payable	200

Transaction 8: Stationery of $50 bought on credit from Green Supplies

This is another type of expense. A business will have many different types of expenditure that it needs to keep in separate T-accounts, both for management accounting purposes, financial reporting purposes and tax purposes. The stationery costs will therefore be recorded in a T-account by a debit entry. This time, however, there is no cash payment and therefore another T-account needs to be set up for the supplier, Green Supplies. Since all transactions have a corresponding debit and credit, Green Supplies' account will be credited with the $50.

Stationery

	$		$
Mr Green	50		

DOUBLE ENTRY BOOKKEEPING : CHAPTER 3

Green Supplies – credit supplier

	$		$
		Stationery	50

Transaction 9: Credit purchases of $1,000 from Blue Supplies

We saw in transaction 5 that purchases require debit entries in expense accounts. The only difference with these purchases for $1,000 is that they are made on credit, rather than paying for them in cash. Therefore, we need to debit purchases with $1,000 and set up a T-account for our credit supplier, Blue Supplies and record a credit of $1,000 in this account.

Purchases

	$		$
Bank	700		
Mr Blue	1,000		

Blue Supplies – credit supplier

	$		$
		Purchases	1,000

Transaction 10: Credit sales of $2,000 to Grey

We saw in transaction 6 that sales are recorded in an income account, with a credit entry. The only difference with these sales is that they are made on credit, rather than the cash being received straight away. Therefore, we will post the credit entry to the sales account in the usual way, but this time we will set up a T-account for Grey and post the debit entry to that account.

Grey – credit customer

	$		$
Sales	2,000		

Sales

	$		$
		Bank	1,050
		Grey	2,000

Transaction 11: Wages of $50

Hopper decides to employ a part-time worker. In the first week, Hopper pays the employee $50 from the business bank account. Again, wages are simply another type of expense account. The double entry is therefore to debit wages with the $50 and credit bank.

Wages

	$		$
Bank	50		

Bank

	$		$
Capital	5,000	Furniture	1,500
Bank loan	1,000	Equipment	2,000
Sales	1,050	Tableware	800
		Purchases	700
		Rent payable	200
		Wages	50

Transaction 12: Full payment of $2,000 received from Grey

When a credit customer pays the balance/part of the balance owing on their account, cash is received into the business. This increase in an asset (cash) is reflected by debiting the bank account with the $2,000. At the same time, there is a reduction in another asset, the receivable's account. This reduction is reflected by a credit entry to the receivable account for $2,000.

Bank

	$		$
Capital	5,000	Furniture	1,500
Bank loan	1,000	Equipment	2,000
Sales	1,050	Tableware	800
Grey- receivable	2,000	Purchases	700
		Rent payable	200
		Wages	50

Grey – receivable

	$		$
Sales	2,000	Bank	2,000

Transaction 13: Full payment by Hopper of $50 to Green Supplies and $1,000 to Blue Supplies

When a business pays an account payable, it reduces a liability – the payables' accounts – but it also reduces an asset – cash at the bank. Reduction of a liability is a debit entry and reduction of an asset is a credit entry. Therefore, we need to debit Green Supplies and Blue's Supplies accounts with $50 and $1,000 respectively, and we need to credit the bank account with the two amounts as well.

Green Supplies – credit supplier

	$		$
Bank	50	Stationery	50

Blue Supplies – credit supplier

	$		$
Bank	1,000	Purchases	1,000

Bank

	$		$
Capital	5,000	Furniture	1,500
Bank loan	1,000	Equipment	2,000
Sales	1,050	Tableware	800
Grey	2,000	Purchases	700
		Rent payable	200
		Wages	50
		Green Supplies	50
		Blue Supplies	1,000

Transaction 14: Partial repayment of $100 against loan

Hopper makes its first loan repayment of $100, which is therefore reducing a liability – the loan – by $100. It is also reducing an asset – cash – by $100. A reduction in a liability is a debit and a reduction in an asset is a credit. Therefore, we need to debit the loan account with $100 and credit the bank account with $100.

Bank loan

	$		$
Bank	100	Bank	1,000

Bank

	$		$
Capital	5,000	Furniture	1,500
Bank loan	1,000	Equipment	2,000
Sales	1,050	Tableware	800
Grey	2,000	Purchases	700
		Rent payable	200
		Wages	50
		Green Supplies	50
		Blue Supplies	1,000
		Loan	100

8 BALANCING AN ACCOUNT

The balance on an account is the amount by which the total value of debit entries and the total value of credit entries in the account are different.

- When total debits exceed total credits, there is a debit balance.

- When total credits exceed total debits, there is a credit balance.

As the number of transactions in a ledger account is updated, the size or value of the remaining debit or credit balance will change.

The examples above should suggest that the balance on the bank account changes continuously, as cash is received or paid out.

FA1: RECORDING FINANCIAL TRANSACTIONS

There are two methods of keeping track of the current balance on an account.

- Whenever a transaction is recorded in the account, the new balance can be calculated and shown in a separate memorandum column in the account. A memorandum column is not part of the double entry. It is used for convenience. In computerised accounting systems, there is always a running balance on accounts showing the up to date position.

- From time to time, an account can be 'ruled off' and the balance calculated. This balance is then recorded in the account.

'Ruling off' accounts might be done only occasionally, say at the end of each financial year. Alternatively, an account can be ruled off more frequently, say monthly.

Consider the following example of Hopper's Coffee with a bank account which needs to be balanced off, all transactions having been entered:

Bank

	$		$
Capital	5,000	Furniture	1,500
Bank loan	1,000	Equipment	2,000
Sales	1,050	Tableware	800
Grey	2,000	Purchases	700
		Rent payable	200
		Wages	50
		Green Supplies	50
		Blue Supplies	1,000
		Loan	100

Use the following 'four step plan' to balance off any ledger account as follows:

Step 1 – sub-total each side of the ledger account to give a value of debits and credits.

Step 2 – the difference between the two sub-totals is the closing balance and this should be added to the side with the small sub-total and reference it as 'balance c/d'.

Step 3 – the ledger account now balances off with an equal value of debits and credits.

Step 4 – carry down the closing balance on the account to the opposite side of the ledger account and reference it as 'Balance b/d'.

This procedure has been applied to the ledger account above so that you can follow how the closing ledger account balance has been determined.

DOUBLE ENTRY BOOKKEEPING : CHAPTER 3

Bank

	$		$
Capital	5,000	Furniture	1,500
Bank loan	1,000	Equipment	2,000
Sales	1,050	Tableware	800
Grey	2,000	Purchases	700
		Rent payable	200
		Wages	50
		Green Supplies	50
		Blue Supplies	1,000
		Loan	100
Step 1	9,050	Step 1	6,400
		Step 2 Balance c/d	2,650
Step 3	9,050	Step 3	9,050
Step 4 Balance b/d	2,650		

There is a debit balance, because total debits ($9,050) exceed total credits ($6,400). The account can be ruled off, or balanced off, as follows:

Bank

	$		$
Capital	5,000	Furniture	1,500
Bank loan	1,000	Equipment	2,000
Sales	1,050	Tableware	800
Gray	2,000	Purchases	700
		Rent payable	200
		Wages	50
		Green Supplies	50
		Blue Supplies	1,000
		Loan	100
		Balance c/d	2,650
	9,050		9,050
Balance b/d	2,650		

This shows that Hopper's Coffee has a positive balance of $2,650 in its bank account. It is a debit balance because cash is an asset.

The total of $9,050 has no particular significance in itself, it merely acts as an arithmetic check on the calculation of the balance carried down.

FA1: RECORDING FINANCIAL TRANSACTIONS

The bank loan account can be balanced in the same way:

Bank loan

	$		$
Bank	100	Bank	1,000
Balance c/d	900		
	1,000		1,000
		Balance b/d	900

This shows that Carl still owes $900 to the bank. It is a credit balance because it is a liability.

ACTIVITY 2

Required:

(a) Balance-off the following Cash account at 30 June.

Cash

		$			$
1 June	Balance b/d	4,200	3 June	Purchases	1,600
				Telephone	
3 June	Sales	3,700	8 June	expenses	850
10 June	Sales	6,100	15 June	Equipment	2,000
15 June	Sales	4,900	28 June	Purchases	3,700
26 June	Sales	8,800	29 June	Salaries payable	14,200

(b) What would a credit balance on the Bank T-account signify?

For a suggested answer, see the 'Answers' section at the end of the book.

ACTIVITY 3

Write up the following cash transactions in main ledger accounts.

Balance off the 'Cash at bank' account.

Transaction	Details
1	Set up the business by introducing $150,000 in cash.
2	Purchase property costing $140,000. Pay in cash.
3	Purchase goods costing $5,000. Pay in cash.
4	Sell goods for $7,000. All cash sales.
5	Purchase goods costing $8,000. Pay in cash.
6	Pay a sundry expense of $100, by cheque.
7	Sell goods for $15,000. All cash sales.
8	Pay wages of $2,000 to an employee.
9	Pay postage costs of $100 by cheque.

Note: A payment by cheque = a payment in cash.

Tip: Remember there is no such account as 'goods'.

For a suggested answer, see the 'Answers' section at the end of the book.

9 CAPITAL EXPENDITURE AND REVENUE EXPENDITURE

There are various examples above where expenditure provides the business with an asset. Alternatively payments may be made to pay off amounts owing.

Expenditure is classified as either capital expenditure or as revenue expenditure, depending on whether the expenditure is of short or long time use.

- **Capital expenditure** (also referred to as **asset expenditure**) refers to expenditure to purchase an asset that will be used for a fairly long time in the business. If the purchased asset is expected to have a useful life of *more than one year*, the expenditure is classified as capital expenditure.

- **Revenue expenditure** (also referred to as **expense expenditure**) is expenditure on expense items, including purchases of goods or materials.

The distinction between capital expenditure and revenue expenditure will become apparent when you go on to study the statement of profit or loss (income statement) and the statement of financial position (balance sheet) (not included in the FA1 syllabus).

In terms of double entry accounting:

- **Capital expenditure** to purchase a long-term asset is recorded with a debit entry in an asset account. For example, if a business purchases a machine for cash, the double entry record will be:

    Dr   Machinery account

    Cr   Bank

- **Revenue expenditure** for materials purchases or other expense items are recorded with a debit entry in an expense account. For example, if a business incurs postage costs and pays for them out of its bank account, the double entry record will be:

    Dr   Postage costs account

    Cr   Bank

Example

A business may purchase a piece of land and a factory for a total of $500,000. It may then build an office next to it, costing $100,000. Two years later it may be necessary to spend $10,000 redecorating the factory and $5,000 repairing the structure of the factory.

The original costs of $500,000 and $100,000 are capital costs because they are spent acquiring and improving non-current assets for continuing use in the business. The subsequent $10,000 and $5,000 are revenue costs because they are spent ensuring the continuing earning capacity of the buildings, but do not add to their capital value.

9.1 NON-CURRENT ASSETS AND CURRENT ASSETS

When a business incurs **capital expenditure** and buys a long-term asset, the 'capital asset' is called a **non-current asset**. This is simply an asset that the business expects to use for more than one year.

When a business acquires an asset that it expects to use or consume within a year then it is referred to as a **current asset**. Inventory is an example of a current asset as businesses do not tend to hold onto inventory for too long because of the increased risks of damage and the storage costs.

The main distinction between current and non-current assets is that current assets will be used by the business within one year, non-current assets will be held onto longer.

Examples of current assets include:

- inventory
- receivables
- cash in a bank account
- petty cash (notes and coins)
- payments in advance.

ACTIVITY 4

Try the following for additional practice to check you understand double entry.

Banner begins a business, Banner's Books, as a second-hand bookseller on 1 February 20X3. The first week's transactions are listed below:

(a) Deposited $5,000 in a business bank account as the opening capital.

(b) Purchased books for $600, paying by cheque.

(c) Sold books for $800 cash.

(d) Purchased books for $300, paying by cheque.

(e) Paid rent of $500, by cheque.

(f) Bought a second-hand van for $2,000, by cheque.

Record the first week's transactions of Banner's Books in the appropriate ledger accounts.

For a suggested answer, see the 'Answers' section at the end of the book.

10 BOOKS OF PRIME ENTRY

In many businesses there are numerous transactions each day, making it very difficult to record individual transactions directly to the nominal (general) ledger. The solution is to group similar transactions together and record them in one of the books of prime entry, also known as books of original entry. Periodically, the totals of each group of transactions are transferred to the nominal (general) ledger. The transferring or posting to the nominal (general) ledger was traditionally performed daily but may be performed weekly or monthly, depending upon the needs of the business.

The main books of prime entry are:

- **sales day book** (a list of all sales made on credit, with details of the date, customer and amount). Sales records and recording sale are considered in more detail in Chapters 5 and 6.

- **purchase day book** (a list of all purchases made on credit, with details of the date, supplier and amount). Purchase records and recording purchases are considered in more detail in Chapters 7 and 8.

- **cash book** (a list of all payments and receipts going through the bank account, including cash sales and purchases and giving details of payee or payer, date and amount). This is considered in more detail in Chapter 9.

- **petty cash book** (a list of all receipts and payments of cash, i.e. notes and coins, and giving details of amounts, reason for transaction and date). This is considered in more detail in Chapter 10.

- **transfer journal**.

The journal or transfer journal deserves some comment here. There are occasions when a transaction needs to be moved from one T-account to another. For example, an error may have been made and a transaction has been recorded in the wrong account. Whenever an amount is moved from one account to another it is important that a record of the movement is kept. This is so that all transactions in a set of accounting records can be traced. The document used to record this transfer is called a journal.

The journal is used to record:

- the purchase and sale of non-current assets on credit (you will see below why these are not recorded in the standard sales and purchases records)

- the correction of errors

- writing off bad or irrecoverable debts (a topic considered in a later chapter)

- opening entries at the beginning of the business or transfer from a manual to a computerised system

- other items not recorded in other books of original entry.

An example journal entry for the credit purchase of equipment is given below. Note the presentation and the narrative explanation of the transaction, which is a requirement for all journal entries.

JOURNAL

			$	$
14 May	Equipment	Dr	10,000	
	Ace Equipment suppliers	Cr		10,000
	Purchase of new equipment on credit			

11 COMPUTERISED ACCOUNTING

Although some businesses use manual accounting records, a significant number have now adopted computerised systems. A fully computerised system will operate under the same principles as a manual system except that all the records will be stored in one place i.e. the hard disk of the computer. This does not necessarily mean that all accounting personnel have access to all records. The system will be broken down into sections in very much the same way as the manual system, with access controlled by a 'password'.

Another difference in a computerised system may be that when the data is printed out, the form of that information may look very different from a manual system particularly with regard to the nominal *(general)* ledger. Whereas in a manual system the nominal *(general)* ledger is a collection of T-accounts, the nominal *(general)* ledger on a computer system will probably appear as an arithmetic listing of debits and credits. This does not mean, however, that the system is not performing double entry – it is; it is simply that the accounts may take the following format:

Motor van account

Date	Details	Dr ($)	Cr ($)	Balance ($)
	Cash at bank	2,000		2,000

As computerised accounts use double entry principles, all you have studied about manual accounts also applies to computerised accounting systems.

Computerised accounting systems make it easier to extract information and reports for accounting staff and managers to assist with management and control of business activities. Examples of reports that many accounting systems normally produce include the following:

- a summary of amounts due from customers, normally broken down by how long amounts have been outstanding from individual customers

- a register of items of property, plant and equipment owned by the business

- a listing of purchase invoices received from suppliers

- a summary of amounts due for payment, so that payments can be prepared and processed

- employee wages and salary payslips, along with a summary of the total of gross pay, deductions and net pay for the workforce as a whole, or by department

- an inventory usage report which summarises receipts and issues into and from inventory during a period of time e.g. a week.

There are, however, some advantages and disadvantages to computerised accounts.

11.1 ADVANTAGES OF COMPUTERS

(a) **Speed**. The computer is very fast – much faster than a clerk or any other type of office machine. This speed can be of value to the business in two ways:

    (i)   High volumes of work can be handled by a computer.

    (ii)   Rapid turn round and response can be achieved.

Thus, one company might value a computer primarily for its ability to cope with large numbers of orders, while another might be more interested in speeding up its order processing.

(b) **Stored program**. Once the programs have been written and tested, the computer can perform large amounts of work with the minimum of labour costs. Only small teams of operators are needed for the largest machines. This is possible because the computer runs under the control of its stored program, and operator activity is limited to loading and unloading peripherals and indicating what work is to be done.

(c) **Decision-making**. The computer can be programmed to undertake complicated decision-making processes. It can handle work to a much higher degree of complexity than other office machines – and often more than the manager.

(d) **File storage and processing**. Large files of data can be stored on magnetic media, which require very little space. More importantly, files thus stored can be reviewed and updated at high speeds, and information can be retrieved from them very quickly.

(e) **Accuracy and reliability**. The computer is very accurate (provided always that its programs are free from faults). It is also very reliable.

11.2 DISADVANTAGES OF COMPUTERS

(a) **Lack of intelligence**. The computer is a machine. It cannot recognise errors made in its program or notice that data is incomplete or incorrect. Errors that would be detected by clerks in a manual system may go unnoticed in a computer-based system. It is therefore necessary to devote the utmost care to the development of computer-based systems in order to foresee every contingency and to test every instruction. Thus, system development is often both prolonged and costly.

(b) **Quantifiable decisions**. The program can only take decisions that can be quantified, for example, that can be expressed as two numbers or amounts that can be compared with each other. It cannot make value judgements of the type involved, in, for example, selecting personnel or deciding whether to take legal action if debts are overdue. The solution indicated by the program may have to be modified because of intangible factors known to the manager but incapable of being expressed in the program.

(c) **Initial costs**. Costs, of hardware, software, site preparation, training and so on tend to be high. Today, software costs often exceed hardware costs.

(d) **Inflexibility**. Owing to the care and attention to detail needed in systems and program development and maintenance, computer systems tend to be inflexible. They take longer and cost more to alter than manual systems.

(e) **Vulnerability**. The more work an organisation transfers to a computer, the greater is its dependence on a single resource. A machine breakdown or damage to the computer, or industrial action by computer staff, may bring the system to a halt.

11.3 INTEGRATED ACCOUNTING PACKAGES

Originally, separate computer programs were written for different parts of the accounting system. However, this is no longer necessary as there are many integrated accounting packages available. Each package varies, but the broad groups are:

(a) **Cash book systems**

This group is merely an electronic version of a manual cash book. Such a system might be suitable for a small business which does not sell on credit and which either provides a service or buys its stock for cash or on credit from a small number of suppliers.

(b) **Basic bookkeeping systems**

These might be suitable for the smaller business selling mainly on a cash basis, requiring basic bookkeeping. Such a system will normally offer basic facilities for maintaining a sales *(receivables)* ledger (the accounts of credit customers), a purchase *(payables)* ledger (the accounts of credit suppliers) and a nominal *(general)* ledger (all other accounts including the bank account, cash account, sales and purchases, etc.). There should be facilities for automatically producing quarterly VAT returns or sales tax reports, a full print out of transactions and perhaps bank reconciliation statements. The package will also generate trial balances, statements of profit or loss and statements of financial position.

(c) **Bookkeeping and accountancy systems**

In addition to offering the basic facilities described above, these packages can cope with a greater number of customer and supplier accounts and offer more sophisticated credit control facilities.

They can generate invoices, print out customers' statements and produce ageing schedules of receivables. They may be able to produce standard letters automatically to send to customers whose accounts are overdue or who have exceeded their agreed credit limit.

Within this group the more advanced packages may incorporate stock control facilities. Separate records are maintained for each stock item recording units purchased and sold and the balance of inventory in hand.

11.4 INTRODUCTION TO ACCOUNT CODES

Every account must be separately identifiable. One method of identification is to give each account its own unique name. However, it is often quicker and more convenient to give accounts their own unique code number as well.

- A code number is usually quicker to write than an account name, so using code numbers can save time.

- Using unique code numbers can reduce the risk of errors, where several different accounts have similar names so that there is a risk that a transaction might be recorded in the wrong account.

- In computerised accounting, it is easier for a computer to process code numbers than account names.

Account codes can be designed to have some significance. For example, a business may have account codes with four digits in the code. If so, it might give the code number 1000 to the owner's capital account, give all asset accounts a code beginning with the number 2, all liabilities a code beginning with a 3, all income accounts a code beginning with 4 and all expense accounts a code beginning with 5. In this way, it is possible to tell immediately from the code whether the account is a capital, asset, liability, income or expense account.

It is usual to record the account codes on source documents before recording the transactions in the accounts. It is important to identify the correct codes to avoid mistakes in the accounting system.

11.5 CODING SYSTEMS

Inputting transactions into the bookkeeping system is normally organised using a system of codes. In most accounting systems all the nominal *(general)* ledger accounts, suppliers, customers, stock items and documents such as cheques and invoices are referenced using codes. This makes it easier to ensure that data is input into the correct account and can also enable the company to conduct additional analyses of data in order to extract useful management information.

Sequential codes

In a sequential system codes are allocated to items in strict numerical order. This means that there is no obvious connection between a code and what it stands for.

For instance in the following system you can have no idea what code 62 would represent.

63   Baked beans
64   Kitchen towels
65   Boxer shorts

Faceted codes

A faceted code is one that is broken down into a number of facets or fields, each of which signifies a unit of information. For instance:

- The first digit:

    1   Fresh foods
    2   Frozen foods
    3   Canned foods
    etc...

- The second digit:

    1   Meat
    2   Pulses
    3   Fruit
    etc...

- The third and fourth digits:

    01   Heinz
    02   Crosse & Blackwell
    03   Own brand
    etc...

A can of Heinz baked beans would therefore have a code of 3201.

Mnemonic codes and significant digit codes

Mnemonic codes are usually in alphanumeric form and incorporate some descriptive element that makes it easy to find the correct code. For example, a customer called 'Robertson' might have a code beginning ROB, e.g. ROB052. A similar concept can be used where items can be distinguished by some kind of measurement. Significant digit codes incorporate digits which are part of the description of the item. For example:

500000 – Jeans
502828 – Jeans – 28" waist, 28" leg
503028 – Jeans – 30" waist, 28" leg

KAPLAN PUBLISHING

FA1: RECORDING FINANCIAL TRANSACTIONS

Block codes and hierarchical codes

Block/hierarchical codes commonly form the basis of nominal ledger coding systems, for instance:

0000 to 0999 – Non-current assets
1000 to 1999 – Current assets
etc...

The first 'block' is allocated to only non-current assets. This means that it is possible to have up to 1,000 different non-current asset accounts.

A hierarchical code structure is a type of faceted code where each digit represents a classification, and each digit further to the right represents a smaller subset than those to the left. This makes it even easier to find items in a list of codes because related accounts are grouped together.

For instance within the 0000 – 0999 non-current assets block, the range 0300 to 0399 may be office furniture assets and 0400 to 0499 may be motor car accounts.

11.6 CHART OF ACCOUNTS

When an accounting system is coded using the block/hierarchical method it is called a chart of accounts. An extract from the default chart of accounts in the widely-used Sage® bookkeeping package is as follows:

Category	Sub-category	Code range		
Non-current assets	Property	0010	to	0019
	Plant and Machinery	0020	to	0029
	Office Equipment	0030	to	0039
	Furniture and Fixtures	0040	to	0049
	Motor Vehicles	0050	to	0059
Current assets	Inventory	1000	to	1099
	Receivables	1100	to	1199
	Bank Account	1200	to	1209
	Deposits and Cash	1210	to	1239
	Credit Card (payables)	1240	to	1240
	Credit Card (receivables)	1250	to	1250

Within each of these sub-divisions Sage provides a number of further default accounts. For instance the Professional Fees range 7600 to 7699 has the following accounts ready set up:

7600	Legal Fees
7601	Audit and Accountancy Fees
7602	Consultancy Fees
7603	Professional Fees

11.7 FEATURES OF A GOOD CODING SYSTEM

An efficient and effective coding system, whether manual or computerised, should incorporate the following features:

- Each item should have a unique code.

- The coding system should have scope for additions and expansion. Codes need to be long enough to allow for the suitable identification of all items, but it should be as brief as possible to save typing time, processing time and storage space.

- Codes should be uniform: for instance if one customer code has three letters and three numbers then all other customer codes should be in the same length and format. This helps to detect missing characters and makes analysis of data easier.

- The use of characters such as dots, dashes, colons and so on is not recommended. A well designed system should avoid confusion between I and 1, O and 0 (zero), S and 5 and so on by only allowing letters or numbers in specific positions (e.g. characters 1 to 3 must be letters; characters 4 to 6 must be numbers).

- The coding system should, if possible, be significant (in other words, the actual code should signify something about the item being coded). If the code consists of alphabetic characters, they should be derived from the item's description or name.

- Controls are needed over the creation and allocation of new codes: for instance this may have to be authorised by the department manager.

- In a manual system there should be an index or reference book of codes. This will be kept automatically in a computerised system.

CONCLUSION

Double entry bookkeeping is fundamental to accounting. If you have a good grasp of this topic you will find it easier to understand complex areas in the future.

The accounting equation shows how assets equal capital and liabilities indicating the duality of double entry: debits equal credits. When preparing ledger accounts the entries are either debit or credit and balances on those accounts are also debit or credit. If the total of all accounts with credit balances are added together, this total should equal the total of all accounts with debit balances. If the totals do not agree, there has been an arithmetical error in the accounting.

Accounts provide indications of how much a business owes, owns or is owed. Different types of account indicate the type of asset, liability, income or expense. Expenditure may be revenue or capital in nature.

The quantity of transactions which take place day to day in modern business are numerous and, because of this, transactions are posted initially to books of original or prime entry such as the cash book, day books and the journal. Computers are also very helpful in dealing with significant information and are nowadays commonly used in bookkeeping.

KEY TERMS

Account – A record of similar transactions, or transactions relating to a particular asset or liability, built up over time.

Accounting equation – Assets = Liabilities + Capital

Asset expenditure – Expenditure on long-term assets (also referred to as capital expenditure).

Assets – An asset is a present economic resource controlled by the entity as a result of past events.

Balance on an account – The amount by which total debit entries exceed total credit entries (debit balance) or total credit entries exceed total debits (credit balance).

Books of prime entry – Books where a transaction is first recorded, such as the sales day book. Also known as books of original entry.

Capital – An owner's investment in the business.

Capital expenditure (also known as asset expenditure) – expenditure on non-current assets expected to be used in the business for more than one year.

Current assets – Assets held for a short time (inventory *(stock)*, receivables *(debtors)*, cash and so on).

Double entry – A system of accounting whereby every transaction is recorded twice, as a debit and a credit entry in two different accounts.

Economic resource – a right that has the potential to produce economic benefits

Inventory – Goods or materials for resale. Sometimes referred to as 'stock'

Journal – A book of prime entry that records transfers from one T-account to another.

Ledger – A set of related accounts.

Liabilities – A liability is a present obligation of the entity to transfer an economic resource as a result of past events.

Nominal (*general*) ledger – A set of accounts for assets, liabilities, capital, income and expenses.

Non-current assets – Long-term assets used in the business over a number of years

Revenue expenditure – Expenditure on expense items.

Separate entity concept – The principle that, from an accounting viewpoint, a business exists separately from its owner.

SELF TEST QUESTIONS

		Paragraph
1	Define an asset.	1
2	Explain the separate entity concept.	2
3	State the accounting equation.	3
4	Give an example of an expense.	4
5	Explain duality.	5
6	What is an account?	6
7	What is a ledger?	6
8	What is contained in the nominal ledger (also called the general ledger or main ledger)?	6
9	Which is the credit side of a T-account and which is the debit side?	6
10	Are increases in an asset debited or credited to the appropriate asset account?	7
11	Are increases in income debited or credited to the appropriate income account?	7
12	Are reductions in expenses debited to the appropriate expense account?	7
13	Are reductions in liabilities credited to the appropriate liability account?	7
14	Is money paid into a business bank account debited or credited to the Bank account in the nominal (general) ledger?	7
15	What is meant by balancing T-accounts and how is that performed?	8
16	Define capital expenditure.	9
17	What is the difference between non-current assets and current assets?	9
18	Identify the main books of prime entry in a business.	10
19	Why are accounts given a code number?	11
20	State two advantages and two disadvantages of computers accounting.	11
21	Describe the importance of coding systems in bookkeeping.	11

EXAM-STYLE QUESTIONS

1 Which of the following is a definition of current assets?

   A   Assets retained for long-term use within the business in order to generate income or make profits

   B   Money or other items owned by the business, which will be converted to money as part of the day-to-day trading activities

   C   The amount owed by the business to the owner

   D   Amounts taken out of the business by the owner for personal use

2 Which one of the following would be a non-current asset?

   A   Inventory

   B   Receivables

   C   Factory premises

   D   Bank overdraft

3 Which parts of the accounting equation are affected by paying off a loan by cash?

   A   Assets, capital

   B   Assets, liabilities

   C   Capital, liabilities

   D   Assets, capital, liabilities

4 Zarina Mohamad has purchased some stationery with a cheque. Which of the following represents the double entry that should be used to record this transaction?

   Account codes

   Bank   4071

   Cash   4072

   Purchases   5001

   Stationery 6137

   A   Dr 4071, Cr 5001

   B   Dr 4072, Cr 6137

   C   Dr 5001, Cr 4072

   D   Dr 6137, Cr 4071

5   Which of the following defines a book of prime entry?

    A   It is where the credit transactions of a business are initially recorded

    B   It is where sales invoices issued and purchase invoices received are recorded

    C   It is where all transactions are initially recorded

    D   It is the only account without a double entry

6   Which of the following is not a book of prime entry?

    A   Sales day book

    B   Petty cash book

    C   Transfer journal

    D   Bank account

7   What is the purpose of the following journal entry?

    Dr   Office equipment $4,000

    Cr   Purchases $4,000

    A   To record the cash purchase of office equipment

    B   To record the credit purchase of office equipment

    C   To correct the error of debiting office equipment to purchases

    D   To correct the error of crediting office equipment to purchases

8   Which of the following is asset expenditure, rather than an expense?

    A   Repair to a delivery van

    B   Business rates

    C   Purchasing office premises

    D   Computers bought for resale by an electronics retailer

9   A debit can represent three of the following. Which is the odd one out?

    A   A decrease in an asset

    B   An increase in an asset

    C   A decrease in a liability

    D   An increase in an expense

10   Which of the following is a disadvantage of computers?

   A   Speed

   B   Accuracy

   C   Vulnerability

   D   File storage and processing

For suggested answers, see the 'Answers' section at the end of the book.

Chapter 4

BANKING: PAYMENTS AND RECEIPTS

This chapter describes the main methods of paying for goods and services. You might already be familiar with much of the content of this chapter, from having a bank account and/or credit card of your own. This chapter covers the central bank clearing system, banks and banking institutions, along with the processing and security features for a range of receipts and payment methods.

CONTENTS

1. Customer/bank relationship
2. Central bank clearing system
3. Types of receipt/payment
4. Preparing a cheque prior to despatch
5. Credit cards, debit cards and contactless payments
6. Automated bank payments
7. Unusual features of receipts and payments media and documentation
8. Banking monies received
9. Handling, storage and security of money
10. Banks and banking institutions

LEARNING OUTCOMES

At the end of this chapter, you should be able to:

- describe the relationship between a bank and its customer
- outline the working of a central bank clearing system
- recognise the obligation owed by a bank to its clients
- understand the content and format of a cheque
- prepare a cheque prior to despatch

- describe the procedure and documentation relating to the use of credit and debit cards
- describe other services offered by banks
- explain the correct procedure to cope with unusual situations associated with payments and receipts
- describe general procedures for dealing with cash, cheques, credit and debit card receipts and payments
- outline the purpose and format of paying-in documents
- understand procedures for banking cash receipts
- describe the key procedures for ensuring safety, security and, where appropriate, confidentiality over the handling of cash and cheques.

1 CUSTOMER/BANK RELATIONSHIP

1.1 RECEIVABLE AND PAYABLE

If a business pays $2,000 into a bank account then the bank owes that money back to the business. The bank is therefore a receivable of the business. Equally, the business is a payable from the bank's point of view.

Alternatively if the bank allows the business an overdraft then the bank is a payable of the business and the business is a receivable in the bank's eyes. The situation in one set of books is a mirror image of the other.

The importance of this relationship is that the bank can use the business's $2,000 in order to invest and hopefully make a profit. This profit does not have to be repaid to the business. This is the bank's to keep. The bank must however repay the $2,000 as and when requested.

Banks provide a number of services to customers and often charge interest and commission. There are pure banking services such as direct debits and standing orders, overdrafts and loans. There are also other services such as the provision of insurance, tax advice and travel facilities.

1.2 BANKERS' OBLIGATIONS

Although a bank does not have to account to its customer for any profit that it makes with the money deposited, it does have a number of obligations to its customer:

- The banker must repay the amount of the deposit on demand or pay it to a third party when requested to by the drawing of a cheque. The bank does not have to pay a cheque in part. For example if a customer has only $100 in their bank account but draws a cheque for $160 then the bank is under no obligation to pay just the $100. It should either pay in full or refuse payment altogether.

- The banker has a duty to honour a customer's cheques up to the amount of the bank balance or agreed overdraft provided that the cheque has been made out correctly.

- The banker must provide the amount of the balance on the account at any time on the request of the customer.

- The banker must provide a statement showing the transactions on the account for an agreed period within a reasonable time of the end of that period. The customer is not obliged to check the statement and therefore any errors made by the bank will usually be binding on the bank.

- The banker also has a contractual duty not to disclose any information regarding the affairs of the customer unless instructed by the customer or compelled by other areas of the law.

- In more general terms the banker is expected to use a professional level of care and skill in dealing with the customer and their account.

1.3 CUSTOMERS' OBLIGATIONS

The main duty of the customer is to ensure that reasonable care is exercised when drawing up cheques. Cheques should be drawn up so as not to mislead the bank and not to facilitate forgery.

2 CENTRAL BANK CLEARING SYSTEM

2.1 CLEARING BANKS

Major high street banks are known as clearing banks, for example, HSBC and Barclays Bank in the UK. These clearing banks settle the amount of cheques drawn on them and payable into their accounts through what is known as the clearing system.

2.2 THE CLEARING SYSTEM

As an example, the clearing system in the UK operates in the following manner:

- All cheques paid into, say, Lloyds Bank branches in a day are sent to Lloyds head office. They are sorted into groups according to the bank that the cheques are drawn on, for example all cheques drawn on HSBC Bank are grouped together.

- This process will take place in each of the clearing bank head offices' clearing departments.

- The end result might be that for that particular day Lloyds requires $18m from HSBC to cover the cheques paid into Lloyds branches that are drawn on HSBC Bank accounts. HSBC in turn requires $24m from Lloyds for cheques paid into HSBC branches drawn on Lloyds' accounts. This is settled by Lloyds paying the difference of $6m to HSBC through the accounts that each of the clearing banks hold at the Bank of England, the central bank for the UK.

- Each individual cheque is then sent to the branch on which it has been drawn. If the cheque is valid and the account has sufficient funds then the account will be debited with the amount of the cheque and the payee's account credited.

- Cheques drawn on other banks or building societies are dealt with in the same system with one of the clearing banks acting as their agent.

- Cheques do not leave the branch if both the drawer (account holder) and the payee (person to whom the cheque is made out) have an account at that branch. Cheques are dealt with at head offices if the drawer and payee have accounts at different branches of the same bank.

Clearing systems may operate differently in countries outside the UK but the principles are similar. The geographical size of a country or accessibility from one city to another may, for example, affect the speed of clearing.

2.3 TIMING OF THE CLEARING SYSTEM

This time taken to process the clearing cheques takes has reduced in recent years. In some cases, such as when the drawer and payee of the cheque have accounts at the same branch of a bank, this may occur within one working day.

2.4 DISHONOURED CHEQUES

The paying bank may not necessarily pay all cheques. For example, if the cheque is incorrectly drawn up or the drawer does not have sufficient funds in the bank account then the drawer's bank will not pay on the cheque. The cheque will be dishonoured. When a customer's cheque is dishonoured this means that the goods or services supplied have not been paid for. The business will look for some other form of payment.

3 TYPES OF RECEIPT/PAYMENT

3.1 CASH

Transactions may also be paid for by notes and coins. A $10 or $50 note legally belongs to the person who holds it and that person may spend it as they wish.

The fact that cash is portable and belongs to the person holding it is also a disadvantage. It can be lost, destroyed or stolen. In quantity, it is also quite bulky.

In terms of security and convenience, bank payments are preferred in business.

3.2 CHEQUES

Cheques are used for a large number of receipts and payments. If you have your own bank account, you are probably familiar with cheques from your personal experience.

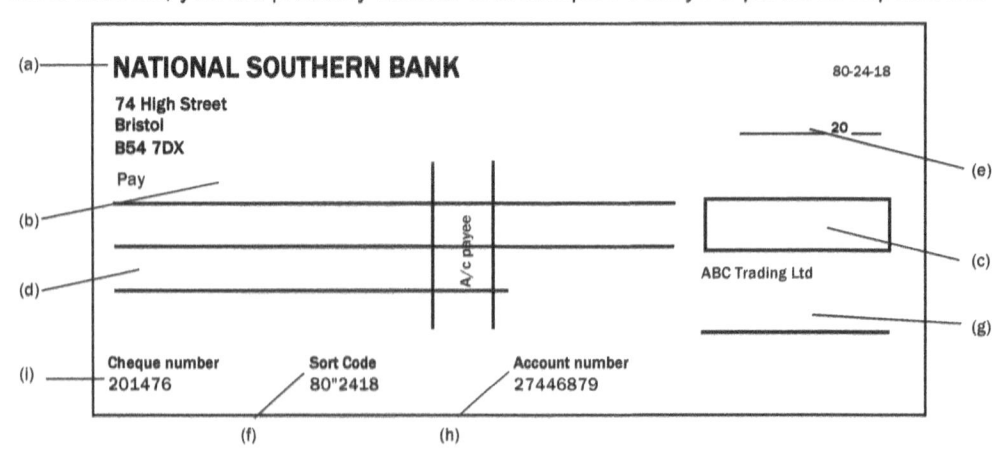

```
(a) ── NATIONAL SOUTHERN BANK                    80-24-18
        74 High Street
        Bristol                                   ──── 20 ──
        B54 7DX                                              (e)
        Pay
(b) ──
                                   A/c payee                 (c)
                                                ABC Trading Ltd
(d) ──
                                                             (g)
        Cheque number   Sort Code      Account number
(i) ──  201476          80"2418        27446879
            (f)            (h)
```

(a) **Bank name and branch** – The cheque identifies the bank and branch of the bank where the payer has the account.

(b) **Payee** – The person the cheque is payable to is called the payee. The payee's name is written on the top line of the cheque, after 'Pay'.

(c)/(d) **Amount** – The amount to be paid is written in both words and numbers. Amounts in pence are not written in words, but shown as figures.

(e) **Date** – The cheque must show a date. If it has not been presented to the bank within six months of this date, the bank will treat it as out-of-date and refuse to accept it. Cheques are sometimes post-dated (dated in advance for some future date). Banks receiving post-dated cheques would refuse to accept them before the actual date on the cheque. Post-dating of cheques is not recommended by banks.

(f) **Bank sort code** – Every branch of every bank has a unique sort code, which is printed on the cheque.

(g) **The name of the account holder and signature of an authorised person (the 'drawer')** – This is the person making the payment by cheque. Cheques written by individuals are signed by the account holder (or one of the account holders, if there is more than one). With business cheques, the name of the individual signing the cheque and the name of the business (the account holder) might be different. For example, cheques written by ABC Limited might be signed by any one of the managing director, chief executive officer, the chief accountant and the deputy chief accountant. The bank will keep a record of the signatures of the individuals who are authorised to sign a cheque on behalf of the business ('authorised signatories').

(h) **Account number** – The account number of the account holder is pre-printed.

(i) **Cheque number** – Each cheque is numbered, in sequence. The cheque number is pre-printed on the cheque.

3.3 CROSSED CHEQUES

A cheque is crossed by drawing (or printing) two parallel vertical lines across it. When a cheque is crossed, the payment has to be made into a bank account, it cannot be paid out in cash. This is a useful security procedure as it prevents cash payments being made to unauthorised persons should the cheque be lost or stolen.

Most cheques are now printed as a crossed cheque and with 'A/c payee' printed between the vertical lines. This is shown below.

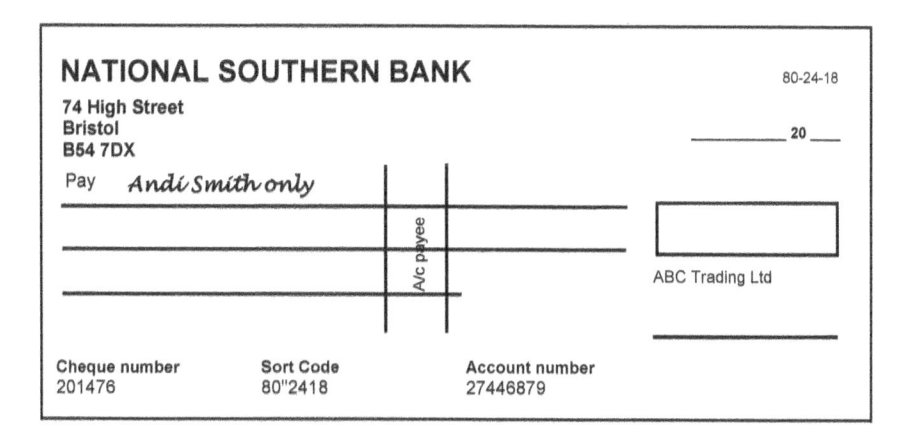

```
NATIONAL SOUTHERN BANK                              80-24-18
74 High Street
Bristol                                             _____ 20 __
B54 7DX
Pay   Andi Smith only
                              |   |
                              | A |
_____| / |
                              | c |                 _____
                              | p |
_____| a |                 ABC Trading Ltd
                              | y |
                              | e |
                              | e |
                              |   |

Cheque number      Sort Code          Account number
201476             80"2418            27446879
```

'A/c payee' stands for 'Account payee'. When a cheque is crossed with A/c payee:

- it must be paid into a bank account, because it is a crossed cheque, and

- it must be paid into the bank account of the person named as the payee on the cheque.

In other words, a cheque crossed A/c payee cannot be endorsed. Endorsement is described in the next section.

Most cheques are crossed A/c payee because it reduces the risk of theft or fraud.

3.4 ENDORSING A CHEQUE

A cheque may be endorsed by the payee unless it is an 'A/c payee' cheque.

Suppose for example that B Brown has written a cheque, payable to G F Dunn, for $500. It can be endorsed by the payee, G F Dunn writing their signature on the back of the cheque. The cheque can then be passed to another person to pay it into their own bank account.

The wide use of 'A/c payee' cheques has significantly reduced the use of endorsements.

ACTIVITY 1

1 Customers have obligations to their bank. Which of the following is a customer's obligation?

    A   To repay the amount of their deposits on demand

    B   Not to disclose any information regarding the affairs of the bank

    C   To use a professional level of care and skill in dealing with their accounts

    D   Not to draw up cheques in a way to facilitate forgery

2 When may a bank return a cheque to the payee?

    (i)   When it is more than six month out of date

    (ii)   When it is unsigned

    (iii)   When the account holder has insufficient funds to cover the cheque

    (iv)   When the cheque is crossed 'A/c payee' and it is presented by the named payee

    A   (i), (ii) and (iii)

    B   (i), (ii) and (iv)

    C   (i), (iii) and (iv)

    D   (ii), (iii) and (iv)

3 What is the effect of endorsing a cheque 'account payee'?

    A It need not go through the clearing system.

    B It cannot be transferred to another person for them to pay the cheque into their bank account.

    C It can be transferred to another person for them to pay the cheque into their bank account.

    D It enables someone other than the account holder to sign a cheque.

For a suggested answer, see the 'Answers' section at the end of the book.

3.5 STANDING ORDERS

Whilst many payments are made by cheque, there are other methods of making payments. For example, it is possible to instruct a bank to make regular payments for a fixed amount to a third party by means of a standing order.

A standing order is an instruction to the bank by the payer to pay a certain amount on a regular basis (usually monthly) to a third party. This removes the need for anyone within the business to remember to make the payment and to write a cheque. The types of regular payments that are made by standing order are items such as insurance premiums or regular donations to charity. The standing order can only be amended or cancelled by the authorised signatory of the bank account which originates the payment.

3.6 DIRECT DEBITS

A bank can also pay a third party on behalf of a customer by a direct debit. This is very similar to a standing order, the main difference being that it is the receiving business that initiates the direct debit and specifies the amount. Also, the amount and frequency of payment can vary with a direct debit.

The types of payments that a business might make using a direct debit include payments of regular bills such as telephone and heating.

3.7 CREDIT TRANSFER

A credit transfer is a further method of instructing a bank to make a payment to a third party. This is usually done by the customer filling out a credit transfer form in favour of the third party. This form is typically attached to the bottom of a bill received by the customer and, when completed, is then handed into the bank and the funds are transferred from the payer's bank account to the payee's bank account.

This method of payment is suitable for one off payments or irregular payments to suppliers. Credit transfer forms (Bank Giro Credit) are often found attached to bills such as gas, electricity and telephone.

3.8 BANKER'S DRAFT

A banker's draft is a payment instrument prepared by a bank at the request of a customer. It can only be paid into an account maintained by the payee named in the draft. The bank will usually require notice from a customer if a banker's draft is required and they will normally charge a fee for its preparation. Upon preparation of the draft, the customer's bank account is immediately charged with the amount of the draft, plus any charges or fees applicable, even though the recipient of the draft ('the payee') may not receive and present it for payment for several days.

In effect, a banker's draft ids a cheque drawn directly upon a bank. The benefit of the banker's draft to the payee is that there is no risk of the draft being dishonoured due to lack of funds on the part of the customer. This form of payment is less popular than it used to be as more individuals and businesses operate bank accounts and there is now a broader range of methods of making receipts and payments between two parties.

3.9 DIRECT PAYMENTS

Many business and personal bank accounts now permit the account holder to make a direct payment to another bank account. The payer needs to have the bank account details of the intended recipient (bank sort code, account number and account name) and is then able to set up a payment authority. The payment authority normally allows the payer flexibility in terms of the amount to be paid and the date of payment.

Individuals may find this beneficial, for example, when paying a tradesperson for work done relating to their property, or as a more convenient alternative to using a cheque. Normally the payer's bank will instigate controls to verify with the payer that the payment authority is valid (i.e. is the account name, bank sort code and account number correct?). The risk of error is reduced by the bank using standard templates for completion for information required.

In addition, following the completion of the payment authority, before a payment is made the bank will instigate further controls to ensure that, for any payment requested, the correct recipient has been selected, and that the date and amount of the payment is correct. Such payments may now appear in the bank account of the recipient within a matter of hours.

Typical controls used in this situation include the bank requesting confirmation from the payer of a confidential password or number code, which may be communicated via the payer's personal mobile phone. There is obviously a risk to the account holder if they set up the payment authority using incorrect details.

4 PREPARING A CHEQUE PRIOR TO DESPATCH

Once supporting documentation for a payment has been correctly authorised, it is ready for payment and the cheque must be drawn up.

- The cheque must be correctly dated with today's date. A post-dated cheque is not strictly valid. Equally, a cheque that is dated more than six months previously will be regarded as 'stale' by the bank and again not valid.

- The cheque should be made out to the correct payee. This means that it should be made out in the full business name of the organisation that is being paid.

- When a cheque is drawn up, not only must it be for the correct amount, but the monetary amount in numbers must agree with the amount stated in words.

- If a cheque payment is for a single invoice or cheque requisition then it is a straightforward matter of copying down the correct amount onto the cheque. However, if the cheque payment is for a number of invoices, and possibly credit notes as well, then these must be correctly totalled in order to arrive at the correct amount for the cheque.

4.1 EXAMPLE

A business, Smith & Co, is about to pay one of its suppliers, Manning & Sons. The sales *(receivables)* ledger record of the amounts owed to Manning & Sons is given below:

Date	Invoice number	Amount $
13 December	105345	382.94
18 December	105448	114.26
20 December	Credit Note 273	102.45
23 December	106293	449.11
12 January	106331	152.83
15 January	106934	119.02
28 January	107018	229.30

It is now 30 January 20X4 and Smith & Co's policy is to pay all invoices net of credit notes for the previous month.

Draw up the cheque that will be sent out to Manning & Sons.

4.2 SOLUTION

Cheque amount

		$
13 December	105345	382.94
18 December	105448	114.26
20 December	Credit Note 273	(102.45)
23 December	106293	449.11
		843.86

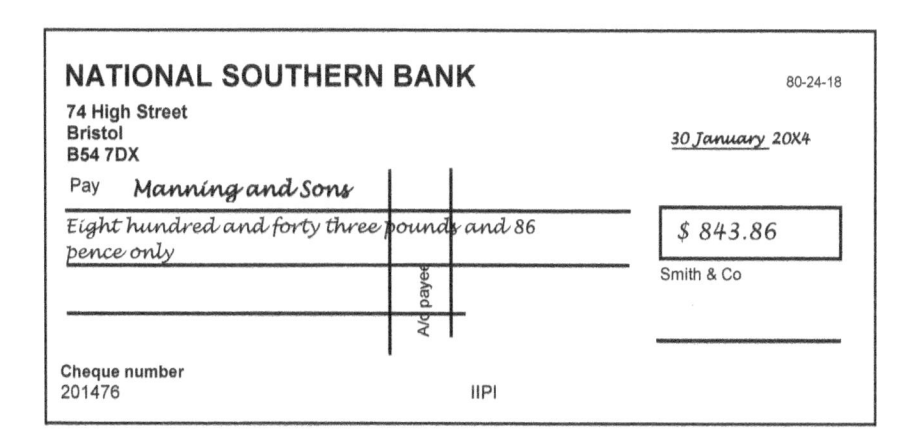

NATIONAL SOUTHERN BANK 80-24-18
74 High Street
Bristol
B54 7DX

30 January 20X4

Pay *Manning and Sons*

Eight hundred and forty three pounds and 86 pence only

$ 843.86

Smith & Co

Cheque number
201476   IIPI

When a cheque has been written it will be removed from the cheque book, signed by the authorised signatory (or signatories) and then sent out to the payee. In order to keep a record of the amount of the cheque payment the counterfoil of the cheque should be completed. The counterfoil of the cheque is the small perforated section that remains in the cheque book when the cheque is removed.

The details to be included on the counterfoil are:

- the date of the cheque
- the payee of the cheque
- the amount of the cheque and
- the amount of any cash discounts taken (see later).

The counterfoil for the cheque payment to Manning & Sons would look like this:

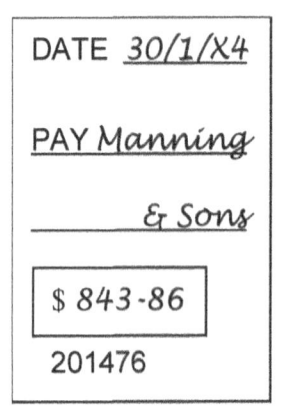

```
DATE  30/1/X4

PAY  Manning
          & Sons

  $ 843-86

  201476
```

4.3 DESIGNATED SIGNATORIES

The individual who sign a cheque is effectively the final person to authorise that expense and payment. The supporting documentation may be authorised and the cheque correctly prepared but it is the cheque signatory who finally signs the cheque and turns it into a valid form of payment. This highlights the importance of the cheque signatory. Many business entities require two designated signatories for a valid cheque.

4.4 EXAMPLE

Each business entity will determine its own system of cheque signatories but a typical example might be as follows:

Amounts up to $5,000	One director
$5,001 to $10,000	Two directors
$10,001 to $20,000	One director plus the finance director
Over $20,000	Managing director/Chief executive officer plus the finance director

ACTIVITY 2

Suppose that the following cheques need to be signed as soon as possible:

	Cheque No.	Amount $
(a)	11723	5,379.20
(b)	11724	1,406.29
(c)	11725	293.50
(d)	11726	20,501.80

Given below are the authorised cheque signatories:

G Gammage	Finance Director
F Freud	Managing Director
P Palim	Marketing Director
T Timms	Finance Manager
S Simon	Production Manager

The cheque signatory limits are:

Amounts up to $1,000	One manager
$1,001 to $2,000	Two managers
$2,001 to $5,000	One director
$5,001 to $10,000	Two directors
$10,001 to $20,000	One director plus the finance director
Over $20,000	Managing director plus the finance director

Who can sign each of these cheques?

For a suggested answer, see the 'Answers' section at the end of the book.

5 CREDIT CARDS, DEBIT CARDS AND CONTACTLESS PAYMENTS

5.1 CREDIT CARDS

Credit cards are available in most countries and many are part of the VISA and MasterCard networks.

Credit cards may be used to purchase goods or services on credit. The customer receives a monthly statement detailing the purchases made and the amount due. If the full amount due is paid off within a specified time scale then there is no interest charge. However, if there is an outstanding amount left on the card, then interest will be charged by the credit card provider on this. There is sometimes also a yearly fee charged for the use of the credit card. A typical credit card is illustrated below.

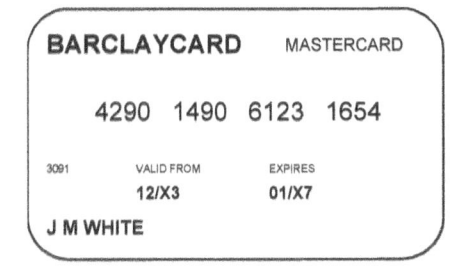

FA1: RECORDING FINANCIAL TRANSACTIONS

The key points to note on the front of the card are:

- the issuing company of the card (e.g. American Express, Morgan Stanley, etc.)
- the card has an individual number unique to that card
- the card will show the date from which it can be used, 'valid from' date, and the date until which it can be used, 'expiry date'. The card is not valid outside of these two dates, and
- the name of the card holder.

The reverse of the card has the following main details:

- a black magnetic strip which has encoded on it all of the details required for a computer to read the card, and
- the card holder's specimen signature.

Cards may also include additional security features such as a photograph of the account holder and holographic images. The UK has introduced a security system called 'chip and pin' under which cardholders key in a personal four digit number when they pay with their card, rather than signing their name.

5.2 DEBIT CARDS

A debit card is a method of making a payment straight from an individual's bank account but without writing a cheque.

If goods are purchased using a debit card (which looks similar to a credit card) then the card is processed in the same way as a credit card with a voucher being signed by the purchaser. The difference is that the purchaser's bank account is debited immediately with the amount of the purchase.

Depending upon the type of debit card that is used, the processing will take place either through the credit card system or through an EFTPOS (Electronic Funds Transfer at Point of Sale) system. EFTPOS enables the instant transfer of funds from the bank account of the purchaser to the account of the seller.

5.3 CREDIT CARDS AND CHARGE CARDS

It is worth briefly distinguishing between a credit card and a charge card.

Credit cards are designed to give the holder choice as to whether to pay off all or only some of the outstanding balance on the card at the end of each month. If a balance remains at the end of the month then the holder will be charged interest on the outstanding amount.

A charge card however differs in this respect as the balance must be cleared in full at the end of each month. Popular examples of charge cards are American Express and Diners Club.

As far as the retailer is concerned the procedures for accepting payment by a credit card or a charge card will be generally the same.

5.4 CONTACTLESS PAYMENTS

In recent years, many banks, retailers and other entities have developed and introduced contactless methods of payment. This may be part of the increased functionality offered by a debit or credit card, or may relate to other devices such as smartcards and smartphones.

When a debit card or credit card is capable of making contactless payments, the following symbol is normally visible on the card.

Similarly, retailers will display the symbol to indicate that contactless payment can be made by their customers.

One of the principal reasons why retailers introduced methods of contactless payment is to improve the speed of making transactions without customers having to sign a receipt or to use their pin number to authorise a transaction. A retailer needs to have a point-of-sale terminal that supports contactless payments. Most modern point-of-sale terminals used by retailers support both contactless payments and payments made using pin numbers. Consequently, contactless payments are often used for transactions of a relatively low value, such as the purchase of drinks and snacks in a coffee house, or to make payment for purchases in a supermarket.

Smartcards may be used for a wide range of activities, including the purchase and use of travel tickets. For example, Transport for London introduced the Oyster card which is a contactless smartcard that records the purchase and use of travel tickets, including season tickets. Examples of similar smartcards that record purchase and use of travel tickets include the PRESTO card in Toronto, the MetroCard in New York and the RioCard in Rio de Janeiro.

Apple Pay uses debit or credit card information linked with the card to make payments. Payments can be made by Apple Pay when using an iPhone, iPad, Apple Watch or Mac. Google introduced a similar system for android devices called Android Pay in the United States of America in 2015 which was introduced in the United Kingdom in the following year. Both payment methods now also include the facility to make payment for purchases within apps. It is possible to use Apple Pay or Android Pay for purchase transactions in excess of the contactless payment limit, in which case it is treated as a normal debit or credit card payment.

As with any payment system, it is essential that there are robust and reliable controls that minimise the risk of error or abuse resulting from loss or theft of any card or device which can be used for contactless payments. One key security feature is that the retailer does not have access to the customer credit or credit card number.

FA1: RECORDING FINANCIAL TRANSACTIONS

Controls that may be applied relating to the security of contactless payments include the following:

- customer choice whether or not to make contactless payments

- the customer has the right to request a receipt as evidence that the transaction that has taken place

- the customer has the right to challenge or query the legitimacy of a contactless payment that appears on their statement

- a maximum monetary limit placed on the value of a contactless payment – either by paying bank or by the retailer to limit their exposure to risk of loss resulting from misuse of lost or stolen cards

- a limit or restriction on the number of contactless payments that can be made before the bank or credit card company require authorisation of a transaction (e.g. by the customer using their 'chip-and-pin' number) to confirm that they are the valid user of the card

- data transmitted following authorisation of a transaction is encrypted and only the paying bank or card company will be able to match the transaction code with the account holder.

6 AUTOMATED BANK PAYMENTS

An automated bank payment is a transfer of money from one bank account to another, without the need for a paper 'transfer document' such as a cheque. Automated payments are often more convenient than paying by cheque. Standing orders and direct debits are common forms of automated payment. Another is BACS.

6.1 BACS PAYMENTS

BACS stands for Banks Automated Clearing System. It is a system for making payments between bank accounts of different banks that reduces the amount of paper work and effort required.

BACS is used:

- for direct debit payments

- for standing order payments

- to make salary payments to employees

- to make payments to regular suppliers (whose banking details are known by the payer).

It is possible to instruct a bank to make BACS payments using a paper instruction, called a BACS payment listing. An example is shown overleaf.

```
┌─────────────────────────────────────────────────────────────────┐
│  NATIONAL SOUTHERN BANK                                         │
│                                                                 │
│  74 High Street, Bristol B54 7DX              Sort Code 80-24-18│
│                                                                 │
│  BACS Payment Listing                                           │
│                                                                 │
│  Payment ref:                  BACS                             │
│  Name of customer:             ABC Trading Ltd                  │
│                                Downland Road                    │
│                                Twyford                          │
│                                Berks                            │
│  Account number:               27446879                         │
│  Date:                                                          │
│  Authority is hereby given to National Southern Bank to make    │
│  the following payments by BACS transfer from the account       │
│  designated above.                                              │
└─────────────────────────────────────────────────────────────────┘
```

Payee	Sort code	Account number	Amount $
		Total	

Please make these payments as soon as possible and debit our account with the total shown above

Authorised signature   Date

Most businesses send the instructions by computer disk to a BACS reception centre, or by electronic communication. This electronic data is then processed at a BACS processing centre, and the payments are then made 'automatically' through the banking system.

7 UNUSUAL FEATURES OF RECEIPTS AND PAYMENTS MEDIA AND DOCUMENTATION

In a perfect world, nothing goes wrong. Ideally, when payments are received from a customer, they should normally be processed without any difficulty or complication. From time to time, however, unusual situations might arise.

- A **cheque might be incorrectly completed** by the customer. When payments by cheque are received through the post, the accounts section should make sure that the cheque has been correctly prepared.

    If a cheque has been incorrectly completed, it should be sent back to the customer. If you come across a cheque that will not be accepted by the bank, you should follow office procedures.

- **Out-of-date cheques**. A cheque that is more than six months out of date will not be processed by the bank. It would be unusual for any cheque to be more than just a few days old. However, there are occasions when a customer writes the wrong year on a cheque. This is often accidental, such as early in a new year. Sometimes, a customer might write in the wrong year deliberately, hoping to delay payment by completing the cheque incorrectly. Out-of-date cheques should be returned to the customer.

- **Credit card limits exceeded**. When a customer pays by credit card, the credit card company might refuse the payment because the customer's credit card limit has been exceeded. When a customer tries to pay by card in a shop, the payment will be rejected on the spot by the automated checking system. However, when a customer pays by post, for example by filling in an order form which includes credit card details, the payment will not be rejected until later.

The credit card payment will be submitted to the bank, but will then be returned when the credit card company rejects it. On receiving notification of a rejected payment, the customer should be informed and asked to pay by a different method.

A supervisor should be informed about unusual situations with large payments because the customer could be deliberately delaying payment, or the attempt at payment might even be fraudulent – for example, a customer might try to pay with a stolen credit card.

7.1 PAYMENT DISAGREES WITH SUPPORTING DOCUMENTATION

Sometimes the amount of a payment might disagree with the supporting documentation. For example:

- A customer might pay an invoice, but send in a payment for the wrong amount. Checking the amount of the payment against the invoice or the customer's ledger account record will reveal the mistake.

- A customer might claim a settlement discount, but calculate the discount incorrectly, and so pay the wrong amount, for example, $90 instead of $95.

In situations where a credit customer is entitled to settlement discount in excess of what has already been accounted for, this will normally be resolved by issuing a credit note to the customer for the additional settlement discount they are entitled to.

Mistakes of this kind can usually be corrected by referring the problem back to the customer. A general rule ought to be, however, that a business should bank the payments it receives, and sort out the discrepancies later. For example, suppose that a business receives a payment of $950 in settlement of an invoice, but on checking it is discovered that the invoice is for $960. The procedure should be to bank the payment for $950 immediately, and contact the customer to ask for the remaining $10.

It would be **bad business practice** to:

- send the incorrect payment back and ask for the correct payment in full, or

- hold on to the payment received without banking it, until the error is corrected.

Occasionally, you may be asked to **check the money from a cash register** against the recorded sales from the till roll. The actual amount of cash collected might be less than the total sales recorded by the cash register. If this happened, some money – possibly notes and coins – have gone missing. It is possible that it may have been stolen. The appropriate course of action might seem obvious:

- carry out the check again, to make sure that you did not make a mistake when counting the money received.

- calculate the amount of money that seems to be missing.

- inform the supervisor.

7.2 REIMBURSEMENT OF EXPENSES TO EMPLOYEES

Problems may also arise in relation to claims made by employees for reimbursement of expenses. Such problems might fall into one of three categories as considered below.

- The claim for payment may not have been authorised in advance. For example, an employee may have bought some stationery for the office and is now seeking reimbursement, without having formerly sought authorisation.

- There may be insufficient supporting evidence. For example, the employee may be claiming for reimbursement of a train fare incurred for attending a training course, but they have failed to produce a receipt.

- The claim exceeds the employee's authorised limits. For example, an employee may have been required to work away and was told not to spend more than $20 per night on dinner. The employee subsequently produces a claim for $30 per night.

Procedures should be in place to ensure that any claim falling under the above headings is referred to a higher-level signatory than the usual signatory. This means that a more senior employee than the person who usually approves of the expenses is required to authorise them. They must treat each claim on a case-by-case basis. This means that they must look at the circumstances surrounding the breach of rules before deciding whether reimbursement should be made.

For example, the employee buying stationery without prior authorisation may have needed, for example, a printer cartridge in order to meet a deadline. He/she may have attempted to contact a more senior employee for authorisation and been unable to contact one. It would be unfair if such reimbursement was denied. Alternatively, they may have bought unnecessary items that were not required, in which case reimbursement should be denied.

ACTIVITY 3

1 Which form of payment allows a purchaser to immediately transfer money from their bank account to the seller's bank account?

   A   Cheque payment

   B   Charge card

   C   Credit card

   D   Debit card

2 Which form of automated payment would be useful in paying wages to employees?

   A   BACS

   B   Credit transfer

   C   Direct debit

   D   Standing order

3   In which of the following instances would a different form of payment be requested for the purchase of goods costing $40?

   A   When a customer pays by cheque

   B   When a customer's credit card company states that the transaction would exceed the set credit limit

   C   When a customer pays by $1 and $2 coins

   D   When a customer is only able to pay by debit card

For a suggested answer, see the 'Answers' section at the end of the book.

8   BANKING MONIES RECEIVED

Payments from customers sometimes go straight into the bank account of the business. Money received through direct debit payments and standing orders, and money received in BACS payments go straight into the bank account. These have to be checked, and recorded in the accounts of the business, but there is no need to bank the money.

In a similar way, payments by credit card through a website are handled automatically by the computer system that processes the payments. A printout is produced of the payments received, but the money goes automatically into the business bank account.

However, when payments are received in notes or coin, or by cheque, the money has to be banked.

8.1   PAYING-IN SLIPS

When money is paid into a bank account, the payments should be accompanied by a paying-in slip. A paying-in slip gives details of:

- the quantities of banknotes and coins paid in

- each cheque paid in

- the total amount paid in.

An **example of a bank paying-in slip** is shown on the following page. If you have your own bank account, you should have paying-in slips of your own, either at the back of your cheque book or in a separate booklet of paying-in slips from the bank.

BANKING: PAYMENTS AND RECEIPTS : CHAPTER 4

Bank Giro Credit					
Date:	29/4/X4		$50	50	00
Code No.	82 09 54		$20	60	00
Bank	National Western Bank		$10	30	00
Branch	Bristol		$5	0	00
Account in the name of	Smith & Co		$2	0	00
Account No.	1 2 3 4 5 6 8 2 1		$1	5	00
Number of cheques	3		50c	1	50
			20c	0	00
Fee	Paid in by / Ref:		Silver	0	25
			Bronze	0	05
			Total cash	146	80
	PLEASE DO NOT WRITE BELOW THIS LINE		Cheques POs, etc.	416	90
			$	563	70

The front side of a paying-in slip gives details of the business bank account, together with a summary of the notes and coins being paid in and the total value of the cheques. The term 'silver' refers to small silver coins of 5c and 10c denomination, and 'bronze' refers to 1c and 2c coins.

Cheques, POs, etc			Brought forward			Brought forward		
30-14-16 Cheque 105326	129	00						
42-08-61 Cheque 215371	81	70						
04-26-35 Cheque 352714	206	20						
Total carried forward			Total carried forward					
						Carried over $	416	90

The reverse side of the paying-in slip is used to itemise the individual cheques.

Similar forms are used, with appropriate changes for relevant currency, in other countries.

FA1: RECORDING FINANCIAL TRANSACTIONS

8.2 PAYING NOTES AND COINS AND CHEQUES INTO A BANK ACCOUNT

To pay notes and coins and cheques into a bank account, the procedures are therefore to:

- Count the notes and coins correctly, and enter the details on the paying-in slip. Many businesses put coins into special bags provided by the bank.

- Write cheque details on the back of the paying-in slip.

- Total the cheque payments and enter this amount on the front side of the paying-in slip, together with the grand total of the amount being banked.

- Take the money to the bank and pay it in. Where large amounts are involved, a business might hire a security firm to take money to the bank.

Example: paying in notes and coins

The contents of a till have been checked and counted at the end of a day. The numbers of each type of note and coin are as follows:

Note/coin	Number
$50	2
$20	43
$10	159
$5	147
$2	20
$1	53
50c	52
20c	226
10c	367
5c	158
2c	362
1c	273

The business will keep a cash float, to put in the till at the start of the next day. The cash float for the following day remains in the business's safe overnight. The remaining cash is to be paid into the bank, using the night deposit box at the local branch of the bank.

Task 1

Work out the total amount of cash from the till for that day.

Task 2

The cash float for tomorrow is to be made up of 10 × $5 notes, 5 × $2 coins, 10 × $1 coins, 10 × 50c coins, 50 × 20c coins, 100 × 10c coins, 100 × 5c coins, 100 × 2c coins and 100 × 1c coins.

Prepare the bank paying-in slip for the amounts of cash to be paid in to the night safe.

Solution

Task 1

Note/coin	Number	Amount $
$50	2	100.00
$20	43	860.00
$10	159	1,590.00
$5	147	735.00
$2	20	40.00
$1	53	53.00
50p	52	26.00
20p	226	45.20
10p	367	36.70
5p	158	7.90
2p	362	7.24
1p	273	2.73
		3,503.77

Task 2

Note/coin	Number in till	Number for cash float	Number to be paid in to bank	Amount $
$50	2	–	2	100.00
$20	43	–	43	860.00
$10	159	–	159	1,590.00
$5	147	10	137	685.00
$2	20	5	15	30.00
$1	53	10	43	43.00
50c	52	10	42	21.00
20c	226	50	176	35.20
10c	367	100	267	26.70
5c	158	100	58	2.90
2c	362	100	262	5.24
1c	273	100	173	1.73
Total				3,400.77

Workings

		$			$
Silver	10c	26.70	Bronze	2c	5.24
	5c	2.90		1c	1.73
		29.60			6.97

Bank Giro Credit				
Date: _____		$50	100	00
Code No.	82 09 54	$20	860	00
Bank	National Western Bank	$10	1,590	00
Branch	Bristol	$5	685	00
Account in the name of		$2	30	00
		$1	43	00
Account No.		50c	21	00
Number of cheques		20c	35	20
Fee	Paid in by / Ref:	Silver	29	60
		Bronze	6	97
		Total cash	3,400	77
	PLEASE DO NOT WRITE BELOW THIS LINE	Cheques POs, etc.		
		$		
	C3 0D92157A C77			

8.3 CHECKING PAYING-IN SLIPS AGAINST RELEVANT DOCUMENTATION

The paying-in slip documents the actual amount of cash, cheques, and credit card vouchers being paid into the bank account. Any discrepancy between the actual amounts of cash, cheques, and credit card vouchers paid in and the documented amounts on the paying-in slip should be picked up by the bank. If any errors have been made on the paying-in slip then this will cause problems with the bank and could lead to a delay in processing the payment into the business bank account.

It is therefore important that the paying-in slip is correct. Once completed the paying-in slip should be reconciled to appropriate supporting documentation for each method of payment.

- The total amount of notes and coins entered onto the paying-in slip should agree with the total of notes and coins counted from the cash register, less any cash float retained for the next day.

- The individual amounts and totals for **cheques** that are entered onto the paying-in slip should be checked either to the original cheques or to any cheque listing or remittance list drawn up. Any cheque listing or remittance list should have been checked against the original cheques when it was drawn up.

- The amount entered as a total for **credit card vouchers** should be checked against the card summary for accuracy. The summary of vouchers should in turn have been checked against the actual credit card vouchers when it was prepared. Banking credit card payments is explained next.

8.4 BANKING CREDIT CARD PAYMENTS

Credit card payments might also have to be paid into a bank account. For example, a shop has to bank its credit card payments from customers. With credit card payments:

- A summary of the credit card voucher payments needs to be prepared for the credit card company. This is handed into the bank.

- In addition, the total amount of credit card payments is included in the paying-in slip, together with the list of cheques and the total for cheque payments.

A card summary is a document giving details of the credit card payments being banked. This is a typical illustration of a card summary.

```
HAVE YOU IMPRINTED THE SUMMARY
WITH YOUR RETAILER'S CARD?

Bank Processing (White)
copy of Summary with your
vouchers in correct order:              ITEMS        AMOUNT

1. SUMMARY           SALES VOUCHERS
2. SALES VOUCHERS    (LISTED OVERLEAF)
3. REFUND VOUCHERS
KEEP Retailer's copies   LESS REFUND
(Blue & Yellow)          VOUCHERS
NO MORE THAN 200
Vouchers to each Summary.  DATE         TOTAL $
DO NOT USE Staples, Pins
Paper Clips
NORTH BANK              BANKING
                        SUMMARY

                                        RETAILER'S SIGNATURE

Complete this summary for every deposit of sales vouchers and enter the total on you
normal current account paying-in slip.
```

(SUMMARY – RETAILER'S COPY)

- The front of the document gives the total of payments, less refund vouchers. (A refund voucher is produced when a customer returns goods to a retailer. The original credit card sales voucher remains valid, but a refund voucher is issued to cancel out the sales voucher.) The 'Items' column is for entering the **number** of sales vouchers and refund vouchers.

- The reverse side of the summary lists the amounts of the credit card vouchers and (if any) the refund vouchers.

	$	c
1		
2		
3		
4		
5		
6		
7		
8		
9		
10		
11		
12		
13		
14		
15		
16		
17		
18		
19		
20		
Total		Carried overleaf

DO NOT TICK OR MAKE ANY MARKS OUTSIDE THE LISTING AREA

Most businesses accept payments from both Visa and MasterCard. If so, a **separate summary voucher is needed for each type of card**.

The summary voucher must also be imprinted with the retailer's own card details, such as the retailer's name and its account number with the credit card company.

Once the card summary has been filled in, the total of the payments (less refunds) is copied on to the reverse side of the paying-in slip, and added to the total of payments by cheque etc.

The credit card vouchers, the card summary and the paying-in slip are then all handed in to the bank.

9 HANDLING, STORAGE AND SECURITY OF MONEY

9.1 WHEN TO PAY MONEY IN TO THE BANK

It is not always possible to bank money received on the same day. However, unless only small amounts are involved, the aim should be to bank payments received as soon as possible.

Money should be banked as soon as possible, for two reasons:

- If payments are not banked, there is a constant risk of theft.

- Paying money into the bank as soon as possible helps to keep the bank overdraft lower, and so keeps interest costs lower.

Many branches of banks have a night safe system, which allows deposits to be put into the bank after the bank has been closed for the day. A business can therefore make payments into a bank by putting the cash, cheques, card vouchers, paying-in slip and card voucher summaries into the bank's night safe. The bank will find the items in the morning and process the payments.

Many businesses prefer to use a night safe rather than hold money in the office overnight, to reduce the risk of loss from theft.

9.2 SECURITY MEASURES

When money is kept in an office, it is important to keep it secure. For example:

- If a lot of money is kept in an office overnight, it should be kept in a safe, rather than a desk drawer.

- Notes and coins should never be left lying around on desk tops or in unlocked drawers. Even small amounts might be stolen.

- When an individual is given the task of taking money to the bank to pay it in, the physical safety of that person should be considered. When very large amounts of notes and coins are involved, the business might hire a security firm to handle payments into the bank. If an employee does the banking, a security measure might be for the employee to be accompanied by someone else. It is also sensible to use different routes to the bank and also different trusted employees. There are instances where long-trusted employees who are routinely employed in banking are influenced by disreputable individuals or, indeed, who suddenly disappear with funds.

It is just as important for a business to ensure safe custody of cheques and remittances received from customers so that they can be properly accounted for and banked. One procedure that a business may adopt to ensure that all monies (including cheques and remittances received) are properly accounted for is to implement a system of segregation of duties between members of staff who may have access to cash, cheques and remittances in order to fulfil their work responsibilities e.g. to update the cash receipts book.

For example, the post received each morning should be opened in the presence of two persons, and a list made of cheques and remittances received. A different individual should then be responsible for updating the cash receipts book. Ideally, the update of other accounting records, such as the general ledger and the individual receivables' ledger accounts should also be performed by different persons.

By allocating responsibility to different members of staff for recording different aspects of a transaction, the risk of error or omission (whether deliberate or unintentional or even theft) should be reduced. It is acknowledged that this may not be possible to achieve in smaller organisations, but elements of this process can normally be adopted in most organisations to minimise the risk of loss or theft or errors in the receipt and recording of cheques and remittances received from customers.

ACTIVITY 4

Here is a final comprehensive exercise relating to paying in money to the bank.

At the end of 16 July 20X5 the cash, cheques and card vouchers from the tills of Bensons Retailers were counted and checked. The total amounts are to be paid into the bank account and the paying-in slip must therefore be prepared.

The amount of cash to be paid into the bank is made up as follows:

Note/coins	Number
$50	1
$20	2
$10	17
$5	51
$2	40
$1	89
50c	258
20c	391
10c	307
5c	219
2c	381
1c	245

The cheques paid into the till during the day have been listed as:

Drawer	Amount $
Unifloss Ltd	279.30
A Amad	27.18
H Knight	55.19
P Dilip	104.72
N C Fisher	31.95
L Lister	82.82
Z Szolai	131.04

The card summary for North Bank card vouchers has already been drawn up and is given on the next page.

BANKING: PAYMENTS AND RECEIPTS : **CHAPTER 4**

	$	c
1	101	23
2	78	19
3	11	21
4	41	30
5	(11	29)
6	5	97
7	23	30
8	10	00
9		
10		
11		
12		
13		
14		
15		
16		
17		
18		
19		
20		
Total	259	91	Carried overleaf

DO NOT TICK OR MAKE ANY MARKS OUTSIDE THE LISTING AREA

Benson Retailers banks with the Brighton branch of Aylesford bank (sort code 16 39 64) and their account number is 17234552.

Complete the paying-in slip given below for the banking for 16 July 20X5.

Cheques, POs, etc		Brought forward		Brought forward		
Total carried forward		Total carried forward				
Date ————		Account ————		Carried over $		

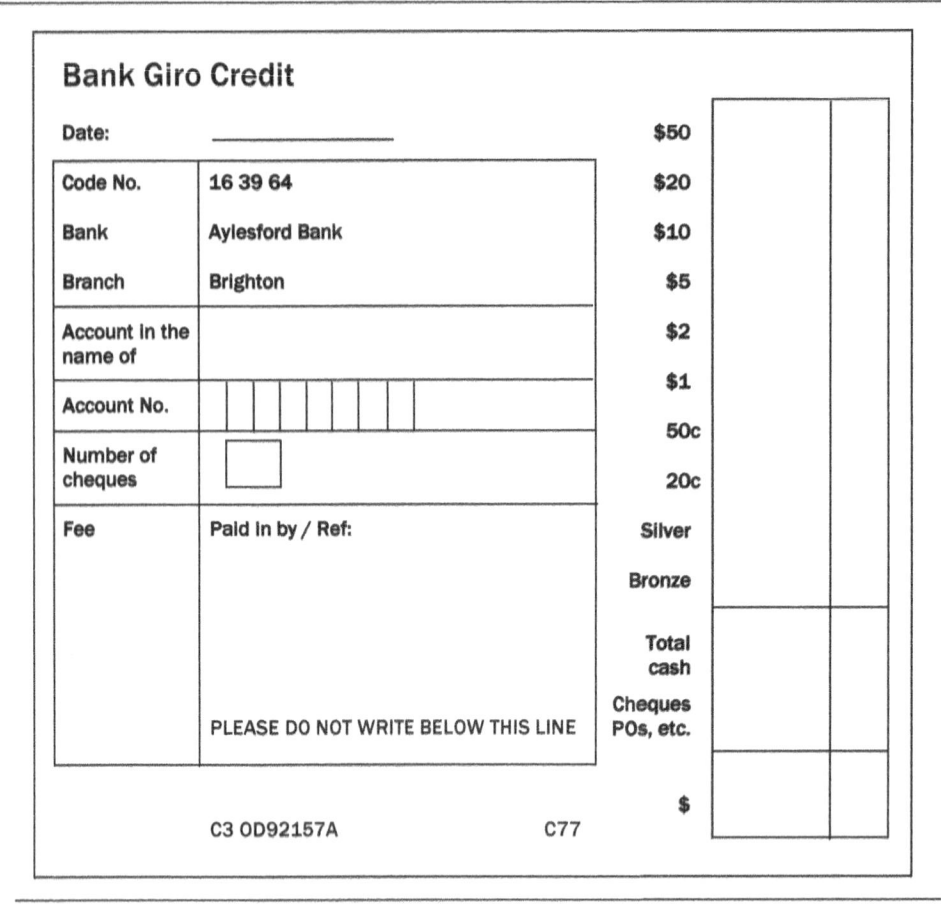

Bank Giro Credit			
Date:		$50	
Code No.	16 39 64	$20	
Bank	Aylesford Bank	$10	
Branch	Brighton	$5	
Account in the name of		$2	
Account No.		$1	
		50c	
Number of cheques		20c	
Fee	Paid in by / Ref:	Silver	
		Bronze	
		Total cash	
	PLEASE DO NOT WRITE BELOW THIS LINE	Cheques POs, etc.	
		$	
C3 0D92157A	C77		

For a suggested answer, see the 'Answers' section at the end of the book.

10 BANKS AND BANKING INSTITUTIONS

10.1 SERVICES OFFERED BY BANKS

High street (or 'retail') banks are usually regarded as providers of a range of banking services to individuals and businesses. This includes operation of cheque or current account services, along with a range of savings and loan account services. Banks are normally subject to strict regulation by government, including authorisation to operate and regular monitoring and supervision to minimise the risk of bank failure or inappropriate conduct. In recent years, the distinction between the services offered by high street banks and other banking institutions has become less marked. However, it is still useful to consider the services traditionally offered by retails banks and other banking institutions.

The range of services provided by banks normally includes the following:

- current account operation, including cheque clearing facilities
- provision of loan and overdraft facilities
- savings accounts and related products
- foreign exchange and currency services
- provision of safe custody or security facilities
- financial advice to individuals and businesses.

10.2 TELEPHONE AND INTERNET BANKING

Most banks now offer personal and business bank accounts that allow telephone and online banking, with some bank accounts based solely upon telephone and internet activity, rather than using the traditional bank branch network to transact business. Such accounts enable the account holder to make regular or ad hoc payments to others provided that they have the bank account details of the intended recipient. Similarly, third parties can make direct payments into another bank account without the need to write and post cheques or visit a bank branch.

Similarly, businesses are now more willing to disclose their bank account details to customers so that they can make direct payment into a nominated bank account following the supply of goods and services. Some businesses also have the facility to link this to their accounting systems so that accounting records are automatically updated to reflect payments received from customers.

Note that there telephone and internet banking is simply another way for account holders to initiate or authorise a range of payments (such as direct payments and standing orders) or to access bank services (such as ordering foreign currency).

Confidentiality and security of data is clearly an important issue for the operation of such accounts. Typically, controls focus upon ensuring that only the account holder can gain access to the bank account details, including the ability to review transactions and statements and entering into new transactions. Although the detail of which controls are applied by an individual bank may differ, they normally have common features.

For example, there may be a multiple-stage access process applying controls such as passwords, pin numbers, personal security questions and account history questions.

To minimise the risk of an account holder making an incorrect payment, there are usually standard template documents to complete to provide the account details of the intended recipient. As the documents are completed, there will normally be a 'logic checks' applied by the bank to ensure that the information appears to be complete, such as checking that the six-digit bank sort code has been provided and falls within accepted number ranges. The account holder is usually asked to check and confirm that the details submitted are correct and complete before the payment request is accepted by the bank. Finally, the bank may also contact the account holder, perhaps using their mobile phone, to send an automated voice or text message stating that a new payment authorisation has been set up and to contact the bank immediately if they have not initiated this account activity.

10.3 SERVICES OFFERED BY BANKING INSTITUTIONS

In addition to high street banks, there are other organisations which are involved in banking activities to a greater or lesser extent. These institutions often focus upon a specialised range of banking activity, rather than provide the broad range of services offered by high street banks. The range of services provided by banking institutions may include the following:

- accepting savings or deposits from customers

- lending money subject to specified criteria or within specified parameters

- providing mortgage facilities

- providing leasing and hire purchase facilities

- providing factoring and invoice discounting services

- providing letters of credit to businesses involved with importing or exporting
- merchant or investment banking activities to provide finance to businesses
- corporate finance advice to businesses.

CONCLUSION

Banks are very important to businesses, providing a convenient and secure place to keep funds and also a source of financing when an organisation is short of cash. In this chapter you have seen how cheques, standing orders and direct debits as well as debit cards are useful ways to pay for goods and services. In addition, credit and charge cards are convenient payment devices too.

Generally most transactions are completed correctly and the cash, cheques, credit card vouchers and so on can be paid into the business bank account using appropriate forms. However, an awareness of problems which can occur may help to identify and avoid potential problems at an early stage. For example, if a cheque is received from a customer, it should be reviewed to ensure that it is complete (e.g. properly prepared, signed and dated, with the amount in words and figures agreed) before it is processed and banked, to avoid having to deal with a cheque returned by the bank.

All transfers of cash, cheques and so on within a business and in transit to the bank need to be handled with care and with appropriate security to avoid loss, theft or destruction and to provide a transaction trail.

KEY TERMS

BACS – Automated payments by bank transfer. BACS is commonly used to pay salaries to employees and to pay regular suppliers.

Charge card – A charge card is similar to a credit card, however, the balance must be paid in full every month.

Credit card – A form of payment whereby the cardholder makes payment to a retailer from an agreed credit facility. The outstanding amount is settled by the cardholder to the credit card company.

Crossed cheque – A cheque is crossed by drawing two parallel vertical lines on it. A crossed cheque must be paid into a bank account.

Debit card – Payment medium allowing instant payment from a customer's bank account to a retailer electronically.

Designated signatory – Person authorised to sign a cheque in defined circumstances.

Direct debit – Order to a bank to make regular payments out of a bank account. The amounts to be paid are notified to the bank by the payee (the account holder having given written authority to the bank for the payee to do this).

Drawer of a cheque – Account holder of person/business writing a cheque.

Payee – The person being paid.

Standing order – An order to a bank to make regular payments out of a bank account. The amount to be paid is notified by the account holder.

SELF TEST QUESTIONS

Paragraph

1	What is the relationship that exists between a bank and its customer?	1
2	State an obligation a bank has to its customers.	1
3	Explain how a central bank clearing system works.	2
4	Identify three separate items which appear on a cheque.	3
5	What does it mean when a cheque is crossed with 'A/c payee'?	3
6	What is meant by endorsing a cheque?	3
7	Give two examples of payments that may be made by direct debit and standing order.	3
8	What details appear on a cheque counterfoil?	4
9	What is meant by a designated signatory?	4
10	Distinguish between a credit card and a debit card.	5
11	What are BACS payments usually used for?	6
12	Explain what makes a cheque invalid.	7
13	Why is it important to reconcile a paying-in slip with its appropriate supporting documentation?	8
14	Are credit card vouchers included on the normal paying-in slip when paying in money at the bank?	8
15	Why should businesses try to pay monies received into their bank account as promptly as possible?	9
16	State a procedure that would improve the security of taking cash to the bank.	9

EXAM-STYLE QUESTIONS

1   What is the bank clearing system?

    A   Agreeing a loan or overdraft between bank and customer

    B   The transfer of cheques between the payee's bank to payment at the drawer's bank

    C   The electronic transfer of funds enabling a supplier to be instantly paid by debit card

    D   Checking customer references before they are given a credit card

2   Which is unique to a bank customer?

    A   Account number

    B   Cheque number

    C   Drawee

    D   Sort code

3   A parent makes a regular monthly payment from their account to their child's bank account to cover living expenses during their time at college or university.

    What method of payment is the parent using?

    A   'Account payee' crossed cheque

    B   BACS

    C   Direct debit

    D   Standing order

4   A bank dishonours a cheque on a partnership account because there are insufficient funds on the account. Who must now pay the outstanding amount?

    A   The bank

    B   The partnership

    C   The payee of the cheque

    D   The person who was the authorised signatory

5   When banking cash, general security procedures should be followed wherever possible. Which of the following is the most risky?

    A   Ensuring that the employee taking the cash to the bank or night safe is accompanied by another employee

    D   Going to the bank or the night safe at different times of day or by a different route

    C   Using the same responsible employee to take the cash to the bank

    D   Using a security firm to transport the cash to the bank if necessary

For suggested answers, see the 'Answers' section at the end of the book.

Chapter 5

SALES AND SALES RECORDS

This chapter explains the procedures for recording income from credit sales, from the preparation of an invoice to recording the income in the accounting records. The chapter introduces the sales day book and sales returns day book, which are the books of prime entry for credit sales. It covers the syllabus area of sales and sales returns.

CONTENTS

1. Source documents for sales and sales returns
2. Types of discount
3. General principles of sales taxes
4. Preparing a sales invoice and credit note
5. Methods of coding data
6. Books of prime entry: day books
7. Sales day book
8. Sales returns day book
9. Function of the primary records: posting transaction details to the ledgers

FA1: RECORDING FINANCIAL TRANSACTIONS

LEARNING OUTCOMES

At the end of this chapter, you should be able to:

- identify and recognise source sales documents
- calculate and record trade and settlement discounts
- understand the general principles sales tax
- calculate sales tax on transactions
- complete sales invoices and process credit notes/debit notes
- record transactions in a sales day book and a sales returns day book
- code sales and customer records and data
- recognise and describe authorisation procedures.

1 SOURCE DOCUMENTS FOR SALES AND SALES RETURNS

1.1 THE PURPOSE OF SALES INVOICES

When a credit sale is made, the cash from the sale is not received immediately. Instead the customer receives the goods or services provided and then pay at some later date. It is therefore usually necessary to create some evidence, and a reminder, of the fact that the customer owes the money for the goods or services. This evidence is created in the form of a sales invoice.

- One copy is sent to the customer as a reminder to pay.
- One or more copies are kept by the seller.

From **the seller's point of view**, the sales invoice serves a number of purposes.

- It is a record of the amount owed by the customer and the date by which the payment is due.
- It provides a record of the sale, and this can be used as a source document to enter the details of the sale into the accounting records.

From **the customer's point of view**, the invoice also has a number of purposes. (To the customer, it is a purchase invoice.)

- It is a reminder of the goods or services that were purchased, the amount payable to the supplier and when the payment is due.
- It provides a record of the purchase, and this can be used as a source document to enter the details of the purchase into the accounting records.

A sales invoice is also an official document for external bodies, such as HM Revenue and Customs in the UK. There are certain legal requirements that a sales invoice must comply with, particularly with regard to sales tax.

1.2 COPIES OF SALES INVOICES

When a sales invoice is prepared, it is produced in multiple copies. The top copy or main copy is sent to the customer. The remaining copies remain with the seller. The seller can use these copies for a variety of purposes:

- to update the accounting records (accounts department)

- to file for reference, for example in the event of a query or complaint by the customer (sales department or customer services department)

- to maintain good business and accounting records.

Records are not only essential for tax purposes, but also other governing bodies and local authorities may require a business to keep certain records. In the UK you need to keep all of your invoices (as well as quotations, order forms, credit notes, delivery notes, till rolls, banking records and other documents) for **six years** in case you are asked for them. Outside the UK, the details of which records must be retained, and for how long, may differ.

1.3 WHEN ARE SALES INVOICES PRODUCED?

In some cases, the sales invoice will be sent out to the customer with the goods or with the person providing the service, so that the customer receives the invoice with the goods or immediately the service is provided. However, it is more usual for goods to be sent to a customer with a delivery note (that the customer might be asked to sign as confirmation of receipt) and for the sales invoice to be sent out separately. This will always be the case if the goods are delivered to one part of the customer's organisation, say its warehouse, and for the invoice to be sent to a different department, such as the accounts department or buying department.

When an invoice is for providing a service, the invoice is usually sent out to the customer after the service has been provided. For example, if an accountant sends an invoice to a client for the hours spent preparing the monthly accounts, then this invoice cannot be sent out until the work has been finished and the number of hours to charge for is known.

In some cases, an invoice might be sent out before the goods or services are provided. For example in most forms of rental agreement, such as the hire of a car, an invoice is sent to the customer before the period of rental begins.

One important point is to determine the contract price to be invoiced in exchange for goods or services provided. This could be based upon, for example, a price list, previous dealings with the customer or normal business practice. Part of this process includes assessing whether a customer will take up the offer of prompt payment or early settlement discount. Consequently, the sales revenue receivable will be variable, depending upon whether the customer takes up the prompt payment discount offer (a lower amount is receivable) or does not pay promptly (the full amount is receivable). This issue is considered in more detail elsewhere in this chapter.

1.4 CONTENTS OF A SALES INVOICE

Most of the essential contents of a sales invoice was covered in Chapter 2. However, there are also some further specific contents that an invoice must contain if the organisation is registered for sales tax or is a registered company.

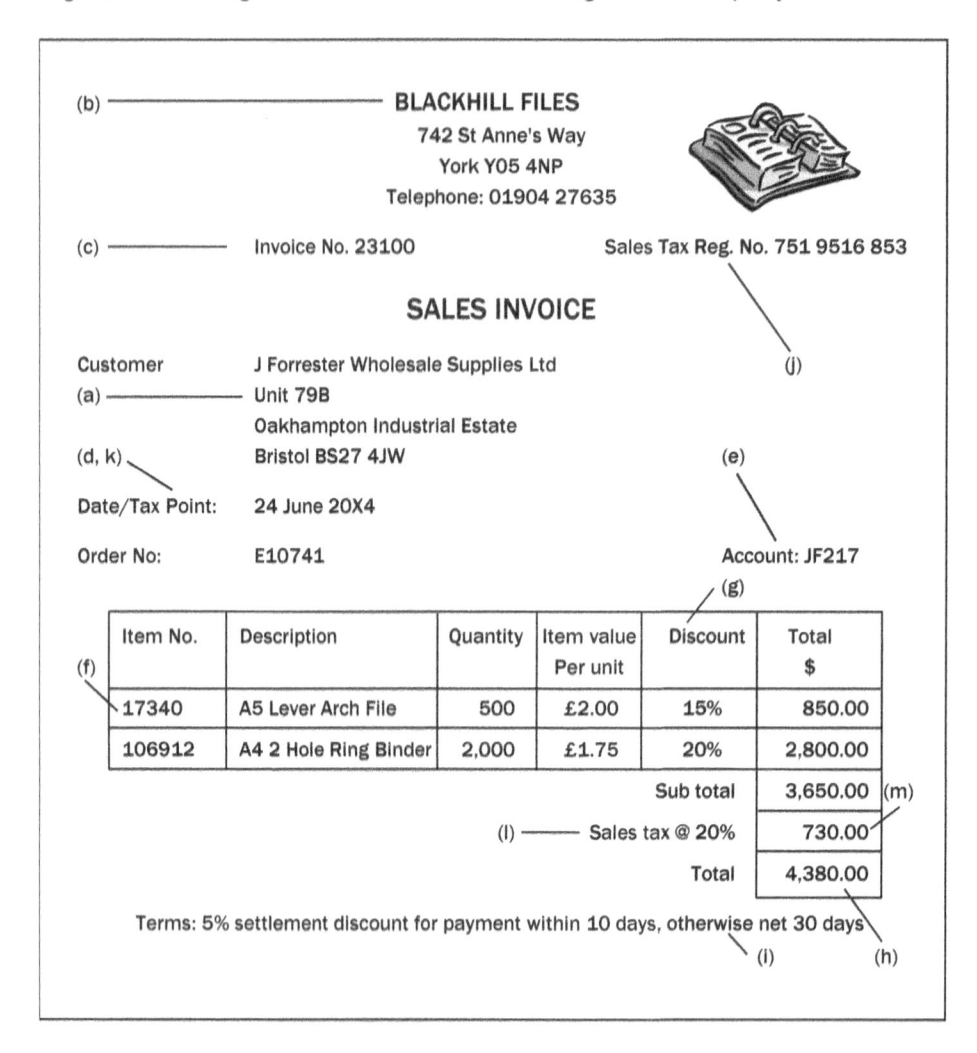

(b) ─────────────── **BLACKHILL FILES**
742 St Anne's Way
York Y05 4NP
Telephone: 01904 27635

(c) ─────── Invoice No. 23100   Sales Tax Reg. No. 751 9516 853

SALES INVOICE

Customer   J Forrester Wholesale Supplies Ltd   (j)
(a) ─────── Unit 79B
              Oakhampton Industrial Estate
(d, k)   Bristol BS27 4JW   (e)

Date/Tax Point: 24 June 20X4

Order No: E10741   Account: JF217
                                                         (g)

Item No.	Description	Quantity	Item value Per unit	Discount	Total $
17340	A5 Lever Arch File	500	£2.00	15%	850.00
106912	A4 2 Hole Ring Binder	2,000	£1.75	20%	2,800.00
				Sub total	3,650.00 (m)
			(l) — Sales tax @ 20%		730.00
				Total	4,380.00

Terms: 5% settlement discount for payment within 10 days, otherwise net 30 days
                                                          (i)   (h)

(a) **Customer name and address**

This is the name and address to which the invoice should be sent (the 'invoice address').

(b) **Name of your business, business address and telephone number**

This shows the customer who the invoice is from, and where to telephone with any queries. The invoice might include some pre-printed payment instructions on the back. In the absence of any other such instructions, this information also shows the customer who to make the payment to and where to send it.

(c) **Invoice number**

Every invoice is given a number. The invoice number must be unique to the invoice so that the invoice can be specifically identified. **When sales invoices are produced, they are numbered sequentially**. This means that if you are asked to prepare some invoices, and you are told that the most recent invoice was numbered 47733, you will number the next invoice 47734, and then the next one 47735, and so on.

SALES AND SALES RECORDS : CHAPTER 5

(d) **Invoice date**

The invoice date is important for accounting purposes, because it indicates the accounting period in which the sale has occurred. The date is also useful as a reference point for when the invoice should be paid.

The invoice date is often the same date as the delivery date, particularly when the delivery note and invoice are both generated by computer at the same time.

(e) **Customer account number or reference**

The customer account number or reference is used internally by the business. Each credit customer (or 'account customer') has a unique number or reference, in the form of a code. Customer account code numbers are used in the accounting system.

(f) **Details of the goods or services supplied**

This information allows both the business and its customers to see details of what is being sold and the price to be paid. Sometimes, this part of the invoice gives a general description of the goods or service. Sometimes, as in this example, the goods or services are itemised in detail, and might show the inventory item code number and description, the quantity sold and the price per unit. The total amount payable for each item, if they are priced separately, is also shown. (If there is no discount to calculate, the total payable for an item is simply the quantity supplied in units multiplied by the price per unit.)

(g) **Trade discounts**

Trade discounts are not always shown on an invoice. Discounts are discussed below.

(h), (l) and (m)

Final total value

The total invoice value must be shown because this is what the customer is being asked to pay. When sales tax is included in the invoice, it is essential to show separately:

- the total payable excluding sales tax
- the sales tax payable
- the total payable including sales tax.

(i) **Settlement terms**

The settlement terms state when the invoice should be paid. These terms are usually agreed when the customer makes an order, but it is certainly worth repeating the terms on the invoice as well. Sometimes, a percentage discount (known as a settlement discount or a prompt payment discount) is given if the invoice is paid earlier than when payment would normally be due.

(j) **Sales tax registration number.**

When a business is registered for sales tax, it is given a unique registration number (by HM Revenue and Customs in the UK). This number must be shown on the invoice.

(k) **Tax point**

This is explained in section 3 of this chapter.

1.5 SETTLEMENT TERMS: TERMS SOMETIMES USED

Some special terms might be used in the settlement terms at the bottom of a sales invoice. It might be useful to know the meaning of the following three terms.

- If settlement is stated as '**net 30 days**' this means that, in the absence of an offer of any settlement discount, the invoice should be paid within 30 days of the invoice date. Similarly, 'net 60 days' means that the invoice should be paid within 60 days of the invoice date. It is normal business practice to use '30 days', '60 days' or '90 days' as meaning '1 month' '2 months' or '3 months' respectively.

- The term '**E & OE**', if it appears on an invoice, stands for 'errors and omissions excepted'. This means that the seller reserves the right to amend any error that is subsequently found on the invoice.

- A sales invoice might include the term '**ex works**'. This means that the price quoted does not include the cost of delivery of the goods. The customer will therefore have to pay for the delivery of the goods separately, perhaps to a haulage firm that makes the delivery.

1.6 PURPOSE OF A CREDIT NOTE

A **credit note** is effectively the reverse of a sales invoice. It is a document sent to a customer stating that they no longer owe money for certain items.

A credit note will be required in the following circumstances when **an invoice has already been sent out** to the customer:

- A customer has returned some or all of the goods because they are damaged or faulty.

- A customer has returned some or all of the goods because they are not the goods that were ordered.

- A customer never received the goods although an invoice was sent out.

- An error made on the original invoice which is corrected using a credit note.

In each case it will be necessary to send out a credit note to the customer in order to reverse or correct the relevant part of the original invoice. This is done instead of cancelling the original invoice and issuing a replacement.

From the **seller's point of view**, the credit note serves the following purposes.

- It indicates that the amount shown on the credit note is no longer due from the customer.

- The details on the credit note are used for entering the information in the accounting records.

From the **customer's point of view**, the credit note serves similar purposes.

- It is evidence that the amount shown is no longer due to the seller.

- It can be used to update the customer's accounting records.

To the seller, the credit note is a credit note issued for 'sales returns'. To the customer, the credit note is a credit note received for 'purchases returns'.

1.7 COPIES OF CREDIT NOTES

It is usual practice to send out the top copy of the credit note to the customer and to use any remaining copies for filing, accounting, control and reference purposes.

1.8 WHEN ARE CREDIT NOTES PRODUCED?

If a customer is given a credit note, it might be reasonable to suppose that the customer is dissatisfied in some way. In order to regain the customer's goodwill, it is important to issue the credit note as soon as possible, to show that the matter has been dealt with promptly.

1.9 CONTENTS OF A CREDIT NOTE

The information required on a credit note is very similar to the information on a sales invoice, although there are some differences. An example of a credit note is given below.

LEWIS.PAPER

47/49 Mill Lane
Manchester M23 6AZ
Telephone: 0161 872 3641

(a) ——————————— **CREDIT NOTE**

(b) ——————— Credit Note No. 23100   Sales Tax Reg. No. 486 4598 220

Customer   J Forrester Wholesale Supplies Ltd
             Unit 79B
             Oakhampton Industrial Estate
             Bristol BS27 4JW

Date/Tax Point: 24 June 20X4

Original Invoice No: 21391 ——————— (c)   Account: 216340

Item No.	Description	Quantity	Item value	Discount	Total $
ST095	A4 Copier Paper Green	20 reams	£5.40 per ream	10%	97.20
				Sub total	97.20
Reason for credit note				Sales tax at 20%	19.44
Goods returned as damaged in transit —— (d)				Credit note total	£116.64

From this, it can be seen that the main differences between a sales invoice and credit note are as follows.

(a) The words '**credit note**' are displayed prominently on the document, to avoid confusion with an invoice.

(b) Instead of an invoice number, there is a unique credit note number. Like sales invoices, credit notes issued are numbered sequentially.

(c) A reference should be provided to the original invoice number to which the credit note relates.

(d) A reason for the credit note being sent out should be included.

Otherwise, credit notes and sales invoices look very similar. To avoid confusion between the two, credit notes might be printed on different coloured paper from sales invoices.

2 TYPES OF DISCOUNT

2.1 TRADE DISCOUNTS

Trade discounts are given to customers for a variety of reasons. The main reason a trade discount is offered is to encourage customers to either purchase more goods over a period of time and/or to encourage them to place larger individual orders.

For example, trade discount may be offered to customers who purchase in excess of, say, 1,000 units of a product within a specified period. Alternatively, trade discount could be offered on any individual order to purchase, say, 100 units or more in a single transaction.

It is normal policy to show the percentage of trade discount on the face of a sales invoice. For example if the list price of goods is $100 and a 10% trade discount is given then this might be shown on the invoice as:

	$
List price	100.00
Less: 10% trade discount	10.00
Net price	90.00

The customer pays the net price. If sales tax is charged, it should be added to the net price, and the customer is required to pay the net price plus sales tax. Different percentages of trade discount might be applied to different products, in which case the relevant percentage discount is normally shown against each product on the invoice before sales tax is calculated, in the following alternative layout:

Product	Description	Quantity	Item price $	Discount	Total $
HS336	Table	1	100.00	10%	90.00
HS472	Chair	6	90.00	5%	513.00
					603.00
Sales tax @ 20%					120.60
					723.60

2.2 SETTLEMENT DISCOUNT

A settlement (or prompt payment) discount is a discount that is offered to a customer if the invoice is paid by a specified date, prior to the end of the normal credit period.

Typically, an invoice will state that payment is due 30 days from the invoice date. However, to persuade the customer to pay early, a percentage discount will be offered if payment is made before the due date. This discount is known as a **settlement discount or prompt payment discount**.

A settlement discount is therefore different in nature to a trade discount. A trade discount is a definite reduction in price that is **given** to the customer. A settlement discount is a reduction in the overall invoice price that is **offered** to the customer. It is for the customer to decide whether to accept this discount and pay the reduced amount within the required timescale, or whether to pay the full invoice amount at some later date.

A **typical wording of a settlement discount** might be '4% cash discount for payment within 14 days otherwise net 30 days'. This may be greatly abbreviated to: '4/14, net 30'.

This means that if the customer decides to pay the invoice within 14 days of the invoice date, 4% can be deducted from the invoice total and only the remaining amount is paid. However, if the customer decides not to accept the settlement discount the full invoice amount should still be paid within 30 days.

In practical terms if a settlement discount is offered to a credit customer, there is no way of knowing, at the point when the invoice is prepared, whether the customer will take advantage of the discount terms offered and pay the reduced amount. This is known as **'variable consideration'** as the seller does not know at the time sales revenue is recorded whether they will receive only the discounted amount or the full amount.

A business could therefore adopt one of the following approaches to deal with this situation:

- prepare the sales invoice for the full amount and, if the customer should pay early to claim the settlement discount, issue a credit note for the discount allowed to the customer. If the customer does not pay early, the full amount is due as normal.

- prepare the invoice for the reduced amount (after applying the settlement discount) on the expectation that the customer will pay early and be entitled to the settlement discount. Subsequently, if the customer does not pay early and is no longer entitled to the discount, the full amount is due and the additional amount received would be treated as if it were a cash sale.

Therefore, **in examination questions**, it will be stated whether a credit customer is expected to take advantage of settlement discount terms or not for the purpose of calculating amounts due from customers, or to calculate and account for amounts received from customers.

For example, consider the situation of a business which sold goods to a customer at a price of $200, and the customer is offered 3% settlement discount for settlement within ten days of the invoice date.

If the customer **is not expected to take advantage** of the early settlement discount terms, the invoice would consist of the following amounts:

	$
List price	200.00
Less: 3% settlement discount	Nil
Amount due from customer	200.00

The accounting entries recorded by the seller would be as follows:

Debit Receivables $200.00

Credit Revenue $200.00

If, as expected, the customer does not take advantage of the settlement discount available, the full amount of $200.00 should be paid by the customer. When the cash is received, the accounting entries to record this would be as follows:

Debit   Cash $200.00

Credit   Receivables $200.00

If however, the customer does take advantage of the settlement discount terms, they will pay $194.00. The total receivable of $200.00 must be cleared, even though only $194.00 has been received. This would be accounted for by making an adjustment to revenue as follows:

Debit   Cash $194.00 (97% of $200.00)

Debit   Revenue $6.00

Credit   Receivables $200.00

If the customer **is expected to take advantage** of the early settlement discount terms, the invoice would consist of the following amounts:

	$
List price	200.00
Less: 3% settlement discount	(6.00)
Amount due from customer	194.00

In this situation, settlement discount allowed is excluded from the accounting records in the same way as trade discount is excluded from the accounting records. The accounting entries initially recorded by the seller would be as follows:

Debit   Receivables $194.00

Credit   Revenue $194.00

Subsequently if, as expected, the customer pays within ten days to take advantage of the early settlement terms, the receipt of cash will be accounted for as follows:

Debit   Cash $194.00

Credit   Receivables $194.00

If the customer does not take advantage of the early settlement terms, the full amount of $200.00 is due. When it is received, the additional variable consideration received is accounted for as if it were an additional cash sale as follows:

Debit   Cash $200.00

Credit Receivables $194.00

Credit Revenue $6.00

ACTIVITY 1

1   Why are sales invoices prepared in multiple copies?

   (i)   To update the accounting records

   (ii) To file for reference in case of customer query

   (iii) For record keeping purposes in the business

   (iv) For sending to the customer

   A   (i), (ii) and (iii)

   B   (i), (iii) and (iv)

   C   (ii), (iii) and (iv)

   D   All the above

2   What may appear on an invoice to indicate that delivery is not included?

   A   E & OE

   B   Ex works

   C   30 days net

   D   Settlement discount

3   How does a customer know to which transaction a credit note relates?

   A   By reference to the credit note number

   B   By reference to the amount of the credit note

   C   By the reason given for the issue of the credit note

   D   By reference to the quoted invoice number on the credit note

FA1: RECORDING FINANCIAL TRANSACTIONS

4 Three office chairs costing $77 each with an agreed trade discount of 10% have been sent to a customer. What is the total of the invoice for the three chairs?

   A $7.70

   B $69.30

   C $207.90

   D $210.00

5 A sale was made to a credit customer at a price of $500, less trade discount of 5%. The customer is expected to take advantage of the early settlement discount terms and receive 4% discount for payment within ten days. What is the total of the sales invoice?

   A $456.00

   B $475.00

   C $480.00

   D $495.00

6 A sale was made to a customer at a price of $1,500. The customer is entitled to 6% trade discount. Early settlement discount of 3% was offered to the customer for payment within ten days, and the customer was expected to take advantage of this offer. Subsequently, the customer did not take advantage of the early settlement discount and paid after 30 days. What accounting entries are required to record the subsequent receipt of cash?

   A   Debit Cash $1,410.00   Credit Receivables $1,410.00

   B   Debit Cash $1,367.70   Credit Receivables $1,367.70

   C   Debit Cash $1,410.00   Credit Receivables $1,367.70

                                    Credit Revenue $42.30

   D   Debit Cash $1,367.70   Credit Revenue $1,367.70

7 A sale was made to a customer at a price of $750. The customer is entitled to 6% trade discount. Early settlement discount of 2% has been offered to the customer for payment within ten days, but the customer is not expected to take advantage of this offer. What is the total of the sales invoice?

   A $690.90

   B $705.00

   C $735.00

   D $750.00

For a suggested answer, see the 'Answers' section at the end of the book.

3 GENERAL PRINCIPLES OF SALES TAXES

An international perspective

Sales tax is one that applies to most business transactions involving a transfer of goods or services. It is often referred to as a tax on consumption as it is the final consumer of the goods and services that usually incurs the cost.

The basic principle is that businesses operate as the agent of the tax authority collecting the tax on their behalf and paying it over to them on a regular basis.

The rates of sales tax around the world vary, and therefore the percentage sales tax used in the exam may vary as well. However, it is not the amount of the tax that is important for the exam, but a keen understanding of the principles involved in accounting for that tax, whatever the rate may be. You will always be given the relevant rate in the exam and you must use this for your calculations.

3.1 BASIC CALCULATION OF SALES TAX

Whenever a sales tax registered business sells anything, it must charge its customers sales tax on all goods or services to which the tax applies.

The basic calculation is to take a percentage of the invoice total (after deducting any trade discounts) and to round this amount down to the nearest cent or penny.

So, for goods with a list price of $50.00 on which a 10% trade discount is allowed, and settlement discount of 3% (which was expected to be taken up by the customer) the net amount would be $43.65 (shown below) on which sales tax at the appropriate rate calculated and added.

List price	$50.00
Less: trade discount	$5.00
Less: settlement discount	$1.35 (i.e. 3% × $45.00)
Net	$43.65

3.2 SALES TAX REQUIREMENTS

If a business is sales tax registered, then it must charge sales tax on its sales and must issue a sales tax invoice. To be a valid sales tax invoice, certain information must be included on the invoice.

(a) **Registration number**

All sales tax registered businesses will have a unique registration number. The requirement to include this number on the invoice enables the tax authorities to determine whether the invoice came from a valid registered business.

(b) **Tax point**

The tax point on an invoice is the date when a transaction is deemed to have taken place for sales tax purposes. It enables the tax on the transaction to be recorded in the correct accounting period. There are quite complex tax point rules, but usually the tax point is the invoice date.

(c) **Rate of sales tax**

The rate of sales tax on an invoice must be shown. Rates vary from country to country and some countries may have more than one rate. The rate you need to apply in the exam will be given to you. Note that the FA 1 syllabus does not include accounting for sales tax on a reduced amount where settlement discount (i.e. prompt payment discount) has been offered. Therefore, sales tax should be calculated on the net amount using the appropriate rate of sales tax.

ACTIVITY 2

Complete the following sales invoice details:

	$
4 widgets at $100 each	400.00
1 grommit at $43 each	43.00
Sub-total	443.00
Sales tax at 20%	
Amount payable	

Terms Net 30 days.

For a suggested answer, see the 'Answers' section at the end of the book.

4 PREPARING A SALES INVOICE AND CREDIT NOTE

You need to understand the administrative procedures that must be carried out before an invoice and credit note are prepared and sent out to the customer, as well as how to prepare them.

4.1 AUTHORISING THE PREPARATION OF AN INVOICE

A business should not send out an invoice to a customer until the appropriate time. Usually, this is after the goods have been delivered or the service has been provided. A person in authority should confirm that the goods or services have been provided, and that an invoice should now be prepared and issued. The person who gives authorisation for an invoice to be prepared is likely to be an office manager, but arrangements will differ between organisations.

The purpose of authorising an invoice, however, is to avoid sending out invoices to a customer for goods or services that have not been delivered.

Credit notes, which reduce the amount owing by the customer, should only be sent out when necessary and be properly authorised.

4.2 FINDING THE INFORMATION FOR A SALES INVOICE

When authorisation has been given for a sales invoice to be prepared, the task will usually fall on someone in the accounts department. The information for preparing the invoice could come from several different sources, such as:

- a customer purchase order
- a price list for items sold by the organisation
- a sales order
- a copy of a price quotation sent to the customer.

Customer details

In many instances businesses deal with the same credit customers (or account customers) again and again over a period of time. If so, it would be usual to keep a file of customer details. The customer details needed to produce sales invoice are likely to be:

- customer name
- customer delivery address
- customer invoice address
- customer telephone number, fax number and e-mail details
- customer account number/code (for internal purposes)
- the agreed discount terms both for trade and settlement discounts.

If goods are supplied to a new customer then there will be no existing customer details and the ordering process should ensure that the relevant invoicing details for the customer are recorded when the order is placed.

Goods details

The main information requirements are:

- the quantity of goods to be invoiced
- the description and/or product coding of the goods
- the price of the goods
- the date of the invoice (usually the despatch date).

The quantity, description, code and price of the goods might be available from the customer's purchase order. However, if the business is unable to fulfil all of the customer's quantity requirements then the actual quantity to be invoiced may have to be identified from the despatch note or delivery note, so that the customer is invoiced only for goods delivered.

The code and price of the goods may be available from the customer's purchase order or a sales order form. Alternatively it might be necessary to look them up from the current price list.

FA1: RECORDING FINANCIAL TRANSACTIONS

Supply of services

If an invoice is to be raised for the provision of a service rather than the supply of goods then the information required is likely to come from different sources. The supply of services will usually involve the customer being charged with the time of the person supplying the service.

The actual time spent on the customer's job can normally be obtained from timesheets or job sheets and the hourly charge-out rate of the employee from the appropriate accounting records.

In many service situations, such as car repairs or machinery repairs, spare parts will also form part of the cost to the customer and therefore part of the invoice. The retail price of such parts will normally be taken from a current price list.

4.3 CHECKING AND APPROVING A COMPLETED INVOICE

When an invoice has been prepared manually, it should be checked against the original documents (the purchase order, price list, and so on) to make sure that there are no errors in the invoice details. In addition, a check should be made that all the required information has been included.

Although procedures vary between organisations, the responsibility for checking invoices might be given to the accounts supervisor. After the invoice has been checked and approved, it should be sent out to the customer.

ACTIVITY 3

Given below are three customer purchase orders, an extract from the current price list and the relevant customer details. The most recent sales invoice number was 33825.

From the information you are required to prepare sales invoices to be sent out with the orders for these goods.

Today's date is 22 June 20X4.

Price list extract

Code	Description	Price $
Y29DI	Plain self-seal envelopes	7.99 per 500
Y29WW	White window envelopes (A4)	8.80 per 500
Y13BP	Economy manila plain (A5)	6.20 per 1,000
Y14BW	Economy manila window (A5)	7.50 per 1,000
Y21BP	Economy manila plain (A4)	10.60 per 1,000
Y22BW	Economy manila window (A4)	11.30 per 1,000
W66MS	Whiteboard marker set (6)	4.90
W67MS	Whiteboard marker set (10)	8.30
W41OD	Document wallets (paper)	4.21 per 50
W42OK	Document wallets (plastic)	15.80 per 100
W55OP	Document zipper wallets (plastic)	8.60 per 10
A91FF	Accordion expanding file	3.40
A34SP	Suspension files (paper)	26.70 per 50
P52LK	Personal lockable file	28.30

Customer details

Name	Accounting code	Address	Discounts agreed	
			Trade	Settlement
DU Enterprises	D46	Finch Estate Dartmouth Devon EX55 99R	5%	Net 30 days
P J Freeman	F12	New Street Plymouth Devon PL4 7ZU	–	3% for payment within 10 days, net 30 days
Tab Design	T03	22 Fairmount Rd Tavistock Devon TA4 8BB	10%	4% for payment within 10 days, net 30 days

P J Freeman is expected to take advantage of the early settlement discount offered.

Tab Design is not expected to take up the early settlement discount offered.

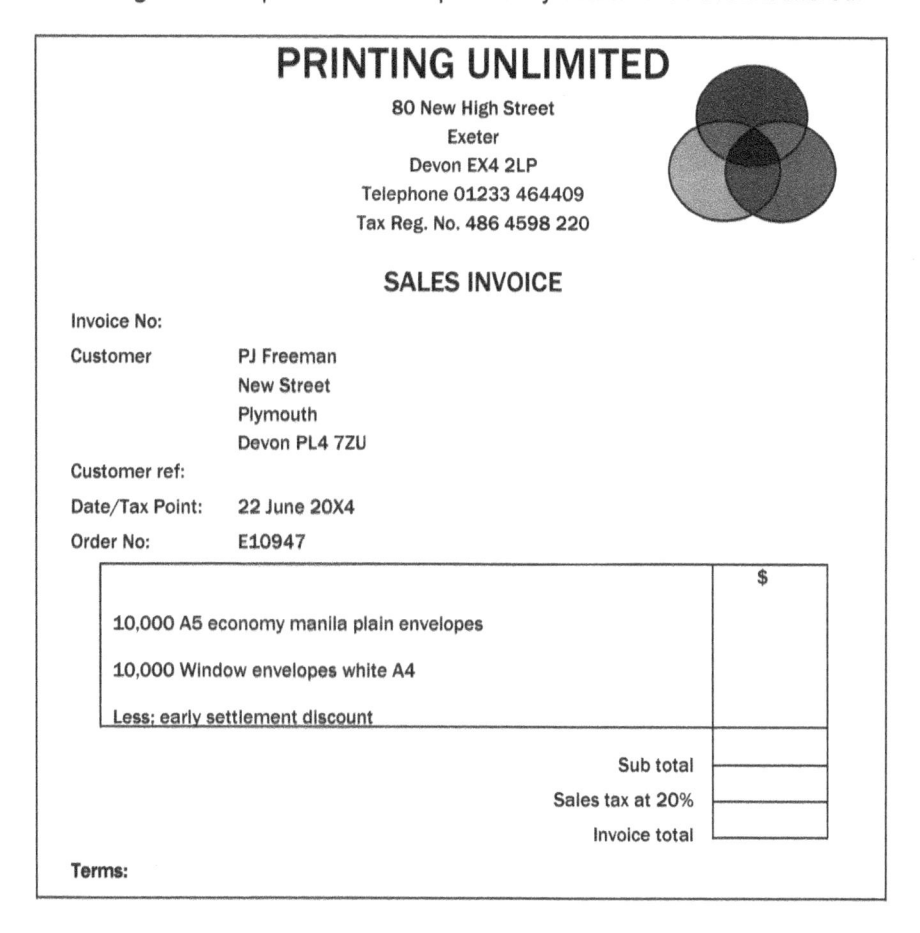

PRINTING UNLIMITED

80 New High Street
Exeter
Devon EX4 2LP
Telephone 01233 464409
Tax Reg. No. 486 4598 220

SALES INVOICE

Invoice No:
Customer: PJ Freeman
New Street
Plymouth
Devon PL4 7ZU
Customer ref:
Date/Tax Point: 22 June 20X4
Order No: E10947

	$
10,000 A5 economy manila plain envelopes	
10,000 Window envelopes white A4	
Less: early settlement discount	
Sub total	
Sales tax at 20%	
Invoice total	

Terms:

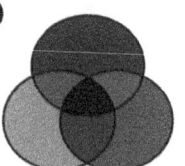

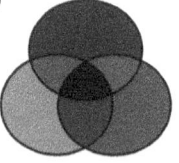

PRINTING UNLIMITED

80 New High Street
Exeter
Devon EX4 2LP
Telephone 01233 464409
Tax Reg. No. 486 4598 220

SALES INVOICE

Invoice No:

Customer   DU Enterprises
                Finch Estate
                Dartmouth
                EX55 99R

Customer ref:

Date/Tax Point: 22 June 20X4

Order No: E10948

	$
200 Suspension files	
500 Document wallets (paper)	
400 Document wallets (plastic)	
Total for goods before discount	
Less: trade discount of 5%	
Sub total	
Sales tax at 20%	
Invoice total	

Terms:

PRINTING UNLIMITED

80 New High Street
Exeter
Devon EX4 2LP
Telephone 01233 464409
Tax Reg. No. 486 4598 220

SALES INVOICE

Invoice No:

Customer   Tab Design
                22 Fairmount Road
                Tavistock
                Devon TA4 8BB

Customer ref:

Date/Tax Point: 22 June 20X4

Order No: E10949

	$
3 Whiteboard marker sets (10)	
1 Personal lockable file	
7 Accordian expanding files	
3,000 Plain self-seal envelopes	
Sub total	
Sales tax at 20%	
Invoice total	

Terms:

For a suggested answer, see the 'Answers' section at the end of the book.

4.4 OBTAINING THE DETAILS FOR A CREDIT NOTE

The procedures and processes for authorising, preparing and checking and approving a credit note are very similar to those for a sales invoice. This is perhaps not surprising, since preparing a credit note is simply the reversal of all or part of an earlier sales invoice, or the correction of an earlier sales invoice.

Remember that when you issue credit notes, they are numbered sequentially.

Customer details

The customer details can be obtained from the file of customer records or from a copy of the original invoice.

Details of goods returned

When a customer returns goods, there should be a check of the quantities returned and their condition. When the goods have been checked, some form of **goods returned note** should be completed. This will include details of the goods returned and usually the reasons for their return. If the reason for the credit note is not goods returned as such but a change in price or an allowance for poor work, then the source document may be a letter, a fax, an e-mail, or even a note on the original invoice.

This information is part of what is required for the credit note. However, as well as knowing the **quantity** of goods returned, we also need to know the price originally charged to the customer. The list price can be found from the price list that was in issue at the date of the original invoice and any trade discount allowed should be identified from the customer details file or a copy of the original invoice.

Correction of invoice errors

If a credit note is to be issued to correct an error on the original invoice rather than for the return of any goods from the customer, then the details for the credit note will normally be available from the original invoice together with any subsequent correspondence with the customer giving details of the amount and reason for the correction.

4.5 SALES TAX ON CREDIT NOTES

When a credit note is issued, the amount of sales tax payable is also reduced. The sales tax on the credit note should be calculated in the same way as on the invoice.

ACTIVITY 4

A credit note needs to be prepared for Tab Design, for sales returns. The amount of the credit note was $28.30 before sales tax at 20%. What should be the total value of the credit note?

For a suggested answer, see the 'Answers' section at the end of the book.

4.6 AUTHORISATION AND APPROVAL OF CREDIT NOTES

Authorisation should be given for the preparation of a credit note. The person in authority might indicate that the credit note should be prepared simply by signing or initialling the source document containing details of the sales return.

Credit notes should be checked for accuracy, probably by the accounts supervisor. After a credit note has been approved, it should be sent promptly to the customer.

5 METHODS OF CODING DATA

Sales invoices and credit notes are source documents for recording the details of the transactions in the accounting records of the business.

5.1 CODING REQUIRED FOR A SALES INVOICE

For a **sales invoice**, the coding should be enough to ensure that:

- the transaction can be recorded properly in the nominal ledger *(general ledger)*, and
- a record is also made of the money owed by the individual customer.

In a manual system, this will normally require several codes.

- For the nominal *(general)* ledger record, the code number for the sales account and for the sales tax account.
- To record the amount owed by the individual receivable the customer's account code. This might be referred to as the customer's **sales ledger account code**.

The sales ledger and sales ledger accounts are explained in the next chapter.

5.2 CODING REQUIRED FOR A CREDIT NOTE

The **coding required for a credit note** should be sufficient to identify the transaction as a sales return or return from a customer, for recording in the nominal *(general)* ledger. In addition, a record should be made of the fact that the debt of the individual customer has now been reduced.

In a manual accounting system, this will normally require several codes:

- For the nominal *(general)* ledger record, the code number for the sales returns account and for the sales tax account.
- To record the reduction in the amount owed by the individual customer, the customer's account code in the sales ledger.

5.3 CODING INVOICES AND CREDIT NOTES: GRID BOX STAMP

There are a variety of methods of coding invoices and credit notes. One commonly used method is to use a stamp to put a grid or table on the document, and then fill it in with the code details.

The grid box can go under a variety of names, but essentially it is a box stamped on to the internal copy of an invoice (or credit note) before the invoice details (or credit note details) are entered in the day books of the accounting system.

The box is filled in both to make a note of the appropriate account code numbers, and as a checklist to make sure that the appropriate procedures for entering the transaction in the accounting system have been carried out.

The typical contents of a grid box are as follows:

Nominal *(general)* ledger account	5003
Additions and calculations checked	✓
Credit note authorisation obtained	Not applicable
Sales ledger (customer) account	S42770
Initial when posted	RGT

Here, the main ledger account code 5003 might be the for the account in the main ledger for domestic sales, and the sales ledger account number will be the customer account number for the customer to whom the invoice was sent.

When the invoice is entered into the sales day book, the final grid box is initialled, to show that the transaction has been entered in the accounting system. It therefore acts as a safeguard to make sure that the same details are not entered again.

The copy of the invoice or credit note is then filed.

6 BOOKS OF PRIME ENTRY: DAY BOOKS

In practice, an accounts office normally sends out large numbers of credit sales invoices and credit notes. If it does, it would be a very time-consuming job to enter the details of each transaction individually in the main accounting records. To improve efficiency in the accounts office, it is therefore usual practice to start recording transactions in the accounting system by making lists of similar transactions. These lists of transactions are drawn up in **books of prime entry**. In this case, credit sales and sales returns are recorded initially in **day books**.

The term 'day book' comes from the fact that a new list of transactions might typically be prepared each day, and the transactions for that day are then transferred to the main accounting records as part of a 'posting' exercise.

Sales day book

The details of every credit sales invoice prepared and issued to customers are recorded initially in the sales day book. The sales day book is therefore used to list credit sales transactions in date order.

Sales returns day book

In some systems, credit notes sent to customers are also recorded in the sales day book, as 'negative sales'. More usually, however, they are listed in a separate sales returns day book.

Purchase day book

All the purchase invoices received by an organisation are recorded initially in the purchase day book when they are received. These include not only invoices from suppliers for purchases of goods but also records of other invoices for expenses such as gas, telephone, electricity, accounting fees and so on.

Purchase returns day book

If any credit notes are received, these too may be entered in the purchase day book as 'negative purchases'. However, it is more usual to record them a separate purchase returns day book.

Cash book

A cash book is used to list cash receipts and cash payments. Cash receipts include money from cash sales, payments by receivables, and sundry other cash receipts. Cash payments include cash paid to suppliers, employees, the tax authorities and so on.

Cash receipts include not just cash and cheques, but also receipts from debit/credit cards. Cash payments are usually payments by cheque and automated transfer payments, by BACS, direct debit or standing order payments.

Petty cash book

The petty cash book records all the transactions through the petty cash box ('cash in hand'). Petty cash and petty cash transactions are explained in a later chapter.

Journal

The use of the journal was covered in Chapter 3.

In this chapter, the books of prime entry that concern us are:

- the **sales day book for invoices** sent out, and
- the **sales returns day book for credit notes** sent out.

7 SALES DAY BOOK

The purpose of the sales day book is to make an initial record of all the credit sales invoices that are sent out to customers. For each invoice the following details should be recorded:

- date and invoice number
- customer name and customer account code number or reference (sales ledger account code)
- the net invoice total, the sales tax and the gross invoice total.

7.1 WHAT DOES A SALES DAY BOOK LOOK LIKE?

The basic information entered in a sales day book will normally be set out as follows (although different styles of layout and presentation are possible):

Date	Invoice number	Customer name	Sales ledger account	Total $	Sales tax $	Net sales $

All this information can usually be taken from the sales invoice. The first three columns, date, invoice number and customer name are self-explanatory. These identify the sales invoice that is being recorded. The total column is the invoice total including sales tax. The sales tax column is for recording the sales tax. The net sales column is for the sales value excluding sales tax. It is the amount shown on the sales invoice as the sub-total before sales tax, after any trade discounts have been deducted.

This book can also include accounting for sales returns, which will be shown as negative amounts or deductions from sales invoices. In some cases, a separate sales returns day book may be maintained – see next section.

Sales ledger account number

To identify the customer to whom each sales invoice has been sent, it is normal practice to show the customer's account code in addition to the customer name. This may be called the sales ledger reference.

Some organisations will include the sales ledger reference on the face of the invoice when it is sent out to the customer. In other systems the sales ledger reference is entered in the grid box when the invoice is authorised as ready for recording in the day book.

Settlement discounts

The sales day book (and the sales returns day book) has no column for settlement discounts. Although a settlement discount is offered when the sales invoice is issued, it is not known whether the customer will take this discount until the invoice is paid or the discount period has elapsed.

Therefore, as discussed earlier, when a sales invoice is prepared the seller will judge or assess whether it is probable that the additional revenue will be receivable. Based upon this judgement or assessment, the sales invoice will then be prepared in one of the following two ways:

- if the customer is expected to pay early to take up the offer of early settlement discount, it is probable that only the lower amount will be received. Accordingly, the invoice will include deduction of early settlement discount in the same way that trade discount is deducted and only the lower amount is expected to be received from the customer.

- if the customer is not expected to pay early to take up the offer of early settlement discount, it is probable that the full amount will be received. Accordingly, the invoice will not include deduction of early settlement discount and the full amount is expected to be received from the customer.

Example

Tyson is a supplier of widgets and has six regular credit customers. At the start of July, none of these customers owed any money. Transactions with these customers during July were recorded in the sales day book as follows:

Sales day book   Folio 36

Date	Details	Invoice	Total $	Sales tax $	Net $
July					
1	Able	3031	864.00	144.00	720.00
1	Baker	3032	960.00	160.00	800.00
1	Charlie	3033	264.00	44.00	220.00
1	Delta	3034	494.40	82.40	412.00
1	Echo	3035	756.00	126.00	630.00
1	Foxtrot	3036	960.00	160,00	800.00
8	Baker	3037	480.00	80.00	400.00
8	Delta	3038	153.60	25.60	128.00
8	Able	3039	378.00	63.00	315.00
8	Foxtrot	3040	720.00	120.00	600.00
			6,030.00	1,005.00	5,025.00

You will see this example again in Chapter 13.

8 SALES RETURNS DAY BOOK

A business may decide to maintain a separate sales returns day book, rather than offset sales returns against the value of credit sales recorded in the sales day book. A sales returns day book is prepared in much the same way as a sales day book, but from details of the credit notes sent out to customers.

The details to be recorded from credit notes are:

- date of credit note
- credit note number
- customer name
- customer account reference (sales ledger account reference)
- credit note total amount (including sales tax)
- sales tax
- subtotal (net amount of sales returns, excluding sales tax).

Example

Tyson makes the following sales returns:

Sales returns day book   Folio 4

Date	Details	Credit note	Total $	Sales tax $	Net $
July					
10	Charlie	C23	168.00	28.00	140.00
10	Delta	C24	96.00	16.00	80.00
			264.00	44.00	220.00

You will see this example again in Chapter 13.

ACTIVITY 5

Pentel Cement Co issued the following sales invoices and credit notes during the week ended 23 January 20X4:

Date	Customer name	Sales ledger reference	Net amount $	Sales tax $	Invoice total $
Sales invoices					
19 Jan	Louch & Co	184	137.32	27.46	164.78
19 Jan	Framells	221	59.29	11.85	71.14
20 Jan	Position Co	002	448.00	89.60	537.60
21 Jan	Reflon Bros	042	338.27	67.65	405.92
22 Jan	Stonecast	114	142.94	28.58	171.52
23 Jan	Piltdown Co	089	551.80	110.36	662.16
Credit notes			Net amount $	Sales tax $	Credit note total $
20 Jan	Piltdown Co	089	88.94	17.78	106.72
22 Jan	Worton & Co	143	51.27	10.25	61.52

The invoice numbers started at 06254 at the beginning of the week and the credit note numbers at CN337.

Record these transactions in the sales day book or the sales returns day book.

For a suggested answer, see the 'Answers' section at the end of the book

9 FUNCTION OF THE PRIMARY RECORDS: POSTING TRANSACTION DETAILS TO THE LEDGERS

All transactions are initially recorded in one or other of the books of prime entry, as a first step towards recording them in the accounts.

However, **the books of prime entry are not part of the double entry accounting system.** After the transactions have been entered into a book of prime entry, their details have to be transferred or 'posted' to the main accounts.

To record invoices and credit notes in the accounts, the following procedures are necessary.

Step 1 Periodically the transactions in the book of prime entry are totalled. The total should be for all the transactions listed in the day book since the previous occasion when a total was taken. This might be daily (as the name 'day book' implies). However, it might be weekly or monthly depending on the volume of transactions entered in the day book and the requirements of the organisation.

The sales day book therefore provides a total of invoices sent to customers, in other words a total for credit sales. The sales returns day book totals the credit notes issued and so gives a total for sales returns.

Step 2 The total from the book of prime entry is posted to the nominal ledger *(general ledger)* where the correct double entry for that type of transaction must be recorded. For example, the total from the sales day book represents credit sales so the double entry in the main ledger should be:

Debit Receivables control account with the total amount owed on the invoices, including sales tax

Credit Sales account (or a particular sales account, such as Domestic Sales) with the total value of sales, excluding sales tax

Credit Sales tax account with the amount of sales tax on the credit sales

Control accounts

The receivables control account is considered in more detail in Chapter 13. It is simply one account which summarises transactions with all credit customers.

Memorandum accounts

As well as making the above entries in the nominal *(general)* ledger, a business also needs to know exactly how much each individual customer owes at any one time. 'Memorandum' accounts are therefore kept for individual receivables. Maintenance of these involves posting credit sales for individual customers to their individual memorandum accounts from the sales day book. Similarly, any subsequent cash received in payment for these credit sales must also be posted to these memorandum accounts, together with any credit notes and other adjustments.

These memorandum accounts **are not part of the double entry system. They are simply a way of keeping a record of how much individual customers owe at any one time.** They are not held in the nominal *(general)* ledger, but instead in a separate sales ledger. This is sometimes referred to as a receivables ledger.

Occasionally, you may encounter a business that uses individual customer accounts as part of its double entry system. This means that it has a cumbersome double entry system involving lots of individual customers' accounts, rather than one receivables control account containing only totals from day book postings (the sales day book, the sales returns day book and the cash book). This kind of system is not to be recommended and you should always assume, in the exam, that individual receivable's accounts **do not form part of the double entry system unless told otherwise.** Such memorandum accounts also exist for accounts payable.

CONCLUSION

In this chapter we have dealt with two main areas:

- preparing sales invoices and credit notes which need to be prepared correctly, checked and properly authorised

- recording sales invoices and credit notes in the day books.

This chapter builds upon and adds to some earlier work so there has been a little repetition but you should now be well acquainted with sales documentation, how it is used in the business and recorded in the day books.

KEY TERMS

Book of prime entry – A 'book' in which details of transactions are listed for the first time as a first step towards recording them in the accounts.

Day book – A name for a book of prime entry.

Posting – Transferring details of transactions from a book of prime entry to accounts in the main ledger to an account in the ledger.

Sales day book – Book of prime entry for recording credit sale transactions (sales invoices).

Sales ledger – A ledger containing accounts for individual credit customers/trade receivable. It is also known as the receivable ledger.

Sales return day book – Book of prime entry for recording details of sales returns (credit notes to customers).

Settlement discount (or cash discount) – Discount for early payment of an invoice.

Tax point – The date on which a transaction is deemed to have taken place for sales tax purposes.

Trade discounts – A discount on the price of goods or services, agreed in advance (and often granted to regular customers or for bulk purchases).

Sales tax invoice – Sales invoice or purchase invoice containing certain information for Sales tax purposes.

SELF TEST QUESTIONS

Paragraph

1	What are 'settlement terms'?	1
2	Outline the main differences between a credit note and a sales invoice.	1
3	Explain what a trade discount is.	2
4	Explain what a settlement discount is.	2
5	Is sales tax levied only on goods, or on both goods and services?	3
6	What is a tax point?	3
7	What customer details do you need to produce a sales invoice?	4
8	How is a grid stamp used in coding?	5
9	List the main books of prime entry.	6
10	What is an analysed day book?	7

EXAM-STYLE QUESTIONS

1   Jacobs Co provides its customers with individual trade discounts from list price. One customer, Caspian, negotiated a 20% trade discount. Caspian's transactions during March were as follows:

   March 12   Purchased goods with a $2,000 list price

   March 14   Returned faulty goods with a $400 list price

   March 20   Paid half of the net balance on the account.

   How much did Caspian owe Jacobs Co at the end of March?

   A $627.20

   B $640

   C $800

   D $1,280

2   Alan Co bought a drill at a cost of $235, sander at $59.20 and a saw at a cost of $70. These are all gross figures, inclusive of sales tax at 20%.

   How much sales tax has Alan Co paid?

   A $60.70

   B $72.84

   C $303.50

   D $364.20

3   Which is the book of prime entry used to list credit notes sent to customers?

    A   Cash book

    B   Journal

    C   Sales day book

    D   Sales returns day book

4   Asap Co is registered to account for sales tax. On 17 June it purchased a cash till for its business at the list price of $4,000. Asap Co is given a trade discount of 25% and the sales tax rate is 20%.

    How much will be the invoice received by Asap Co, inclusive of sales tax?

    A $833

    B $1,000

    C $3,600

    D $4,800

5   Campion Co is not registered for sales tax. It provides office services to various farming customers. If the customers pay early Campion Co allows settlement discounts as follows:

    | Cash on receipt of invoice | 3% |
    | Payment within 7 days | 2% |
    | Payment within 14 days | 1% |
    | Payment in 30 days | Nil |

    How much would a customer be invoiced, and expected to pay, if the sales value of services provided was $520 and the customer was expected to pay 10 days after invoicing?

    A $520.00

    B $514.80

    C $509.60

    D $504.40

6   Who initials a box on a coding grid on a sales invoice?

    A   The person authorising the initial purchase

    B   The person delivering the goods sold

    C   The person posting entries about the sale

    D   The person taking delivery of the goods purchased

FA1: RECORDING FINANCIAL TRANSACTIONS

7 Why are sales invoices authorised?

    A   To prevent invoicing someone who has not received the goods or services ordered

    B   To ensure that the invoice is paid on time

    C   To ensure that the invoice is correctly posted to the correct book of prime entry

    D   To indicate the need for a credit note

For suggested answers, see the 'Answers' section at the end of the book.

Chapter 6

RECORDING SALES

This chapter takes the process of recording sales further, following Chapter 5. It takes the day books and looks at the transfers to the sales ledger and nominal (general) ledger. The chapter then goes on to consider the monitoring and control of receivables as well as what happens when they do not pay what they owe. This chapter covers the syllabus area for recording sales.

CONTENTS

1. Posting sales day book totals
2. Posting sales returns day book totals
3. Computerised ledgers
4. Statements of account
5. Aged receivables analysis
6. Communication with customers
7. Provision of credit facilities
8. Credit limits
9. Irrecoverable debts
10. Allowance for receivables

LEARNING OUTCOMES

At the end of this chapter, you should be able to:

- maintain a manual nominal (general) and receivables ledger to record sales

- describe a computerised receivables ledger

- prepare, reconcile and understand the purpose of customer statements

- understand the purpose of and prepare an aged receivables analysis

- communicate efficiently and effectively with customers

- explain the benefits and costs of offering credit facilities to customers

- understand the importance of credit limits

- recognise the existence and impact of irrecoverable debts and the allowance for receivables

- record the accounting treatment of irrecoverable debts and the allowance for receivables.

1 POSTING SALES DAY BOOK TOTALS

The sales day book is a book of prime entry for credit sales. From the sales day book, the details have to be transferred (or 'posted') to the main ledger and entered in the appropriate main ledger accounts, as part of the double entry accounting system. Remember that the main ledger is also known as the nominal *(general)* ledger.

These transaction details are not posted one by one. Instead, as we saw in the previous chapter, the entries in the sales day book are **totalled** and the **total figure for credit sales is posted** to the main sales account and receivables control account in the nominal *(general)* ledger. Each individual transaction is also posted to the individual memorandum customer accounts in the sales ledger (also known as the receivables ledger).

The system described above assumes that a control account is maintained and the memorandum accounts are not part of the double entry system. As control accounts are not covered in detail until Chapter 13, for the remainder of this chapter, we shall assume that no control account is kept and the individual customer accounts **are** part of the double entry system.

As we have seen, a simple sales day book has the following columns:

- the gross column or total column, which is the total amount owed by the customers on the invoices

- the sales tax column, which is the amount of sales tax payable

- the net column which is the value of the credit sales to the business itself.

RECORDING SALES : CHAPTER 6

Therefore in order to transfer the total credit sales for a period to the main ledger accounts, the postings should be as follows:

Dr The receivables account with the gross amounts of invoices

    Cr Sales tax account with the sales tax column total

    Cr Sales account with the net column total

Example

Suppose that an organisation had a sales day book for 11 January 20X6 as follows:

Sales day book

Date	Invoice number	Customer name	Customer ref	Total $	Sales tax $	Net $
11/1/X6	0725	F Wells	FW03	106.93	17.82	89.11
11/1/X6	0726	Fargo Ltd	FL09	166.27	27.71	138.56
11/1/X6	0727	Smith Jones	SJ01	112.96	18.82	94.14
				386.16	64.35	321.81

Show the double entry required and post these amounts to the correct main ledger accounts for the day. The main ledger account codes are 2001, 2002 and 2003 for the three respective customers, 3152 for the sales tax account and 5001 for sales.

Solution

Double entry:

Dr	F Wells		$106.93
Dr	Fargo Ltd		$166.27
Dr	Smith Jones		$112.96
	Cr	Sales tax account	$64.35
	Cr	Sales account	$321.81

F Wells 2001

	$		$
Sales (SDB)	106.93		

Fargo Ltd 2002

	$		$
Sales (SDB)	166.27		

Smith Jones 2003

	$		$
Sales (SDB)	112.96		

Sales tax account 3152

$		$
	Sundry receivables (SDB)	64.35

Sales account 5001

$		$
	Sundry receivables (SDB)	321.81

The sales day book is sometimes marked up with the main ledger code for each column (total, sales tax and net), plus a note of whether each total will be debited or credited to the account.

Date	Invoice number	Customer name	Customer ref/code	Total $	Sales tax $	Net $
11/1/X6	0725	F Wells	FW03/2001	106.93	17.82	89.11
11/1/X6	0726	Fargo Ltd	FL09/2002	166.27	27.71	138.56
11/1/X6	0727	Smith Jones	SJ01/2003	112.96	18.82	94.14
				386.16	64.35	321.81
					CR: 3152	CR: 5001

1.1 ANALYSED SALES DAY BOOK

If the sales day book is analysed then this will normally mean that the accounting records will also be analysed in this way.

The implications for the posting of the sales day book are that instead of there being just one single sales account, there will be a sales account for each area of analysis.

Therefore there will be an individual sales account for each of the sales analysis columns in the sales day book.

ACTIVITY 1

You are given the following main ledger codes:

Receivables:	Forks Ltd	1001	sales tax account	2000
	BL Lorries	1002	North sales account	5000
	MA Meters	1003	South sales account	5500

Required:

Use these account codes and post the following sales day book entries to the main ledger accounts.

Date 20X6	Invoice number	Customer	Sales ledger ref	Total $	Sales tax $	North sales $	South sales $
15/9	68	Forks Ltd	S2175	24,000	4,000	20,000	
18/9	69	BL Lorries	S3018	4,800	800		4,000
30/9	70	MA Meters	S2609	2,928	488	2,440	
				31,728	5,288	22,440	4,000

For a suggested answer, see the 'Answers' section at the end of the book.

2 POSTING SALES RETURNS DAY BOOK TOTALS

Credit notes are recorded in a separate sales returns day book. Totals are posted periodically to the main ledger.

The double entry is as follows:

Dr Sales returns account (net cost of the goods returned)

Dr Sales tax account (sales tax charged on goods returned)

    Cr Individual customers' accounts (total cost of goods returned)

These figures are taken from the relevant columns in the sales returns day book.

ACTIVITY 2

A sales returns day book for 20 September 20X4 shows the following:

Date	Credit note number	Customer	Customer ref/code	Total $	Sales tax $	Net $
20/9	5513	Rollit Co	K08/1004	38.61	6.43	32.18
20/9	5514	Marcus Ltd	M12/1005	71.88	11.98	59.90
20/9	5515	Alans Ltd	A03/1006	53.55	8.92	44.63
				164.04	27.33	136.71
					Code 2410	Code 3000

Record these figures for the day in the nominal *(general)* ledger accounts.

For a suggested answer, see the 'Answers' section at the end of the book.

3 COMPUTERISED LEDGERS

If a business uses a computerised system for the receivables ledger, the bookkeeping is the same as with a manual ledger. The presentation is just slightly different from the 'T' account layout of manual ledger accounts.

A benefit of a computerised accounting system is that the transaction has only to be entered once on the issue of the invoice (which itself may be generated by an integrated system). For example, the initial entry may be keyed into the account of the individual customer. The double entry to sales and sales tax will be made automatically. There is no need to call up the latter accounts on screen. This reduces the possibility of error.

4 STATEMENTS OF ACCOUNT

4.1 THE PURPOSE OF A STATEMENT OF ACCOUNT

A statement of account, often called simply a statement, sets out the transactions that a business had with a particular customer since the previous statement.

A statement covers a specified period of time (e.g. a month) and shows:

- the balance on the account at the start of the period covered by the statement
- invoices sent to the customer during the period
- credit notes sent to the customer during the period
- payments by the customer during the period
- the balance on the account at the end of the period, which is 'now'. In other words, it shows the current balance on the customer's account, stating what the customer currently owes.

Remember that trade discount and early settlement discount expected to be taken by a credit customer will not be included in the statement of account as they are excluded from invoice amounts.

A statement is simply a list of the transactions on the customer's account. The information is readily available from the **customer's account in the sales ledger**, where all the transactions are recorded.

There are two common reasons for producing statements and sending them to customers.

- It might be the policy of the organisation to send out statements regularly, perhaps every month or three months, to remind the customer about the position on the account. Sending a statement might prompt the customer to make a payment.

- A customer might ask for a statement of account, possibly because it wants to check the details of the transactions shown on the account, and either for some reason cannot rely on its own records or suspects that there is a mistake and wants to identify the discrepancy and resolve it.

4.2 PREPARING A STATEMENT OF ACCOUNT

There isn't any standard format for preparing a statement of account. Usually, however, a statement is printed on headed paper, and begins by stating the name of the credit customer, the account number and the (current) date of the statement.

The statement will start by showing the balance on the customer's account at the start of the period covered by the statement.

The transactions with the customer, such as invoices sent out and payments received, should be listed. One way of doing this is to list the transactions in date order. It is also usual for a statement to show the balance on the account after each transaction.

Finally, the current balance (closing balance) is shown.

The statement might also remind the customer about the credit terms, to help him to identify which invoices, if any, are now due for payment.

Example

You work for Viking Paper Limited in the sales ledger section, and you have been asked to prepare a statement of account for a credit customer, Clivedon Co, for the month of March.

The account for Clivedon Co in the sales ledger shows the following information:

Clivedon Co   Account 32558

		$			$
01/03	Balance b/f	25.00	08/03	Bank	25.00
05/03	SDB – 15093	97.52	15/03	Bank	97.52
12/03	SDB – 15142	116.40	23/03	Bank	116.40
19/03	SDB – 15221	230.49	26/03	SRDB – CN147	12.70
			31/03	Balance c/f	217.79
		469.41			469.41
01/04	Balance b/f	217.79			

SDB refers to the sales day book   SRDB refers to the sales returns day book

Task

Prepare a statement of account for March for this customer.

Solution

The statement of account itemises the transactions during the month in date order, and shows the balance on the account after each transaction. It ends with a statement of the current balance on the account.

FA1: RECORDING FINANCIAL TRANSACTIONS

Viking Paper Limited
Viking House, 27 High Road, Sheffield S16 6HD
STATEMENT OF ACCOUNT

Clivedon Co
(Address)
Account 32558

Date	Transaction details	Amount $	Balance $
01/03	Balance, start of March	25.00	25.00
05/03	Invoice – 15093	97.52	122.52
08/03	Payment received	(25.00)	97.52
12/03	Invoice – 15142	116.40	213.92
15/03	Payment received	(97.52)	116.40
19/03	Invoice – 15221	230.49	346.89
23/03	Payment received	(116.40)	230.49
26/03	Credit note – CN147	(12.70)	217.79
Amount due at statement date			**217.79**

ACTIVITY 3

Another customer of Viking Paper has requested a statement for March. The customer's account in the sales ledger shows the following details.

T Smith & Co   Account 31702

Date	Details	$	Date	Details	$
01/03	Balance b/f	90.11	15/03	Bank	250.50
02/03	SDB – 15021	160.39	23/03	Bank	115.73
09/03	SDB – 15100	115.73	25/03	SRDB – CN156	14.56
16/03	SDB – 15183	66.25	30/03	Bank	66.25
23/03	SDB – 15257	228.37			
27/03	SDB – 15302	14.56			
30/03	SDB – 15347	93.62	31/03	Balance c/f	321.99
		769.03			769.03
01/04	Balance b/f	321.99			

Prepare a statement of account for March for this customer.

For a suggested answer, see the 'Answers' section at the end of the book.

5 AGED RECEIVABLES ANALYSIS

Credit customers do not always pay on time, and it might be necessary to chase them for payment. In many organisations, there are standard procedures for checking on overdue payments and taking measures to persuade customers to pay.

Management should also want to know how efficient the accounts department has been at collecting debts.

An aged receivables analysis is a report that is both useful for identifying late payers and for providing information about receivables and debt collection efficiency to management.

An aged receivables analysis is a report listing all the receivables of a business, how much they owe, and for how long the money has been owed. Typically, unpaid debts are analysed into amounts that have been outstanding for less than one month, for between one and two months, for between two and three months and for over three months. However, the analysis can vary from one organisation to another.

5.1 PREPARING AN AGED RECEIVABLES ANALYSIS

An aged receivables analysis is prepared by producing a list of all the current receivables of the business, and recording how much they currently owe. This information can be extracted from the sales ledger accounts.

The total debt of each customer is then analysed according to the dates of the unpaid invoices.

An analysis is typically presented as follows. In this example, there are just three credit customers, but in reality there could be a large number of them.

Aged receivables analysis as at (date)

Credit customer	Total owing	Outstanding for			
		Less than 30 days	30–60 days	60–90 days	More than 90 days
	$	$	$	$	$
T Grainger	551.86	279.30	272.56	–	–
C N Lawson	713.59	–	–	279.03	434.56
Burden & Co	518.47	219.50	248.30	50.67	–
Total	1,783.92	498.80	520.86	329.70	434.56

Notes

1   Although the columns are headed 'Less than 30 days', '30–60 days' and so on, it is common practice to assume that there are 30 days in a month, so less than 30 days means less than one calendar month and 30–60 days really means between one and two months.

2   For each customer, the total of the unpaid debts in the 'Outstanding for' columns add up to the total amount currently owed by the customer, as shown in the 'Total owing' column.

3   It is usual to show grand total figures at the end of the report, because these provide useful information for management.

If a business normally allows up to 30 days' credit to customers, it will expect most unpaid debts to be in the 'Less than 30 days' column. Most other unpaid debts should be in the 30–60 days column. However, if a business normally allows only 30 days' credit, but it has a large amount of unpaid debts in the '60–90 days' and 'More than 90 days' columns, then its debt collection procedures are probably poor and inefficient.

When staff in the sales ledger or debt collection section contact each customer to encourage them to pay, the initial focus will be on the debts that have been unpaid for the longest time.

5.2 USING AN AGED RECEIVABLES ANALYSIS

An aged receivables analysis can be used to identify which customers are taking longer than they should to pay their debts, and should therefore be contacted or followed up to request payment.

- If the organisation offers the same credit terms to all its customers, there may be a standard rule about how to prioritise which customers to follow up. For example, if an organisation allows 30 days credit to all its credit customers, the standard procedure might be to follow up all receivables who have a debt that has been outstanding (i.e. unpaid) for 60–90 days or longer. In the example above, both C N Lawson and Burden & Co would be followed up for some of their unpaid debts if this rule were applied.

- If the organisation offers different credit terms to different customers, it is important to know what the credit terms are for each individual customer. These can be entered on the receivables analysis list, next to the customer's name. There might then be a standard office rule that customers should be followed up for debts where payment is more than one month overdue.

Some organisations might follow up slow payers sooner, for example within a few days of the debt becoming overdue.

6 COMMUNICATION WITH CUSTOMERS

The accounts department of an organisation communicates with customers from time to time.

- A customer might have a question or a complaint about an invoice or a credit note.

- The accounts department might have to follow up a customer whose debt is overdue for payment.

There are some important guidelines for dealing with customers.

- It is essential to be polite at all times, and to deal with the customer in a courteous and professional way. A business relies on its customers for sales and profits, and many will continue to be customers of the business a long time into the future, if they are treated properly.

- It is also important to have all the information to hand for dealing with a customer. For example, if you are following up a customer for an overdue payment of a debt, you should obtain the office copy of all the relevant invoices (and credit notes, if there are any) from the unpaid invoices file. When you write to the customer, or speak to the customer on the telephone, you should then have everything you need to respond fully to any questions and comments.

6.1 PROCEDURES FOR FOLLOWING UP OVERDUE PAYMENTS

It is an unhappy fact of business that many credit customers will not pay promptly unless they are pressed into complying with the agreed credit terms. An organisation has to decide on a policy for following up overdue debts that encourages customers to pay but at the same time does not annoy them and create ill will for the future. It may not be immediately obvious but sometimes an efficient and understanding approach at such a time may encourage customer loyalty. In any case, it is unlikely that the staff working in the customer's accounts department have anything to do with selecting suppliers or placing orders. Any loss of goodwill on their part is unlikely to affect future sales.

A debt collection policy might be as follows:

- Send out invoices promptly, having made sure that they are complete and accurate. The invoice should state clearly what the credit terms are. The customer should not be given an excuse for paying late!

- Offer a settlement discount for early payment, to encourage customers to pay early and get the benefit of the discount.

- When a customer raises a query about an invoice, the query should be dealt with promptly to the customer's satisfaction. Until the problem is resolved, the customer is unlikely to pay the invoice.

- When it is agreed that a credit note should be issued to the customer, prepare the credit note and send it promptly. Until the customer has received the credit note, they are unlikely to pay the balance owing.

- The organisation might send statements of account to its credit customers regularly, perhaps every month, as a reminder of how much they owe.

- When a debt becomes overdue for payment, there should be established procedures for writing to the customer, or telephoning the customer.

Procedures vary between organisations.

- An organisation might write to customers about overdue debts, a certain length of time after payment has become due. The first 'reminder letter' should be polite.

- If the customer has not paid within, say, two weeks, someone in the accounts department might telephone the customer (especially business customers) and ask if there is a problem with paying the invoice. In these telephone conversations, it should often be possible to get the customer to agree to make the payment promptly.

- If the customer still fails to pay, a more strongly worded letter might be sent, by a more senior person such as an accounts department supervisor. Even this letter should be polite and professional in its tone.

- If the customer still fails to pay, the matter might be taken up by a manager, or referred to a 'specialist' debt collection department.

6.2 WRITING TO A CUSTOMER: 'HOUSE STYLE'

If you are asked to write to a customer to remind him to pay an outstanding debt, the letter should be short but clear. As stated above, it should also be polite and professional in tone.

You will probably be expected to use a 'house style' when you write a letter. Since reminder letters are often fairly standard in content, there should be a 'proforma' standard letter that you can copy and adapt.

Start and end of a letter

If you are writing to a person whose name you know, for example Mr/Ms Foxton, your letter should use the following conventions:

Start: Dear (name)

End: Yours sincerely, (followed by your name and possibly also your position in your organisation)

For example:

Dear Mr/Ms Foxton

Yours sincerely,

B Trout

Accounts Clerk

There should be space between the 'Yours sincerely' and your printed name to write your signature.

If you are writing to a department or an organisation rather than to an individual person, your letter should use the following conventions:

Start: Dear Sirs

End: Yours faithfully, (followed by your name and possibly also your position in your organisation).

Letter title

Letters from your organisation might be given a title or heading, to inform the recipient immediately what it is about.

For example:

Unpaid invoice number 44825

Contact name and number

Reminder letters to customers should always include information to enable the customer to get in contact with you, by telephone, fax, e-mail or even letter, to ask any questions or make any response to your letter. This information may be included in the pre-printed heading on the letter paper. If not, you should include it within the wording of the letter itself.

Example

A first reminder letter to a customer might look something like this:

Viking Paper Limited Viking House, 27 High Road Sheffield S16 6HD
S T Stratton 3 Down Industrial Estate Hatton road London E4 6YE 3 May 20X4   Dear Mr/Ms Stratton
Unpaid invoice 100754
We note from our records that we are currently owed the sum of $400.00 by you in connection with an invoice, number 100754 and dated 15 March, which is still unpaid. Payment is overdue, and we should therefore be grateful if we could now have your payment. If you have sent a payment within the last day or so, please ignore this letter. If you wish to raise any query in connection with the invoice, please contact me. My telephone number is 0114 999000.   Yours sincerely   C Merridew Sales ledger clerk

7 PROVISION OF CREDIT FACILITIES

Often the first communication with a customer is about the amount and duration or extent of credit that a business will allow.

Businesses provide credit facilities for various reasons:

- People may not be able to buy goods immediately for cash. If they cannot buy immediately, they may not purchase the goods or services provided by the business.

- Competitors may offer credit facilities so the business may lose sales if it does not offer credit as well.

- The ability to buy now, pay later may encourage people to buy goods and services which they might not otherwise purchase.

The provision of credit, however, is not without its costs. These can be summarised as follows:

- The finance costs involved in funding working capital. These may take the form of interest payments on an overdraft, if the company has one.

- The costs of running a sales ledger and maintaining and reconciling control accounts. If all sales were for cash, the accounting system for this area would be very simple!

- The costs of assessing credit worthiness, including staff costs, credit reference agency costs, etc.

- The staff costs of chasing debts. These can be high, involving the employment of specific credit control staff, as well as management time for larger debts.

- The cost of default. If a customer fails to pay for goods/services at a later date, the seller has lost not only the amount they incurred in providing the goods or services but also any profit they would have made.

- Legal costs associated with recovering monies when a credit customer defaults on a debt.

8 CREDIT LIMITS

As discussed above, it is a risk for a business to offer credit to its customers because they may not be able to pay at a later date. To try to ensure that the customer is able to deal with credit facilities satisfactorily, the supplier will, if satisfied with enquiries on the finances of the customer, base credit facilities on:

- amount, say a limit of $1,000 in total with an individual item limit of $250

- time, for example, payment within 30 days.

There are various ways in which the suppliers arrive at the limits provided:

- from bank references from the potential customer's bank

- from references from other credit suppliers to the potential customer

- by reference to a computer program which aims to calculate creditworthiness based on information provided by the potential customer

- by interviewing the potential customer.

It is common for credit limits to be reviewed periodically and revised in the light of experience. For example, a limit of $200, payment within 30 days may be offered initially. If the account is run in accordance with the credit facilities offered for a year, the limit may be raised to $500. If it is not operated well, the limit may be kept at the same level, reduced or the account may be closed.

A well-run account generates income and profits for the supplier at little cost. It is, admittedly, more expensive in terms of administration to allow credit than simply to deal in cash. It may also leave the business a little short of cash when credit is first offered because it has to wait for income. However, credit facilities should, hopefully, generate a greater level of sales overall.

Risks are that the receivables do not pay at the end of the credit period and that the quality of credit customers is poor and that the business has to spend money on administration monitoring and chasing the credit customers for payment.

RECORDING SALES : CHAPTER 6

9 IRRECOVERABLE DEBTS

9.1 THE BASIC SITUATION

When a sale is made to a credit customer, the sale and related receivable are recorded immediately even though the cash has not yet been received. This is because the business is reasonably certain that the customer will pay the amount due within a certain period of time.

However, some customers do not pay within a reasonable time and it may appear unlikely that the amounts due from them will ever be paid.

An **irrecoverable debt** is a debt for which payment is reasonably certain not to be received. An irrecoverable debt is sometimes referred to as a bad debt. The most common instances of irrecoverable debts are where a credit customer has become bankrupt (legally unable to pay debts) or gone out of business and is unable to pay the amount due.

If the debt is unlikely to ever be paid then this must be recognised in the accounts. This is done by writing off the irrecoverable debt. The write-off is recorded initially in the journal, and is then posted from the journal to the irrecoverable debts (expense) account and the trade receivables control account in the nominal *(general)* ledger. As a separate exercise, the individual sales ledger account must also be updated.

Writing off an irrecoverable debt means that it is removed from the customer's account and is an expense charged to the business. Note, however, that the original sale entry is not reversed. The double entry required to complete this is:

Dr   Irrecoverable debts expense

and either:

Cr   Individual account of the receivable (if the individual sales ledger accounts form part of the double-entry system)

or:

Cr   Receivables control account (if the business maintains a receivables ledger control account as part of the double-entry system)

An irrecoverable debt is removed entirely from the accounting records. After the write-off, there will be no record remaining of that debt ever having existed. It is therefore extremely important that this write off is properly authorised by an appropriate responsible official before it takes place.

Example

It is 31 July 20X4 and an amount owing from T P Coleman totalling $338.90 is to be written off as this customer can no longer be traced and the debt has been outstanding for a considerable period of time.

Task

Show the journal entry and accounting entries necessary to write off this debt. The previous journal entry was numbered 1041. The irrecoverable debts account is coded B3 and the account of T P Coleman is coded D1. Note – this business includes the individual sales ledger accounts as part of the double-entry accounting system,

KAPLAN PUBLISHING

Solution

Journal entry

Entry number	Date	Account name	Folio ref	Debit $	Credit $
1042	31 July	Irrecoverable debts expense	B3	338.90	
		T P Coleman	D1		338.90

Being the write off of an irrecoverable debt owing from T P Coleman.

Nominal *(general)* ledger

Irrecoverable debts expense account   B3

Date		$	Date		$
31 July	T P Coleman (Journal 1042)	338.90			

Sales ledger

T P Coleman account   D1

Date		$	Date		$
31 July	Balance b/d	338.90	31 July	Irrecoverable debt (Journal 1042)	338.90

Note that the business should not send out a final statement to the customer including the irrecoverable debt entry. This would indicate to the customer that the business has no further interest in recovering the amount outstanding. Sometimes amounts written off as irrecoverable debts are repaid partially or in full and this is considered in the following section.

9.2 IRRECOVERABLE DEBTS RECOVERED

It is possible that a debt which was previously written off as irrecoverable in one accounting period, perhaps because the customer was in financial difficulties, that all or part of the amount due is then unexpectedly received in a subsequent accounting period.

In the previous section, the accounting entries required to write off an irrecoverable debt were stated as:

Dr   Irrecoverable debts expense

Cr   Receivables (either the sales ledger account of the receivable or the receivables ledger control account as appropriate)

When cash is received from a credit customer the normal double entry is:

Dr   Cash

Cr   Receivables

When an irrecoverable debt is recovered, the credit entry (above) cannot be taken to receivables as the debt has already been removed from the receivables balance. Instead the accounting entry is:

Dr   Cash

Cr   Irrecoverable debts expense

Some businesses may wish to keep a separate 'irrecoverable debts recovered' account to separate the actual cost of irrecoverable debts in the accounting period.

Example

If the previous example is continued, it is now January 20X6 and $250.00 has just been received from T P Coleman.

Task

Show the accounting entries required to record the receipt of cash from T P Coleman in January 20X6.

Solution

Dr   Cash $250.00

Cr   Irrecoverable debts expense $250.00

Note that, regardless of whether individual sales ledger accounts or a receivables control account is maintained in the nominal ledger, they remain unaffected.

10   ALLOWANCE FOR RECEIVABLES

10.1 THE BASIC SITUATION

There may be some amounts due from credit customers where there is some cause for concern that they may not be fully recovered but they are not yet regarded as irrecoverable and written-off. Such amounts due may be considered to be 'doubtful' and an allowance is required recognise that such amounts may not be fully recovered.

Any amount regarded as 'doubtful' remains within receivables, but a separate 'allowance for receivables' ledger account is established. The allowance is a credit balance. This is netted off against trade receivables in the statement of financial position to give a net figure for receivables that are regarded as probably recoverable.

The allowance should consist only of specific amounts where, for example, the customer is known to be in financial difficulty, or is disputing an invoice, or payment is already overdue, or is refusing to pay for some other reason (e.g. a faulty product), and therefore the amount owing may not be fully recovered. Therefore, an allowance can only be established where there is some evidence or indication that a particular receivable may not be recovered in part or in full.

To account for an allowance against receivables, the accounting entries are as follows:

Dr   Irrecoverable debts expense

Cr   Allowance for receivables

Normally the allowance is assessed and adjusted at each accounting year-end. An increase in the allowance from one year-end to another is accounted for as follows:

Dr   Irrecoverable debts expense

Cr   Allowance for receivables

A decrease in the allowance from one year-end to another is accounted for as follows:

Dr   Allowance for receivables

Cr   Irrecoverable debts expense

Example

At 1 January 20X6, J Stamp had trade receivables totalling $68,000 and an allowance for receivables of $3,400. During the year ended 31 December 20X6, J Stamp made credit sales of $354,000 and collected cash from receivables of $340,000.

At 31 December 20X6, J Stamp reviewed the receivables' listing and identified $2,000 that was to be accounted for as irrecoverable. In addition, at that date, it was estimated that further amounts totalling $5,000 were overdue and that an allowance should be made for this amount.

Task

Prepare the trade receivables control account, irrecoverable debts account and allowance for receivables account for the year ended 31 December 20X6.

Solution

Nominal (general) ledger accounts

Trade receivables ledger control account

Date		$	Date		$
1 Jan X6	Balance b/d	68,000	31 Dec X6	Irrecoverable debt	2,000
	Sales day book	354,000		Cash rec'd	340,000
			31 Dec X6	Bal c/d	80,000
		422,000			422,000
1 Jan X7		80,000			

Allowance for receivables

Date		$	Date		$
			1 Jan X6	Balance b/d	3,400
31 Dec X6	Balance c/d	5,000	31 Dec X6	Irrecoverable debts	1,600
		5,000			5,000
			1 Jan X7	Balance b/d	5,000

RECORDING SALES : CHAPTER 6

Irrecoverable debts expense account

Date		$	Date		$
31 Dec X6	Receivables w/off	2,000			
	Allowance for receivables	1,600	31 Dec X6	P&L expense	3,600
		3,600			3,600

Note that the Change in the allowance for receivables required (from $3,400 to $5,000 = $1,600) is accounted for as follows:

Dr   Irrecoverable debts expense $1,600

Cr   Allowance for receivables $1,600

ACTIVITY 4

Arch Ltd has the following accounts in its sales ledger on 31 August:

Sales ledger

P Casey

Date		$	Date	$
31 July	Balance b/d	210.25		
4 Aug	Sales	50.25		

H Smith

Date		$	Date	$
28 Feb	Balance b/d	8.40		

K Wild

Date		$	Date	$
30 June	Balance b/d	74.30		

T Major

Date		$	Date	$
30 Apr	Balance b/d	170.50		

1   Prepare a suitable aged receivables analysis for the four accounts for Arch Ltd.

2   Arch Ltd writes off any accounts which have been outstanding for six months. Prepare journal and ledger account entries to write off any accounts in this category.

3   Suggest how Arch Ltd should deal with T Major whose balance has been outstanding for some time.

For a suggested answer, see the 'Answers' section at the end of the book.

CONCLUSION

This chapter looked at the posting of transactions from the books of prime entry (sales day book and sales returns day book) to the main or nominal *(general)* ledger and the individual customer accounts in the receivables ledger.

The chapter then looked at statements that reflect the ledger accounts of customers. These are useful in checking the records of customer and supplier.

The chapter then progressed to review the usefulness of credit facilities in potentially increasing the income of a business. Credit limits need monitoring and this further increases the need for communication between customer and supplier. Most business relationships are straightforward and productive, but sometimes difficulties occur. In particular, there can be delays in the receipt of funds from credit customers and businesses need to monitor this by using the aged receivable analysis. However, even with careful monitoring and control, some customers will be unable to pay and the business may need to write off the debts.

Finally, the chapter considered the accounting entries required to write-off an irrecoverable debt and also to record the accounting entries required to establish, increase or reduce the allowance for receivables. Accounting entries required to record an irrecoverable debt, or establishing, increasing or reducing an allowance for receivables are first recorded in the journal.

KEY TERMS

Aged receivables analysis – List of credit customers (and amounts owed), analysed according to how long it has been since the invoice was issued.

Allowance for receivables – The allowance established to recognise that an amount due from one or more credit customers may not be fully recovered.

Irrecoverable debt – A debt for which payment is reasonably certain not to be received.

Posting – Transferring details of transactions from a book of prime entry to accounts in the main or nominal *(general)* ledger.

Sales day book – Book of prime entry for recording credit sale transactions (sales invoices).

Sales ledger – A ledger containing accounts for individual credit customers/accounts receivable. Also known as the receivables ledger.

Sales returns day book – Book of prime entry for recording details of sales returns (credit notes to customers).

SELF TEST QUESTIONS

Paragraph

1 An entry in the sales day book leads to entries in the ledger accounts. What are those entries? 1

2 When would a business have more than one sales account? 1

3 Give a benefit of using a computerised sales ledger. 3

4 What is the purpose of a statement of account? 4

5 What is the purpose of preparing an aged receivables analysis? 5

6 What is the usual layout for an aged receivables analysis? 5

7 Why should communication with customers be polite and professional? 6

8 What is the benefit to a business of giving its customers credit facilities? 7

9 What is an irrecoverable debt? 9

10 State the double entry for writing off an irrecoverable debt. 9

EXAM-STYLE QUESTIONS

1 Which one of the following is the correct posting of totals from the sales day book?

   A Dr Nominal *(general)* ledger sales account, Cr Customers' accounts in sales ledger

   B Dr Nominal *(general)* ledger sales account, Cr Cash book

   C Dr Customers' accounts in Nominal *(general)* ledger, Cr Nominal *(general)* ledger sales account

   D Dr Cash book, Cr Nominal *(general)* ledger sales account

2 Which one of the following would normally be recorded using the journal?

   A Irrecoverable debts

   B Expenses paid

   C Purchases

   D Sales

3 Which of the following would increase overdue balances in sales ledger accounts?

   A Improved debt collection methods

   B Offering larger settlement discounts for credit sales

   C Reducing credit limits

   D Speedier payments by customers

4   What is a statement of account?

    A   It is a copy of the customer's account sent out by the supplier

    B   It is a copy of the supplier's account sent out by the customer

    C   It is a document recording a credit sale

    D   It is a document recording sales returns

5   What is an aged receivables analysis used for?

    A   To monitor cash

    B   To monitor discounts

    C   To monitor outstanding amounts from credit purchases

    D   To monitor outstanding amounts from credit sales

For suggested answers, see the 'Answers' section at the end of the book.

Chapter 7

PURCHASES AND PURCHASE RECORDS

Most businesses purchase a wide variety of goods and services from suppliers. As a general rule, businesses prefer to buy goods and services on credit, although some small items might be purchased with notes and coins out of 'petty cash'.

This chapter explains the typical procedures for ordering goods or services on credit, receiving delivery, receiving a purchase invoice, checking the invoice and identifying and sorting out any discrepancies. It also covers the recording of purchases and purchase returns in the books of prime entry.

The chapter covers the syllabus area for purchases and purchase returns.

CONTENTS

1. Buying goods or services
2. Source documents
3. Suppliers' invoices and supporting documents
4. Credit notes
5. Authorising and coding
6. Purchase day book
7. Purchase returns day book

LEARNING OUTCOMES

At the end of this chapter, you should be able to:

- identify and recognise source purchase and expenditure documents
- complete purchase invoices and process credit notes
- calculate and record trade and settlement discounts
- record transactions in a purchase day book and a purchase returns day book
- code purchases and supplier records and data.

# 1 BUYING GOODS OR SERVICES

The procedures for buying goods or services were explained in an earlier chapter but a brief reminder might be useful here.

1.1 PURCHASE REQUISITION

Expenditure by a business must be properly authorised. If there were no rules about authorising spending, there would be nothing to stop any employee of a business making whatever expenditure they chose.

The rules for authorisation vary from one organisation to another, and it is important to know who can authorise different types and amounts of expenditure.

Expenditure should not be approved for payment unless there is evidence that it has been properly authorised. Proper authorisation is normally evidenced by a piece of paper, signed by the person giving the authority to spend. This authorising document is often called a **purchase requisition**.

The expenditure should be approved by an individual who is in a position to authorise it. Following authorisation, a purchase requisition becomes an authority to spend.

1.2 METHODS OF PURCHASING

A business might buy goods or services in different ways.

- Once authority has been obtained, an item can be ordered verbally, by telephone. For example, suppose that there is flooding in a washroom due to a blocked drain. After authority has been obtained to get the fault repaired, a plumber can be called in by telephone.

- Occasionally, an item may be purchased by internet after the authority has been given, although the person making the purchase will probably be required to pay immediately by credit or debit card.

- Business to business transactions also take place over the internet with customers buying from suppliers.

- For large expenditure, an organisation might ask one or more suppliers to submit **a price quotation**. The organisation specifies the goods or services that it wants to buy, and suppliers who are invited to 'bid' for the work each submits a price quotation. One of these quotations is then authorised – usually the lowest-priced bid.

- A common method of ordering goods and services from a supplier is to prepare and submit a written purchase order.

2 SOURCE DOCUMENTS

You will recognise many of the following from studying sales transactions.

2.1 PURCHASE ORDER

A purchase order is a written request by an organisation for the supply of a specified quantity of goods or a service.

Large organisations might have a specialist purchasing department, with buyers whose job is to process purchase requisitions. They may ask different suppliers to submit price quotations, or they might select a supplier and try to negotiate a good price.

Having agreed the purchase terms with a supplier, the buyer prepares a formal purchase order. One copy goes to the supplier, and is the formal order. At least one other copy is retained, as documentary evidence for use in checking later on.

An example of a purchase order was shown in an earlier chapter.

When services are purchased, the 'purchase order' can take the form of a written contract, specifying the nature of the service and the agreed price.

2.2 DELIVERY NOTE/ADVICE NOTE AND GOODS RECEIVED NOTE

When a supplier delivers goods, a **delivery note** is given to the person accepting the goods, for example the storekeeper.

The physical goods received are checked against the delivery note, and any discrepancies between them should be spotted and reported. For example, the delivery note might say that 10 boxes have been delivered, but in fact only 8 boxes have been delivered.

The condition of the goods should also be checked. If some or all of the goods appear to be in bad condition, the person accepting the delivery can do one of three things:

- Reject the entire consignment of goods and refuse to accept any of them.

- Reject the goods that appear to be damaged or in poor condition, and accept the rest.

- Accept all the goods, but agree with the delivery firm what the condition of the goods is, and make a record of this on all copies of the delivery note.

If goods have been accepted in unsatisfactory condition, or if some goods have been rejected, this fact should be recorded on both copies of the delivery note – the copy retained by the supplier and the copy provided by the supplier. Similarly, if the actual quantity of goods received differs from the quantity shown on the delivery note, this too should be recorded on both copies of the delivery note.

2.3 RECORDING SERVICES PROVIDED

When services are provided, a documentary record is often kept to confirm that the work has been done. An example is work carried out by an outside contractor on the customer's premises.

It is quite common for such services to be charged for by the hour. Examples are the cost of temporary accounting staff and office workers supplied by an employment agency.

When services are provided on a time-charged basis, there should be:

- a contract for the work, in which the rate for the work is specified

- a timesheet, showing how many hours have been worked by the individual each day. Typically, a timesheet is prepared each week. It should be checked by a manager or supervisor and signed as confirmation that the stated hours have actually been worked.

An example of a timesheet is shown below. This is a timesheet for work done by an engineer who works for another firm. It is prepared by the individual's employer, Telesouth Installation Engineers, and checked and confirmed by R Ruan, an employee of the customer, J Forrester Wholesale Supplies.

TIMESHEET			
Telesouth Installation Engineers			
Engineer	D Huan		
Customer site:	J Forrester Wholesale Supplies		
Week ending:	Friday 16 June 20X4		
Day	Hours worked	Weekday hours	Weekend hours
Saturday	0		0
Sunday	0		0
Monday	9am – 5pm	8	
Tuesday	9am – 5pm	8	
Wednesday	9am – 5pm	8	
Thursday	9am – 5pm	8	
Friday	9am – 5pm	8	
Total hours		40	0
Signature of customer	R Ruan		

2.4 PURCHASE INVOICE

The supplier usually submits an invoice when the goods or services are delivered, or soon after. The sales invoice issued by the supplier is a purchase invoice to the customer. Whereas a sales invoice represents income, purchase invoices represent expenditure.

Invoices are often addressed to the accounts department, and it is at this stage that the accounts staff become involved in checking and recording the expenditures.

3 SUPPLIERS' INVOICES AND SUPPORTING DOCUMENTS

You are aware of invoices and credit notes from earlier chapters so this chapter moves straight on to processing documents rather than looking at the basic documents again.

3.1 CHECKING INVOICES AGAINST SUPPORTING DOCUMENTATION

When purchase invoices are received from suppliers, they must be checked. If there is any problem with an invoice, it should be followed up with the supplier immediately. Three types of check may be required:

- that the invoice details are correct

- that there is a document such as a purchase order or authorised price quotation, showing that the goods or services detailed on the invoice were in fact ordered

- that the goods ordered were all delivered and in good condition, or that the service was delivered to the buyer's satisfaction.

The individual who does these checks needs to compare the invoice details with other documents, in particular the purchase order (or contract or price quotation) and the delivery note.

This means that the accounts department should hold a copy of this supporting documentation. A copy of the appropriate documents should therefore be sent to the accounts department when they are created or received. Within the accounts department, there should be a system of filing these documents so that they can be traced easily when the purchase invoice is received.

- Purchase orders for which no invoice has yet been received can be filed in purchase number order.

- The delivery note should be attached to the purchase order when the goods have been delivered. The supplier's delivery note should show the purchase order number, which means that it should be easy to match by number the delivery note with the filed copy of the purchase order.

- The supplier's invoice should also give the purchase order number as a reference, so that the invoice can be matched with the purchase order.

3.2 CHECKING THE INVOICE DETAILS FOR CALCULATION ERRORS

Each purchase invoice should be checked to make sure that its details are correct.

If an invoice has been prepared manually rather than by computer, there is always a chance of an **error in the arithmetic**. There might be an error in multiplying a quantity by a price, or in adding up a column of figures.

The recommended procedure should therefore be to **check all the calculations** on an invoice. If there appears to be an error, the supplier should be contacted, probably by telephone, and asked to confirm error and issue a credit note or an amended invoice to resolve the problem.

Example

You are asked to check an invoice from Frost Supplies that includes the following details.

Item		Quantity	Price per unit $	Total $
456213	Widgets	250	12.45	3,112.50
478002	Grommits	145	14.67	2,177.15
				5,299.65

Here, there are two errors in the calculations, and if the quantities and unit prices are correct, the invoice should be for the following amount.

Item		Quantity	Price per unit $	Total $
456213	Widgets	250	12.45	3,112.50
478002	Grommits	145	14.67	2,127.15
				5,239.65

The invoice is for $60 too much.

To resolve this problem, you should contact the supplier and ask for confirmation that the invoice is incorrect.

- The supplier should agree to send a **credit note** for $60.

- You should write a note on the invoice stating that a credit note for $60 should be expected from the supplier.

- It should be office procedure that the invoice should not be processed further until the credit note has been received. The incorrect invoice and the supporting documentation should be held together until the credit note is received.

The fact that such errors may be queried gives businesses an incentive to check sales invoices before sending them out. If customers need to delay the recording and processing of an invoice to resolve queries then the payment for the invoice may be delayed. Some businesses only make payments weekly or even monthly and so even a slight delay in processing could lead to an even longer wait for the payment.

3.3 CHECKING THE SALES TAX CALCULATION

You might need to take particular care with the calculation of the sales tax. Remember that when the supplier offers a settlement discount for early payment of the invoice, the sales tax should be calculated on the assumption that it will not be reduced to account for the settlement discount. Accounting for a reduced amount of sales tax due to settlement discount is excluded from the FA 1 syllabus.

When sales tax is charged, you should also check that the invoice is appropriate for the relevant sales tax. The supplier's sales tax registered number should be shown on the invoice.

ACTIVITY 1

Here is a supplier's invoice. You are required to determine if the calculations have been correctly carried out.

MARCHANT PAPER LTD
74 High Road
Leeds LS14 0NY
Telephone: 0191 328 4813
Tax Reg. No. 947 4565 411

SALES INVOICE

Invoice No: 47914
Customer: J Forrester Wholesale Supplies Ltd
Unit 79b
Oakhampton Industrial Estate
Bristol BS27 4JW
Date/Tax Point: 2 March 20X3
Order No: E9471

Item No.	Description	Quantity	Item value	Discount	Total $
EE27	Envelopes A5	20,000	£8.50 per 1,000	7%	258.10
EE29	Envelopes A4	20,000	£12.75 per 1,000	5%	242.25
RE20	Recycled A4 envelopes	30,000	£11.50 per 1,000	8%	217.40
				Total before taxes	717.75
				Sales tax at 20%	143.55
				Total	861.30

Terms: 5% cash discount for payment within 30 days
Carriage paid
E&OE

For a suggested answer, see the 'Answers' section at the end of the book.

FA1: RECORDING FINANCIAL TRANSACTIONS

The following is a comprehensive activity to help you revise earlier studies of documents.

ACTIVITY 2

Given below are three purchase invoices and related purchase orders and goods received notes. Should these purchase invoices be passed for payment?

LIGHTING INVENTORY LTD

14 High Road
Crowborough
East Sussex
Telephone 01673 892014
Tax Reg. No. 226 1429 292

SALES INVOICE

Invoice No: 497731
Customer: Fielden Lighting Ltd
Crowhurst Road
Wareham
Kent

Date/Tax Point: 20 May 20X6

Supply of:	Total ($)
27 Brandish light fittings	510.30
14 Farell light fittings	216.44
19 Barnstable wall mounts	240.92
Sub total	967.66
Sales tax at 20%	193.53
Invoice total	1,161.19

Terms: Net cash within 30 days
E&OE

SUMMERHILL SUPPLIES

27 High Road
Knebworth
Herts
Telephone 01985 621058
Tax Reg. No. 221 7438 319

SALES INVOICE

Invoice No: FL 493
Customer: Fielden Lighting Ltd
Crowhurst Road
Wareham
Kent

Date/Tax Point: 20 May 20X6

	Total ($)
4 PC 21 Light fittings	194.60
11 TL 15 Wall fittings	441.57
12 MT 06 Lamp stands	387.76
	1,023.93
Less: trade discount	56.27
Sub total	967.66
Sales tax at 20%	193.53
Invoice total	1,161.19

Terms: Net cash within 30 days
E&OE

Stonewall Stationery

Merrydown Court
Wadhurst
Telephone: 01673 492492
Tax Reg. No. 496 3211 566

SALES INVOICE

Invoice No: 13382
Customer: Fielden Lighting Ltd
Crowhurst Road
Wareham
Kent
Date/Tax Point: 18 May 20X6
Order No: E5561

Item No.	Description	Quantity	Item value	Discount	Total $
106924	2 Hole Files – A4	25	£1.50	10%	33.75
17240	Lever Arch Files	40	£2.50	15%	85.00

Total before taxes 118.75
Sales tax at 20% 23.75

Terms: 5% cash discount for payment within 30 days
Otherwise net 60 days
E&OE

Total 142.50

Fielden Lighting

Crowhurst Road
Wareham
Kent
Telephone: 01673 472841
Tax Reg. No. 742 8287 974

PURCHASE ORDER

Order No: 5566
To: Lighting Inventory Ltd
14 High Road
Crowborough
E. Sussex
Date: 30 April 20X6

Please supply:
- 20 Barnstable wall mounts
- 20 Brandish light fittings
- 14 Farell light fittings

Delivery to: As above

Fielden Lighting

Crowhurst Road
Wareham
Kent
Telephone: 01673 472841
Tax Reg. No. 742 8287 974

PURCHASE ORDER

Order No: 5561

To: Stonewall Stationery
             Merrydown Court
             Wadhurst

Date: 20 April 20X6

Please supply:
  25 × 106924
  40 × 17240

Delivery to: As above

Fielden Lighting

Crowhurst Road
Wareham
Kent
Telephone: 01673 472841
Tax Reg. No. 742 8287 974

PURCHASE ORDER

Order No: 5568

To: Summerhill Supplies
             27 High Street
             Knebworth
             Herts

Date: 30 April 20X6

Please supply:
  12   MT06 Lamp stands
   6   PC21 Light fittings
  11   TL15 Wall fittings

Delivery to: As above

GOODS RECEIVED NOTE

Supplier	Lighting Inventory Ltd		No. 4615
Supplier DN no.	XX41		
Date:	18 May 20X6		
Time:	1:07pm		

Ref..	Item delivered	Quantity	Condition
	Farell light fittings	14	OK
	Brandish light fittings	20	OK
	Barnstable wall mounts	15	OK

Received in good condition
Signed .... *PHarman* ....
Print name.... P Harman ....

GOODS RECEIVED NOTE

Supplier	Summerhill Supplies		No. 4621
Supplier DN no.	F316		
Date:	20 May 20X6		
Time:	10:43am		

Ref..	Item delivered	Quantity	Condition
	TL15 wall fittings	11	OK
	PC21 light fittings	4	OK
	MT06 lamp stands	12	OK

Received in good condition
Signed .... *P Harman* ....
Print name.... P Harman ....

GOODS RECEIVED NOTE

Supplier: Stonewall Stationery
Supplier DN no.: 4411
Date: 10 May 20X6
Time: 5:12pm

No. 4617

Ref..	Item delivered	Quantity	Condition
17240	Files	40	OK
106924	Files	25	6 damaged and returned

Received in good condition

Signed .... P. Harman ....

Print name ..... P. Harman .....

For a suggested answer, see the 'Answers' section at the end of the book.

3.4 CHECKING INVOICES FOR SERVICES

There are fewer items to check on an invoice for services than on an invoice for goods.

- Invoices for services should be checked for arithmetical accuracy, if they have been manually prepared.

- The amount charged should be checked against supporting documentation if it exists. For example, an invoice for the services of temporary office staff should be checked against the time sheets of the individual or individuals.

In many cases, however, there might be insufficient supporting documentation in the accounts department. For example:

- If an invoice is received for quarterly rent of premises or for rent of machinery, the accounts department might not have a copy of the rental agreement and so cannot check the invoice for accuracy.

- Regular invoices for gas, electricity, telephone charges and water supplies cannot be checked for reasonableness by the accounts staff.

- There might be other regular invoices for repeated services, such as monthly invoices for office cleaning services or six-monthly invoices for waste disposal services.

In such cases, the invoice should be referred to a person who is in a position to **authorise the invoice for payment**. This could be an office manager, for example. Authority can be evidenced by signing or initialling the invoice, whatever the established procedure happens to be in the organisation.

4 CREDIT NOTES

When a customer returns goods, it is normal business practice to keep the original invoice unchanged and to send a credit note to the customer.

It is much more convenient administratively to do this. By the time it is recognised that the sales invoice is incorrect, the invoice has probably been recorded in the sales day book and the ledgers. Rather than cancel the first invoice and issue a new one, it is simpler to issue a credit note that has the effect of reducing the amount owed by the credit customer.

Similarly, when there is an error in a purchase invoice, the supplier will normally want to issue a credit note rather than cancel the first invoice and issue a new one.

This is normal accepted practice. However, an incorrect purchase invoice should not be processed for payment until the credit note has been received.

Example

You receive an invoice from Crab Co for 600 units of product PQR costing $4 each, and the invoice is for $2,400 plus sales tax of $480, which is $2,880 in total.

On checking the documentation, you find that although 600 units were ordered and delivered, the delivery note contains a hand-written note that 100 units were delivered in a damaged condition.

You should contact the supplier and explain the problem. The supplier's copy of the delivery note should also include a note that 100 units were delivered in a damaged condition, and if this is the case, the supplier should agree not to charge for the 100 units. The supplier should therefore promise to send you a credit note for $400 plus sales tax of $80, or $480 in total.

You should hold on to the invoice, and you should not process it until the credit note has been received. When the credit note is received, it should be checked and if it is acceptable, the invoice and credit note should be processed together.

4.1 CHECKING CREDIT NOTES

When credit notes are received, they should be checked for accuracy.

- Check the accuracy of the arithmetic, if the credit note has been prepared manually.

- Check that the credit note is for the correct amount. The best way to do this is probably to write a note about the discrepancy on the invoice. When the credit note is received, it should then be a fairly simple matter to check that the credit note deals with the discrepancy you have noted on the invoice.

5 AUTHORISING AND CODING

5.1 AUTHORISING PURCHASE INVOICES

Purchase invoices should be authorised for payment before they are actually paid. There are two ways in which invoices might be approved.

- The purchase invoices might be checked in the accounts department, against supporting documentation. If the invoice appears to be correct, it should be noted to show that the checks have been carried out, and then approved by a person with the required authority in the accounts department. This could be the accounts supervisor.

- If the accounts department is unable to carry out the checks on the invoices, a copy of the invoice should be sent to a person who can check and confirm the accuracy of the invoice. This may be the manager responsible for the expenditure e.g. the purchasing manager. When the invoice has been authorised (with a signature of the appropriate person) it should be returned to the accounts department.

If a discrepancy has been found and the supplier has agreed to provide a credit note, the invoice should not be approved until the credit note has been received, and the invoice should then be approved at the same time as the credit note.

This process of approving invoices is important, because unless it is carried out properly and according to established office procedures, there is a risk that payments will be made that should not have been made. Similarly, credit notes should also be authorised prior to processing to ensure that any amounts owed to suppliers are correctly accounted for.

5.2 EXPENSE ACCOUNT CODES, ASSET ACCOUNT CODES AND SUPPLIER ACCOUNT CODES

Asset expenditure (i.e. capital expenditure) and revenue expenditure (i.e. expenses) must be distinguished from each other. In addition, different types of asset expenditure and different types of expense are categorised according to their nature.

There is an account in the main ledger for each category of expenditure. These are commonly referred to as **expense accounts**. Although each expense account has an identifying name, it is also given a code number.

Asset expenditure results in the purchase of an asset for the business, and there are **asset accounts** in the main ledger for different categories of asset expenditure, such as land and buildings, plant and machinery, equipment and motor vehicles.

Just as there are individual accounts in a sales ledger for each credit customer, a business maintains individual accounts for each supplier. These **supplier accounts** are held in the **purchase ledger or payables' ledger**. Each supplier account has both a name and an identifying account number or code.

When expenditure is recorded in the accounting system, the accounts codes are used. This means that for each purchase invoice or credit note received, we need the expense account code or asset account code and also the supplier account code in order to enter the transaction in the accounting system.

Two codes are therefore added to a supplier's invoice (or credit note):

- the main ledger code, identifying the type of expense, e.g. purchases, telephone expenses or assets

- the payables' ledger code identifying the supplier.

5.3 NUMBERING PURCHASE INVOICES

It is common practice, for reasons of internal control, to give all purchase invoices received an internal sequential number. (Similarly credit notes received from suppliers are given an internal sequential number.)

This number must be written on the invoice or credit note itself, in addition to the supplier code and main or nominal *(general)* ledger codes.

5.4 GRID BOX STAMP (OR FRONT SHEET)

A purchase invoice should not be entered into the accounting system and processed for payment unless it has been properly authorised. Where the invoice is authorised after checks carried out in the 'purchase ledger section' of the accounts department, there should be visible evidence that the checks have been completed and either:

- the invoice is correct, or
- a discrepancy was found, but a credit note has now been received from the supplier.

Evidence of the check should be:

- written on the invoice, perhaps as an authorising signature
- entered into a grid stamped on to the invoice by the clerks in the purchase ledger section
- written on a front sheet attached to the invoice by the clerks in the purchase ledger section.

The same stamped grid or front sheet can also be used to write in the main ledger code for the expenditure and the supplier account code.

An example of a front sheet is shown on the following page.

The following details should be entered on either the invoice or a front sheet:

- **Date**. This is the date the invoice is received by the accounts department. If a supplier is chasing for payment of an invoice, this date can be used to check when the invoice was received, and so how long it has been unpaid.

- **Agreed to purchase order**. There should be evidence that the invoice has been checked and agrees with the purchase order. In the example above, the front sheet does this by having space for the purchase order number and for tick boxes to show that the prices, discounts and credit terms on the invoice are the same as those shown on the purchase order. There could be another tick box to confirm that the quantities delivered are correct.

- **Agreed to delivery note**. There should also be evidence that the invoice has been checked against the delivery note, and that the quantities on the invoice are the actual quantities delivered in good condition. In the front sheet above, the evidence is provided by entering the delivery note number, and by means of tick boxes for checks on the quantities and their condition.

- **Calculations checked**. There should be evidence to show that the invoice has been checked to make sure that the calculations are correct. In the front sheet above, there are tick boxes to show that specific calculations have been checked. (**Note: Price extensions** are the multiplication of the quantity by the unit price for each item delivered.)

- **Discrepancies.** If any discrepancies or errors have been found, a note should be written to explain how they are being resolved. If the supplier has agreed to send a credit note, the details should be noted.

- **Supplier account reference.** The supplier account code should be found and noted. It can be found in a list of supplier account codes for the purchase ledger. This may be held in a file in alphabetical order of supplier names.

- **Main ledger account reference.** The main ledger expense account code or asset account code for the expenditure should be found and noted. This can be found from a list of main ledger codes.

- **Signature and date.** When all the items have been checked, and the codes obtained, the document should be signed and dated by the checker.

- **Invoice authorised for payment.** After the invoice has been checked, it should be authorised. Authorisation is evidenced by the signature of the person giving the approval (and possibly also the date of approval).

- **Invoice (and credit note, if there is one) entered in the day book.** When the invoice is returned to the accounts department, it will be entered into the accounting records (the purchase day book) and this should be recorded on the checklist. This final tick should make sure that the invoice is not entered into the day book twice.

Purchase invoice check list

Date invoice received	31 May 20X4
Purchase order number	19853
Prices	✓
Discounts	✓
Terms	✓
Delivery note number	AB5612
Quantities	✓
Condition	✓
Calculations checked	
Price extensions	✓
Totals	✓
Sales tax	✓
Date discrepancies notified	
To supplier	None
To department manager	None
Supplier account reference	P4234
Main ledger account reference	500312
Signature: G.T. Hobbs	Date: 8 June 20X4
Approved for payment: B.B Barnes	Date: 10 June 20X4
Day book	✓

ACTIVITY 3

1. A business invoices a customer for $400 plus sales tax at 20%. The business offers all customers a settlement discount of 2% if payment is received within 7 days.

    What is the total on the invoice, including sales tax at 20%?

    A $480.00

    B $489.60

    C $470.40

    D $392.00

2. An invoice was received from a non-sales tax registered supplier for $300. Checking against the original order the customer noted that the agreed trade discount of 20% has been omitted as has a cash discount of 5%.

    For how much should the invoice have been?

    A $228.00

    B $240.00

    C $252.00

    D $285.00

3. An invoice is received for a magazine subscription.

    How should this invoice be dealt with?

    A   It should be paid immediately.

    B   It should be diarised until the latest date when any cash discount can be claimed and paid then.

    C   It should be matched up with documentation providing evidence of the order, be authorised and then paid.

    D   It should be rejected.

    For a suggested answer, see the 'Answers' section at the end of the book.

6 PURCHASE DAY BOOK

The first step in accounting for a purchase invoice is to enter its details into a book of prime entry, known as the **purchase day book**.

Similarly, the first step in accounting for a credit note from a supplier is to enter it into a book of prime entry, known as the **purchase returns day book.**

These books of prime entry are not a part of the accounting ledgers, but like the sales day book and the sales returns day book, they are a primary record in which accounting transactions can be recorded prior to posting them to the ledgers.

6.1 BATCHING TRANSACTIONS FOR PROCESSING

A business might receive large numbers of invoices each day. It is usual to process them in manageable amounts or batches, or, if there are few invoices each day, wait until there are enough to be worthwhile processing. If there is a large number of purchase invoices, dividing them into batches means that purchase ledger clerks can be given only as many to process as they can handle. If there are any errors in entering the invoice details into the accounting system, it should be easier and quicker to track down the error by tracing it to a single batch of transactions.

6.2 PURCHASE DAY BOOK

A purchase day book is similar to a sales day book, but it records purchase invoice details rather than sales invoices. Another difference between a purchase day book and a sales day book is that a purchase day book normally has a large number of analysis columns, whereas a sales day book normally has only a few.

There should be an analysis column in the purchase day book for every expense account in the nominal *(general)* ledger. Some businesses will also record purchase returns as negative amounts or deductions from the number and value of credit purchase invoices received and recorded. Alternatively, some businesses may choose to maintain a separate purchase returns day book – see later in this chapter.

This is difficult to show conveniently in a text book, but the following simplified example shows what a purchase day book should look like.

What a purchase day book looks like

Date	Supplier – name and code	Total	Sales tax	Purchases	Gas & Electric	Telephone and postage	Rent	Motor expenses	Sundry expenses
		$	$	$	$	$	$	$	$
			2165	4001	4002	4003	4004	4005	4006

There will probably be many other columns in a 'real' purchase day book, and so each 'folio' of the day book might stretch across two pages of a physical accounts book. Each purchase invoice is recorded on one line of the day book.

- **Date**. This should be the date on the purchase invoice.

- **Purchase invoice number**. There might be a column for entering the purchase invoice number, when purchase invoices are given an internal (sequential) number. This column is not included in the example above.

- **Supplier name and code.** There might be separate columns for name and account code. The supplier details are entered here.

- **Total.** This is the total amount payable, which is the total shown on the invoice. It includes sales tax, where payable.

- The remaining columns are analysis columns, and the total of the entries in the analysis columns should add up to the total value of the invoice, as shown in the total column.

- **Sales tax.** This is the amount of sales tax payable, as shown on the invoice.

- **Expense (or asset) columns.** The amount of the expense **excluding sales tax** should be entered in the relevant column, to indicate the nature or category of the expense.

- **Nominal *(general)* ledger codes.** The nominal *(general)* ledger account code numbers should ideally be shown on each page. Each analysis column for expenditure should have a unique expense account (or asset account) in the nominal *(general)* ledger.

Example

Bobble Co is a car parts distributor. It has six credit suppliers. At the beginning of July, Bobble Co did not owe any of these suppliers money. Transactions with these suppliers during July were recorded in the purchases day book as follows:

Purchases day book

Date	Details	Invoice	Total	Sales tax	Net
July			$	$	$
1	Ace	6031	1,728.00	288.00	1,440.00
1	Bays	6032	1,920.00	320.00	1,600.00
1	Campo	6033	528.00	88.00	440.00
1	Dans	6034	988.80	164.80	824.00
1	Eastern	6035	1,512.00	252.00	1,260.00
1	Field	6036	1,920.00	320.00	1,600.00
8	Bays	6037	960.00	160.00	800.00
8	Dans	6038	307.20	51.20	256.00
8	Ace	6039	756.00	126.00	630.00
8	Fields	6040	1,440,00	240.00	1,200.00
			12,060.00	2,010.00	10,050.00

This example will be revisited in Chapter 13.

ACTIVITY 4

Suppose that a business received the following invoices in the post on 3 May 20X5:

Supplier	Type of expense	Supplier ref code	Net $	Sales tax $	Gross $
G J Kite	Purchases	K06	225.10	45.02	270.12
BT	Telephone	BT01	268.41	53.68	322.09
Yelson Ltd	Purchases	Y03	113.90	22.78	136.68
Henn Garage	Car repairs	H02	810.00	162.00	972.00
Dino & Co	Purchases	D09	58.48	11.69	70.17
T Tortelli	Purchases	T11	552.68	110.53	663.21
Lynn Partners	Rent	LP02	800.00	160.00	960.00
Franco Bros	Purchases	FB08	120.00	24.00	144.00

Enter these invoice details in the following purchase day book.

Date	Supplier	Supplier account number	Total $	Sales tax $	Purchases $	Motor $	Rent $	Telephone $	Power $

For a suggested answer, see the 'Answers' section at the end of the book.

6.3 DISCOUNTS

Settlement discounts

Notice that there is no column in the purchase day book for settlement discounts received. When a settlement discount is received, it is recorded in the cash payments book, which is described in a later chapter. This is because it is not known with certainty, at the time of purchase, whether settlement discounts offered will be taken up.

Trade discounts

Remember, as explained in Chapter 5, that these are usually given to customers because of regular buying or quantities purchased. The effect of a trade discount is to reduce the selling price from the published list price. The calculation of the trade discount is usually shown on the invoice recording the transaction.

Consequently, if a business makes a purchase in relation to which it receives a trade discount, such discount will not be recorded in any account.

The value of the purchase or debt created is the net value shown on the invoice. It will therefore be this amount that is recorded in the purchase day book.

7 PURCHASE RETURNS DAY BOOK

A business can choose to maintain a separate day book to record supplier credit notes received, rather than simply deducting or offsetting credit notes from suppliers against purchase invoices summarised in the purchases day book. This is called the purchase returns day book (or returns outwards day book). The purchase returns day book is similar to a sales returns day book, except that it records supplier credit notes received rather than credit notes issued to customers.

Like the purchase day book, the purchase returns day book has analysis columns. However, the items for which there might be supplier credit notes are usually quite small. For example, it would be unusual to get credit notes for expenditures on rent, local business tax, gas bills, electricity bills, telephone bills, postage charges, motor repair costs and so on. This means that the day book might have as little as two analysis columns, one for returns of purchases and one for Sales tax.

The items to be entered into the purchase returns day book for each credit note might therefore be simply:

- date

- credit note number. There might be a column for writing in the credit note number, when credit notes are given an internal (sequential) number. (This column is not shown in the example below)

- supplier name

- supplier's reference number (supplier account number)

- the gross amount of the credit note (including sales tax)

- the sales tax on the goods returned

- the net cost of the goods returned, excluding sales tax.

Example

A business received a credit note from a supplier, Vast Chemicals, for $480. The credit note was dated 5 November. The credit note is for a quantity of chemical items that were returned to the supplier as unsatisfactory. These had a cost of $400 and sales tax at 20% is $80. The supplier's account code number is P9704.

The entry in the purchase returns day book might look like this:

Date	Supplier	Supplier account number	Total $	Sales tax $	Purchases $
05/11	Vast Chemicals	P9704	480.00	80.00	400.00
	Main ledger codes			2165	1800

Note

- Each number column in the purchase returns day book represents an account in the main ledger, and hypothetical account numbers have been entered in the example above.

- The sales tax column is for the sales tax account in the main ledger.

- The purchases column does not represent the purchases account in the main ledger, but the **purchase returns account.**

CONCLUSION

When purchase invoices and credit notes have been checked, and any discrepancies have been resolved, the details of the purchase invoices and credit notes should be recorded in the accounting system. The procedures for recording expenditure in the accounts are similar to the procedures for recording credit sales and sales returns which were described in an earlier chapter.

KEY TERMS

Price extensions – The multiplication of the quantity by the unit price for each item.

Price quotation – Document sent to a potential customer quoting price for some goods or a service. If signed and accepted by the customer, it becomes a purchase order from the customer.

Timesheet – Record of time spent by an employee on certain work or jobs.

SELF TEST QUESTIONS

		Paragraph
1	What is a purchase requisition?	1
2	When is a timesheet used?	2
3	State three checks to do when receiving a purchase invoice from a supplier.	3
4	What would you do if you checked an invoice and found that the goods on the invoice disagreed with the details on the purchase order and delivery note?	3
5	What should you check on a credit note when you receive one?	4
6	List and explain the different codes you will meet with purchase and expenses documentation.	5
7	Compare a purchase day book with a sales day book.	6
8	Why are there likely to be fewer columns in a purchase returns day book than a purchase day book?	7

EXAM-STYLE QUESTIONS

1   What sometimes takes the place of a purchase order when services are purchased?

   A   A written contract specifying nature of the service and agreed price

   B   A delivery note listing the service and price agreed

   C   A completed timesheet

   D   A purchase requisition

2   An individual bought 20 units of inventory at $50 per unit their business. The supplier allowed a trade discount of 10% and charged sales tax at 20%.

   What is the total invoice price that the supplier should charge the customer?

   A $900.00

   B $1,000.00

   C $1,080.00

   D $1,200.00

3   Jinx Co received an invoice for $450 and, subsequently a credit note for $50 as reimbursement for damaged goods. What entries should be made in the books of prime entry?

   A $400 posted to the purchase day book

   B $400 posted to the purchase returns day book

   C $450 posted to the purchase day book, $50 to the purchase returns day book

   D $50 posted to the purchase day book, $450 to the purchase returns day book

4   Cube Co, a business entity, is registered to account for sales tax. In the last week, its purchases were $960 inclusive of sales tax and its sales were $400 exclusive of sales tax.

   The rate of sales tax is 20%.

   How much sales tax will be receivable or payable for this week?

   A $160 payable

   B $160 receivable

   C $80 payable

   D $80 receivable

For suggested answers, see the 'Answers' section at the end of the book.

Chapter 8

RECORDING PURCHASES

When expenditure is incurred, a record should be entered in the accounting system. Purchases on credit are recorded in the nominal (general) ledger and a payables ledger. This chapter explains the procedures for recording purchases in the ledgers. It also considers supplier statements and monitoring of payables in the aged payables analysis. This chapter covers the syllabus area for recording purchases.

CONTENTS

1 Posting to the nominal *(general)* ledger

2 Computerised ledgers

3 Statements

4 Aged payables analysis

5 Communication with suppliers

LEARNING OUTCOMES

At the end of this chapter, you should be able to:

- maintain a manual nominal (general) and purchase or payables ledger to record purchases

- describe a computerised payables ledger

- prepare, reconcile and understand the purpose of supplier statements

- understand the purpose of and prepare an aged payables analysis

- communicate efficiently and effectively with suppliers.

1 POSTING TO THE NOMINAL *(GENERAL)* LEDGER

1.1 POSTING FROM THE PURCHASE DAY BOOK TO THE NOMINAL *(GENERAL)* LEDGER

Each column of figures in the purchase day book represents an account in the nominal *(general)* ledger. There are columns for:

- total payables (the total column)
- sales tax
- each expense account in the nominal (general) ledger, and possibly some asset accounts too.

The total values of the entries in each column are the total amounts invoiced by suppliers, the sales tax on those invoices, and the total amount of expenditure for each item of expense.

These total figures in each column are posted to the nominal *(general)* ledger as follows.

- **Debit**: Each expense account with the total for the appropriate column in the purchase day book. For example, debit the purchases account in the nominal *(general)* ledger with the total value of the purchases column, and debit the motor vehicle expenses account with the total of the motor vehicle expenses column. These totals will be net of sales tax.

- **Debit**: The sales tax account in the nominal *(general)* ledger with the total of the sales tax column.

- **Credit**: payables control account with the total including sales tax.

You will recognise that this is similar to the approach seen earlier for sales.

Memorandum accounts

As well as needing to know the total amount owed to credit suppliers at any one time, shown in the control account, it is also necessary to know exactly how much each individual credit supplier is owed. This is achieved by the use of memorandum accounts (see Chapter 5). In the case of suppliers, these are maintained in the payables ledger.

Don't forget, unless told otherwise in the exam, memorandum accounts are not part of the double entry system for a business. They are an essential part of any business' record keeping but using them as part of the double entry system, rather than using the payables control account, is a cumbersome option.

Control accounts are discussed in more detail in Chapter 13; for the remainder of this chapter, we shall consider the individual supplier accounts to be part of the double entry system.

ACTIVITY 1

Total the columns in the purchase day book and post them to the relevant nominal *(general)* ledger accounts.

Purchase day book   Folio PDB35

Date	Supplier	Supplier account number	Total	Sales tax	Purchases	Motor expenses	Rent	Telephone
			$	$	$	$	$	$
03/05	G J Kite	3011	270.12	45.02	225.10			
	Brit Telecom	3012	322.09	53.68				268.41
	Yelson Ltd	3013	136.68	22.78	113.90			
	Henn Garage	3014	972.00	162.00		810.00		
	Dino & Co	3015	70.17	11.69	58.48			
	T Tortelli	3016	663.21	110.53	552.68			
	Lynn Prtnrs	3017	960.00	160.00			800.00	
	Franco Bros	3018	144.00	24.00	120.00			
	Ledger code			3050	5001	5002	5003	5004

For a suggested answer, see the 'Answers' section at the end of the book.

1.2 POSTING FROM THE PURCHASE RETURNS DAY BOOK TO THE NOMINAL (*GENERAL*) LEDGER

Totals in the purchase returns day book are calculated in a similar way, and the totals are posted to the nominal *(general)* ledger as follows.

- **Debit**: Accounts of individual suppliers in the payables ledger with the total cost of goods returned, including sales tax.

- **Credit**: Purchase returns account with the net cost of goods returned, excluding sales tax.

- **Credit**: sales tax account with the sales tax charged on goods returned. This is the total of the sales tax column in the day book.

In most organisations, a purchase returns account only exists for the purchase returns of purchases of raw materials and/or goods for resale. Where a credit note relates to other types of expense, such as purchases of stationery, the purchase returns day book should have an analysis column for each different type of return. The total of any returns column, except for purchase returns, should be posted as a credit entry to the expense account. For example, returns of stationery purchases would be posted as a credit entry to the stationery expenses account in the nominal *(general)* ledger.

FA1: RECORDING FINANCIAL TRANSACTIONS

ACTIVITY 2

A purchase returns day book for 21 April 20X3 shows the following:

Purchase returns day book (PRDB)

Date	Credit note number	Supplier	Supplier ref/code	Total $	Sales tax $	Purchase returns $	Stationery $
21/4	CN211	Cutler Ltd	C09/3050	56.80	9.46	47.34	
21/4	CN7631	Platter Bros	P03/3051	27.46	4.57		22.89
21/4	CN0972	Linden Ltd	L06/3052	10.74	1.79	8.95	
				95.00	15.82	56.29	22.89
	Main ledger code				3215	4406	6322

Post the relevant figures for the day to the main ledger accounts.

For a suggested answer, see the 'Answers' section at the end of the book.

2 COMPUTERISED LEDGERS

The purchase ledger (also called the bought ledger, the payables' ledger or the accounts payable ledger) may be operated through a computerised system. The format of the purchases ledger may be different than a manual one, but the principles of double entry are the same.

Most computerised systems are 'integrated'. This means that when, for example, a purchase is entered onto the system (in the purchases day book) the system automatically updates all of the ledgers in the nominal *(general)* ledger, as well as updating the memorandum accounts.

Example

A business maintains a control account for payables in the nominal *(general)* ledger. It purchases materials for $1,000 on credit from its supplier, M Tang. The purchase ledger clerk enters this in the purchase day book. The system automatically updates the purchases account, the sales tax account (if the business is appropriately registered) and the payables' control account in the nominal *(general)* ledger. Also, it automatically updates the individual memorandum account for M Tang in the payables ledger.

In a computerised system such as this, the total of the individual balances on the credit suppliers' memorandum accounts will always reconcile with the total on the payables' control account (see Chapter 13.) This is because one transaction initiates lots of entries on the system. Whilst this reduces the potential for incorrect transfer of information, if the original entry is wrong, all the accounts (including the memorandum accounts) will also be wrong.

3 STATEMENTS

3.1 BALANCING A SUPPLIER'S ACCOUNT

A supplier's account in the payables ledger provides a record of all the transactions with the supplier. It shows the amount of invoices received, credit notes received, payments made and discounts received. It also shows the amount currently owing to the supplier, which is the current balance on the account.

If there is any disagreement with the supplier about how much is owed, the account can be checked to obtain the necessary details, or find a cross-reference to the page in the book of prime entry where the transaction was recorded (which in turn can lead you back to the source documentation).

Recording transactions in a supplier's account and calculating the balance is done in the same way as for customer accounts in the sales ledger. Periodically, say at the end of each month, the supplier's account is ruled off, and the closing balance is carried forward.

Example

The following transactions occurred with a new supplier, MNP, in May and June.

6 May: Purchased goods on credit, costing $987 including sales tax at 20%.

24 May: Purchased goods on credit for which the invoice price is $1,168 including sales tax. The supplier has offered an early settlement discount of 4% ($40) on this invoice.

5 June: Purchased goods on credit for which the invoice price is $1,752. The supplier has offered an early settlement discount of 4% ($60) on this invoice.

12 June: Purchased goods on credit for $141 including sales tax.

12 May: Received a credit note for $188.

3 June: Paid the supplier $1,927. Part of this payment was to settle the 24 May invoice, and the settlement discount of $40 was taken.

The supplier account number is 71003.

Task

Show the supplier's account for May and June, and carry forward the balance on the account at the end of June.

Solution

			MNP account				71003
Date	Details	Folio	$	Date	Details	Folio	$
12/05	Purchase returns	PRDB	188	6/05	Purchases	PDB	987
3/06	Bank	CPB	1,927	24/05	Purchases	PDB	1,168
3/06	Disc. rec'd	CPB	40	5/06	Purchases	PDB	1,752
30/06	Balance c/d		1,893	12/06	Purchases	PDB	141
			4,048				4,048
				1/07	Balance b/d		1,893

Notes

1. The closing balance on the account is calculated by adding up the total of the entries on the debit side ($2,155) and the total of all the entries on the credit side ($4,048). The credit entries exceed the debit entries by $1,893 ($4,048 – $2,155), so there is a credit balance of $1,893 on the account.

2. The credit balance in this example represents the unpaid invoices of 5th and 12th June: ($1,752 + $141 = $1,893).

3. The account is ruled off by entering the closing balance to carry forward on the debit side, to make the two column totals equal above the line, and to bring forward the balance below the line, on the credit side of the account.

3.2 SUPPLIERS' STATEMENTS

Many organisations will tend to make their payments at a particular time each month, for example on the last Friday of each month. During the month it is quite possible that several invoices may have been received from the same supplier.

In order to summarise the invoices that have been sent out and the total amount owed, the supplier may send the organisation a statement.

A statement can be used to check that the supplier's records agree with the position as shown in the supplier's purchase ledger account. If there is any discrepancy, the difference should be investigated, and where necessary taken up with the supplier.

An example of a supplier's statement is given below. It is addressed to J Forrester Wholesale Supplies Ltd from Disks and Labels Ltd.

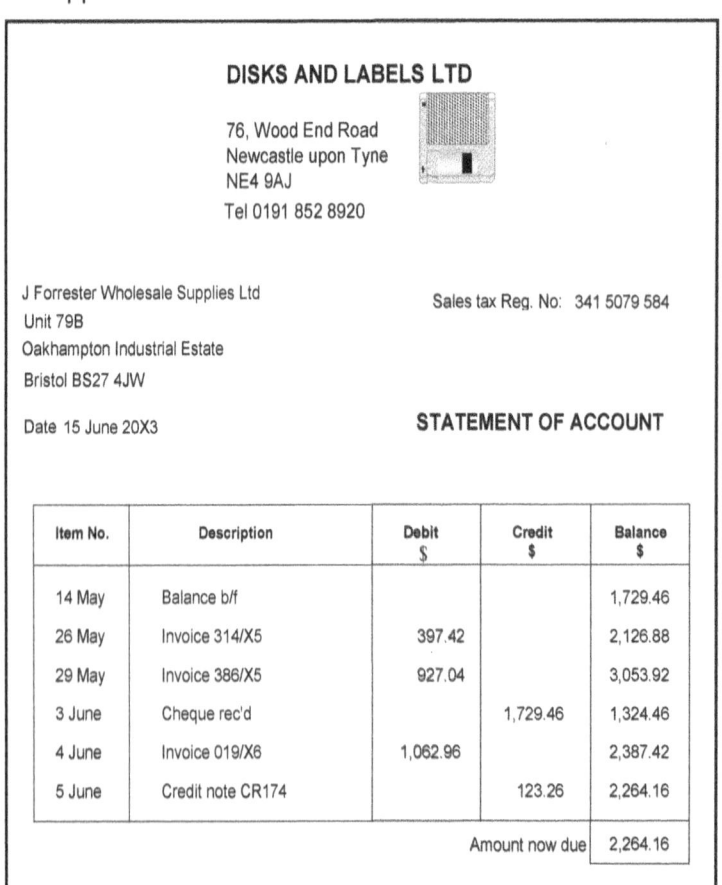

DISKS AND LABELS LTD

76, Wood End Road
Newcastle upon Tyne
NE4 9AJ

Tel 0191 852 8920

J Forrester Wholesale Supplies Ltd
Unit 79B
Oakhampton Industrial Estate
Bristol BS27 4JW

Sales tax Reg. No: 341 5079 584

Date 15 June 20X3

STATEMENT OF ACCOUNT

Item No.	Description	Debit $	Credit $	Balance $
14 May	Balance b/f			1,729.46
26 May	Invoice 314/X5	397.42		2,126.88
29 May	Invoice 386/X5	927.04		3,053.92
3 June	Cheque rec'd		1,729.46	1,324.46
4 June	Invoice 019/X6	1,062.96		2,387.42
5 June	Credit note CR174		123.26	2,264.16
			Amount now due	2,264.16

A statement shows the following amounts:

- the balance brought forward as owing at the beginning of the period
- the invoices issued during the period
- the credit note issued in the period (deducted from the total due to be paid)
- the account balance after each transaction
- the balance (amount currently due) at the statement date.

Essentially, a statement should contain the same information as the supplier account in the payables ledger. Any differences should be followed up and resolved.

Note, however, that in this supplier's statement, the transactions are shown as 'debits' and 'credits'. The 'debit' column lists invoices that John Forrester owes, but in John Forrester's accounts these are purchase invoices and will be listed as credits! You have to get used to this 'mirror image'. The debts that we **owe** to our **supplier** are **owned** by the supplier. The amount owed to the supplier is their **receivable**.

3.3 CHECKING A STATEMENT

The following example illustrates the checking of a statement.

Suppose that the invoices shown on the statement above were checked and invoice 386/X5 from 29 May appears as follows:

DISKS AND LABELS LTD

76, Wood End Road
Newcastle upon Tyne
NE4 9AJ
Tel: 0191 852 8920

J Forrester Wholesale Supplies Ltd
Unit 79B
Oakhampton Industrial Estate
Bristol BS27 4JW

Date   29 May 20X3

Invoice No: 386/X5
Tax Reg. No. 341 5079 584
Order No: 227P
DN No: 1489

INVOICE

Item No.	Description	Quantity	Item value $	Total $
P180	Boxed disks	15	5.15	77.25
			Total before taxes	77.25
			Sales tax @ 20%	15.45
				92.70

Terms: Net 30 days

An error has been made on the statement from Disks and Labels as the invoice on 29 May has been included in the balance as $927.04 rather than the correct amount of $92.70.

The actual amount due from J Forrester to Disks and Labels is therefore substantially less than that which appears on the statement.

Amount due:

	$
Balance b/f	1,729.46
26 May Invoice 314/X5	397.42
29 May Invoice 386/X5	92.70
4 June Invoice 019/X6	1,062.96
	3,282.54
Less: Cheque received	1,729.46
Credit note CR 174	123.26
	1,429.82

When this discrepancy has been discovered, Disks and Labels Ltd should be informed of the error that they have made on the statement by letter so that it can be amended and a replacement statement issued. Either the purchasing manager or the payables ledger supervisor should probably write this letter.

4 AGED PAYABLES ANALYSIS

In exactly the same way as customer balances can be analysed in terms of their age, so too can suppliers' balances. We refer in this case to an aged payables analysis.

An aged payables analysis is a report showing amounts owed to credit suppliers, analysed in terms of the number of days each amount has been outstanding.

4.1 THE PURPOSE OF AN AGED PAYABLES ANALYSIS

An aged debt analysis relating to credit customers is an important tool of management control. By referring to amounts overdue, managers can initiate appropriate action to chase slow payers. This is obviously not an important consideration in the reverse situation (money owed to credit suppliers) and as a result, most businesses make less use of their payables analysis than of their receivables analysis.

Despite this, there are good reasons why managers should pay attention to the aged payables analysis. One reason is the need to maintain good relationships with trusted suppliers. If an organisation is consistently late in paying its debts, suppliers may retaliate by reducing the level of customer service, withdrawing favourable trading terms, or, in the last resort, refusing to make further supplies. To avoid this issue, it makes sense to monitor suppliers' balances to ensure that debts due are paid in good time.

It is also a good idea for a business to monitor amounts owed to ensure that settlement discounts are claimed and not missed.

4.2 PREPARING AN AGED PAYABLES ANALYSIS

An aged payables analysis is prepared in exactly the same way as the aged debt analysis. The layout of the report, also, is the same as we have already seen in the aged debt analysis. The only difference, obviously, is that the starting point is the ledger accounts for credit suppliers rather than credit customers. In addition the periods used are likely to be shorter, clearly highlighting the typical periods offered for settlement discounts.

5 COMMUNICATION WITH SUPPLIERS

When looking at communicating with customers the focus was on developing, monitoring and maintaining good relations to encourage customers to develop and maintain long relationships. Contented customers are also likely to recommend the business to others.

In the case of suppliers, good communications are focused on maintaining continued supplies. In addition, as occasionally goods need to be returned because of damages or problems with the goods, it is important to have a good line of communications to ensure replacements are quickly received.

As mentioned earlier in the chapter, communications can take place over statements and any disagreements between the accounting records of supplier and customers.

The points about being polite and professional covered in the chapter in respect of communication with customers also apply with suppliers.

CONCLUSION

Purchase transactions are first entered in the books of prime entry and then transferred to the nominal *(general)* ledger and the payables ledger. This completes the process of recording expenditure in the accounting system. Supplier statements can be produced to confirm the transactions which take place on the ledger accounts of suppliers.

Sometime later, suppliers will be paid what they are owed. The procedures for paying suppliers and recording the payments in the accounting system will be described in the next chapter. Before making payments it is useful for a business to monitor when they are due and whether discounts may be claimed. An aged payables analysis is used for careful monitoring.

KEY TERMS

Aged payables analysis – List of payables, analysed according to how long it is until payment is due.

Purchase day book – Book of prime entry for recording purchase transactions on credit (purchase invoices).

Payables ledger – A ledger containing accounts for individual suppliers.

Purchase returns day book – Book of prime entry for recording details of credit notes from suppliers (purchase returns).

SELF TEST QUESTIONS

		Paragraph
1	How are totals in the purchase day return book posted to the main ledger?	1
2	Give a reason for checking a supplier's statement.	3
3	What is an aged payables analysis?	4
4	Why should management be interested in an aged payables analysis?	4
5	Give a reason for maintaining good communications with suppliers.	5

EXAM-STYLE QUESTIONS

1 Which of the following will appear as a debit balance in the ledger accounts?

    A   Trade payables

    B   Purchases

    C   Purchase returns day book

    D   Trade creditors

2 Which of the following does not appear on a supplier statement?

    A   Balance b/f

    B   Balance c/f

    C   Payments/Bank

    D   Trade discount

3 Which is not a reason for maintaining an aged payables analysis?

    A   To avoid customers becoming bad debts

    B   To take advantage of settlement discounts

    C   To check payments are made on time

    D   To avoid suppliers withdrawing credit terms

For suggested answers, see the 'Answers' section at the end of the book.

Chapter 9

RECORDING RECEIPTS AND PAYMENTS

When payments are received from customers, the money has to be banked. The procedures for banking money were explained in an earlier chapter. In addition, a record of the receipts has to be made in the accounting system. The same is true also for payments made by the business. This chapter explains how receipts and payments are recorded. It focuses on the syllabus areas recording payments and monies received and authorising and making payments.

CONTENTS

1 Recording payments and monies received

2 The cash book

3 Manual nominal *(general)* ledger and receivables ledger

4 Posting receipts and payments from the cash book to the main ledger

5 Computerised records

6 Authorising and making payments

LEARNING OUTCOMES

At the end of this chapter, you should be able to:

- identify the documentation accompanying payments and receipts

- recognise the importance of accurately recording all payments and receipts

- identify the main ways to ensure that only authorised payments are made

- record payments and receipts in the cash book, nominal (general) ledger, payables and receivables ledger (manual or computerised).

1 RECORDING PAYMENTS AND MONIES RECEIVED

1.1 RECEIPTS FROM CREDIT CUSTOMERS AND FROM CUSTOMERS WITHOUT CREDIT ACCOUNTS

Businesses receive money from credit customers who are paying invoices and from customers who do not have a credit account. From an accounting perspective, there is an important difference between receipts from credit customers and receipts from customers without a credit account.

- **Receipts from credit customers** have to be recorded, not just in the nominal (general) ledger, but also in the individual account of the customer in the receivables ledger, so that the account is kept up to date.

- **Receipts from customers without a credit account** are treated as cash sales. These receipts might come through takings in a cash register or through orders by post, telephone or e-mail, where payment is by cheque or credit card.

Credit sales have already been recorded in the main ledger. When a credit customer eventually pays, the accounting records have to be updated to show that the customer has paid the money owed. Cash sales have not been recorded in the main ledger yet, and when money is received for cash sales, both the sale and the receipt have to be recorded.

1.2 CHECKING RECEIPTS AGAINST RELEVANT SUPPORTING INFORMATION

When a business receives money for cash sales, the amount received has to be checked to make sure that all the money is there. The total value of receipts in notes and coins, cheques, and credit and debit cards should be calculated separately, to get three separate totals. The total value of receipts by cheque and by credit and debit cards is found by going through the cheques and credit/debit card vouchers one by one and adding up their total value. Some calculators produce a printed list of the individual cheque or credit/debit card voucher amounts.

When the total value of receipts has been calculated in this way, it might be possible to the compare this total with a till roll (for cash received through a cash register) or a printout of credit card receipts (for receipts taken and recorded through a credit card machine). The two totals should be equal.

1.3 REMITTANCE LIST

When money is received from credit customers, it is important to make sure that each receipt is properly recorded. A common method of doing this is to start by preparing a remittance list or cash received list. A remittance list is simply a list of each receipt, with details of who the money has come from and the amount of the receipt.

The following is a typical remittance list:

Customer name	Account number	Amount received $
A C Bryan	1037	265.40
Flowers Limited	1002	319.64
E Patel	1053	396.61
P Taylor	1025	236.98
F Willis	1129	326.89
Young Fashions	1042	115.79
Perry & Co	1079	163.26
L Connor Limited	1023	115.37
O McGovern	1152	327.36
J Shepard	1116	372.45
Cole and Porter	1014	325.67
P Smith	1046	235.89
D Iqbal	1103	117.80

The account number here is the customer's account number, which is the account number in the receivables ledger. This number might be obtainable from the remittance advice from the customer, if there is one, or from the copy of the invoice held by the accounts office.

A remittance list might also be drawn up by a small business that does not have a cash register but receives money from customers through the course of each day. In this case, all receipts from customers would be recorded immediately on the remittance list.

Example

H Chan works for Bradshaw Electrical Repairs. H Chan carries out repairs to household appliances and is called out to repair washing machines, fridges and other household items. For each call out, a fee is charged that is paid either in cash or by cheque.

When H Chan finishes each job, a receipt is completed and handed to the customer, giving details of the amount charged and acknowledging that the customer has paid. H Chan keeps a carbon copy of each receipt, and from these carbon copies a remittance list of all of the receipts from customers during the day can be drawn up.

A remittance list might look something like this:

Date	Customer	Work done	Amount $
12 June	F Bond	Washing machine repair	62.30
12 June	V Assam	Fridge repair	41.78
12 June	T Poll	Freezer repair	56.02
			160.10

The remittance list is a document for recording receipts from customers. Each day or week, the details from the remittance list should be entered in the cash book.

FA1: RECORDING FINANCIAL TRANSACTIONS

1.4 BATCHING TRANSACTIONS

When a business receives a large number of receipts, it is often a good idea to split them up into manageable batches of transactions, and to process each batch separately.

1.5 CHECKING RECEIPTS FROM CREDIT CUSTOMERS AGAINST THE INVOICE

When money is received from a credit customer, the receipt should be matched with the invoice that the customer is paying. Sometimes, a customer might pay several invoices at the same time.

2 THE CASH BOOK

Details of receipts should now be recorded in the accounting system. The first step is to make a record in the cash book, which is a **book of prime entry**.

The cash book is sometimes kept in two separate parts, a cash receipts book for recording receipts and a cash (or cheque) payments book for recording payments.

The purpose of a cash receipts book is to record:

- receipts from credit customers settling invoices
- all other receipts, including those for cash sales.

Each payment by a credit customer must be recorded individually. Receipts from cash sales can be recorded as a total. Often the cash book is updated every day, so the cash sales entry is likely to be total cash sales for the day.

A cash receipts book will contain several columns, typically as follows:

FOLIO CRB14

Date	Reference	Total	Receivables	Cash sales	Sales tax	Other
		$	$	$	$	$

2.1 ENTERING RECEIPTS IN THE CASH RECEIPTS BOOK

Details of receipts are entered in the cash book as follows:

Date This is the date the money is received.

Reference This could be one column or several columns. It is needed to identify who the receipt is from or what it is for.

- It might show the name of the credit customer, the account number and possibly the number of the invoice being paid.

- For cash sales, it might simply state 'Cash sales'.

- For other items of income, it might be used to indicate the nature of the receipt, such as 'bank interest received'.

The details in the reference column usually indicate the other part of the double entry. For example if the cash receipts are from sales the details should read 'sales'.

Total The total amount of the receipt is entered in the Total column.

The other columns are analysis columns.

Receivables If the receipt is a payment by a credit customer, the total amount of the receipt should be entered in the receivables column. There is no need to separate the amount of the payment that is for sales tax, and nothing is entered in the sales tax column. The sales tax on credit sales is recorded earlier, when the sales invoice is recorded in the sales day book, and so there is no need to record it again.

Remember! Sales tax on a credit sales invoice is only recorded once, in the sales day book. It is **never** recorded again in the cash receipts book.

Cash sales If the receipt is for cash sales, the total amount received is shown in the total column. The cash sales column is used to record the amount of the sales **excluding sales tax.**

Sales tax This column is used to record any sales tax received for anything **except** credit sales invoices. If the item recorded is cash sales, the cash sales column should show the amount of the sale excluding sales tax and the tax on the sale should be shown in the sales tax column. The amount in this column and the amount in the cash sales column will add up together to the amount in the total column.

The reason for recording the sales tax on receipts from cash sales (and on other sources of income, if any) is that sales tax is recorded for the first time in the accounting system at this point.

This is illustrated in the example overleaf.

Other A business might occasionally receive money from other sources, such as interest on a bank deposit account, or receipt of cash from a bank loan. If other receipts are uncommon, a single column may be used to record them, and the Reference column will be used to explain the nature of the receipt.

On each row of the cash receipts book, the figure in the Total column should agree to the sum of the amounts in the receivables, Cash sales, sales tax and other columns.

Example

The following amounts were received on 19 October 20X6.

(a) Payment of invoice number 69 by BL Lorries (account number S239), total $4,700.

(b) Payment of invoice number 70 by MA Meters (account number S314), total $2,820.

(c) Payment of invoice number 78 by Tanktop Limited (account number S205), total $3,100.

(d) A cash sale of $1,200 including sales tax at 20%.

Task

Write up the cash receipts book and total each of the columns.

Solution

Cash receipts book   FOLIO CBR14

Date	Reference	Total $	Rec'bles $	Cash sales $	Sales tax $
19.10.X6					
	BL Lorries, a/c S239	4,700	4,700		
	MA Meters, a/c S314	2,820	2,820		
	Tanktop Ltd, a/c S205	3,100	3,100		
	Cash sale	1,200		1,000	200
		11,820	10,620	1,000	200

Notes

1 In a manual accounting system, each page in the cash book is numbered sequentially, for reference purposes. The page number is referred to as its 'folio' number. Here, the page of the book has been given an imaginary folio number of CBR14.

2 Cash sale. Sales tax = $1,200 × (20/120) = $200. The value of the cash sale to the business is $1,200 × (100/120) = $1,000. These are the figures entered in the sales tax and Cash Sales columns, and together they add up to the $1,200 in the Total column.

3 Receipts entered in the cash receipts book should be banked intact in order to reduce the risk of fraud or error. If the business needs cash for petty cash payments then it should cash a cheque. Most receipts will normally be in the form of cheques.

ACTIVITY 1

The following remittance list has been prepared showing receipts today, 1 June:

Customer name	Account number	Amount received $
A C Bhatt	1037	265.40
Flowers Limited	1002	319.64
E Murphy	1053	396.61
P Taylor	1025	236.98
F Willis	1129	326.89
Young Fashions	1042	115.79
Perry & Co	1079	163.26
L Connor Limited	1023	115.37
O McGovern	1152	327.36
J Shepard	1116	372.45
Cole and Porter	1014	325.67
P Smith	1046	235.89
D Smith	1103	117.80

The summary information from the cash register printout for 1 June was as follows:

Totals	$
Cash	1,151.50
Cheques	513.71
Credit/debit card (agreed to end of day reconciliation)	815.74
	2,480.95

These details agree with the amount of cash, cheques and card vouchers in the till. Sales tax within cash register receipts amounts to $413.49.

Enter these amounts in the cash receipts book.

For a suggested answer, see the 'Answers' section at the end of the book.

3 MANUAL NOMINAL *(GENERAL)* LEDGER AND RECEIVABLES LEDGER

3.1 THE USE OF PRIMARY RECORDS

We do not enter all transactions in the ledger as and when they arise. In a business with many transactions that would soon lead to the ledger becoming cluttered. Instead, we group similar transactions together in books of prime entry and, at intervals, we total these transactions. Only this periodic total is then entered in the ledger.

3.2 THE RECEIVABLES LEDGER

The sales ledger comprises accounts for credit customers and was described in an earlier chapter.

The impact of this system is that each transaction involving a credit customer – whether a sale or a cash receipt – needs to be reflected in both the individual account in the receivables ledger and in the nominal *(general)* ledger.

4 POSTING RECEIPTS AND PAYMENTS FROM THE CASH BOOK TO THE MAIN LEDGER

4.1 POSTING RECEIPTS FROM THE CASH BOOK TO THE MAIN LEDGER

The cash book is a book of prime entry, and the next step in recording the receipts is to transfer or 'post' the entries in the cash book to the relevant accounts in the ledgers. The rules for doing this are as follows.

Take the totals in the columns of the cash receipts book, or on the cash receipts side of the cash book, and:

- **Total cash received**

    DEBIT this total in the 'Bank' account in the nominal *(general)* ledger if one exists. The 'Cash' and 'Bank' accounts in the cash book may well be those ledger accounts, particularly if the cash book is not analysed.

- **Receivables**

    CREDIT this total in the receivables control account. Amounts received from individual customers must also be recorded in their personal memorandum accounts in the receivables ledger.

- **Cash sales**

    CREDIT this total in the 'Sales' account in the main ledger.

- **Sales tax**

    CREDIT this total in the relevant account in the main ledger. The sales tax on cash sales is payable to the government.

    The total value of credit entries in the receivables, cash sales and sales tax columns (and Other Receipts column) should add up to the amount of the debit entry in the Total column for cash received and paid into the bank account.

Example

The following entries have been made in the cash receipts book for 19 October.

FOLIO CBR14

Date	Reference	Total $	Rec'bles $	Cash sales $	Sales tax $
19.10.X6					
	BL Lorries, a/c S239	4,700	4,700		
	MA Meters, a/c S314	2,820	2,820		
	Tanktop Ltd, a/c S205	3,100	3,100		
	Cash sale	1,200		1,000	200
		11,820	10,620	1,000	200

Task

Post these entries to the nominal *(general)* ledger and receivables ledger. Assume that individual customer accounts are part of the double entry system and no control account is maintained for receivables.

Solution

These totals should be posted to the ledgers as follows.

Bank (main ledger)

Date	Details	Folio	$	Date	Details	Folio	$
19.10.X6	Sundry receivables	CBR14	10,620				
19.10.X6	Sales	CBR14	1,200				

BL Lorries (sales ledger)

Date	Details	Folio	$	Date	Details	Folio	$
				19.10.X6	Bank	CBR14	4,700

MA Meters (sales ledger)

Date	Details	Folio	$	Date	Details	Folio	$
				19.10.X6	Bank	CBR14	2,820

Tanktop Ltd (sales ledger)

Date	Details	Folio	$	Date	Details	Folio	$
				19.10.X6	Bank	CBR14	3,100

Sales (main ledger)

Date	Details	Folio	$	Date	Details	Folio	$
				19.10.X6	Bank	CBR14	1,000

Sales tax (main ledger)

Date	Details	Folio	$	Date	Details	Folio	$
				19.10.X6	Bank	CBR14	200

4.2 THE CASH BOOK CONTAINING MAIN LEDGER ACCOUNTS

In the example above, the cash receipts book is a book of prime entry, and there is an account in the nominal *(general)* ledger called the 'Bank' account. There would also be a separate 'Cash' account.

An alternative approach is a **three column cash book** which is drawn up as follows:

Cash book

Date	Details	Fo	Cash $	Bank $	Date	Details	Fo	Disc $	Cash $	Bank $
6.7.X4	Balance	b/d	125	386	9.7.X4	Rent	21			1,000
7.7.X4	Sales	301		220	9.7.X4	H. Batt	504	20		380
8.7.X4	T. Kaye	442		190	9.7.X4	Travel expenses	603		43	

Any cash receipts and payments are included in the column headed cash and the same approach is used for bank transactions. Discounts received are also included in the columns headed 'Disc'. This is a memorandum column and is not part of the double entry. 'Fo' is short for folio and includes the relevant account code for the double entry. In other words in the example above the code for sales is 301. It is 442 for the customer account of T. Kaye and so on.

Here, the cash book serves two purposes:

- It is a book of prime entry for recording receipts and payments.

- It also includes two nominal *(general)* ledger accounts – cash and bank – and is part of the double entry system.

When the cash book (receipts and payments) is also a part of the double entry system, there is no requirement to post the total amount of cash received to a Cash or Bank account. This is because the posting is done when the receipts are entered in the cash book and totalled.

Cash books include a further memorandum column in businesses registered for sales tax to record the relevant tax on cash transactions. Remember that sales tax on credit transactions is recorded on the issue or receipt of invoice and so no further entry should be made on payment to the supplier or receipt from the customer.

Whether three column cash books or cash receipts and cash payments books are used, the double entry system is very similar. The use of cash receipts and cash payments allows easier analysis of transactions.

ACTIVITY 2

The primary records for a business show the following for 20 April:

Cash register receipts	$
Cash	441.68
Cheques	227.44
Credit/debit cards	129.79
	798.91

The sales tax in these cash receipts amounts to $133.15.

Cheques received in the post from credit customers were as follows:

Value of cheque from D Middleton, account 5469	884.84

Record this information in the cash receipts book and then post the totals to the relevant accounts.

For a suggested answer, see the 'Answers' section at the end of the book.

4.3 CASH PAID DIRECTLY INTO THE BANK ACCOUNT

Many businesses receive cash directly into their bank accounts, by means of

- BACS payments, and

- standing order receipts and direct debit receipts.

In such cases, the business might not know about the receipt until it receives a bank statement, although the customer is likely to send a notification of payment when paying by BACS.

If the bank statement contains previously unidentified receipts, the procedures are much the same as described already for receipts by cheque.

- Check that the correct amount has been paid. The bank statement should give some information to help with identifying who the money has come from.

- Enter the amounts received in the cash receipts book on the date you are aware of the items.

- Post the totals from the cash receipts book to the relevant accounts in the main ledger.

- A similar approach is used when recording payments made in cash or by cheque.

4.4 CASH BOOK (CASH OR CHEQUE PAYMENTS BOOK)

The cash payments book is a list of all the payments made from the business bank account, by cheque and by other methods such as BACS.

There has to be a source document from which the details of payments can be copied into the cash payments book. It is usually convenient to prepare a listing of payments, taking details from the cheque itself and the invoice, cheque requisition or expense claim form.

There may be a variety of types of payment, other than payments to suppliers, so it is common in an accounting system to find an analysed cash payments book. This is similar to an analysed cash receipts book, but might have many more columns. In an analysed cash payments book, each payment is recorded on a separate line of the book, and we should find columns for:

- the payment date

- the cheque number (cheques should be numbered **sequentially**)

- details of who the payment is to

- in the case of credit suppliers, the purchase *(payables)* ledger account number

- the total amount of the payment

- analysis columns, showing the nature of the payment for the purpose of posting details to the main ledger

- a memorandum column to show any early settlement discount received.

There might be a large number of analysis columns in a cash payments book, but the example below gives an impression of what it might look like.

Date	Cheque number	Payee/ supplier account number	Total	Payables	Sales tax	Insurance	Wages and salaries	Petty cash	Other	Discount received
			$	$	$	$	$	$	$	$

Completing the cash payments book

- **Date.** This is the date of the payment.

- **Cheque number.** Where payment is by cheque, the cheque number should be shown. Cheques should be in sequential number order. If they are not, there could be a serious security problem with a missing cheque. If payment is by another method, such as BACS, the payment method should be shown here.

- **Payee, supplier account number.** This column is for entering the identity of the payee. If the payment is to a trade payable, the payable's account number in the payables ledger should be shown too.

- **Total.** This column is for showing the total amount of the payment. It is the actual amount of money being paid out of the bank account of the business.

- **Payables.** If the payment is to a supplier, and the expenditure has already been recorded in the purchases day book, main ledger and payables ledger, **the total amount of the payment** should also be entered in this column. This includes the sales tax element in the payment.

- **Other analysis columns.** The other analysis columns are for providing an analysis of payments other than payments to credit suppliers. They should be used for payments to suppliers who do not provide credit facilities (where the payment is supported by a cheque requisition), for payments of expenses, for payments of wages and salaries and for withdrawals of money from the bank for petty cash. Where there is an amount for sales tax in the payment, the tax should be shown separately in the sales tax column, and the analysis columns for the expense should show the amount excluding sales tax. Each column should represent an account in the main ledger (an expense account or the sales tax account).

- **An entry should not be made in the sales tax column for payments to payables.** It should only record the sales tax in other payments.

- **Settlement discounts received.** There should also be a column for recording any settlement discounts received (taken from suppliers). It is a memorandum column only, because it does not represent a payment of cash from the business bank account. It is needed for posting details of settlement discounts received to the main ledger. An entry should only be appropriate for this column when the payment is made to a supplier.

ACTIVITY 3

FFP makes the following payments in respect of various credit invoices and other items. Enter these transactions into the cash payments book.

- Payment of $4,230 on 23/7/X4 to N Hudson. A settlement discount of $130 was taken. This was paid by cheque (cheque number 1003). The payables ledger reference code is P4153.

- On 24/7/X4, $2,350 to G Fazaal in respect of an outstanding invoice, by cheque (cheque number 1004). The payables ledger reference code is P4778.

- On 28/7/X4, purchase of inventory, **not on credit**, of $960 including sales tax of $160 (cheque number 1005).

- On 30/7/X4, payment of a salary by cheque of $2,500, using cheque number 1006. (There is no sales tax on wages and salaries).

For a suggested answer, see the 'Answers' section at the end of the book.

FA1: RECORDING FINANCIAL TRANSACTIONS

4.5 TOTALLING THE CASH PAYMENTS BOOK

The columns of the cash payments book should be totalled. The accuracy of the adding up should be checked by adding up the totals of all the analysis columns (**but not the total in the discounts received column**).

ACTIVITY 4

Following on from the previous activity, total each of the columns of the cash payments book and check that the totals agree with each other.

For a suggested answer, see the 'Answers' section at the end of the book.

ACTIVITY 5

On 22 June 20X3 Viking Paper made three cheque payments. The original documents for these transactions are given below.

Task

Write up the relevant details of these documents in the cash payments book, and total all relevant columns.

Payables ledger references are the following:

Computer Supplies	PL 32
Step Wholesale Supplies	PL 56

Viking Paper always takes advantage of any settlement discounts offered from suppliers.

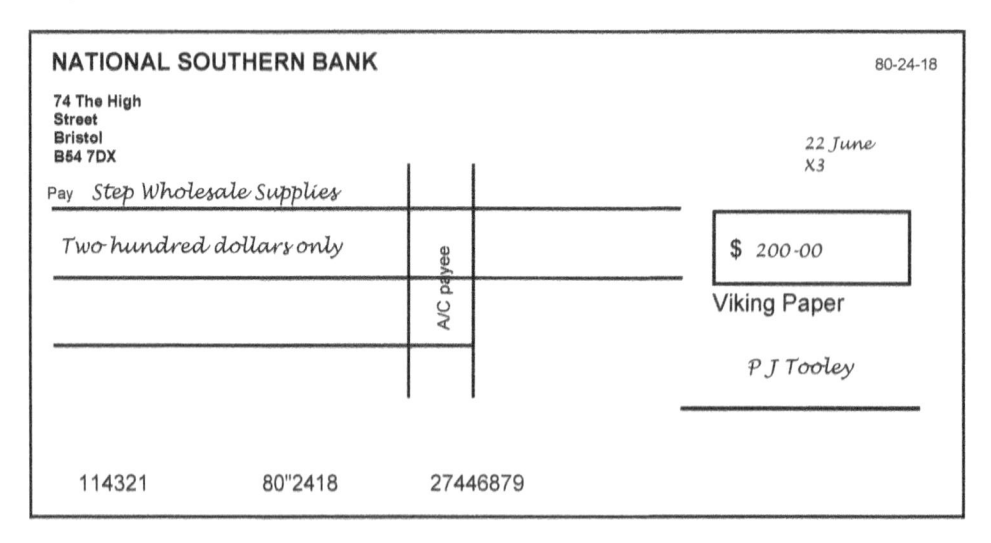

NATIONAL SOUTHERN BANK 80-24-18

74 The High Street
Bristol
B54 7DX

22 June X3

Pay *Step Wholesale Supplies*

Two hundred dollars only

A/C payee

$ 200-00

Viking Paper

P J Tooley

114321   80"2418   27446879

---

204   KAPLAN PUBLISHING

RECORDING RECEIPTS AND PAYMENTS : CHAPTER 9

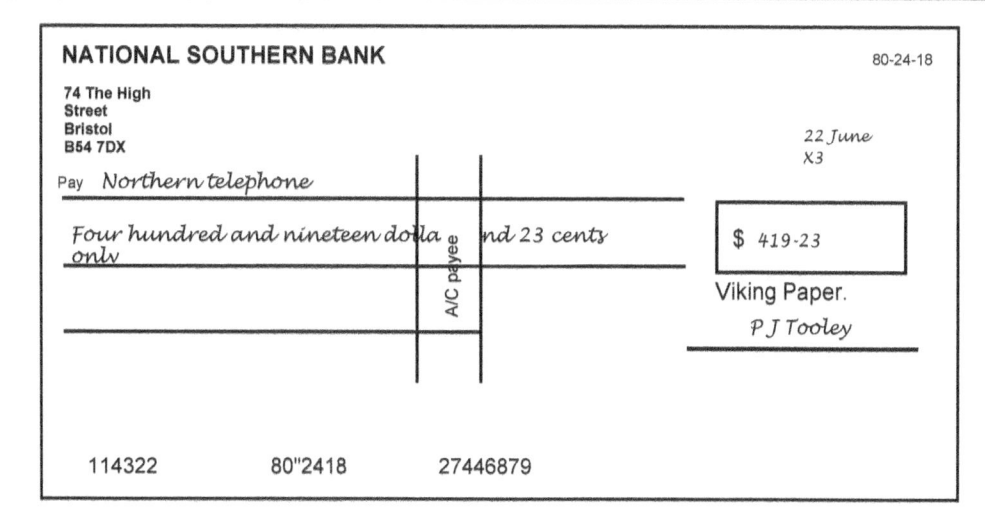

```
NATIONAL SOUTHERN BANK                          80-24-18
74 The High
Street
Bristol
B54 7DX                                         22 June
                                                X3
Pay  Northern telephone

     Four hundred and nineteen dollars and 23 cents
     only                                       $ 419-23

                          A/C payee
                                                Viking Paper.
                                                P J Tooley


     114322      80"2418       27446879
```

Note: Payment of the telephone bill, which includes Sales tax at 20%

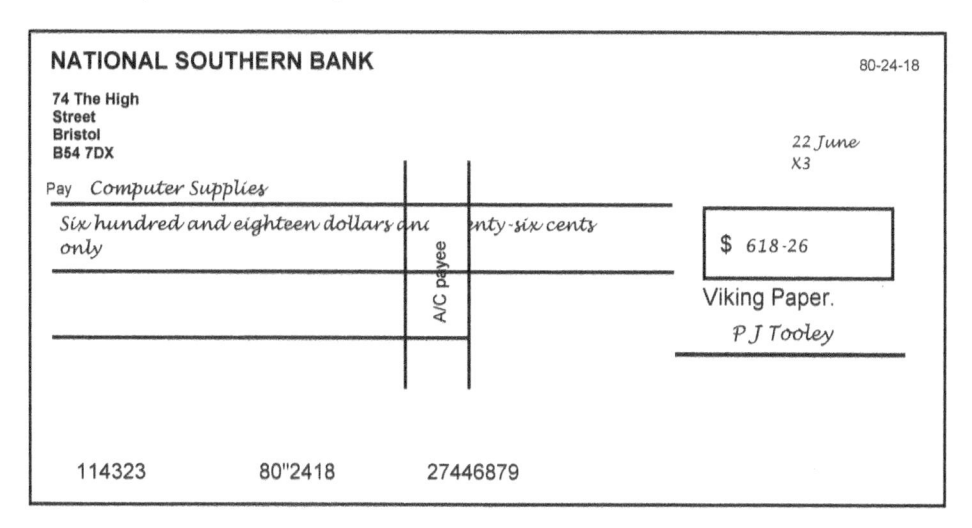

```
NATIONAL SOUTHERN BANK                          80-24-18
74 The High
Street
Bristol
B54 7DX                                         22 June
                                                X3
Pay  Computer Supplies

     Six hundred and eighteen dollars and twenty-six cents
     only                                       $ 618-26

                          A/C payee
                                                Viking Paper.
                                                P J Tooley


     114323      80"2418       27446879
```

Note: A discount of $32.54 was taken on this payment to Computer Supplies.

For a suggested answer, see the 'Answers' section at the end of the book.

4.6 POSTING TRANSACTIONS FROM THE CASH PAYMENTS BOOK TO THE NOMINAL *(GENERAL)* LEDGER

The cash payments book is used to record all the payments out of the business bank account. However, the cash payments book is a book of prime entry, and the transaction details have to be transferred or posted to the nominal *(general)* ledger if the cash book does not also include the ledger accounts.

Each column in the cash payments book represents an account in the nominal *(general)* ledger.

- The total column is for the Cash at bank account or Bank account.

- The sales tax column is for tax payable to or receivable from the tax authorities.

- The payables column is for the payables control account (or individual accounts where a control account is not maintained).

- Each of the other columns represents an expense account in the nominal *(general)* ledger (or possibly an asset account).

- There is also a Discount received account in the main ledger.

The rules for posting the transactions to the main ledger are as follows.

- **Credit** **Bank account**, with the total in the Total column
- **Debit** **Sales tax account**, with the total in the sales tax column
- **Debit** **Payables control account with the total in the payables *column*** or accounts of individual **payables** with the relevant amounts
- **Debit** The relevant **expense account** (or asset account) with the total in the analysis column for that expense

4.7 CASH BOOK AS A NOMINAL *(GENERAL)* LEDGER ACCOUNT AND A PART OF THE DOUBLE ENTRY SYSTEM

When the cash book contains the ledger accounts of cash and bank as well as being a book of prime entry, the cash receipts side of the cash book is the debit side of the main ledger account, and the cash payments side is the credit side of the main ledger account.

Since the cash book is a main or nominal *(general)* ledger account as well as a book of prime entry, there is no need to post transactions from the total column to a main ledger account, because the transactions are recorded in the main ledger account already.

4.8 POSTING DETAILS OF CASH PAYMENTS TO THE PAYABLES LEDGER

When a payment is made to a supplier, the details of the transaction must be posted to the supplier's account in the payables ledger, so that the account can be kept up to date. Similarly, discounts received (settlement discounts taken from the supplier) must also be recorded in the supplier's account.

Details of payments to individual suppliers and of discounts received should therefore be posted from the cash payments book to the relevant supplier's account in the payables ledger. (This is similar to the process of posting receipts from customers and discounts allowed from the cash receipts book to the receivables ledger accounts. However, you should remember that any settlement discounts allowed are adjusted against revenue, rather than accounted for in a separate 'discounts allowed expense account.)

Posting to the payables ledger is needed only for payments to credit suppliers, and not for other payments.

For each transaction in the cash payments book showing a payment to a credit supplier, the posting should be:

- **Debit the supplier's account** in the payables ledger with the amount paid.

When a settlement discount is taken from a supplier, an additional posting should be:

- **Debit the supplier's account** with the amount of the discount received.

Example

On 30/07/07 Barker Co made a payment to its credit supplier, Bushells (supplier account number B0003), for $1,980 with cheque number 00052. The amount relates to supplies on which no sales tax arises. This relates to an invoice for $2,000, against which Barker Co has received a settlement discount of $20.

Make the necessary postings to the cash book and show the double entries that will be made to the memorandum account for Bushells. Show the double entries to the ledger accounts, assuming that a payables ledger control account is maintained.

Solution

Cash payments book (book of prime entry)

Date	Cheque number	Payee/ supplier account number	Total	Payables	Sales tax	Insurance	Wages and salaries	Petty cash	Other	Discount received
			$	$	$	$	$	$	$	$
30/06/07	00052	B0003	1,980	1,980	0					20

Bushells memorandum account in the payables ledger.

Bushells

Date	Details	Folio	$	Date	Details	Folio	$
30.06.07	Bank	CBR1	1,980		Balance b/d		2,000
30.06.07	Discounts rec'd	CBR1	20				

In the nominal *(general)* ledger total payments to suppliers will be posted to the payables ledger control account (see Chapter 13) and the cash account. If you assume that there are no other transactions that day, the double entry will be:

Dr Payables ledger control account $1,980

Cr Cash control account $1,980

Similarly, the total discounts received must be posted to the nominal *(general)* ledger accounts:

Dr Payables ledger control account $20

Cr Discounts received $20

FA1: RECORDING FINANCIAL TRANSACTIONS

ACTIVITY 6

1. A sole trader introduced $1,000 by cheque into the business by cheque. What is the double entry to record this transaction?

    A   Dr Cash; Cr Capital

    B   Dr Bank; Cr Capital

    C   Dr Capital; Cr Cash

    D   Dr Capital; Cr Bank

2. Jang operates a three column cash book. Jang pays for paper for the printer at a local store in cash. The list price of the paper is $25 but Jang is offered a trade discount of 20%. Sales tax must be added to the cost and is charged at 20%. How should this transaction be recorded in Jang's accounting records?

    A   Dr Stationery $20; Cr Cash $20

    B   Dr Stationery $20; Dr Sales tax $4.00; Cr Cash $24.00

    C   Dr Stationery $25; Cr Cash $25

    D   Dr Stationery $25; Dr Sales tax $5.00; Cr Cash $30.00

For suggested answers, see the 'Answers' section at the end of the book.

5 COMPUTERISED RECORDS

In a business that uses an integrated accounting system or simply a computerised cash book the effect is similar to the use of a three column cash book. Each transaction that is posted to the system leads to the automatic completion of the double entry. Cash and bank accounts are part of the double-entry system.

Remember that, whether a business uses computerised or manual accounting records, it needs to record and retain the same information. Users of computerised records therefore need to be familiar with how information is presented so that they understand the information they are using. For example, debits may be presented as positive (plus) items and credits may be presented as negative (minus) items in a computerised document that lists transactions, rather than presenting transactions in ledger account format..

6 AUTHORISING AND MAKING PAYMENTS

It is obviously extremely important that payments are only made for genuine goods, services and expenses incurred by the organisation. Therefore if a cheque is required for payment of an item, there must be sufficient evidence of that item existing for the payment to appear reasonable.

Computerised accounting systems may also generate payments in the form of automated direct payments and electronically-produced cheque payments to suppliers and others owed money by a business. In these situations, it is vital that a suitably authorised person (a senior member of staff not directly involved in the process to raise and authorise payments) regularly reviews and approves transactions. It is also important that any payments made, in whatever form they may take, are subject to appropriate checks and controls to confirm that they are valid payments for goods and services received. No payments should be made without appropriate authorisation.

CONCLUSION

The management and control of cash is of fundamental importance to any business. In a past chapter we looked at the procedures for dealing with cash receipts and payments, ensuring that cheques received and their supporting cheque guarantee cards are valid, dealing with credit and debit card payments and operating the cash register. We have also noted the importance of checking monies received to any supporting documentation, checking the calculation of an entitlement to discounts and issuing written receipts.

In this chapter you saw how receipts and payments are recorded in the cash and bank accounts of the business. Remember:

- a receipt of cash is recorded as a debit in the cash or bank account

- a payment is credited to the cash or bank account

- sales tax is recorded when the sales tax liability occurs which is when a cash sale or purchase takes place or the date when an invoice was created in respect of credit transactions

- sales tax and discounts received columns in a cash book are memorandum columns.

KEY TERMS

Cash book – Book of prime entry for recording receipts into and payments from the business bank account. May also includes the ledger account for cash and bank.

Settlement discount (or cash discount) – Discount for early payment of an invoice. Recorded in the nominal *(general)* ledger as discounts received.

Trade discounts – A discount on the price of goods or services, agreed in advance (and often granted to regular customers or for bulk purchases).

SELF TEST QUESTIONS

Paragraph

1	Where do receipts from credit customers have to be recorded?	1
2	What is a remittance list?	1
3	Draw up a typical three column cash book.	4
4	When is sales tax posted to the cash book?	4
5	Why would a cash payments book generally include more analysis columns than a cash receipts book?	4

FA1: RECORDING FINANCIAL TRANSACTIONS

EXAM-STYLE QUESTIONS

1   Which of the following is the correct posting to record a cash purchase of $600 from Georgio Caterers?

   A   Dr Purchases $600; Cr Georgio Caterers $600

   B   Dr Georgio Caterers $600; Cr Purchases $600

   C   Dr Purchases $600; Cr Cash $600

   D   Dr Cash $600: Cr Purchases $600

2   The total of the discounts in the cash payments book for April 20X7 is $80. One part of the double-entry required to reflect this will be recorded in the trade payables ledger control account.

   What is the other accounting entry required to properly record this transaction in the nominal ledger?

   A   Dr Revenue

   B   Cr Revenue

   C   Dr Discount received

   D   Cr Discount received

3   Sales tax is recorded in the cash book:

   A   When a sale is made on credit

   B   When a cheque is received from a credit customer

   C   When a cash sale takes place

   D   When discounts are received

4   Which columns are part of the double entry in a three column cash book?

   (i)   Bank

   (ii)   Cash

   (iii) Discount received

   (iv) Sales tax

   A   (i) and (ii)

   B   (i) and (iii)

   C   (ii) and (iii)

   D   (iii) and (iv)

5   What is the book of prime entry to record cash sales?

   A   Cash book

   B   Journal

   C   Sales day book

   D   Sales ledger

For suggested answers, see the 'Answers' section at the end of the book.

Chapter 10

MAINTAINING PETTY CASH RECORDS

Most business expenditure is paid for out of the business bank account, by cheque, BACS transfer, direct debit, or other payment methods. Occasionally, however, small items of expense need to be paid for in cash. Cash might be needed for bus fares, for example, or to buy a packet of biscuits for the office from the local shop. Spending by cash has to be controlled carefully, to prevent theft, and properly recorded.

This chapter explains the nature of petty cash, how petty cash systems are organised and operated and how expense items are recorded in the accounting system. It covers the syllabus area of maintaining petty cash records.

CONTENTS

1 Operation of petty cash

2 Documentation

3 Authorisation

4 Security of cash

5 Queries and problems

6 Manual petty cash book

7 Imprest and non-imprest methods

8 Petty cash reconciliation

LEARNING OUTCOMES

At the end of this chapter, you should be able to:

- recognise the types of transaction likely to be paid out of petty cash
- account for petty cash using imprest and non-imprest methods
- exercise control over petty cash and recognise how control can be maintained
- record petty cash claims
- reconcile the petty cash to cash in hand.

FA1: RECORDING FINANCIAL TRANSACTIONS

1 OPERATION OF PETTY CASH

1.1 HOW PETTY CASH WORKS

The way the petty cash system of an organisation works is usually as follows:

Step 1   An employee personally pays for a business expense, such as coffee for the office or a taxi fare to a meeting, and obtains a receipt for the payment.

Step 2   The employee then reclaims the expense from the organisation through the petty cash system, by signing a petty cash voucher and handing over the receipt for the money spent.

Step 3   The expense must be recorded as a business expense in the ledger accounts of the organisation. This process is explained later.

2 DOCUMENTATION

To ensure that the petty cash system is not abused and that payments are made only for valid business expenses, there must be some system of authorisation for petty cash claims.

In addition, for accounting purposes, all payments out of petty cash must be properly documented.

2.1 PETTY CASH VOUCHERS

The initial record of any petty cash claim is a petty cash voucher. Blank petty cash vouchers are obtainable from stationery suppliers in pads, and each voucher is torn off the pad when it is used. An example of a blank voucher is shown below:

Petty Cash Voucher	No. _____	
Date _____		
For what required	AMOUNT $	¢
Signature _____		
Authorised _____		

Notes on filling in a voucher

- Petty cash vouchers should be given a unique identification number. For control purposes, they should be numbered sequentially by the person in charge of petty cash.

- Each voucher should be dated (with the date it is filled in and authorised).

- The details of the expenditure and the amount should be included in the voucher. If there is a receipt, this should be attached by a staple or paper clip.

- The person claiming the petty cash should sign the voucher.

- The person authorising the claim should also sign the voucher.

3 AUTHORISATION

Authorisation of petty cash claims is an important issue. Each organisation should have a policy about who is permitted to authorise petty cash claims. The following alternative approaches might be considered:

The person responsible for the petty cash, the petty cashier, may be given responsibility for authorisation of all petty cash claims.

An employee or director other than the petty cashier, such as the chief accountant, may be required to authorise all petty cash claims.

The petty cashier may authorise all claims up to a certain amount, whilst another official authorises claims above this amount.

3.1 AUTHORISATION PROCEDURE

The person authorising the petty cash claim must make two checks.

- The claim should be supported by adequate documentation proving the expense is for valid business purposes.

- The claim should not exceed the petty cash limits of the organisation. Claims above a certain amount should be made as an expenses claim, for payment by cheque or BACS, and not as a petty cash claim for payment in cash.

The petty cashier should refuse to make a payment out of petty cash unless the claim has been properly authorised, as evidenced by the signature on the petty cash voucher.

3.2 SUPPORTING DOCUMENTATION

To make sure that a petty cash claim is for a valid business expense then each claim must normally be supported by documentation proving that the expense is genuine. Before the petty cash claim is authorised, this supporting documentation must be checked.

Most types of petty cash claim are for straightforward office expenses such as the purchase of coffee, biscuits, stamps, bus and taxi fare, and so on.

FA1: RECORDING FINANCIAL TRANSACTIONS

In these cases, a simple receipt or till roll receipt is sufficient evidence of the payment for the expense. For bus fares, the ticket itself might be used as the evidence.

However, if the payment includes sales tax that can be reclaimed from the tax authorities, a proper sales tax receipt showing the supplier's name and sales tax registration number is required. Most till roll receipts do show this information.

In each case the supporting documentation should be attached to the petty cash claim.

Sales tax as part of the expense

Provided there is a valid tax receipt (i.e. a written receipt containing the supplier's sales tax registration number), the sales tax included in a cash payment can be claimed back from the tax authorities. To record the sales tax properly, the amount of the tax should be shown in the petty cash voucher. The voucher will therefore show the expense exclusive of tax, the sales tax and the total expense inclusive of tax. The sales tax should be itemised on the tax receipt.

ACTIVITY 1

Below is a till receipt. Sales tax is set at 20%:

Price's Stationers

15 Reams A 4 paper	$17.80
200 Envelopes	$5.00
Total	$22.80

Received with thanks 30/5/X7

Sales tax registration: 72 38 237 840

Task

Complete the petty cash voucher.

Petty Cash Voucher	No. _____
Date _____	

	AMOUNT	
For what required	$	¢
Supporting documentation		

Signature _____

Authorised _____

For a suggested answer, see the 'Answers' section at the end of the book.

3.3 NO SUPPORTING DOCUMENTATION

Some expenses claimed from petty cash may not have a supporting receipt. For example, the employee may simply have lost the receipt, or an employee might have paid for a train fare to a meeting, and the ticket might have been collected.

For such cases, most organisations have a policy that the claim can still be authorised if it is deemed to be reasonable. This might involve authorisation by the manager responsible for the claimant's work, as this manager is most likely to be able to judge whether, say, a journey, did take place and was a valid business expense.

3.4 PAYMENTS IN ADVANCE

In some instances, an employee might not have enough cash to purchase the item out of their own money and then reclaim it from petty cash later. The employee will therefore ask the petty cashier for cash in advance to pay for the item or the expense. Any such payment must be authorised by an appropriate person.

When the expenditure has been incurred, the employee will normally be required to provide appropriate documentation of the actual expense (typically, a receipt) and return any change to the petty cashier.

In such cases, a petty cash voucher is initially filled in for the amount of cash taken, and when the change is returned, the voucher is then altered to show the actual amount of the spending.

Example

The managing director's assistant is required to buy some light refreshments for this evening's board meeting but does not have enough personal cash on hand to do so.

The assistant makes a claim from petty cash for $10, the estimated price of the items required. The actual expense is $8.47, which includes sales tax at 20%.

How would this be dealt with?

Solution

Step 1 The petty cashier must obtain authorisation for the cash payment from an appropriate person, such as the managing director or chief accountant. Therefore a petty cash voucher is completed for $10 and suitably authorised.

Petty Cash Voucher	No. 698		
Date 3 April 20X9			
For what required		AMOUNT $	¢
Refreshments including sales tax @20%		10	00
Signature MD's Assistant			
Authorised Chief accountant			

Step 2 The managing director's assistant buys the goods which actually cost $8.47 including sales tax. The assistant returns the change of $1.53 to the petty cashier together with a receipt for $8.47.

Step 3 The receipt is attached to the petty cash voucher and the voucher is altered to show the actual amount of the goods purchased. The net amount is sales tax is $8.47 × (100/120) = $7.06. The sales tax element is $8.47 − $7.06 = $1.41.

Petty Cash Voucher	No. 698	
Date 3 April 20X9		
For what required	AMOUNT $	¢
Refreshments	7 ~~10~~	06 ~~00~~
VAT	1	41
Total	8	47
Signature MD's Assistant		
Authorised Chief accountant		

4 SECURITY OF CASH

Petty cash is usually kept in a metal tin or 'box' with a lock and key. Inside the petty cash tin, there are notes and coins (and a pad of petty cash vouchers) and payments of petty cash expenses are made from the money in the tin. Every so often the petty cash is topped up by withdrawing more cash from the bank account, by writing a cheque for 'Pay cash'.

Clearly, there is a security problem with petty cash, and it is important that:

- the petty cash tin is kept in a secure place, such as a locked desk drawer, to deter theft

- only one or possibly two designated individuals should be permitted to make payments from the tin.

To reduce the risk of loss, a business should only keep as much cash in petty cash as it considers reasonably necessary, so that if the petty cash tin is stolen, the amount of the loss might not be large.

5 QUERIES AND PROBLEMS

Occasionally, when petty cash claims are being processed, a query may arise. Possible reasons for this include:

- a petty cash voucher might not have been signed by an authorised person

- the person making the claim should be told that petty cash claims cannot be paid without proper authorisation. The claimant should be asked why authorisation has not been obtained.

There could be a perfectly understandable reason for this. For example, there might be only two people permitted to authorise claims, and they might both be absent. There should be established procedures for dealing with such problems. Usually, the query should be referred to someone more senior for a decision.

On the other hand, the claimant might simply not have tried to obtain the necessary authorisation. If this is the case, the claimant should be asked to do so.

- There might be insufficient supporting documentation as evidence of the expense. For example, the claimant might have forgotten to obtain a receipt, or the claim may be for a local bus fare and there is no receipt. Unless there are established procedures for dealing with such situations, the query should be referred to a more senior person for a decision.

- If the petty cash claim exceeds the limit for payments in cash out of petty cash, the claimant should be asked to make an expenses claim on an expenses claim form.

6 MANUAL PETTY CASH BOOK

Although payments out of petty cash are usually quite small, they have to be accounted for. A petty cash book is used for recording transactions involving petty cash, just as a cash book is used to record transactions involving receipts into and payments from the bank account.

Most of the transactions recorded in the petty cash book are payments for expenses. However, money withdrawn from the bank account to top up petty cash are also recorded. **(Top-ups of petty cash are recorded in the petty cash book as cash received and in the cash book as a cash payment.)**

Recording petty cash transactions in the petty cash book is similar to recording bank transactions in the cash book.

- However, since payments into petty cash are only withdrawals of cash from the bank, there is no need for any analysis columns on the cash receipts side of the book.

- On the other hand, payments out of petty cash could be for a wide range of different expenses, so there will be a large number of analysis columns on the cash payments side.

The payments side of the petty cash book should therefore have columns for:

- the petty cash voucher number
- brief details of the expense
- the total amount of the expense
- analysis columns, including a column for sales tax.

6.1 RECORDING PETTY CASH PAYMENTS

The source documents for recording petty cash payments in the petty cash book are the petty cash vouchers. At regular intervals, perhaps every time the petty cash is topped up, these petty cash vouchers should be written up in the petty cash book.

- Each voucher represents one petty cash transaction, and should be entered on one line of the book.

- The vouchers should be recorded in consecutive number order (according to their identifying number).

The payments are analysed in the petty cash book so that the expenses can be posted to the relevant accounts in the nominal *(general)* ledger. There should be an analysis column in the petty cash book for each expense account in the main ledger for which petty cash expenses might be incurred.

When an expense includes sales tax, the amount of the expense in the Total column should be for the total spending, including the sales tax. In the analysis columns, however, the sales tax is shown separately, and the other analysis columns record the expense excluding the tax.

Example

Given below are a number of petty cash vouchers.

Task

Write up the petty cash book to record these transactions.

Petty Cash Voucher	No. 340			Petty Cash Voucher	No. 341		
Date 22/3/X3				Date 22/3/X3			
For what required		AMOUNT $	¢	For what required		AMOUNT $	¢
Postage stamps		7	10	Stationery (inclusive of 20% VAT)		28	00
Signature P Nelson				Signature V Bacon			
Authorised J Falk				Authorised J Falk			

MAINTAINING PETTY CASH RECORDS : CHAPTER 10

Petty Cash Voucher	No. 342
Date 22/3/X3	

For what required	AMOUNT $	¢
Rail fare	6	40

Signature R Andrew
Authorised J Falk

Petty Cash Voucher	No. 343
Date 26/3/X3	

For what required	AMOUNT $	¢
Tea, coffee	3	49

Signature M Baston
Authorised J Falk

Petty Cash Voucher	No. 344
Date 26/3/X3	

For what required	AMOUNT $	¢
Taxi (no VAT invoice)	2	40

Signature M Johnson
Authorised J Falk

Petty Cash Voucher	No. 345
Date 26/3/X3	

For what required	AMOUNT $	¢
Rail fare	11	40

Signature R Andrew
Authorised J Falk

Solution

Petty cash book

Date	Receipts $	Voucher/ Ref no	Details	Total payment $		Sales tax $		Travel expenses $		Office expenses $		Postage $		Stationery $		Sundry $
22/3		340	Stamps	7	10							7	10			
22/3		341	Stationery	28	00	4	66							23	34	
22/3		342	Rail fare	6	40			6	40							
26/3		343	Refreshments	3	49					3	49					
26/3		344	Taxi	2	40			2	40							
26/3		345	Rail fare	11	40			11	40							

FA1: RECORDING FINANCIAL TRANSACTIONS

7 IMPREST AND NON-IMPREST METHODS

7.1 IMPREST SYSTEM FOR PETTY CASH

Money is continually paid out from petty cash. From time to time the cash is topped up so that it does not run out. There are several systems for topping up the money in petty cash. The most common is called the imprest system.

A petty cash box is started with a certain amount of cash. This amount of cash is known as the **imprest amount.** This should be enough cash to cover foreseeable petty cash expenses for, say, two to four weeks. The aim is to avoid having to top up petty cash too often, but at the same time avoid having too much cash in the petty cash tin, where it could be at risk of theft.

Completed petty cash vouchers are put into the petty cash tin whenever money is taken out of the tin. Periodically, the amount of cash in the tin is topped up to the original imprest amount. When this happens, the petty cash vouchers in the tin should be taken out, and filed somewhere else. (Before they are filed away, they should be used to record the transactions in the petty cash book. This is explained later.)

The amount of cash required to top up the petty cash is therefore the amount of money taken out since the last time it was topped up. This should be the total value of the vouchers in the petty cash tin.

A check can therefore be made, when petty cash is topped up, that the amount required to top up the petty cash is the total value of the vouchers in the tin. This is a useful security check, to prevent theft of money from the tin. Indeed, the cash tin can be checked at any time and the total of the cash on hand plus the value of the petty cash vouchers should come to the imprest total.

The petty cash box is topped up with cash obtained by cashing a cheque at the bank.

ACTIVITY 2

The petty cash system of HHG is operated on an imprest system, and the imprest amount is $100. The money in petty cash is topped up every week.

At the end of one particular week, there are petty cash vouchers in the tin for $4.67, $12.90, $2.99, $5.06 and $16.25.

How much cash should have to be drawn from the bank to restore the petty cash balance to $100?

For a suggested answer, see the 'Answers' section at the end of the book.

7.2 NON-IMPREST SYSTEM

Most petty cash systems operate with an imprest system, because there is an in-built check to make sure that cash is not stolen. However, it is also possible to set up a system that is not an imprest system, and simply to pay a fixed amount of money into petty cash every so often, to top it up.

For example, suppose that an organisation thinks that petty cash expenditure should be about $50 every week, and it wants to top up the petty cash every two weeks. Withdrawals from petty cash are made using the procedures already described. A petty cash box could be set up with an initial amount of $100 in it. Every two weeks, a further $100 would be drawn from the bank account and paid into the petty cash box.

This system could work well if petty cash expenditure each week is in fact just less than $50. However, problems might be encountered if expenditure is higher than expected in any two-week period, so that the petty cash box might run out of cash. Equally if expenditure were significantly less than $50 each week, then a large surplus would begin to grow in the petty cash box, possibly increasing the risk of losses through theft.

As the imprest system is more common, the remainder of the chapter is based on this system.

7.3 RECORDING PETTY CASH RECEIPTS

When cash is received into the petty cash box it is normally the cash being topped up to the imprest amount (or any other amount in a non-imprest system). Therefore, the cash that is going into the petty cash tin is coming out of the bank account.

The petty cash book will simply show the amount of cash that was paid into the petty cash box and the date of the receipt.

Example

A petty cash system has an imprest amount of $50. On 26 March there is only $1.21 left in the petty cash box and vouchers showing claims of $48.79.

Task

Calculate the amount of cash to be paid into the petty cash box on 26 March 20X3 and enter this amount in the petty cash book.

Solution

The amount of cash to be paid into the petty cash box is $48.79. This covers the claims made during the period and tops up the cash to the imprest amount of $50.

The entry in the petty cash book would be shown as follows:

Date	Receipts	Payments			
		Voucher number	Details	Total payment	Sales tax
	$			$	$
26/3	48.79		Bank		

Cash book entry

The cash being paid into the petty cash box is cash that is being taken out of the bank account. Therefore the cash payments book will also show a payment on the same date for the amount of cash required, in the example above $48.79.

7.4 TOTALLING THE PETTY CASH BOOK

When the entries have been made into the petty cash book, each of the columns of the payments side must be totalled in order for the amounts to be posted to the nominal *(general)* ledger. It is normally convenient to post transactions from the petty cash book when the petty cash is topped up.

ACTIVITY 3

On 1 May 20X3 $100 (the imprest amount) was paid into the petty cash box of an organisation, to set up a petty cash system for the first time. During the week ended 8 May the following petty cash vouchers were put into the petty cash box as the claims were paid:

Petty Cash Voucher	No. 832
Date 1 May X3	
For what required	AMOUNT $ ¢
Printing letterheads (including 20% VAT)	31 50
Signature B Gordon	
Authorised P Cash	

Petty Cash Voucher	No. 833
Date 1 May X3	
For what required	AMOUNT $ ¢
Taxi (no VAT invoice)	7 40
Signature A McDougall	
Authorised J Falk	

Petty Cash Voucher	No. 834
Date 3 May X3	
For what required	AMOUNT $ ¢
Tea, coffee	8 23
Signature S P Oak	
Authorised P Cash	

Petty Cash Voucher	No. 835
Date 4 May X3	
For what required	AMOUNT $ ¢
Stationery (including 20% VAT)	12 49
Signature J Wilson	
Authorised P Cash	

Petty Cash Voucher No. 836			Petty Cash Voucher No. 837		
Date 5 May X3			Date 5 May X3		
For what required	AMOUNT $	¢	For what required	AMOUNT $	¢
Taxi (VAT invoice attached) Tax @ 20%	11	30	Train fare	6	50
Signature B Phipps			Signature J Wilson		
Authorised P Cash			Authorised P Cash		

On 8 May the amount of cash required to top up the petty cash box to $100 again was put into the box in cash.

Task

Write up all of these entries in the petty cash book. Ensure that the payments side is totalled and that all of the totals cross-cast.

For a suggested answer, see the 'Answers' section at the end of the book.

7.5 POSTING THE PETTY CASH BOOK

When the petty cash book has been totalled, the total amounts are then posted to the relevant accounts in the nominal *(general)* ledger, as follows:

For cash paid into the petty cash box

- Debit   Petty cash account with the money transferred from the Bank account.

- Credit Bank.

For expense payments out of the petty cash box

- Credit petty cash account with the total of payments. (This is the total of the Total column on the payments side of the petty cash book.)

- Debit sales tax account with the total in the sales tax analysis column.

- Debit the appropriate expense account with the total for each expense analysis column.

FA1: RECORDING FINANCIAL TRANSACTIONS

ACTIVITY 4

Record the following transactions in the petty cash book and post the month end totals to the main ledger.

The balance brought down on the petty cash account on 1 September 20X4 is the imprest amount of $50.

Date

2nd	Coffee purchased for $1.89 (no sales tax)
4th	Repair to light switch $12.00 ($2.00 sales tax)
10th	Taxi fare $5 (no sales tax)
15th	Pay cleaner $15 (no sales tax)
25th	Repairs $5.88 ($0.98 sales tax)

The imprest float was restored on 30 September.

For a suggested answer, see the 'Answers' section at the end of the book.

7.6 THE PETTY CASH BOOK AS A NOMINAL *(GENERAL)* LEDGER ACCOUNT

It was explained in an earlier chapter that the cash book is a book of prime entry, but it can also be used as a main ledger account as well.

The same applies to the petty cash book. The petty cash book itself can be used both as a book of prime entry, for recording petty cash transactions, and also as the nominal *(general)* ledger Petty cash account.

When this happens, the cash receipts side of the petty cash book is the debit side of the ledger account, and the cash payments side is the credit side of the account.

8 PETTY CASH RECONCILIATION

Each time the petty cashier pays out a sum of money from the petty cash box then this payment must be supported by a valid, authorised petty cash voucher. Each petty cash voucher is, in turn, kept in the petty cash box until the petty cash box is due to be topped up to the imprest amount.

8.1 CASH AND VOUCHERS

At any point in time the actual amount of cash in the petty cash box plus the vouchers in the box should be equal to the starting amount in the petty cash box, the imprest amount.

For control purposes it is important that this is checked at regular intervals. Depending upon the volume of transactions, this could be several times per week.

ACTIVITY 5

A petty cash system is run with an imprest amount of $200. Each Friday, just before the petty cash is topped up to $200, the amount of cash is counted and the vouchers in the petty cash box are totalled. On this particular Friday the cash in the petty cash box was made up as follows:

4 × $20 notes

2 × $10 notes

2 × $5 note

5 × $1 coins

3 × 50¢ coins

7 × 20¢ coins

15 × 10¢ coins

6 × 5¢ coins

4 × 2¢ coins

9 × 1¢ coins

The petty cash vouchers in the petty cash box were the following:

Petty Cash Voucher	No. 731		Petty Cash Voucher	No. 732	
Date 19/6/X5			Date 19/6/X5		
For what required	AMOUNT $	¢	For what required	AMOUNT $	¢
Rail fare Taxi	11 _4_ 15	30 _60_ 90	Tea biscuits	6	73
Signature S Pilau			Signature P Peers		
Authorised J Morris			Authorised J Morris		

FA1: RECORDING FINANCIAL TRANSACTIONS

Petty Cash Voucher	No. 733		
Date 20/6/X5			
For what required		AMOUNT $	¢
Milkman		21	90
Signature P Peers			
Authorised J Morris			

Petty Cash Voucher	No. 734		
Date 19/6/X5			
For what required		AMOUNT $	¢
Rail fare		27	00
Taxi x 2		8	60
		<u>35</u>	<u>60</u>
Signature F T Winter			
Authorised J Morris			

Task

Prove the imprest amount of $200.

For a suggested answer, see the 'Answers' section at the end of the book.

8.2 DIFFERENCES ARISING

In Activity 5, the reconciliation of cash and vouchers showed that there were no differences arising. The cash plus the vouchers totalled the imprest amount.

However, in some instances, when the reconciliation is carried out there may be differences. Whenever a difference arises this must be investigated immediately. Possible reasons for differences might be:

(a) petty cash vouchers being made out for an incorrect amount, but the correct amount being paid out in cash

(b) the incorrect amount being paid out in cash, and

(c) money being stolen from the petty cash box.

ACTIVITY 6

On Monday 3 January 20X2, just before the petty cash box was due to be topped up to the imprest amount of $50, the cash and vouchers in the petty cash box were counted.

The cash in the box was made up as follows:

        1 × $5 note

        2 × $1 coins

        6 × 50¢ coins

        5 × 20¢ coins

        3 × 10¢ coins

        2 × 5¢ coins

        24¢ in small denomination coins

MAINTAINING PETTY CASH RECORDS : CHAPTER 10

The following vouchers were in the box:

Petty Cash Voucher	No. 1142
Date 29/12/X1	
For what required	AMOUNT $ ¢
Stamps	6	50
Signature G Jones	
Authorised P Smith	

Petty Cash Voucher	No. 1143
Date 30/12/X1	
For what required	AMOUNT $ ¢
Taxi	7	00
Signature P	
Authorised P Smith	

Petty Cash Voucher	No. 1144
Date 30/12/X1	
For what required	AMOUNT $ ¢
Windowcleaner	21	00
Signature G Jones	
Authorised P Smith	

Petty Cash Voucher	No. 1145
Date 30/12/X1	
For what required	AMOUNT $ ¢
Bus fare	1	20
Signature S Cameron	
Authorised P Smith	

Petty Cash Voucher	No. 1146
Date 30/12/X1	
For what required	AMOUNT $ ¢
Photocopying	1	66
Signature G Jones	
Authorised P Smith	

Task

Reconcile the cash and vouchers in the petty cash box to the imprest amount. Give possible reasons for any difference that is discovered.

For a suggested answer, see the 'Answers' section at the end of the book.

CONCLUSION

We have now looked at how most payments are made by a business and recorded in the accounting system. Even the smallest amounts must be justifiable, be properly evidenced and authorised. Then this expenditure must be recorded correctly. This occurs in the petty cash book, a book of prime entry.

The petty cash book may be kept on the imprest or non-imprest system.

Petty cash should be reconciled regularly.

KEY TERMS

Imprest system – System commonly used for petty cash, whereby the total amount of cash in the petty cash tin is periodically topped up to a given limit. At all times, the petty cash vouchers plus the money in the tin should be equal to this limit.

Petty cash voucher – Document kept in the petty cash giving details of money paid out and the reasons for the expense.

SELF TEST QUESTIONS

Paragraph

1	How should petty cash vouchers be numbered?	2
2	What two checks must the person authorising a petty cash claim make?	3
3	What document should ideally support a petty cash claim?	3
4	Could petty cash claims be paid with no supporting documentation?	3
5	Explain how petty cash is kept secure.	4
6	What is meant by the imprest system?	7
7	How are top-ups of petty cash recorded?	7
8	State three reasons why the total of cash and vouchers in a petty cash box might not equal the imprest amount.	8

EXAM-STYLE QUESTIONS

1   The petty cash can be checked at any time, even if the petty cash book is not up to date. Which of the following formulae is used for checking the petty cash?

    A   Petty cash vouchers – Cash held = Imprest

    B   Imprest + Petty cash vouchers = Cash held

    C   Imprest + Cash held = Petty cash vouchers

    D   Petty cash vouchers + Cash held = Imprest

2   The business for which you work is registered for sales tax. The following petty cash amounts include sales tax at 20%.

    - $1.18
    - $2.31
    - $4.60
    - $5.00
    - $2.87
    - $3.91
    - $6.21
    - $1.85
    - $2.33
    - $4.96

    How much will be shown in the sales tax column in the petty cash book?

    A $5.87

    B $7.04

    C $35.22

    D $29.35

3   A petty cash system is run with an imprest amount of $200. Each Friday just before the petty cash is topped up to $200 the amount of cash is counted and the vouchers in the petty cash box are totalled. On this particular Friday, the cash in the petty cash box amounted to $97.80 and the petty cash vouchers $102.20. How much will be needed to restore it to its nominal amount of $200?

    A $102.20

    B $97.80

    C $4.40

    D $200.00

For suggested answers, see the 'Answers' section at the end of the book.

Chapter 11

PAYROLL

For many businesses, a major item of expense is the cost of its work force, referred to as 'payroll costs'. This chapter explains how wages and salary payments are calculated and paid. It covers the syllabus area for payroll.

CONTENTS

1. Payroll system
2. Processing the payroll
3. Basic pay calculations
4. Overtime pay, bonuses and commission
5. Authorisation
6. Security and control
7. Accounting for payroll

LEARNING OUTCOMES

At the end of this chapter, you should be able to:

- understand payroll systems

- understand the duties of employers in relation to taxes, state benefit contributions and other deductions

- record hours worked: timesheets, clock cards

- calculate gross wages for employees paid by hour, by output (piecework) and salaried workers

- define and calculate bonuses, overtime and commission given the details of each scheme

- describe the documentation required for recording various elements of wages and salaries

- recognise the need for payroll to be authorised and identify appropriate authorisation, security and control procedures

- make other deductions from wages – trade union subscriptions, payroll saving, pension contributions and payroll giving

- identify various methods for making payments to employees

- account for payroll costs and payroll deductions.

1 PAYROLL SYSTEM

The payroll is a list of the employees of the organisation and the money due to each.

A payroll list is produced each time that employees are paid.

- Wage earners are paid weekly.

- Salary earners are paid monthly.

Sometimes, employees earn a fixed amount every week or every month. Sometimes there are variations in the amount employees earn, due to overtime payments or bonuses or commissions which add to their pay.

1.1 GROSS PAY AND NET PAY: DEDUCTIONS

The total amount earned in a week or month by an employee is referred to as **gross pay.**

This is not the amount of money that the employee receives, because deductions are taken away from the gross pay, and the employee receives just the gross pay less deductions. This is known as the employee's **net pay.**

The deductions from pay are usually a combination of:

- statutory deductions, and

- non-statutory or voluntary deductions.

Statutory deductions are deductions from pay that are made by law, for example: income tax and social security. These are deducted from gross pay by the employer and paid to the relevant taxation authority. In this manner an employer acts as the agent of the taxation authority, both calculating and collecting taxation and social security amounts.

For example; in the UK income tax for employees is deducted under the 'Pay As You Earn' scheme along with National Insurance and paid over to HM Revenue and Customs by their employers.

Non-statutory **deductions** are voluntary deductions from pay that the employee chooses to make. Examples of these are:

- subscriptions to a trade union

- contributions by the employee to a pension scheme.

	$
Gross pay	A
Less:	
Statutory deductions	(B)
Non-statutory deductions	(C)
Net pay or 'take-home' pay	A – B – C

What this means is that when an employee is paid, only the net pay or take-home pay is received, and the employer pays the other amounts deducted to other organisations ('external agencies') such as Revenue and Customs, a trade union and a pension scheme organisation.

1.2 OTHER DEDUCTIONS

The employer and employee may agree that other deductions should be made from the employee's salary. Examples are:

(a) pension contributions

(b) deductions under a payroll charitable donation scheme

(c) deductions under a payroll savings scheme

(d) trade union subscriptions

(f) deductions under holiday pay schemes

(g) certain other voluntary deductions agreed by the employer (for example, fees for use of the company sports club).

FA1: RECORDING FINANCIAL TRANSACTIONS

ACTIVITY 1

The following figures have been extracted from a trader's records in respect of wages and salaries for July:

(i)	Wages and salaries (gross)	$6,300
(ii)	Income tax	$1,600
(iii)	Employees' pension contributions	$600
(iv)	Employer's pension contributions	$700

1 What is the total amount the trader will have to pay for wages and salaries for July?

- A $4,100
- B $4,800
- C $6,300
- D $7,000

2 What is the net pay received by employees?

- A $4,100
- B $4,200
- C $4,800
- D $5,600

For a suggested answer, see the 'Answers' section at the end of the book.

2 PROCESSING THE PAYROLL

To process the payroll, an employer must, **for each employee**:

- Calculate the gross wage or salary for the period.
- Calculate the income tax payable out of these earnings.
- Calculate the employee's state benefit contributions that are deductible.
- Calculate any non-statutory deductions.
- Prepare a **payslip** showing the gross pay, deductions and net pay.
- Make the payment of net pay to the employee.
- Calculate the employer's state benefit contributions.

For all employees collectively, the employer must:

- Make the payments of all the deductions from pay and the employer's state benefit contributions to the appropriate other organisations.

- Record the payroll costs in the accounting system.

2.1 PAYSLIPS

A payslip will accompany each payment of salary or wages to an employee. It shows how the amount paid has been arrived at and how much income tax and state benefit contributions have been deducted.

Other deductions will also be shown on the payslip.

Getting a payslip means that even if the employee receives wages or salary payments directly into a nominated bank account, the employee is notified of the payment and how much it is, upon receiving the payslips. Payslips might be distributed to employees at work, posted to their home address or available via the employer's secure website.

A payslip must show details of:

- gross pay

- deductions (itemised separately)

- net pay (net pay is sometimes called 'take-home pay').

However, there isn't a standard layout for a payslip and so payslips of different employers can look very different.

An example is shown below:

Dickson Engineering					
Employee:		T Cardew		Employee no.	
NI No:	TY 45 67 78 L	Tax code: 473L		Date: 11/01/04	Tax period: Wk 40
PAY FOR WEEK ENDING: 11/01/04		Hours	Rate $	AMOUNT $	$
Basic		40.0	7.50	300.00	
Overtime		5.0	15.00	75.00	
Shift allowance		2	10.00	20.00	
GROSS PAY				395.00	
Pension (Employer's pension contribution $25.00)				15.00	
Trade union subscription				10.00	
TOTAL PAY				370.00	16,605.00
PAYE				57.92	2,711.32
Employees' social security (Employer's social security $36.71)				30.85	
NET PAY				281.23	

2.2 MAKING PAYMENTS TO EMPLOYEES

Most employers will have a set day on which employees should be paid, and it is the payroll department's responsibility to ensure that wages are paid on the correct due days.

Weekly paid employees will be paid at least once a week, normally on the same day each week. Usually the pay day will be either Thursday or Friday.

Monthly paid employees will be paid once a month, and there will be a formula for determining the pay day. For example, this may be:

- the last day of the calendar month
- the last Thursday or Friday of the calendar month
- the same date each month, such as the 26th.

Employees may be paid their wages in several ways:

- in cash (but this is now very uncommon)
- by cheque
- by bank giro transfer
- through the Banks Automated Clearing System (BACS).

Making payments by these methods has been described in an earlier chapter.

2.3 PAYMENTS TO OUTSIDE AGENCIES

Payments are made regularly by an employer to outside agencies, such as tax authorities, pension schemes, trades union, and so on.

The supporting documentation for these payments is the payroll itself.

When these payments are made, they are recorded in the cash payments book, and from the cash payments book they are posted to the appropriate nominal *(general)* ledger accounts.

ACTIVITY 2

1 Which of the following does not appear on a payslip?

   A   Gross weekly wage for the employee

   B   Tax paid to date by the employee in the tax year

   C   Deductions paid by the employee

   D   Details of the employee's expected pension

2 Which is the most convenient way for a large employer to pay salaries electronically?

   A   BACS

   B   Bank giro transfer

   C   By cash

   D   By cheque

For a suggested answer, see the 'Answers' section at the end of the book.

3 BASIC PAY CALCULATIONS

3.1 ELEMENTS OF GROSS PAY

The amount of pay to which an employee is entitled may be earned in a variety of different ways. These include:

(a) Basic pay, such as:
   (i)   wages paid according to the number of hours worked
   (ii) salaries, for salaried staff
   (iii) wages paid according to the output of the employee.

(b) Other pay, such as:
   (i) overtime pay, for extra hours worked by the employee
   (ii) shift pay, to compensate for unsocial hours.

(c) Bonuses and commission, such as:
   (i) bonuses paid under bonus schemes, based on productivity, or profitability
   (ii) commission paid, normally based on sales.

3.2 BASIC PAY FOR HOURLY PAID EMPLOYEES

Some employees are paid on the basis of a set amount for every hour that they work. This may be so even if they have agreed to work a certain number of hours per week. If hours in excess of the agreed amount have been worked, or hours are worked outside set times, they may be paid at a different rate, as overtime. Overtime is discussed more fully later.

Workers paid on the basis of an hourly rate normally receive their pay weekly.

3.3 RECORDING HOURS

If an employee is paid according to the number of hours worked, there must be a method of recording the hours worked.

The exact method will vary according to the type and size of the business, but some examples are described below.

(a) **Clock cards**

Each employee has a card which is inserted into a machine when at the start of the working days, and again at the end of the working day. The machine records on the card the times of starting and stopping work.

An example of the format of a clock card is given below. In this example the employee has 'clocked on' at 08.49 on Monday morning by inserting the clock card into a machine which stamps the time on the card. When the employee next places the card in the machine – breaking for lunch at 12.12 on Monday – the card slips further down into the machine and therefore the time stamp appears above the previous one. The employee returns to work at 12.55 on Monday and 'clocks off' at 16.42. Tuesday shows a similar pattern.

The example contains space for the payroll department to analyse the time between basic time and overtime. It may also contain space to record the basic pay and overtime pay, and deductions.

Week no . . . . Name		Ending	
Time	Day	Basic	Overtime
16.22	Tu		
13.07	Tu		
12.01	Tu		
08.29	Tu		
16.42	Mo		
12.55	Mo		
12.12	Mo		
08.49	Mo		

(b) **'Smart' cards**

Clock cards may be replaced by smart cards. These record the same information, but it is recorded on the magnetic strip on the card. Smart cards may also be used for other purposes not related to the payroll.

(c) **Timesheets**

Each employee is required to fill in a list of the hours worked on a standard form, known as a timesheet. The timesheet may require additional information, such as what tasks the employee carried out, and how long each task took. After completion, the timesheet is then, usually, authorised by the supervisor/manager.

Weekly, fortnightly or monthly, timesheets may also be used. These are more common among professional salaried staff, such as solicitors or accountants, who are not paid on an hourly basis, but where the employer needs to know the time spent on each client, so that the client can be charged accordingly. Normally the employee will need to keep daily records which are summarised, so that entries are not omitted.

A simple timesheet for an hourly paid worker may look like this:

Week no				Ending		
Name			Payroll No			
Job no	Start	Finish	Quant	Check	Hours	Cost
L12	M0830	1230				
	M1330	1700				
	T0830	1100	1,000	JK	10.00	

The timesheet should also record idle time. Idle time is when the employee is unable to complete a task because of something outside their control, for example waiting for a replacement part to be delivered. The cost of each job is completed later by the payroll department.

A weekly timesheet for a professional salaried employee may look like this:

Week no			Ending . . . .
Name		Staff no	
Client number	Name		Hours
B088	Brown J		9.50
D301	Doe J		11.50
S111	Smith J		12.25
AA01	Administration		1.75
		Total	35.00

The weekly timesheet may contain space for the daily totals, or they may be kept by the employee separately. If the employee is paid overtime, there will be space to record this on the timesheet.

In addition to calculating the amounts owed to employees, businesses need to keep track of the costs incurred in manufacturing, perhaps for control purposes or perhaps even to arrive at a selling cost for a job or product.

One simple approach to keeping track of costs is to have a system of **job cards**. These might be used in circumstances where each job undertaken has the potential to be unique, such as work done on cars in garage workshops.

Each job is given an identifying number and the time and materials applied to it can then be recorded on a job card.

JOB COST RECORD			
Job no .... Customer			
Date started .... Date completed			
Materials			
Part no	Quantity used	Unit cost	Total cost
TOTAL			
Labour			
Employee no	Hours used	Hourly rate	Total cost
TOTAL			
Overhead			
TOTAL JOB COST			

Example

A garage repairing cars for customers has three employees. Whenever one of the employees is working on a car, they are required to complete a job card for that particular job. Upon completion of the job, the customer is then invoiced for the total on the job card. A typical job card for one recent repair is shown below.

JOB COST RECORD			
Job no ....107/2007.......		Customer ....Bakewell..........	
Date started ..... 13/06/2007 ...		Date completed ..13/06/2007.....	
Materials			
Part no	Quantity used	Unit cost	Total cost
QV3	4	$12.20	$48.80
TT43	2	$52.40	$104.80
TOTAL			$153.60
Labour			
Employee no	Hours used	Hourly rate	Total cost
2	6	$28	$168
TOTAL			$168
Overhead			$16.80
TOTAL JOB COST			$338.40

This form of record will enable the business to justify charging a customer a particular amount for work done on a vehicle, or to enable it to determine whether or not it made a profit or a loss on a job that was done for a fixed cost.

An alternative form of record is better suited to manufacturing, particularly where there are complicated manufacturing processes that may be undertaken in different sequences or combined in different ways. These documents are called **route cards**.

ROUTE CARD			
Project	Product	Identification	
Manufacturing process / supplier		Batch ID / date	
Operation	Comments	Initial	Date

Example

Building a customised truck body may be tackled in a variety of different ways. Perhaps painting can be done before or after certain fabrication work has been completed, perhaps electrical work can be done at different stages in the process, and so on. A route card might be prepared in advance to give staff an indication of how a unit or a batch should be made. If staff are empowered to make such decisions themselves then the card should be filled in as the work progresses so that the approach being taken can be reviewed regularly and any lessons drawn for future reference. A simplified example of a completed route card for the manufacture of a customised truck is shown below:

ROUTE CARD			
Project: Alpha	**Product**: Big Tow	**Identification**: T0256	
Supplier		batch ID / date	
Metal Co		207960T	
Wheel Co		4XT346	
Electrical Co		43578	
Paint Co		3217TYH	
Operation	**Comments**	**Initial**	**Date**
Frame construction	None	TA	16/06/07
Wheel welding	None	BT	27/06/07
Electrical installation	Authorisation of GT received for overrun	FA	28/06/07
Painting	None	YH	03/07/07

3.4 CALCULATING BASIC PAY

To calculate basic pay for hourly paid workers (excluding overtime), the hourly rate is simply multiplied by the numbers of hours worked.

Example

An employee worked 35 hours during a particular week. How much was the employee be paid if their hourly rate is $4.50 per hour?

Solution

Their pay will be 35 hours @ $4.50 = $157.50

3.5 BASIC PAY FOR SALARIED STAFF

Some employees are paid a set amount on the basis that they work for a standard number of hours every week. The amount that they are paid is usually expressed as an annual sum.

For example, an employee may be paid $12,000 per annum, for working from 9.00am till 5.00pm Monday to Friday (with a one hour lunch break), and with an entitlement to 20 days holiday (in addition to public holidays).

Such employees are often referred to as salaried staff, and their earnings referred to as salary. There is no difference in principle between the treatment of wages and salary on the payroll. Salaried staff usually receive their pay monthly.

When an employee is paid an agreed annual salary, the salary will be spread evenly over the year. The spreading disregards the periods over which holidays are taken, so that the employee knows precisely how much pay they will receive.

The way in which the salary is spread is:

(a)	Weekly paid	1/52 of the annual salary
(b)	Fortnightly paid	2/52 of the annual salary
(c)	4-weekly paid	4/52 of the annual salary
(d)	Monthly paid	1/12 of the annual salary

Some salaried staff may be entitled to overtime if they work in excess of the agreed hours. Others may not be entitled to overtime, or only after they have worked a certain number of extra hours.

Overtime is discussed more fully later.

3.6 BASIC PAY FOR EMPLOYEES PAID BY PIECEWORK

If an employee is paid by piecework, it means that payment is made according to the number of items produced by the employee. It usually applies where a high number of small items are produced. It would clearly be inequitable to apply piecework where an employee was expected to complete only a handful of items each week as pay would fluctuate too greatly.

Piecework is often used as an incentive for the workers to work harder, as they can see a direct correlation between their output and their pay.

Piecework can only be applied if an employee's output can be recorded. This is usually done using a job card. A card is prepared for every job, and records the time spent on that job by every employee.

The rate of pay for employees paid by piecework is expressed as so much pay for a given number of items. It might be an amount per item, per 100 items, or even per 10,000 items, depending on the level of expected output.

The formula is:

Basic pay = Number of units produced × Rate of pay per unit

Piecework schemes can also offer higher rates where more than a certain number of items is produced. For example, an employee may be paid $5 each for the first 100 boxes of components packed, and $6 for any extra boxes packed.

Sometimes the piecework system is backed up by a minimum wage. For example, an employee may be paid $6 for every 100 buttonholes, but not less than $80 per week.

In the simplest case, the employee's basic pay will be the number of items produced, multiplied by the rate per item.

This will need to be modified where there are differential rates, by applying the appropriate rates to the appropriate number of items.

If a minimum wage is guaranteed, the basic pay will need to be increased to this level if the pay calculated using piecework rates is lower.

Example

Employees A, B and C are each paid by piecework. The terms of their employment are as follows:

(a) Employee A is paid a flat rate of $1.33 for every box produced. In a given week, Employee A produced 121 boxes.

(b) Employee B is paid $0.99 for every box produced, with a guaranteed minimum wage of $80 per week. In a given week, Employee B produced 75 boxes.

(c) Employee C is paid $1.33 each for the first 125 boxes produced, and $1.47 for each subsequent box. In a given week, Employee C produced 145 boxes.

How much basic pay will each employee receive that week?

Solution

They will receive the following amounts of basic pay:

			$
(a)	Employee A:	121 boxes @ $1.33	160.93
(b)	Employee B:	75 boxes @ $0.99 =	74.25
		guaranteed minimum wage of	80.00
(c)	Employee C:	125 boxes @ $1.33	166.25
		20 boxes @ $1.47	29.40
		145	195.65

ACTIVITY 3

A business manufactures packing cases and employs a number of people on a piece rate scheme of $3.00 for each packing case made. If an employee produces more than 100 packing cases in a week, any extra packing cases produced over 100 are paid at a rate of $4.00 per packing case. All employees have a guaranteed minimum weekly wage of $300.

In the last week an employee produced 109 packing cases.

What was the employee's gross pay for the last week?

A $300

B $327

C $336

D $436

For a suggested answer, see the 'Answers' section at the end of the book.

4   OVERTIME PAY, BONUSES AND COMMISSION

4.1   OVERTIME

Normally an employee is required to work for a set number of hours every week. There may however be occasions where the employer will ask the employee to work for longer hours. Overtime is the time worked over and above the employee's basic working week.

Overtime must not be confused with flexitime. In a flexitime system an employee is allowed to work extra hours earlier in the week or month, in return for which fewer hours need to be worked later on. The overall number of hours worked in a given time period (e.g. a month) remains constant.

4.2   HOURLY PAID WORKERS

Hourly paid workers may be paid overtime at various different rates. For example, the hourly rate of overtime may be the same as the basic rate of pay or higher than the basic rate of pay.

It may either be expressed as a higher monetary amount, or as a proportion of basic pay, such as 'time and a half'.

The hourly rate of overtime may vary according to when the overtime is worked. For example the evening rate may be 'time and a half', whereas the weekend rate may be 'double time'.

The hourly rate may vary with the number of overtime hours worked. For example the first 5 hours may be at 'time and a half', and additional hours at 'double time'.

4.3 CALCULATING OVERTIME PAY – WEEKLY PAID WORKERS

The overtime pay is the number of hours of overtime worked, multiplied by the rate at which overtime is paid.

Example

An employee normally works a 35 hour week, and is paid $5 per hour. In one week the employee worked 12 hours of overtime, one hour each week day, and 7 hours on Saturday.

How much is the overtime pay if:

(a) the employee is paid time and a half for all overtime hours?

(b) the employee is paid time and a half for evening overtime and double time for weekend overtime?

(c) the employee is paid time and a half for the first 8 hours overtime and double time thereafter?

Solution

The employee's overtime pay is:

$

(a) Basic rate of pay $5 per hour
    Overtime rate of pay $5 × 1½ = $7.50 per hour
    Overtime pay   12 hours @ $7.50 per hour   90.00

$

(b) Basic rate of pay $5 per hour
    Overtime rate of pay – evenings $5 × 1½ = $7.50 per hour
    Overtime rate of pay – weekends $5 × 2 = $10.00 per hour
    Overtime pay   5 hours @ $7.50 per hour   37.50
    7 hours @ $10.00 per hour   70.00

    Total   107.50

(c) Basic rate of pay $5 per hour
    Overtime rate of pay – first 8 hours $5 × 1½ = $7.50 per hour
    Overtime rate of pay – excess hours $5 × 2 = $10.00 per hour
    Overtime pay   8 hours @ $7.50 per hour   60.00
    4 hours @ $10.00 per hour   40.00

                                                              100.00

4.4 SALARIED STAFF

Not all salaried staff are paid overtime for any additional hours worked. If they are, the rate at which overtime is paid may vary according to when the overtime is worked, in precisely the same way as for weekly paid employees.

The difference is that the pay of salaried staff is usually expressed as an annual rate, and this must be converted to an hourly rate before the overtime can be calculated.

This is done by dividing the annual salary by 52 to give the weekly salary, and further dividing this by the number of hours an employee is contracted to work for.

It should be noted that the contract of employment may override this calculation, setting a rate of overtime pay.

Example

Employee K works a 35-hour week for an annual salary of $18,200. Employee K is expected to work up to 5 hours of overtime for no extra pay, but thereafter will be paid overtime pay at the rate of time and a half.

One week Employee K works 8 hours of overtime. What is Employee K's overtime pay?

Solution

Employee K's basic hourly rate of pay is:

$18,200 × 1/52 × 1/35 = $10.00

The hourly rate of overtime pay, at time and a half, is:

$10.00 × 1½ = $15.00

Employee K will not be paid for the first 5 hours of overtime, so overtime pay is as follows:

(8 − 5) hours = 3 hours @ $15 = $45.00

4.5 BONUSES

Bonus schemes are schemes under which employees receive additional amounts of earnings, as a reward for good work, on top of their normal pay.

The essence of a bonus scheme is that additional pay will be earned if targets are achieved or exceeded. The scheme should set out the exact details and the dates of payment.

Examples of bonuses which may be earned are:

(a) If the department's output exceeds a set limit, a bonus may be paid for every extra unit.

(b) If the sales exceed a target in any one month, a proportion of the excess is divided between the sales force.

(c) If the company's profits exceed target, every employee may receive a bonus based on their basic pay.

(d) If an employee achieves a certain quality of work, a bonus may be earned.

(e) If a long-term contract is completed early, each employee may receive a bonus related to how early the contract is completed.

(f) If the company's profits increase by a set percentage, the senior managers receive a bonus related to their basic pay.

Example

Supersales Ltd operates various bonus schemes.

1   Normal output of the toy department is 1,000 dolls per week. For every doll produced in excess of 1,100 per week, each employee of the department receives an extra 5¢.

2   If the total sales in the retail outlets exceed $1 million in any one month, 2% of the excess is shared between the sales team.

3   If the company's profits exceed $90 million, every employee receives a bonus of one week's pay.

4   If a junior employee receives a top grade assessment from their supervisor on four consecutive occasions, that employee receives a bonus of $10.

5   Supersales has several contracts spanning 9 months or more. Each employee involved in the contract receives a bonus of one day's pay for every week by which the contract is completed early.

6   If the company's annual profits increase by 5% or more per annum, the senior managers receive a bonus of 1% of their basic annual pay.

The following additional information is relevant:

(a) Employee T works in the toy department, and is paid $100 per week. In one week, 1,230 dolls were produced.

(b) Employee S is a member of the sales team, and is paid $150 per week. In April, sales were $1.7 million. Employee S's proportionate share of the bonus is 0.5%.

(c) Employee R is a junior employee paid $65 per week. Employee R received four consecutive top grade assessments. Employee R was employed on one of the long-term contracts, which was completed two weeks early.

(d) Employee P is a senior manager, and is paid $36,000 per annum.

The company's profits for the year have just been announced as $92 million, a 5.5% increase over the previous year.

What bonuses will each employee receive?

Solution

(a) **Employee T**

	$
Scheme 1. 130 extra dolls @ 5p	6.50
Scheme 3. Profits exceed $90m, one week's pay	100.00
Total bonus	106.50

(b) **Employee S**

	$
Scheme 2 Total bonuses 2% × $(1.7–1)m = $14,000	
Terence's share 0.5%	70.00
Scheme 3. Profits exceed $90m, one week's pay	150.00
	220.00

(c) **Employee R**

	$
Scheme 3. Profits exceed $90m, one week's pay	65.00
Scheme 4. 4 top grade assessments	10.00
Scheme 5. Contract completed 2 weeks early	
2 days pay 2/5 × $65	26.00
	101.00

(d) **Employee P**

	$
Scheme 3. Profits exceed $90m, one week's pay	
1/52 × $36,000	692.31
Scheme 6. Profits increased by 5.5%, 1% of basic pay	360.00
	1,052.31

FA1: RECORDING FINANCIAL TRANSACTIONS

ACTIVITY 4

Employee B and C work for a company which operates the following bonus schemes:

1. A bonus of $10 for every complete $1m by which sales exceed $100 million in any one month.

2. A bonus of $5 for every 10 boxes of components produced by any one worker in one week in excess of 1,000 boxes.

3. A bonus of 10% of the week's pay for any week in which the department's output exceeds 10,000 boxes.

In one week Employee B produced 980 boxes, and Employee C produced 1,030 boxes. The department as a whole produced 10,500 boxes. The figures for the previous month showed that sales were $102.7 million. Employees B and C have basic weekly pay of $120 and $130 respectively.

What bonus will they each receive?

For a suggested answer, see the 'Answers' section at the end of the book.

4.6 COMMISSION

In some jobs, employees may be remunerated by a basic salary, plus an additional amount specifically related to that employee's performance.

Commission is an amount paid to an employee based on that employee's performance.

Commission is most commonly paid to salesperson, based on the volume of sales that they have achieved in a given period. In some cases they may have a very low basic salary, so that commission forms the largest part of their pay.

In its simplest form, commission will usually be expressed as a percentage of sales achieved in the previous period e.g. 1% of sales.

Commission may also be paid at different scales, so that the higher the sales, the higher the commission. For example, a salesperson may be paid 2% commission on the first $10,000 of sales, 2.5% on the next $10,000, and 3% on any additional sales.

This basis may be appropriate where an employee sells a large number of small value items. If the salesperson instead sells higher value contracts, the level of commission may vary with the value of the contract. For example, the rate of commission may be 2% for contracts worth up to $10,000, 2.5% for contracts worth up to $20,000, and 3% for larger contracts.

Since the incentive is for the employee to make a large volume of sales, it is important for the employer to ensure that the salesperson is rewarded only for good sales. The commission scheme may contain a proviso that the commission will only be paid only when the customer has paid, or when the customer's creditworthiness has been checked.

Example

A salesperson receives a commission of 2% on all sales of machinery, with an additional 0.5% for any item of machinery selling for more than $10,000. In addition the sales person receives a further 0.5% on sales in excess of $100,000 per month.

During July the salesperson's total sales amounted to $110,000. Included in this were two expensive machines, one selling for $12,000, and the other for $17,000.

How much commission did the salesperson earn?

Solution

The salesperson earns commission of:

	$
Basic commission $110,000 × 2%	2,200
Expensive machines $(12,000 + 17,000) × 0.5%	145
Sales over $100,000 $(110,000 – 100,000) @ 0.5%	50
Total commission	2,395

ACTIVITY 5

Employee K is paid commission of 5% on the first $20,000 of sales, and 7.5% on any sales in excess of this amount. However, Employee K is only paid the commission when either the customer has paid for the order, or has taken out a financing agreement.

In October Employee K made sales of $35,000. However, two customers declined to pay or take out a financing agreement. One had ordered goods costing $1,500, and the other goods costing $2,500.

How much commission will Employee K receive?

For a suggested answer, see the 'Answers' section at the end of the book.

5 AUTHORISATION

5.1 WHY IS AUTHORISATION REQUIRED?

Where an employee is paid on the basis of hours worked, or work done, pay will vary from week to week. It is the payroll department's responsibility to calculate gross pay each payday.

The payroll department can only calculate gross pay on the basis of the documentation they receive recording the employee's hours of work or work done. The employee often prepares this documentation. It should not be possible for an employee to overstate the hours worked, or work done, as this would result in them being overpaid. It is therefore important that any documentation prepared by the employee is reviewed and approved by a responsible person, such as a manager.

Any overtime worked must also be authorised prior to working.

5.2 HOW SHOULD THE DOCUMENTATION BE AUTHORISED?

The documentation completed by the employee should be authorised by the employee's supervisor, or other person in a managerial capacity. The records should be countersigned to indicate that they have been authorised.

The time at which the authorisation is required may vary, for example:

- hourly paid workers who complete timesheets may need to have them countersigned each time they complete a different job

- hourly paid workers who complete job cards may need to get them authorised when the job covered by the card is finished

- salaried staff completing weekly timesheets may have them authorised at the end of the week. This is particularly important when overtime is paid.

5.3 WHAT IF THE DOCUMENTATION IS NOT AUTHORISED?

Where a defined procedure for authorisation was not followed, the payroll department should refer the documentation back for authorisation before calculating the gross pay.

5.4 AUTHORISATION OF RATES OF PAY

The rate at which an employee is paid will be recorded on the payroll records. Only changes to the rates of pay which are authorised and notified through the personnel department should be recorded.

5.5 JOB CODES

Most of the documents which are used for recording an employee's hours worked also record the jobs on which the employee has worked. As well as being used to calculate the employee's pay, the documents are used to show the labour costs of the various jobs. The timesheets must contain the correct job codes so that the labour costs were allocated properly.

5.6 DEPARTMENT CODES

As well as job codes, the documentation may include department codes. This records not only the job that was done, but the department for which the work was carried out. This may be important when allocating the cost of idle time, or administration time.

5.7 AUTHORISATION OF THE PAYROLL

It is also normal for a responsible person within an organisation to review and approve the payroll before it is processed and payment made to employees. This is a final check of reasonableness to ensure that it is in line with expectations. The review and authorisation may be accompanied by a summary of employee joiners and leavers since the previous payroll to understand why employee numbers have changed. It may also be accompanied by a summary of factors to explain other changes from expectations, such as payment of bonus or overtime in excess of normal practice.

6 SECURITY AND CONTROL

6.1 INTRODUCTION

All the information held on the payroll is highly confidential and must be kept secure.

The information is highly sensitive as most employees will not know what other employees at similar grades are paid, or what the salary scales of more senior employees are.

Other information is personal to the employee, such as whether the employee has joined the staff pension scheme, or contributes to charities through the payroll giving scheme.

6.2 PRESERVING CONFIDENTIALITY

The steps that should be taken to preserve confidentiality include:

- not discussing an employee's pay details with another employee
- not leaving letters or other documents about an employee's pay lying around
- not leaving computers unattended during processing of the payroll
- putting files, papers and discs away in locked cupboards, or in the payroll department where unauthorised personnel do not have access
- not allowing access to payroll files to unauthorised personnel.

6.3 SECURITY

Processing the payroll results in large sums of money paid to employees and outside agencies.

Where cash is involved, it must be kept in a safe between the time it is collected from the bank and the time when wage packets are prepared, and between the completion of that task and the distribution of the wage packets. It is advisable for the wage packets to be prepared in a locked room if possible. Certainly, access to unauthorised personnel should be denied during this period. Payment of wages in cash is now uncommon.

If payments of wages and salaries are made by bank transfer, or by cheque, the cheque book and transfer details must similarly be retained in a secure place.

6.4 THE ROLE OF THE PERSONNEL DEPARTMENT

The main responsibilities of the personnel department are:

(a) the recruitment of new employees

(b) preparing records of the employees' personal details

(c) updating records of the employees' personal details

FA1: RECORDING FINANCIAL TRANSACTIONS

(d) keeping any other records concerning the employees, such as:

(i) records of absences, and the reasons

(ii) details of pay reviews

(iii) notes of progress interviews

(iv) training records.

In some cases the personnel department will also be responsible for processing the payroll. In other words, the payroll function will be one part of the personnel department. More often, the two functions are separate, but there is a certain amount of overlap. For example, the personnel department will keep details of an employee's rate of pay and hours of work, and contributions (if any) to the company pension scheme. These details are also needed by the payroll department.

The separation between personnel and payroll is useful in maintaining controls over the payroll as it enables records to be compared:

- to ensure that employees who have left the organisation are not still being paid

- to highlight whether 'dummy employees' have been invented by employees in payroll as a way of committing fraud.

Controls applied within payroll will aim to ensure that employees are correctly paid the right amount at the right time and with correct deductions. Proper authorisation and checking provides much of that control.

7 ACCOUNTING FOR PAYROLL

Payroll costs are a form of expenditure for an employer, and the expenditure must be recorded in the accounting system. Here is an example of a payroll record for an organisation with only two employees. It employs P Smith and M Brown.

Week 40

Employee	Gross pay $	Pension $	Income tax $	Employee's state benefit $	Net pay $	Employer's pension $	Employer's state benefit $
P Smith	395.00	15.00	57.92	30.85	291.23	15.00	36.71
M Brown	406.25	22.00	64.77	41.33	278.15	15.00	43.82
	801.25	37.00	122.69	72.18	569.38	30.00	80.53

A normal weekly payroll will look something like this, but with a longer list of employees. The payroll shows not just the gross pay, deductions for tax and net pay of the employees. It also shows the additional payroll costs of the employer, and in this example, these consist of:

- Employer's state benefit contributions.

- The employer's contributions to a pension scheme for employees. These contributions are in addition to gross pay, and are not deductions from the employees' wages.

7.1 POSTING PAYROLL DETAILS TO THE NOMINAL (GENERAL) LEDGER

Payroll costs are an expense for the employer, and the expense should be recorded in an expense account in the main or nominal *(general)* ledger.

The net wages or salaries have to be paid to the employees immediately. The various deductions from pay have to be paid to the outside agencies to which they are payable, and the employer's state benefit contributions and pension contributions also have to be paid to outside agencies. These payments are likely to occur some days after the employees have been paid their net pay so, for a short time, the amounts payable to the outside agencies are unpaid liabilities of the organisation. Until the money is paid to the agencies, these agencies are **payables** of the organisation.

In posting the payroll details to the nominal *(general)* ledger:

- The cost of the payroll, in other words the payroll expense, is recorded in an expense account. This might be called the wages and salaries expense account.

- The amounts payable to the employees and to the various outside agencies, in other words the liabilities of the organisation, are recorded in another nominal *(general)* ledger account. This might be called the wages and salaries payable account, or the wages and salaries control account.

Posting the payroll to the main ledger should be completed in the following steps:

Step 1   Gross pay

Take the total for gross pay and:

Dr Wages and salaries expense account

Cr Wages and salaries control account

Step 2   Additional contributions by the employer (state benefit and pension contributions)

Take the total of each type of contribution by the employer to total payroll costs and:

Dr Wages and salaries expense account

Cr Wages and salaries control account

Step 3   Take-home pay for employees

This is paid to the employees immediately, so by the time the payroll is recorded, the money has already been paid.

Take the total of net pay (take-home pay) from the payroll, and:

Dr Wages and salaries control account

Cr Bank account

Step 4 Amounts payable to outside agencies

When the payroll details are posted to the nominal *(general)* ledger, these payments are unlikely to have been made yet, so the amounts are still payable, and the outside agencies are payables.

Take each column in the payroll that represents an amount owing to an outside agency. These are the columns for deductions from employees' pay and the columns for the employer's state benefit contributions and pension scheme contributions. For each of these totals:

Dr Wages and salaries control account

Cr A payable account for the outside agency.

At the end of this process, the balance on the Wages and Salaries Control account should be nil.

These steps are shown in the following T accounts.

Wages and salaries control account

	$		$
Bank (net wages and salaries paid)	X	Wages and salaries expense account:	
		Gross pay	
		Employer's state benefit	X
		Employer's pension contribution	X
Taxation authority	X		X
Pension scheme payable	X		
Payables for any other non-statutory deductions	X		
	——		——
	X		X
	——		——

The balance on the wages and salaries control account should be nil.

Wages and salaries expense account

	$		$
Wages and salaries control account:			
Gross wages and salaries	X		
Employer's state benefit	X		
Employer's pension contribution	X		

There is a debit balance on this account, because it is an expense account.

Taxation authority account

	$		$
		Wages and salaries control account:	
		Income tax deductions	X
		Employees' state benefit	X
		Employer's state benefit	X

There is a credit balance on this account, because it is a liability account, representing a payable of the organisation.

Pension payable (non-statutory deductions) account

$		$
	Wages and salaries control account:	
	Employees' contributions	X
	Employer's contributions	X

There is a credit balance on this account, because it is a liability account, representing a payable of the organisation.

The example here does not have any other payables) for non-statutory deductions, but if there are any such deductions, such as employee subscriptions to a trade union or gifts by employees to a charity, these would be accounted for in a similar way. There would be a debit entry for the deduction in the Wages and salaries control account and a credit entry in the payable account for the external agency (trade union, charity, and so on).

Bank account

$		$
	Wages and salaries control account:	
	Net wages (take-home pay)	X

Payments out of the Bank account are recorded as credit entries.

ACTIVITY 6

Here are the totals from TTC's January payroll:

Total gross pay	$6,172.20
Total employer's state benefit	$488.20
Total income tax	$1,029.96
Total employees' state benefit	$445.20
Total net pay	$4,697.04

Task

Post the above to the relevant main ledger accounts and balance the control account.

For suggested answers, see the 'Answers' section at the end of the book.

FA1: RECORDING FINANCIAL TRANSACTIONS

ACTIVITY 7

Post the following payroll to the appropriate nominal *(general)* ledger accounts, and balance the control account.

Week 40

Employee	Gross pay $	Pension $	Income tax $	Employees' state benefit $	Net pay $	Employer's pension $	Employer's state benefit $
P Smith	395.00	15.00	57.92	30.85	291.23	15.00	36.71
M Brown	406.25	22.00	64.77	41.33	278.15	15.00	43.82
	801.25	37.00	122.69	72.18	569.38	30.00	80.53

For suggested answers, see the 'Answers' section at the end of the book.

7.2 PAYMENT METHODS

Businesses may use a range of methods to pay their employees as follows:

- cash payment, with an employee receiving their individual pay packet containing their net pay in notes and coins plus payslip each week. This may be appropriate when there are relatively few employees and there is little handling of notes and coins to enable wage packets to be prepared each week, or perhaps if an employee does not have a bank account.

- cheque payment, with an employee receiving a cheque for their net pay plus payslip, each week or month as appropriate. This may be appropriate when there may be some variation in weekly or monthly pay (perhaps due to overtime or bonus payment) for each employee.

- direct or automated payment of the net pay into the individual bank account of an employee each week or month as appropriate, with payslip provided separately. This is appropriate for employers who have a significant number of employees and where a business operates automated and computerised systems and processes.

CONCLUSION

Wages and salaries are often one of the largest items of expenditure for businesses. Payroll is the part of an organisation which deals with wages and salaries.

Wages and salaries are calculated as gross pay less various deductions for income tax, state benefit contributions and other deductions including, perhaps, pensions. Payments are made by BACS, cash, cheque and so on.

Gross pay is calculated in a variety of ways based on hours worked, sometimes including overtime, on the amount of work completed or as a proportion of an annual salary. Bonuses and commissions are sometimes paid as incentives.

As the elements of wages and salaries may be quite complex, it is important that they are correctly documented and authorised. Records as well as the actual pay need to be kept secure and carefully controlled.

Payroll is calculated and payment made by cash or some form of bank transfer. Wages and salaries are, therefore, ultimately paid from the cash book. Nominal *(general)* ledger entries record additional aspects of payroll including deductions.

KEY TERMS

Gross pay – Money due to an employee *before* deductions for income tax and NIC, etc.

Net pay – Money payable to an employee *after* deductions for income tax, NIC, etc.

Payroll – List of employees and the wages or salaries due to each.

Payslip – Document given to each employee giving details of pay and deductions from pay.

State benefit contributions – Amount paid by employees (and possibly the employer) to the state for purposes of social security.

SELF TEST QUESTIONS

Paragraph

1	Define a payroll system.	1
2	What is the difference between gross pay and net pay?	1
3	How is the total cost of wages and salaries to the employer calculated?	1
4	List four deductions from an employee's pay.	1
5	What must an employer do to process the payroll?	2
6	Give two ways of recording hours.	3
7	What is meant by 'piecework'?	3
8	What is the difference between overtime and flexitime?	4
9	Give two examples of when a bonus might be paid.	4
10	What is commission and who gets it?	4
11	How should payroll documentation be authorised?	5
12	Explain the steps to be taken when posting the payroll to the main ledger.	7

FA1: RECORDING FINANCIAL TRANSACTIONS

EXAM-STYLE QUESTIONS

1   An employee works as a fruit-packer and paid according to the number of boxes of fruit packed. By what method of remuneration is the employee paid?

    A   Commission

    B   Paid by the hour

    C   Piecework

    D   Salaried

2   An employee is paid a basic salary of $2,000 for the month. Income tax on the salary is $350 and state benefit contributions amount to $180. The employer also pays state benefit contributions of $210.

    In June the employee is also entitled to a bonus of $100 on which no tax or other deductions are payable.

    How much was the employee's take-home pay for June?

    A $1,260

    B $1,360

    C $1,540

    D $1,570

3   An employee earns a basic wage rate of $5.00 per hour for a 35-hour week and at the rate of time-and-a-half for any additional hours worked. Last week the employee worked 43 hours.

    What is the employee's gross pay for last week?

    A $175

    B $215

    C $235

    D $322.50

4   From which account are wages and salaries paid directly to employees?

    A   Bank

    B   Payroll

    C   Wages and salaries control

    D   Wages and salaries expense

For suggested answers, see the 'Answers' section at the end of the book.

Chapter 12

BANK RECONCILIATIONS

The purpose of this chapter is to explain how the entries in the cash book can be checked against a bank statement, in order to identify and correct any errors or omissions in the cash book. It also explains how this checking process is summarised in a bank reconciliation statement. This chapter covers the syllabus area of bank reconciliations.

CONTENTS

1. General bank services and operation of bank clearing system
2. Function and form of banking documentation
3. Bank reconciliation statement
4. Errors and omissions in the cash book

LEARNING OUTCOMES

At the end of this chapter, you should be able to:

- recognise the need to reconcile the cash book with the bank statement periodically
- identify the main reasons for any discrepancies between the cash book and the bank statement, such as errors, unanticipated receipts and payments and timing differences
- correct cash book errors and/or omissions
- reconcile the corrected cash book balance with the bank statement through adjustments for uncleared and uncredited cheques.

1 GENERAL BANK SERVICES AND OPERATION OF BANK CLEARING SYSTEM

This was covered earlier in the textbook but it will be useful to summarise here.

A business uses the cash book to record every receipt of money into its bank account and every payment from its bank account. In theory, the balance on the account shown in the cash book should be the same as the amount of money that is actually in the bank account. In practice, however, this is not the case, and the cash book balance rarely, if ever, agrees with the amount that is in the bank account according to the bank.

There are several reasons for this.

1.1 CHEQUES, RECEIPTS, ELECTRONIC PAYMENTS, CHARGES AND INTEREST

With cheques and credit transfers, there are timing differences between recording the receipt or payment in the cash book and the actual transfer of money into or out of the bank account.

- **Making payments by cheque.** When a business pays a supplier by cheque, the payment will usually be recorded in the cash book when the cheque is written and sent. The supplier should receive the cheque through the post a day or so later, but might not pay the cheque into the bank immediately. When the cheque is paid in, the transfer of money from the payer's bank account to the payee's bank account does not happen instantly. There is a further delay, usually of two or three days, due to the time it takes for the cheque payment to be 'cleared' through the banking system. Thus, it could take a week or more from the recording of a cheque payment in the business' books to appear in the bank's records.

- **Receiving payments by cheque.** When a business receives a payment by cheque, it should record the receipt in the cash book immediately, and it is good business practice to pay the cheque into the bank as soon as possible (ideally, on the same day). Even so, the payment of money into the bank account will take two or three days, due to the 'clearing' delay and so there will be a further difference between the business' record and the bank's.

- **Dishonoured cheques.** When a customer pays by cheque, the payer's bank might refuse to honour it. When a cheque 'bounces', it is sent back with a message 'refer to drawer', but it can take a few days before this happens. As far as the business is concerned, the money has been received from the customer and entered in the cash book. When it finds out that the cheque has been returned and/or dishonoured, it will have to reflect this in the cash book. In the meantime, both the bank and the business will have different balances due to the timing of the recording of the problem.

- **Receiving payments by credit transfer.** A similar delay occurs when payments are received from customers by credit transfer.

- **Receipts by direct debit, standing order or BACS.** A business might record the transactions in its cash book on the dates that the payments are due. However, if it does this, it will need to check later that the money has actually gone into its bank account. A customer might, for example, cancel a standing order payment. When this occurs, the entry of a cash receipt in the cash book would be wrong. A business might therefore wait for confirmation from the bank that the direct debits and standing order transactions have taken place before recording them in the cash book.

- **Payments by standing order.** A business which makes payments by standing order might record the payments in the cash book on the due payment dates. (The details of the payments can be obtained from the schedule the business should keep.) When a business makes payments by direct debit, however, the amount of the payment can vary each time. For example, if telephone bills are paid by direct debit, the amount payable each time will depend on the cost of the telephone calls. Direct debit payments cannot therefore be recorded in the cash book until the business has received notification, from the supplier or the bank, of the amount paid.

- **Electronic receipts and payments.** Businesses may pay and receive funds electronically, say through BACS. Receipts are particularly difficult to predict as to when they will arrive in the bank account. A business might wait for confirmation from the bank that such transactions have taken place before recording them in the cash book.

- **Bank charges.** Individual customers of banks do not usually pay any bank charges provided they keep their account 'in credit'. For a business bank account, however, a bank charges for its services. Bank charges are deducted from the money in the account, and notified to the business on the next bank statement. Until it receives a bank statement, the business does not know how much the bank charges are and so cannot record them in the cash book. Bank charges are recorded as a cash payment in the cash book when the bank statement is received. The same is true of bank interest paid for, say, loans and overdrafts.

Similarly, if a business has a deposit account and received interest on its bank balance, the amount of interest receivable is not known, and so cannot be recorded, until after a bank statement has been received.

2 FUNCTION AND FORM OF BANKING DOCUMENTATION

Account holders with a bank receive a bank statement at regular intervals, typically every month or even every week. A bank statement shows all the payments and receipts through the account that have been processed by the bank since the previous bank statement.

A bank statement might look something like this:

SouthEast Bank plc
High Street, Borchester BO1 2ER

Account number 22353712

		Paid out $	Paid in $	Balance $	
2 July	Balance b/f			345.00	
3 July	Cheque 23457	100.00		245.00	
5 July	Cheque 23454	278.00		33.00	o/d
6 July	BGC T J Smith		425.00	392.00	
9 July	DD Cheshire Gas	45.00		347.00	
9 July	Bank charges	56.00		291.00	
10 July	BAC Fullaway Limited		230.00	521.00	
11 July	SO BV Properties	400.00		121.00	
12 July	BGC Reach plc		314.00	435.00	
12 July	Cheque 23455	499.00		64.00	o/d
15 July	Balance c/f			64.00	o/d

Notes on the bank statement

1 When a business has money in its bank account, the money is an asset. Assets are shown as a debit balance in the cash at bank account in the nominal *(general)* ledger. To the bank, however, the situation is a 'mirror image' opposite. To the bank, when a customer has money in their account, the bank 'owes' the customer and the customer can withdraw the money at any time. The customer's bank balance is therefore a liability and in the accounting system of the bank, this is recorded as a credit entry in the customer's account. This is why we often speak of 'being in credit' at the bank. We are describing the position from the bank's point of view.

When an account is overdrawn, the business owes money to the bank. In the business' nominal *(general)* ledger account, this is recorded as a credit balance. To the bank, the situation is again the opposite. The customer owes the bank money, and is therefore a receivable of the bank. Receivables are assets, and so to the bank, the overdrawn balance is an asset. In a bank statement, it is normally assumed that the account is in credit. However, if the account is overdrawn, this is shown by o/d (for overdrawn).

2 For each transaction, the bank statement shows the date it was processed by the bank and the money was actually paid into or out of the account. The amount of the receipt or payment is shown, together with the resulting balance on the account.

3 For payments by cheque, the cheque number is shown.

4 Payments and receipts by standing order, direct debit and BACS are usually shown by the letters SO, DD and BAC respectively.

5 Receipts by cheque are shown by the letters BGC or the words 'bank giro credit', together with some description to identify the receipt or the payment.

3 BANK RECONCILIATION STATEMENT

For the reasons explained earlier, the balance on the account shown by the bank statement will rarely be the same as the current balance in the cash book in the nominal *(general)* ledger.

A bank statement is used to check that the cash book details are correct. This is done by checking the details in the bank statement and the details in the cash book, and making sure that they are in agreement with each other. Since the balance in the bank statement and the balance in the cash book are different, this exercise involves checking the difference in the two balances, and making sure that the differences can be properly explained. This is a **bank reconciliation**.

Bank reconciliations are important because they are a check on the accuracy of the cash book.

- If any errors have been made they should be identified and corrected.

- The cash book should be updated to include any receipts or payments that have not yet been recorded, such as standing order and direct debit payments, BACS receipts and bank charges.

ACTIVITY 1

1 Why does a business reconcile its cash book with the bank statement periodically?

   A   It is a statutory requirement.

   B   It speeds up the posting to the accounts.

   C   It is a control measure checking for errors and omissions.

   D   It enables the business to correct mistakes with the accurate bank records.

2 The business bank balance recorded in the cash book is $165.40. Reference to the bank statement shows that a standing order of $10.00 to a supplier has not been recorded in the cash book but that every other item is the same in both the cash book and bank statement. The omitted standing order is then included, updating the cash book.

   What are the balances shown in the cash book bank account and on the bank statement after the updating?

   A   Cash book: Bank $155.40 Cr; Bank statement: Bank $155.40 Dr

   B   Cash book: Bank $155.40 Dr; Bank statement: Bank $155.40 Cr

   C   Cash book: Bank $175.40 Cr; Bank statement: Bank $175.40 Dr

   D   Cash book: Bank $175.40 Dr; Bank statement: Bank $175.40 Cr

For a suggested answer, see the 'Answers' section at the end of the book.

3.1 PREPARING A BANK RECONCILIATION

A bank reconciliation involves several sequential steps.

Step 1

First, if possible **the opening balance on the bank statement and the opening balance in the cash book should be reconciled**. (The two opening balances will be different, for the same reasons that the two closing balances are different!)

This is done by looking for receipts or payments during the period that explain the difference. For example, if the opening balance on the bank statement is $3,000 and the opening balance in the cash book is $4,500, the difference might be explained by a receipt (bank giro credit or BGC) for $1,500 during the period. This might be a receipt that was recorded in the cash book in the previous period, but which was not actually paid in by the bank until the current period. In other words, the difference in the two opening balances should be explained by 'timing differences' between when a payment or receipt was recorded in the cash book and when the payment or receipt was processed by the bank.

Transactions that explain the difference between the two opening balances should be ticked in the bank statement.

These various steps are used in an illustrative example later in the chapter so you can see each step in action.

Step 2

Next, **individual transactions in the cash book should be matched with the same transactions in the bank statement**. If there are matching transactions in the cash book and the bank statement, we don't need to worry about them anymore.

When transactions are matched, it is usual to mark it in both the cash book and the bank statement with a tick.

Step 3

The difference in the two closing balances must be explained by transactions in the bank statement and transactions in the cash book that have not yet been ticked.

There might be some receipts or payments shown in the bank statement that are not yet recorded in the cash book. These could be standing order payments, direct debit payments, BACS transactions or bank charges. **The cash book should be updated to record all these transactions on the date the reconciliation takes place.** No effort should be made to squeeze any items in earlier or to change earlier postings.

For standing orders and direct debits, the schedule of payments or receipts should be checked, to make sure that they have all been made as expected.

When items in the bank statement are entered in the cash book, they should be ticked in the bank statement to show that they have been dealt with.

Step 4

After updating the cash book, there will be a new balance on the cash book, but it is likely to be different from the balance on the bank statement. There will be some items in the cash book that have not been ticked because they do not appear on the bank statement.

These items will be:

- Payments received and entered in the cash book, but not yet appearing on the bank statement because the bank has not yet processed them. These transactions are commonly referred to as **outstanding lodgements**.

- Payments by cheque entered in the cash book but not yet appearing on the bank statement because the bank has not yet processed them. These transactions are termed **unpresented cheques**.

Outstanding lodgements and unpresented cheques should explain the difference between the updated cash book balance and the bank statement balance. These transactions should appear on the next bank statement, and will be used to reconcile the two opening balances when the next bank reconciliation is carried out on receipt of the next bank statement.

Step 5

Prepare a bank reconciliation statement. This is a simple statement that sets out the reasons for the differences between the two closing balances.

Bank reconciliation statement as at [date]		
	$	$
Closing balance in the bank statement		3,451.00
Unpresented cheques		
Cheque 13578	45.00	
Cheque 13580	291.00	
Cheque 13583	138.00	
		(474.00)
		2,977.00
Outstanding lodgements		
Receipt VBF Limited	200.00	
Receipt S Dowding	37.00	
		237.00
Closing balance in the cash book		3,214.00

Study this sample reconciliation carefully, to make sure that you understand why unpresented cheques have been subtracted and outstanding lodgements have been added.

- Unpresented cheques are payments recorded in the cash book but not yet in the bank statement. The cash book balance will therefore be lower than the bank statement balance, by the amount of these payments.

- Outstanding lodgements are receipts recorded in the cash book but not yet in the bank statement. The cash book balance will therefore be higher than the bank statement balance, by the amount of these payments.

3.2 ILLUSTRATIVE EXAMPLE

The following example is quite long, but try to follow carefully the steps in the reconciliation process. It uses a typical computerised accounts format for the cash book.

Shown below is the cash book of Bradley Trading for the week ended 31 May 20X5, together with the bank statement at 31 May 20X5. You are also given a bank reconciliation statement for the week ended 24 May 20X5, and details of bank paying-in slips for the week.

Cash book – Bank

Date 20X5	Details	Reference/ Cheque number	Receipts Debit $	Payments Credit $	Balance $
May					
27	Opening balance				6,194.33
27	Cumnor Ltd		76.93		6,271.26
27	Holmes & Sons		119.11		6,390.37
27	Cash sales		490.68		6,881.05
27	Skipper Ltd	12791		44.80	6,836.25
27	Wessex Water	SO		294.00	6,542.25
27	Hill & Co	12792		117.23	6,425.02
27	GW Rail	12793		87.00	6,338.02
28	Wood House		29.48		6,367.50
28	Cash sales		251.09		6,618.59
28	W R Smith	12794		32.89	6,585.70
28	Binder & Sons	12795		918.20	5,667.50
29	Cash sales		365.70		6,033.20
29	Wills Insurance	DD		750.00	5,283.20
29	GW Rail	12796		111.00	5,172.20
29	Shatter & Co	12797		98.60	5,073.60
30	Temple & Co		48.60		5,122.20
30	Grove Ltd		194.20		5,316.40
30	Cash sales		208.45		5,524.85
30	P W Resistor	12798		59.21	5,465.64
30	Proffice	12799		115.34	5,350.30
31	Cash sales		441.92		5,792.22
31	Scroll & Sons	12800		643.12	5,149.10
31	GW Rail	12801		17.90	5,131.20
31	Trapp Garage	12802		33.23	5,097.97

BANK RECONCILIATIONS : CHAPTER 12

Statement of Account

NATIONAL WESTERN BANK   Sheet number 27
66 The Long Way
Bristol BS2 4NY

Account number 17742001

Date	Details	Payments	Receipts	Balance
20X5				
27 May	Balance b/f			6,347.33
27 May	SO: Wessex Water	294.00		6,053.33
28 May	12790	153.00		5,900.33
29 May	Wills Insurance	750.00		5,150.33
30 May	3729: CC		686.72	
	12791	44.80		5,792.25
31 May	3730: CC		280.57	
	12793	87.00		
	Bank charges	14.00		5,971.82

SO standing order   DD direct debit
CC cash and/or cheques   O/D Overdrawn

Bank reconciliation statement for the week ended 24 May 20X5

	$
Balance as per bank statement	6,347.33
Unpresented cheques:	
12790	153.00
Balance as per cash book	6,194.33

Paying-in slip details

27 May 20X5

Cheques:	$
Cumnor Ltd	76.93
Holmes & Sons	119.11
	196.04
Cash sales	490.68
	686.72

28 May 20X5

Cheques:	$
Wood House	29.48
Cash sales	251.09
	280.57

29 May 20X5

	$
Cash sales	365.70

30 May 20X5
Cheques:

	$
Temple & Co	48.60
Grove Ltd	194.20
	242.80
Cash sales	208.45
	451.25

31 May 20X5

	$
Cash sales	441.92

Required:

Task 1

Compare the cash book entries and the bank statement details, ticking off each item in turn as it is correctly matched.

Task 2

Update the cash book to include the transactions shown in the bank statement that are not yet in the cash book.

Task 3

Calculate the closing balance on the cash book as at 31 May.

Task 4

Prepare a bank reconciliation statement as at 31 May.

3.3 SOLUTION

Tasks 1, 2 and 3

First of all, reconcile the opening balance on the bank statement with the opening balance in the cash book. We know from the previous week's bank statement that the difference is due to an unpresented cheque, number 12790. This is shown in the bank statement for the current week, so we can tick off this item in the bank statement.

Next we need to match and tick off the corresponding transactions during the week that appear in both the cash book and the bank statement. Here, the receipts need to be checked first of all by comparing the paying in slips with the bank statement, and then identifying the receipts in the cash book.

The only item in the bank statement that is not in the cash book is the $14 for bank charges. This should be entered in the cash book. The nominal *(general)* ledger entries to record bank charges will be: Debit Bank charges account; Credit Cash at bank account.

Having entered the bank charges, the bank account can be 'balanced off'.

Statement of Account

NATIONAL WESTERN BANK   Sheet number 27

66 The Long Way

Bristol BS2 4NY

Account number 17742001

Date	Details	Payments	Receipts	Balance
20X5				
27 May	Balance b/fwd			6,347.33
27 May	SO: Wessex Water	✓ 294.00		6,053.33
28 May	12790	✓ 153.00		5,900.33
29 May	Wills Insurance	✓ 750.00		5,150.33
30 May	3729: CC		✓ 686.72	
	12791	✓ 44.80		5,792.25
31 May	3730: CC		✓ 280.57	
	12793	✓ 87.00		
	Bank charges	14.00		5,971.82

SO standing order   DD direct debit

CC cash and/or cheques   O/D Overdrawn

Paying-in slip details

27 May 20X5

Cheques:	$	
Cumnor Ltd	76.93	✓
Holmes & Sons	119.11	✓
	196.04	
Cash sales	490.68	✓
	686.72	✓

28 May 20X5

Cheques:	$	
Wood House	29.48	✓
Cash sales	251.09	✓
	280.57	✓

29 May 20X5

	$
Cash sales	365.70

30 May 20X5
Cheques:

	$
Temple & Co	48.60
Grove Ltd	194.20
	242.80
Cash sales	208.45
	451.25

31 May 20X5

	$
Cash sales	441.92

Cash book – Bank

Date	Details	Reference/ Cheque number	Receipts Debit	Payments Credit	Balance
20X5			$	$	$
May					
27	Opening balance				6,194.33
27	Cumnor Ltd	✓	76.93		6,271.26
27	Holmes & Sons	✓	119.11		6,390.37
27	Cash sales	✓	490.68		6,881.05
27	Skipper Ltd	✓12791		44.80	6,836.25
27	Wessex Water	✓ SO		294.00	6,542.25
27	Hill & Co	12792		117.23	6,425.02
27	GW Rail	✓ 12793		87.00	6,338.02
28	Wood House	✓	29.48		6,367.50
28	Cash sales	✓	251.09		6,618.59
28	W R Smith	12794		32.89	6,585.70
28	Binder & Sons	12795		918.20	5,667.50
29	Cash sales		365.70		6,033.20
29	Wills Insurance	✓ DD		750.00	5,283.20
29	GW Rail	12796		111.00	5,172.20
29	Shatter & Co	12797		98.60	5,073.60
30	Temple & Co		48.60		5,122.20
30	Grove Ltd		194.20		5,316.40
30	Cash sales		208.45		5,524.85
30	P W Resistor	12798		59.21	5,465.64
30	Proffice	12799		115.34	5,350.30
31	Cash sales		441.92		5,792.22
31	Scroll & Sons	12800		643.12	5,149.10
31	GW Rail	12801		17.90	5,131.20
31	Trapp Garage	12802		33.23	5,097.97
31	**Bank charges**		**–**	**14.00**	**5,083.97**
	Column totals		**8,420.49**	**3,336.52**	

Task 4

Bank reconciliation statement
for the week ended 31 May 20X5

	$	$
Balance as per bank statement		5,971.82
Unpresented cheques:		
12792	117.23	
12794	32.89	
12795	918.20	
12796	111.00	
12797	98.60	
12798	59.21	
12799	115.34	
12800	643.12	
12801	17.90	
12802	33.23	
		(2,146.72)
Outstanding lodgements		
29 May	365.70	
30 May	451.25	
31 May	441.92	
		1,258.87
Balance as per cash book		5,083.97

4 ERRORS AND OMISSIONS IN THE CASH BOOK

The main reason for comparing the cash book and the bank statement is to identify any errors or omissions in the cash book, and to put them right. Where the reason for an error or omission is not clear, the problem should be brought to the attention of the appropriate person in the organisation.

4.1 CASH BOOK ERRORS

Errors might occur in the cash book because a cash receipt or payment is entered as the wrong amount. This should be discovered when comparing the cash book with the bank statement.

When an error occurs, the cash book should be amended, and the correct amount entered.

4.2 CASH BOOK OMISSIONS

It is also likely that some items in the bank statement might not yet have been entered in the cash book. For example, bank charges, standing order payments and direct debit payments (or receipts) and receipts by BACS transfer might not have been entered in the cash book. The cash book should be updated and these entries recorded.

Occasionally, a transaction might have been omitted from the cash book by mistake. The bank statement should provide enough information to track down the omitted item, and enter it correctly in the cash book.

ACTIVITY 2

Suppose additional receipts of $300 are shown on the bank statement but do not appear in the cash book.

The receipts comprise $200, dividend receipts from owning shares in another company and $100, interest received from the bank on current account balances.

How would these omissions be dealt with?

For a suggested answer, see the 'Answers' section at the end of the book.

ACTIVITY 3

Given below is the cash book for an organisation and its most recent bank statement, together with the previous bank reconciliation statement as at the end of March 20X7.

Bank reconciliation statement as at 31 March 20X7

	$	
Balance as per bank statement	65.60	
Unpresented cheques:		
144680	100.00	
Balance as per cash book	34.40	OD

Cash book – Bank

Date	Details	Reference/ Cheque number	Receipts Debit	Payments Credit	Balance
20X7			$	$	$
April					
1	Opening balance			34.40	34.40 Cr
1	Turner Ltd		110.29		75.89
1	Collins & Co	144682		41.28	34.61
1	Long Ltd	144683		25.67	8.94
1	Jimmy Dino	144684		171.93	162.99 Cr
2	Danton & Co	144685		231.71	394.70 Cr
3	Water rates	SO		98.20	492.90 Cr
4	Simone Ltd		338.97		153.93 Cr
5	M Smith		10.15		143.78 Cr
10	Grossman	144686		319.06	462.84 Cr
19	Butch Ltd	144687		86.21	549.05 Cr
21	Grape & Co		430.06		118.99 Cr
22	Mothball Ltd		341.36		222.37
25	Betty Ltd	144688		89.24	133.13
28	South Ltd	144689		303.13	170.00 Cr
29	Oak & Sons	144690		475.00	645.00 Cr
30	ABC & Co		549.19		95.81 Cr
30	P D Plant	144691		61.35	157.16 Cr

BANK RECONCILIATIONS : CHAPTER 12

Statement of Account

Larry Bank
5 High Cross
Edinburgh EH1 2WS

Sheet number 247

Account number 34267115

Date	Details	Payments	Receipts	Balance
20X7				
1 April	Balance b/f			65.60
2 April	BGC: 47619		110.29	175.89
3 April	SO: Tartan Water	98.20		77.69
4 April	144684	171.93		
	144682	41.28		
	144680	100.00		235.52 O/D
7 April	144683	25.67		
	BGC: 47620		338.97	77.78
8 April	BGC: 47621		10.15	
	144685	231.71		143.78 O/D
13 April	144686	319.06		462.84 O/D
24 April	BGC: 47622		430.06	
	144687	86.21		118.99 O/D
25 April	BGC: 47623		150.00	
	BGC: 47624		341.36	372.37
30 April	Bank interest		3.40	
	Bank charges	27.50		
	Balance c/f			348.27

SO standing order DD direct debit
BGC bank giro credit O/D Overdrawn

Task 1

Reconcile the opening balances on the bank statement and in the cash book. Then compare all the entries in the bank statement with the entries in the cash book, and tick off the matching items.

Task 2

Identify any errors and other discrepancies. Explain how the BGC item dated 25 April for $150.00 would be dealt with.

Task 3

Correct any errors you find in the cash book, and enter any transactions that have so far been omitted from the cash book.

FA1: RECORDING FINANCIAL TRANSACTIONS

Task 4

Balance off the cash book (which also acts as the cash at bank account in the main ledger). Show the balance carried down on 30 April 20X7 and the balance brought down as at 1 May.

Task 5

Prepare a bank reconciliation statement as at 30 April.

For a suggested answer, see the 'Answers' section at the end of the book.

CONCLUSION

Bank reconciliations are used to compare the bank account as recorded in the business' ledger account against the bank's records of the bank account. The reconciliation highlights any discrepancies such as errors and omissions. These are investigated and any necessary corrections made in the business bank account. If an error has been made by the bank, then the business communicates with its bankers.

Once the cash book has been updated, the bank reconciliation statement is drawn up to reconcile the closing balances in the cash book and the bank statement. It is usually necessary to include any unpresented cheques and outstanding lodgements in this statement.

KEY TERMS

Bank reconciliation statement – Statement reconciling the balance of the cash book, bank account, and the bank statement.

SELF TEST QUESTIONS

		Paragraph
1	What information appears on a bank statement?	2
2	What are outstanding lodgements?	3
3	What are unpresented cheques?	3
4	What is the general format of a bank reconciliation statement?	3

BANK RECONCILIATIONS : CHAPTER 12

EXAM-STYLE QUESTIONS

1   After checking a business cashbook against the bank statement, which of the following items could require an entry in the cashbook?

    (i)   Bank charges

    (ii)   A cheque from a customer, which was dishonoured

    (iii)   Cheque not presented

    (iv)   Deposits not credited

    (v)   Credit transfer entered in bank statement

    (vi)   Standing order entered in bank statement

    A   (i), (ii), (v) and (vi)

    B   (iii) and (iv)

    C   (i), (iii), (iv) and (vi)

    D   (iii), (iv), (v) and (vi)

2   The balance on the bank account for a business at the end of May was a debit of $269.36. It was then discovered on receipt of the bank statement that a standing order for $40 had been omitted from the cash book and the bank interest on a deposit account of $15.20 had been credited to the business account.

    What is the correct balance on the bank account at the end of May?

    A $324.56

    B $294.16

    C $244.56

    D $214.16

3   The bank reconciliation statement of High Ltd shows outstanding lodgements of $2,300 and outstanding cheques to suppliers of $2,000. The company's bank account in the ledger shows a debit balance at $12,500.

    What balance does the bank statement of High Ltd show?

    A $12,200

    B $12,500

    C $12,800

    D $16,800

4   ABC's accounting records show that its business bank account is overdrawn by $1,000. The balance on the bank statement is only $500 overdrawn.

Assuming there are no errors in the bank statement, what could account for the difference?

A   Bank charges of $500 charged by the bank

B   A decrease in bank overdraft of $500

C   Unpresented cheques posted to suppliers totalling $500

D $500 paid into the bank has yet to be added to the balance

For suggested answers, see the 'Answers' section at the end of the book.

Chapter 13

CONTROL ACCOUNTS

The purpose of this chapter is to explain how balances in the control accounts and the payables' and receivables' ledgers can be checked against each other and reconciled, and how these 'control total' checks can be used to identify errors in the ledgers. The chapter then goes on to consider what type of errors might be found by control account reconciliations, and how these errors are corrected. This chapter covers the syllabus area for control accounts.

CONTENTS

1 Control accounts

2 Receivables' ledger control account

3 Payables' ledger control account

4 Discrepancies on reconciliation of the receivables' ledger control account

5 Payables' ledger control account reconciliation

LEARNING OUTCOMES

At the end of this chapter, you should be able to:

- understand the need for internal checks

- complete postings to control accounts and understand the link to books of prime entry

- understand the need for individual receivables' and payables' accounts and understand the link to books of prime entry

- explain the purposes of control accounts:
    - as a check on the accuracy of entries in the individual accounts
    - to establish a total of receivables and payables at any time
    - to identify errors in the completion of the day book and in posting the totals from books of prime entry
    - as an internal check

- perform a basic control account reconciliation

- identify errors which would be highlighted by performing a control account reconciliation.

1 CONTROL ACCOUNTS

1.1 THE USE OF CONTROL ACCOUNTS FOR CHECKING

- **Totals** – A control account is a 'totals' account. For example, a receivables' ledger control account is used to record the total value of transactions with credit customers.

- **Check on accuracy** – An important benefit of using control accounts, as the name 'control' might suggest, is that they can be used to check the accuracy of the accounting records and prevent errors from remaining unidentified. This can be achieved, for example, by comparing the information in books of prime entry with the information in either the receivables' or payables' ledger.

- **Identifying errors** – Control accounts can be used to carry out reconciliations, in order to check the accuracy of, for example, day books or the ledgers.

Control accounts are a useful internal check on transactions.

2 RECEIVABLES' LEDGER CONTROL ACCOUNT

The receivables' ledger control account is used to record transactions with credit customers.

2.1 PREPARING THE CONTROL ACCOUNT

Transactions affecting credit customers are:

- sales invoices
- credit notes for sales returns
- payments by customers.

These transactions are entered in books of prime entry, and then posted to the ledgers.

- The day books and cash book are subtotalled and the **total** value of transactions with credit customers is posted to accounts (including the receivables' ledger control account) in the nominal *(general)* ledger.

- The value of individual transactions is posted to the individual memorandum accounts of the credit customers in the receivables' ledger.

Amounts posted to the receivables' ledger control account are part of the double entry bookkeeping system. A proforma receivables' ledger control account is presented below for reference. Note that the amounts posted from the sales day book and the sales returns day book are the gross amounts inclusive of sales tax as these amounts must be paid by the credit customer to the business in due course.

Receivables' ledger control account

Ref		$	Ref		$
	Balance b/d	X			
SDB	Sales/Sales tax	X	SRDB	Sales returns/ Sales tax	X
			CB	Bank	X
			JNL	Irrecoverable debts	X
				Contra with PLCA	X
				Balance c/d	X
		X			X
	Balance b/d	X			

Amounts posted to the individual memorandum accounts in the receivables' ledger are not part of the double entry system. The receivables' ledger is a 'memorandum' record comprising entries from the books of prime entry and is used to break the balance shown in the receivables' ledger control account down into amounts due from individual customers.

At regular intervals, perhaps weekly or monthly, the total for sales on credit according to the sales day book is recorded:

Dr Receivables' ledger control

Cr Sales

Cr Sales tax

Immediately afterwards, the individual sales listed in the sales day book are charged to the appropriate memorandum accounts in the receivables' ledger.

In a similar vein, receipts recorded in the cash book are totalled and recorded:

Dr Bank/cash

Cr Receivables' ledger control account.

Again, the individual customers' memorandum accounts are updated with the detail of the separate transactions.

Both the receivables' ledger control account and the receivables' ledger accounts (i.e. the memorandum accounts) contain similar information, albeit in a different format. The control account shows the total owed by all customers and the receivables' ledger shows the total owed by each individual customer (making it possible to arrive at the total owed by adding the individual balances together). This provides the opportunity to reconcile totals from the books of prime entry for sales against the receivables' ledger balances.

Example

Tyson is a supplier of widgets and has six regular credit customers. At the start of July, none of these customers owed any money. Transactions with these customers during July were recorded in the books of prime entry as follows:

Sales day book Folio 36

Date July	Details	Invoice	Total $	Sales tax $	Net $
1	Able	3031	864.00	144.00	720.00
1	Baker	3032	960.00	160.00	800.00
1	Charlie	3033	264.00	44.00	220.00
1	Delta	3034	494.40	82.40	412.00
1	Echo	3035	756.00	126.00	630.00
1	Foxtrot	3036	960.00	160,00	800.00
8	Baker	3037	480.00	80.00	400.00
8	Delta	3038	153.60	25.60	128.00
8	Able	3039	378.00	63.00	315.00
8	Foxtrot	3040	720.00	120.00	600.00
			6,030.00	1,005.00	5,025.00

Sales returns day book Folio 4

Date July	Details	Credit note	Total $	Sales tax $	Net $
10	Charlie	C23	168.00	28.00	140.00
10	Delta	C24	96.00	16.00	80.00
			264.00	44.00	220.00

Cash book (extract, receipts) Folio CB41

Date July		Bank $
20	Able	864.00
20	Delta	398.40
20	Echo	765.75
20	Foxtrot	1,680.00
		3,708.15

The totals of these transactions would be posted to the receivables' ledger control account as follows:

Receivables' ledger control account

Ref		$	Ref		$
SDB36	Sales/Sales tax	6,030.00	SRDB4	Sales returns/ Sales tax	264.00
			CB41	Bank	3,708.15

The above are the totals from the books of prime entry.

Sales account

Ref		$	Ref		$
			SDB36	Total sales	5,025.00

Sales tax account

Ref		$	Ref		$
SRDB4	Total sales returns	44.00	SBD36	Total sales	1,005.00

Sales returns account

Ref		$	Ref		$
SRDB4	Total sales returns	220.00			

In addition to posting the totals to the nominal *(general)* ledger, the individual transaction details are posted to the receivables' ledger accounts, as follows:

Able account

Ref		$	Ref		$
SDB36	Sales Inv 3031	864.00	CB41	Bank	864.00
SDB36	Sales Inv 3039	378.00			

Baker account

Ref		$	Ref		$
SDB36	Sales Inv 3032	960.00			
SDB36	Sales Inv 3037	480.00			

Charlie account

Ref		$	Ref		$
SDB36	Sales Inv 3033	264.00	SRDB4	Sales returns Credit note 23	168.00

Delta account

Ref		$	Ref		$
SDB36	Sales Inv 3034	494.40	SRDB4	Sales returns Credit note 24	96.00
SDB36	Sales Inv 3038	153.60	CB41	Bank	398.40

Echo account

Ref		$	Ref		$
SDB36	Sales Inv 3035	756.00	CB41	Bank	765.75

Foxtrot account

Ref		$	Ref		$
SDB36	Sales Inv 3036	960.00	CB41	Bank	1,680.00
SDB36	Sales Inv 3040	720.00			

The entries in the individual memorandum accounts in the receivables' ledger should in total match the entries in the receivables' ledger control account. In addition, the balance on the control account should equal the sum of the balances on the individual memorandum accounts. After all, the control account balance is meant to represent the total amount owed to the business by its credit customers.

The ledger accounts can then be balanced and reconciled. The reconciliation of the control account total balance to the total of the balances of the individual customer accounts is shown below.

You might prefer to attempt this exercise yourself before reading on as this is fairly straightforward.

2.2 RECEIVABLES' LEDGER CONTROL ACCOUNT RECONCILIATION

For each account, the closing balance is the difference between the total debits and the total credits.

Receivables' ledger control account

Ref		$	Ref		$
SDB36	Sales/Sales tax	6,030.00	SRDB4	Sales returns/ Sales tax	264.00
			CB41	Bank	3,708.15
				Balance c/d	2,057.85
		6,030.00			6,030.00
	Balance b/d	2,057.85			

Able account

Ref		$	Ref		$
SDB36	Sales Inv 3031	864.00	CB41	Bank	864.00
SDB36	Sales Inv 3039	378.00		Balance c/d	378.00
		1,242.00			1,242.00
	Balance b/d	378.00			

Baker account

Ref		$	Ref		$
SDB36	Sales Inv 3032	960.00			
SDB36	Sales Inv 3037	480.00		Balance c/d	1,440.00
		1,440.00			1,440.00
	Balance b/d	1,440.00			

Charlie account

Ref		$	Ref		$
SDB36	Sales Inv 3033	264.00	SRDB4	Sales returns Credit note C23	168.00
				Balance c/d	96.00
		264.00			264.00
	Balance b/d	96.00			

Delta account

Ref		$	Ref		$
SDB36	Sales Inv 3034	494.40	SRDB4	Sales returns Credit note C24	96.00
SDB36	Sales Inv 3038	153.60	CB41	Bank	398.40
				Balance c/d	153.60
		648.00			648.00
	Balance b/d	153.60			

Echo account

Ref		$	Ref		$
SDB36	Sales Inv 3035	756.00	CB41	Bank	765.75
	Balance c/d	9.75			
		765.75			765.75
				Balance b/d	9.75

There is a credit balance on Echo's account. This is because Echo has paid more than the amount of the debt, and the business therefore owes money to Echo. Echo's account is 'in credit'.

Foxtrot account

Ref		$	Ref		$
SDB36	Sales Inv 3036	960.00	CB41	Bank	1,680.00
SDB36	Sales Inv 3040	720.00			
		1,680.00			1,680.00

Reconciliation statement

Individual account balances	$
Able	378.00
Baker	1,440.00
Charlie	96.00
Delta	153.60
Echo (minus value, because credit balance)	(9.75)
Foxtrot	0
Total of individual account balances	2,057.85
Balance on control account	2,057.85

Here, the total of the individual receivables' ledger account balances agrees with the balance on the control account. This should be expected, so there appears to be no error.

ACTIVITY 1

The receivables' ledger control account for an organisation for the week commencing 1 January is given below. The organisation has five credit customers and the individual ledger accounts for these customers are also shown below.

Reconcile the total on the control account with the total of the individual customer's accounts in the receivables' ledger.

Receivables' ledger control account

			$			$
1 Jan	Bal b/d		2,508.24	5 Jan	Bank	936.02
5 Jan	Sales	SDB	883.26			

Receivables' ledger

Gunn & Co

			$			$
1 Jan	Bal b/d		114.50	5 Jan	Bank	114.50
5 Jan	Sales	SDB	77.40			

Jane & Sons

			$			$
1 Jan	Bal b/d		624.76	5 Jan	Bank	517.03
5 Jan	Sales	SDB	337.49			

Lees Ltd

			$			$
1 Jan	Bal b/d		253.91	5 Jan	Bank	150.00
5 Jan	Sales	SDB	271.76			

Rupert Ltd

			$			$
1 Jan	Bal b/d		95.60	5 Jan	Bank	64.50
5 Jan	Sales	SDB	47.40			

J T Mumby

			$			$
1 Jan	Bal b/d		1,419.47	5 Jan	Bank	89.99
5 Jan	Sales	SDB	149.21			

For a suggested answer, see the 'Answers' section at the end of the book.

3 PAYABLES' LEDGER CONTROL ACCOUNT

The payables' ledger control account is used to record transactions with credit suppliers.

3.1 PREPARING THE CONTROL ACCOUNT

A similar reconciliation can be carried out between the payables' ledger control account with the individual supplier accounts in the payables' ledger. The purpose of the reconciliation is the same – to check that there appear to be no errors, or to discover any errors that might have been made.

Transactions with suppliers are recorded in both the books of prime entry and the payables' ledger. The transactions relating to credit purchases from suppliers are:

- purchase invoices

- credit notes for purchase returns

- payments to suppliers

- settlement discounts taken from suppliers (discounts received).

These transactions are entered in books of prime entry, and then posted to the ledgers.

- The day books and cash book are subtotalled and the total value of transactions with suppliers is posted to accounts (including the payables' ledger control account) in the nominal *(general)* ledger.

- The value of individual transactions is posted to the individual accounts of the suppliers in the payables' ledger.

FA1: RECORDING FINANCIAL TRANSACTIONS

A proforma payables' ledger control account is presented below for reference. Note that the amounts posted from the purchases day book and the purchase returns day book are the gross amounts inclusive of sales tax as these amounts must be paid to the supplier in due course.

Payables' ledger control account

Ref		$	Ref		$
				Balance b/d	X
PRD	Purchase returns/ Sales tax	X	PDB	Purchases/ Sales tax	X
CB	Bank	X			
CB	Discounts received	X			
	Contra with RLCA	X			
	Balance c/d	X			
		X			X
			Balance b/d		X

3.2 PAYABLES' LEDGER CONTROL ACCOUNT RECONCILIATION

Reconciliation is very similar to the approach with the receivables' ledger control account and the receivables' ledger.

The total of all the amounts posted to the payables' ledger accounts should add up to the same as the amount posted to the payables' ledger control account.

It also means that **at any time, the balance on the control account should be equal to the total of all the balances on the individual supplier accounts in the payables' ledger**.

Example

Bobble Co is a car parts distributor. It has six credit suppliers. At the beginning of July, Bobble Co did not owe any of these suppliers money. Transactions with these suppliers during July were recorded in the books of prime entry as follows:

Purchases day book

Date	Details	Invoice	Total	Sales tax	Net
July			$	$	$
1	Ace	6031	1,728.00	288.00	1,440.00
1	Bays	6032	1,920.00	320.00	1,600.00
1	Campo	6033	528.00	88.00	440.00
1	Dans	6034	988.80	164.80	824.00
1	Eastern	6035	1,512.00	252.00	1,260.00
1	Field	6036	1,920.00	320.00	1,600.00
8	Bays	6037	960.00	160.00	800.00
8	Dans	6038	307.20	51.20	256.00
8	Ace	6039	756.00	126.00	630.00
8	Fields	6040	1,440.00	240.00	1,200.00
			12,060.00	2,010.00	10,050.00

Purchase returns day book
Internal
Folio 4

Date	Details	Credit note ref	Total $	Sales tax $	Net $
July					
10	Campo	C23	336.00	56.00	280.00
10	Dans	C24	192.00	32.00	160.00
			528.00	88.00	440.00

Cash book (extract, payments)
Folio CB52

Date		Bank $	Discounts received $
July			
20	Ace	1,728.00	
20	Dans	796.80	
20	Eastern	1,531.50	
20	Fields	3,276.00	84.00
		7,332.30	84.00

The totals of these transactions would be posted to the payables' ledger control account as follows:

Payables' ledger control account

Ref		$	Ref		$
PRD B5	Purchase returns/ Sales tax	528.00	PDB 50	Purchases/ Sales tax	12,060.00
CB52	Bank	7,332.30			
CB52	Discounts received	84.00			

The above are the totals from the books of prime entry.

Purchases account

Ref		$	Ref		$
PDB 50	Total purchases	10,050			

Sales tax account

Ref		$	Ref		$
SRDB4	Total purchases	2,010.00	SBD36	Total purchase returns	88.00

Purchase returns account

Ref		$	Ref		$
			PRD B5	Total purchase returns	440

Discounts received account

Ref		$	Ref		$
			CB52	Payables' ledger control account	84.00

Discounts are posted from the cash book above which, of course, includes the ledger account for the bank account.

In addition to posting the totals to the nominal *(general)* ledger, the individual transaction details are posted to the memorandum accounts in the payables' ledger, as follows:

Ace account

Ref		$	Ref		$
CB52	Bank	1,728.00	PDB50	Purch Inv 6031	1,728.00
			PDB50	Purch Inv 6039	756.00

Bays account

Ref		$	Ref		$
			PDB50	Purch Inv 6032	1,920.00
			PDB50	Purch Inv 6037	960.00

Campo account

Ref		$	Ref		$
PRDB5	Purch returns Credit note 23	336.00	PDB50	Purch Inv 6033	528.00

Dans account

Ref		$	Ref		$
SRDB4	Purch returns Credit note 24	192.00	PDB50	Purch Inv 6034	988.80
CB52	Bank	796.80	PDB50	Purch Inv 6038	307.20

Eastern account

Ref		$	Ref		$
CB52	Bank	1,531.50	PDB50	Purch Inv 6035	1,512.00

Fields account

Ref		$	Ref		$
CB52	Bank	3,276.00	PDB50	Purch Inv 6036	1,920.00
CB52	Discount received	84.00	PDB50	Purch Inv 6040	1,440.00

The entries in the individual memorandum accounts in the payables' ledger should in total match the entries in the payables' ledger control account. In addition, the balance on the control account should equal the sum of the balances on the individual memorandum accounts. After all, the control account balance is meant to represent the total amount owed by the business by its credit suppliers.

CONTROL ACCOUNTS : CHAPTER 13

The ledger accounts can then be balanced and reconciled. The reconciliation of the control account total balance to the total of the balances of the individual supplier accounts is shown below.

You might prefer to attempt this exercise yourself before reading on as this is straightforward, and has already been done for the receivables' ledger.

3.3 PAYABLES' LEDGER CONTROL ACCOUNT RECONCILIATION

For each account, the closing balance is the difference between the total debits and the total credits.

Payables' ledger control account

Ref		$	Ref		$
PRD B5	Purchase returns/ Sales tax	528.00	PDB 50	Purchases/ Sales tax	12,060.00
CB52	Bank	7,332.30			
CB52	Discounts received	84.00			
	Balance c/d	4,115.70			
		12,060.00			12,060.00
				Balance b/d	4,115.70

Ace account

Ref		$	Ref		$
CB52	Bank	1,728.00	PDB50	Purch Inv 6031	1,728.00
	Balance c/d	756.00	PDB50	Purch Inv 6039	756.00
		2,484.00			2,484.00
				Balance b/d	756.00

Bays account

Ref		$	Ref		$
			PDB50	Purch Inv 6032	1,920.00
	Balance c/d	2,880.00	PDB50	Sales Inv 6037	960.00
		2,880.00			2,880.00
				Balance b/d	2,880.00

Campo account

Ref		$	Ref		$
PRDB5	Purch returns Credit note 23	336.00	PDB50	Purch Inv 6033	528.00
	Balance c/d	192.00			
		528.00			528.00
				Balance b/d	192.00

Dans account

Ref		$	Ref		$
SRDB4	Sales returns Credit note 24	192.00	PDB50	Purch Inv 6034	988.80
CB52	Bank	796.80	PDB50	Purch Inv 6038	307.20
	Balance c/d	307.20			
		1,296.00			1,296.00
				Balance b/d	307.20

Eastern account

Ref		$	Ref		$
CB52	Bank	1,531.50	PDB50	Purch Inv 6035	1,512.00
				Balance c/d	19.50
		1,531.50			1,531.50
	Balance b/d	19.50			

There is a debit balance on Echo's account. This is because Bobble Co has paid more than the amount of the debt, and Eastern therefore owes money to Bobble Co. Eastern's account is 'in debit'.

Fields account

Ref		$	Ref		$
CB52	Bank	3,276.00	PDB50	Purch Inv 6036	1,920.00
CB52	Discount received	84.00	PDB50	Purch Inv 6040	1,440.00
		3,360.00			3,360.00

Reconciliation statement

Individual account balances	$
Ace	756.00
Bays	2,880.00
Campo	192.00
Dans	307.20
Eastern (minus value, because debit balance)	(19.50)
Fields	0
Total of individual account balances	4,115.70
Balance on control account	4,115.70
Discrepancy	0

Here, the total of the individual payables' ledger account balances agrees with the balance on the control account. This should be expected, so there appears to be no error.

Try the following activity using the same approach.

ACTIVITY 2

The Porter Emporium is a retailer of household furniture. It purchases goods for resale from five suppliers. The following transactions for the month of April were recorded:

Purchase day book   Folio PDB50

Date April	Details	Internal invoice ref	Total $	Sales tax $	Net $
6	Piper	780	675.60	112.60	563.00
6	Romeo	781	741.60	123.60	618.00
7	Sierra	782	517.20	86.20	431.00
10	Tango	783	1,080.00	180.00	900.00
14	North Electric	784	225.12	37.52	187.60
14	Victor	785	428.40	71.40	357.00
20	Romeo	786	225.60	37.60	188.00
28	Tango	787	960.00	160.00	800.00
28	Victor	788	633.60	105.60	528.00
30	Sierra	789	489.60	81.60	408.00
			5,976.72	996.12	4,980.60

Note: The other analysis columns are not shown. However, all the transactions relate to the purchase of goods for resale, with the exception of the invoice from North Electric, which is an invoice for electricity charges.

Purchase returns day book   **Folio PRDB8**

Date	Details	Internal credit note ref	Total	Sales tax	Net
April			$	$	$
10	Piper	C66	288.00	48.00	240.00
14	Sierra	C67	360.00	60.00	300.00
			648.00	108.00	540.00

Cash book (extract, payments)   **Folio CB65**

Date		Bank	Discounts received
April		$	$
29	Tango, cheque 257453	2,008.00	32.00
29	Piper, cheque 257454	387.60	
29	Romeo, cheque 257455	225.60	
29	North Electric, cheque 257456	228.12	–
		2,849.32	32.00

Tasks

1   Post the transaction totals to the relevant ledger accounts.

2   Post the transactions with individual suppliers to the individual supplier accounts in the payables' ledger. You should assume that North Electric has an account in this ledger.

3   Draw up and balance the payables' ledger control account.

4   Calculate the balances on each supplier account in the payables' ledger.

5   Reconcile the total balance on the control account with the total of the balances on the individual supplier accounts, and identify any discrepancy.

For a suggested answer, see the 'Answers' section at the end of the book.

4 DISCREPANCIES ON RECONCILIATION OF THE RECEIVABLES' LEDGER CONTROL ACCOUNT

If everything is accounted for correctly, there should never be any discrepancy when reconciling a receivables' ledger control account balance with the total of the balances in the receivables' ledger. Similarly, unless there has been an error, there should never be any discrepancy when reconciling a payables' ledger control account balance with the total of the balances in the payables' ledger.

Unfortunately, errors can occur, especially in manual accounting systems. This will normally be due to errors in the postings from a day book or the cash book.

In a computerised system each transaction is input only once and both the receivables' ledger and the receivables' ledger control account are updated using the same information, so there should be fewer arithmetical errors. Discrepancies should not arise unless there is an error in the bookkeeping program.

When the receivables' ledger control account balance is reconciled with the total of the balances on the individual customer accounts in the receivables' ledger, discrepancies might arise for any of the following reasons.

- There is an arithmetic error adding up a column total in the sales day book, the sales returns day book or the cash (receipts) book columns.

- There might be an incorrect posting. For example, the total value of invoices might be $3,478.90, but this might be copied incorrectly into the sales account and receivables' ledger control account as $3,748.90.

- An error might occur preparing the listing of the individual customer account balances. In other words, there might be an error in the reconciliation process, with a customer account balance copied into the list incorrectly, or possibly omitted from the list altogether. Another mistake might be to treat any credit balance on a customer account as a debit balance.

Some of these types of error will be considered below in more detail, together with the accounting treatment necessary to amend them.

4.1 ERROR IN THE DAY BOOK TOTALS

An error may occur when adding up the totals in a day book or the cash book.

For example, suppose the sales day book is undercast by $300. In other words, the sales day book total is $300 less than it should be due to a casting (addition) error.

This casting error will affect the total in the sales day book. This figure is taken to the receivables' ledger control account which will be $300 short. The addition error does not affect the postings to the individual accounts in the receivables' ledger which should be correct and the error will not be discovered until the reconciliation takes place.

As a result, the balance in the control account will be $300 lower than the total of the individual memorandum account balances.

The existence of an error should be found by a discrepancy of $300 when making a control account reconciliation. When the discrepancy is found, someone has to go back to the ledgers and the day books and try to identify where the error has occurred and what has caused it. When the cause of the error has been identified, it should be corrected.

To correct an error, it is important to establish first of all exactly what has been done wrong. When a day book has been totalled incorrectly, is the error in just one column of the day book, or has the same mistake been made in more than one column? In the example above, we would need to establish whether it is just the total column for invoices issued that is $300 too low, or whether the total in the sales column is also undercast by $300.

Let's assume here that both the column for the total amount of invoices sent out and the total for sales have been undercast by $300. To correct this error, we would need to increase total receivables in the receivables' ledger control account and increase total sales in the sales account.

4.2 INCORRECT RECEIVABLES' LEDGER ENTRY: TRANSPOSITION ERROR OR COPYING ERROR

An error might occur when transferring (posting) the details of an individual transaction in the day book to the customer account in the receivables' ledger.

For example, suppose a transposition error occurs and an invoice for $890 to J Longshaw has been entered correctly in the day book but posted to J Longshaw's account in the receivables' ledger as $980.

In this case, there should be no error in the total figures in the day book, and so the receivables' ledger control account total should be correct. The error will be in J Longshaw's account in the receivables' ledger, and the balance on J Longshaw's account will be $90 ($980 – $890) too high.

The existence of an error will be found by a control account reconciliation. When the cause of the error has been detected, the corrective action required is to reduce the amount owing by J Longshaw in the receivables' ledger. This will reduce the total of the account balances in the receivables' ledger. This error would be corrected by:

    Cr   J Longshaw account in the receivables' ledger $90

4.3 INCORRECT RECEIVABLES' LEDGER ENTRY: POSTING TO THE WRONG SIDE OF AN ACCOUNT

Another type of error in posting is to record a debit item as a credit or a credit item as a debit. Entering a transaction on the wrong side of an account will make the account balance incorrect, by double the size of the amount posted. For example, suppose that there is a sales return by customer D Flint for $150, which is correctly entered in the sales returns day book. However, when posting the details to D Flint's account in the receivables' ledger, the sales return might be debited to the account instead of credited. If this happens, the balance on the account will be $300 (2 × $150) more than it should be.

Here is another example.

The receipt of a cheque for $250 from H Gregg was correctly recorded in the cash (receipts) book, but was debited to H Gregg's account in the receivables' ledger instead of credited.

The error here is in the posting of the receivables' ledger. A debit of $250 was recorded in H Gregg's account instead of a credit of $250. Therefore the debit of $250 will need to be cancelled by a credit, and the credit of $250 put through, all in H Gregg's account in the receivables' ledger. The correcting entry is therefore

    Credit H Gregg account in the receivables' ledger $500

The total of all the balances on the individual customer accounts in the receivables' ledger will be reduced by $500 when the correction is made.

4.4 CUSTOMER OMITTED FROM LIST OF ACCOUNT BALANCES

Another error that could occur in a control account reconciliation is to miss out a customer's account balance from the list of account balances in the receivables' ledger. When this happens, the control account balance and the total of the individual account balances will fail to agree.

For example, in doing a control account reconciliation, a balance of $700 owing from J Hudson might be omitted from the list of balances from the receivables' ledger. The accounting entries in the ledgers are all correct, and the error is simply to miss out an account from the list of balances.

The corrective action is to add the omitted balance to the list of receivables' ledger account balances, increasing the total of balances in the receivables' ledger by $700.

4.5 THE MECHANICS OF A RECEIVABLES' LEDGER CONTROL ACCOUNT RECONCILIATION

When errors are found in a control account reconciliation, the reasons for the errors have to be found and the errors corrected. A statement can then be produced to show that, after correcting the errors, the control account total now agrees with the total of the individual balances in the receivables' ledger accounts.

One way of doing this is as follows.

- When errors are found in the receivables' ledger control account, the necessary corrections to the account should be made, and an amended (corrected) control account balance should be obtained.

- When errors occur in the total of individual account balances, the adjustments to the list of balances are shown on the control account reconciliation.

An example of a reconciliation is given below, using illustrative figures:

Reconciliation of receivables' ledger control account and list of receivables' ledger balances at 31 March 20X5

	$
Total list of balances originally extracted from receivables' ledger	582,980
Errors in the receivables' ledger balances	
Less: Transposition error on posting to T White account	(900)
Add: Balance omitted, B Harris	2,810
Adjusted list of receivables' ledger balances and receivables' ledger control account balance	584,890

ACTIVITY 3

The receivables' ledger control account for a business at the end of the month of April showed a balance of $3,765.20. However, the list of balances of individual customer accounts in the receivables' ledger totalled $4,137.20.

The difference was investigated and the following errors were discovered.

- The sales day book was undercast by $300.

- A credit note for $97.50 had been recorded in the sales returns day book as $79.50 but correctly recorded as $97.50 in the sales ledger account of the individual customer.

- An individual customer account balance of $674.90 was listed in the total listing as $764.90.

Correct the control account and then reconcile the corrected balance to the list of receivables' ledger account balances.

For a suggested answer, see the 'Answers' section at the end of the book.

4.6 CORRECTING ERRORS: THE JOURNAL

If amendments to control accounts are identified as being needed as a result of undertaking a reconciliation of control accounts and the ledgers, the journal should be used as the book of prime entry to record the adjustments.

If a member of the accounts department staff is to put through an amendment to the ledger, this amendment must be authorised by a responsible official and then clearly noted.

Each entry in the transfer journal is known as a **journal entry**. The format of a journal entry was shown in a previous chapter.

Each journal entry should show the following information:

- a consecutive transaction number (for example, J001, J002, J003 and so on)
- the date of the journal entry
- the name and code of the ledger account(s) to be debited
- the name and code of the ledger account(s) to be credited
- the amounts to be debited and credited
- a brief description of the reason for the journal entry
- a proper authorisation of the journal entry.

Example

The sales day book has been undercast for the week ended 10 May by $500. As a result, the posting to both the sales account and a customer's account has been $500 less than it should have been. This error must be amended and the instruction is to be given in the journal.

The ledger codes for the sales account and the receivables' ledger control account are ML05 and ML37 respectively.

The previous journal entry was numbered 336.

The required journal entry to amend the error is:

Entry number	Date	Account name	Folio ref	Debit $	Credit $
337	10 May	Receivables' ledger control	ML37	500.00	
		Sales	ML05		500.00

Correction of undercast of the Sales Day Book for the week ended 10 May.

5 PAYABLES' LEDGER CONTROL ACCOUNT RECONCILIATION

A receivables' ledger control account reconciliation can reveal the existence of discrepancies between the control account balance and the total of the balances on the individual customer accounts in the receivables' ledger. In the same way, a purchase or payables' ledger control account reconciliation can reveal the existence of discrepancies between the control account balance and the total of the balances on the individual supplier accounts in the payables' ledger.

If the two totals do not agree, there must be one or more errors. The discrepancy should therefore be investigated to find the cause of the error, and the error should be corrected.

5.1 POSSIBLE ERRORS

The main types of error that are likely to occur in a manual accounting system are as follows:

- Errors in totalling the day books columns. A column in the purchase day book, purchase returns day book or cash (payments) book might be added up incorrectly.

- Incorrect posting, either to the nominal *(general)* ledger accounts or to the payables' ledger accounts, or an amount could be incorrectly transferred to the memorandum accounts. A number may simply be copied incorrectly when the posting is made. Alternatively, a posting might be made incorrectly as a debit entry in an account when it should be a credit entry, or might be made as a credit entry when it should be a debit entry.

- A discount received might be omitted from either the payables' ledger control account or an individual supplier's account in the payables' ledger.

- Errors made when listing the individual supplier account balances.

Each of these types of error will be considered in more detail below together with the accounting treatment required to amend them.

5.2 INCORRECT TOTALS IN A DAY BOOK OR THE CASH BOOK

There might be errors in totalling a column of figures in the purchase day book or the purchase returns day book. When this happens, an incorrect posting will be made to the nominal *(general)* ledger, and the error will affect the payables' ledger control account.

Suppose that the total column of the purchase day book is overcast by $100. The business is not registered for sales tax, and this total figure is used to post to both the payables' control account and purchases account in the nominal *(general)* ledger. This means that the balances in both the purchases account and the payables' control account are too high by $100.

The correcting entry to put the double entry right would therefore be:

Dr	Payables' ledger control account		$100	
	Cr	Purchases		$100

FA1: RECORDING FINANCIAL TRANSACTIONS

5.3 ERROR IN POSTING INVOICE DETAILS

An error might be made in posting to the payables' ledger if the amount of an invoice (or a credit note or a payment) is copied incorrectly. For example, the value of invoices from suppliers might be posted correctly to the day book, totalled correctly, meaning that the control account balance is correct, but an error might be made posting the value of an individual invoice to the supplier's account in the payables' ledger. The existence of this error would be revealed by a control account reconciliation and, when the cause of the error is discovered, it should be corrected.

For example, suppose that an invoice from a supplier, Fenwick Ltd, has been entered in the purchase day book at its correct amount of $247.56. However, when it was posted to Fenwick Ltd's account in the payables' ledger, the amount posted was $274.56. The total in the purchase day book and the postings to the nominal *(general)* ledger were correct.

The only error is in the individual supplier's account which has been credited with $27.00 too much. The correcting entry is to **debit** Fenwick Ltd's account with $27.00 in the payables' ledger. This will correct the double entry.

5.4 INCORRECT ENTRY IN THE PAYABLES' LEDGER

Another type of error is to record a transaction as a debit instead of a credit entry, or as a credit instead of a debit entry. When this happens, the balance on the account affected will be incorrect by twice the amount posted.

For example, suppose a payment of $400 to a supplier C Long was incorrectly entered as a credit entry in C Long's personal account in the payables' ledger.

A payment should in fact be a debit entry in the individual supplier's account, not a credit entry. The C Long account will have an incorrect balance that is too high by $800 (2 × $400). The following entries are required to correct this:

- a debit entry of $400 in order to cancel out the incorrect credit entry

- a further debit entry of $400, being the correct entry for the transaction.

Therefore there should be a total debit entry of $800.

The error is in the payables' ledger only, and does not affect the control account or the day book.

5.5 DISCOUNT RECEIVED OMITTED

A discount received might not be posted to either the payables' ledger control account or, alternatively, to the account of an individual supplier in the payables' ledger. If either situation occurs, there will be a discrepancy in the control account reconciliation.

For example, suppose that the discount received column total in the cash (payments) book for a particular week was $93.50. The discounts received were correctly posted to the individual supplier accounts in the payables' ledger, but the total for discounts received was not posted to the nominal *(general)* ledger.

Both the payables' ledger control account and the discounts received account will be wrong.

The correcting entry to put the double entry right would therefore be:

Dr	Payables' ledger control account		$93.50	
	Cr	Discounts received		$93.50

KAPLAN PUBLISHING

CONTROL ACCOUNTS : CHAPTER 13

5.6 SUPPLIER ACCOUNT BALANCE OMITTED

When the listing of individual supplier balances is prepared for a control account reconciliation, a balance might be omitted. This will cause a discrepancy when the reconciliation is carried out. When the error is found, the missing balance should be added to the total of individual supplier account balances.

5.7 PAYABLES' LEDGER CONTROL ACCOUNT RECONCILIATION

In principle, a payables' ledger control account reconciliation is performed in the same way as a receivables' control account reconciliation. A similar reconciliation statement can be produced.

Example

Rodin Co extracts a list of balances from its payables' ledger on 30 June 20X5 and arrives at a total figure of $1,535. The balance on the payables' ledger control account is $1,885. Further examination of the accounting records reveals the following errors.

(a) The purchase day book total for the month was overcast by $80.

(b) An invoice for $1,458 from Ball Ltd was posted to the individual account in the payables' ledger as $1,548.

(c) An invoice for $156 from T E Ltd was debited to the supplier's account in the payables' ledger.

(d) A balance of $48 owing to Radcliffe had been omitted from the list of balances.

Task

Show how the payables' ledger control account is adjusted for these errors and produce a reconciliation of the payables' ledger control account and the list of payables' ledger balances.

Solution

Step 1 Read through the errors and decide how each one affects the control account and/or the list of balances.

(a) The purchase day book total is $80 too high. Consequently, the entries made to the purchases account and payables' ledger control account in the nominal *(general)* ledger are also $80 too high. The corrective action needed is to reverse $80 of purchases by debiting the payables' ledger control account and crediting the purchases account.

    Dr PLCA $80
      Cr Purchases $80

This error will not affect the individual supplier accounts.

(b) The amount posted to the account of Ball Ltd is $90 too much. The error should be corrected by debiting Ball Ltd's account by $90 in the payables' ledger.

    Dr Ball Ltd account $90

KAPLAN PUBLISHING

(c) The invoice from T E Ltd should have been credited, not debited, and as a result the balance on T E Ltd's account is too low by $312 (2 × $156). The error should be corrected by crediting T E Ltd's account by $312 in the payables' ledger.

(d) Add the omitted supplier's balance of $48 to the list of balances from the payables' ledger.

Step 2 Open up a control account and bring down the balance given, before adjustment. This is a credit balance, because payables' are a liability. Put through any adjustments noted in Step 1 that affect the control account, and find the amended balance.

Payables' ledger control account

	$		$
Purchases	80	Balance b/d	1,885
Amended balance c/d	1,805		
	1,885		1,805
		Amended balance b/d	1,805

Step 3 Produce a control account reconciliation. Start with the total of the list of balances originally extracted, put through any adjustments noted in step 1 which affect the list of balances and find the amended total which should agree with the new control account balance.

Rodin Co

Reconciliation of payables' control account and list of payables' ledger balances at 30 June 20X5

	$
Total list of balances originally extracted from payables' ledger	1,535
Errors in the payables' ledger balances	
Less: Reduction in balance on Ball Ltd account	(90)
Add: Increase in balance on T E Ltd account	312
Add: Account omitted from the list: Radcliffe	48
Adjusted total of payables' ledger balances and payables' ledger control account balance	1,805

ACTIVITY 4

The balance on the payables' ledger control account for an organisation is $24,461.92 at the end of March 20X4. The total of the list of individual supplier accounts at the same date was $21,836.27.

When the difference was investigated, the following errors were identified:

- The cash (payments) book total in the 'payables' column for a particular day, of $1,400.37, had not been posted to the nominal *(general)* ledger account.

- Discounts received for the period totalling $853.20 had not been posted to the nominal *(general)* ledger.

- A supplier balance of $372.08 was omitted from the list of balances.

Produce a payables' ledger control account reconciliation statement.

For a suggested answer, see the 'Answers' section at the end of the book.

CONCLUSION

In this chapter we have looked at how the different types of control account are used as a check on how effectively the business is maintaining its accounting records. We have also seen how the journal is used to process and document amendments, and how discrepancies in the control account reconciliations must be resolved or referred to the appropriate person.

A business should perform regular internal checks on all of the assets such as receivables' that it holds, to verify the accuracy of its accounting records. Similarly, there should be regular checks on the accuracy of the total debts owed to suppliers. Checking through reconciliations is an important 'internal control' within any accounting system.

KEY TERMS

Payables' ledger – Often referred to as the 'list of payables" or 'memorandum' this is the summary of amounts owed to individual suppliers. This does not form part of the double entry nominal ledger system.

Payables' ledger control account – This is where the double entries relating to amounts owed to suppliers are made. This forms part of the nominal ledger.

Receivables' ledger – Often referred to as the 'list of receivables' or 'memorandum' this is the summary of amounts owed by individual customers. This does not form part of the double entry nominal ledger system.

Receivables' ledger control account – This is where the double entries relating to amounts due from customers are made. This forms part of the nominal ledger.

FA1: RECORDING FINANCIAL TRANSACTIONS

SELF TEST QUESTIONS

		Paragraph
1	What are the purposes of control accounts?	1
2	Which two figures are compared in a receivables' control account reconciliation? Why might these two figures not agree?	2, 4
3	What two figures are compared in a payables' control account reconciliation? Why might these two figures not agree?	3, 5

EXAM-STYLE QUESTIONS

1   The balance on an organisation's receivables' ledger control account was $3,172. It was then discovered that the sales day book for the period had been undercast by $30 and discounts received of $40 had not been posted at all. What is the correct balance in the control account?

   A $3,202

   B $3,242

   C $3,102

   D $3,272

2   In a receivables' ledger control account, which of the following lists is composed only of items which would appear on the credit side of that account?

   A   Cash received from customers, sales returns, irrecoverable debts written off, contras against amounts due to suppliers in the payables' ledger control

   B   Sales, cash refunds to customers, irrecoverable debts written off

   C   Cash received from customers, interest charged on overdue accounts, irrecoverable debts written off, increase in allowance for receivables

   D   Sales, cash refunds to customers, interest charged on overdue accounts, contras against amounts due to suppliers in the payables' ledger control

3   The total of the payables' ledger control account should equal the total of:

   A   The receivables' ledger control account

   B   The individual suppliers' balances

   C   The individual customers' balances

   D   Credit purchases

For suggested answers, see the 'Answers' section at the end of the book.

Chapter 14

THE TRIAL BALANCE

The purpose of this chapter is to demonstrate the drafting of an initial trial balance as a check on the accuracy of the accounts in the nominal (general) ledger. The trial balance highlights arithmetical errors and the chapter explains how to identify and correct these. There are some errors which the trial balance cannot identify and these are explained. This chapter covers the syllabus area for the trial balance.

CONTENTS

1. Initial trial balance
2. Identification of errors
3. Suspense account

LEARNING OUTCOMES

At the end of this chapter, you should be able to:

- compile an initial trial balance
- identify errors which would be highlighted by the extraction of a trial balance
- identify and explain different types of errors:
    - errors of commission
    - errors of principle
    - errors of omission
    - single entry
    - transposition errors
    - casting errors
- distinguish between compensating and non-compensating errors
- explain the function of a suspense account
- correct errors using journal entries.

1 INITIAL TRIAL BALANCE

In a manual accounting system, accounts are 'ruled off' or 'balanced off' from time to time, possibly at each month end, and the balance on the account is carried forward as an opening balance at the start of the new period.

- A debit balance on an account is shown as an opening balance brought down on the debit side of the account.

- Similarly, if there is a credit balance on an account, the opening balance brought down at the start of a period should be on the credit side of the account.

When preparing a trial balance, remember that account balances in the ledger are:

	Balance
Assets	**Debit**
Liabilities	**Credit**
Capital	**Credit**
Drawings (withdrawals of capital)	Debit
Income (sales)	**Credit**
Discounts received, purchases returns	Credit
Expenses	**Debit**
Wages, heat and light, sales returns, irrecoverable debts	Debit

Within the nominal *(general)* ledger, all transactions are recorded as a debit entry in one account and a credit entry in another account, and the total value of debit entries and credit entries must always be the same. If they are not, something has gone wrong.

A trial balance checks whether the ledger accounts are correct, insofar as the total debit balances and total credit balances are equal.

The format of a trial balance is a list of accounts with a column for debit balances and a column for credit balances.

Trial balance at (date)

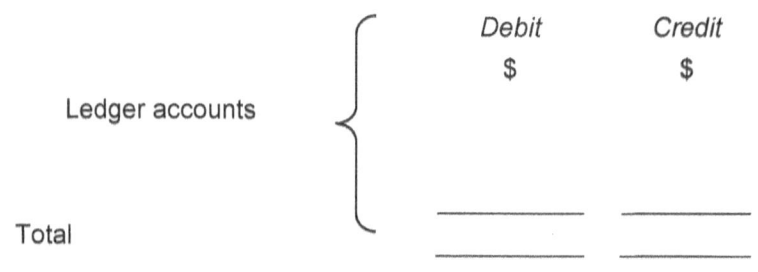

	Debit	*Credit*
	$	$
Ledger accounts		
Total		

A trial balance is a memorandum listing of all the nominal *(general)* ledger account balances.

1.1 THE REASON FOR A TRIAL BALANCE

There are three main reasons for preparing a trial balance.

- At the end of the financial year, a trial balance is used as a starting point for preparing a statement of comprehensive income and a statement of financial position. This is something you will study in the future.

- A trial balance shows the current balances on all the asset, liability, capital, income and expense accounts. This can provide useful information to management.

- In a manual accounting system, preparing a trial balance is a procedure for identifying certain types of errors in the accounts. If the total of debit balances and the total of credit balances are not equal, there must have been a mistake (or several mistakes) in entering transactions in the ledger accounts. When the existence of an error has been identified, the next step is to carry out an investigation, and try to find where the double entry mistake or mistakes have happened. When the error has been found, it should be corrected.

Errors in recording transactions as double entry items in the ledger are much more likely to occur in a manual accounting system than in a computerised accounting system. This is because in a computerised system, most transactions are recorded as double entry items automatically, without the risk of human error.

Each organisation will have its own procedures for preparing a trial balance, and some will produce a trial balance more frequently than others. An organisation with a manual accounting system, however, should produce a trial balance fairly frequently, say monthly or weekly, so that if any errors have been made, their existence will be identified sooner rather than later, and tracking down the cause of the error or errors should be a quicker process.

1.2 PRODUCING AN INITIAL TRIAL BALANCE

An initial trial balance is a trial balance produced by listing all the accounts in the ledger with their debit or credit balances. It is referred to as an 'initial' trial balance because:

- if the total debits and total credits are not equal, the initial trial balance will have to be corrected

- a trial balance is used to prepare a statement of comprehensive income and a statement of financial position and in this process, an 'extended' trial balance is prepared.

There are two stages in preparing an initial trial balance.

Step 1 Balance off all the accounts in the nominal *(general)* ledger.

Step 2 List all the accounts in the ledger, with their debit or credit balance, and add up the total debit balances and the total credit balances.

Remember that the trial balance includes only the accounts within the double entry system. It does not include memorandum accounts in the receivables or payables ledger, for example.

Example

If you think you understand the procedure for preparing an initial trial balance, you might like to attempt preparing your own solution to this example before you read the explanation provided.

Below are the ledger accounts of Avylon as at 31 December 20X4.

Required:

Balance the accounts, bring down the balances (as opening balances brought forward) and show all the balances in a trial balance.

Bank

Date	Details	$	Date	Details	$
	Capital	1,000		Motor car	400
	Sales	300		Purchases	200
	K Long	100		S Stone	200
	Loan	600		Drawings	75
				Rent	40
				Insurance	30

Capital

Date	Details	$	Date	Details	$
				Bank	1,000

Motor car

Date	Details	$	Date	Details	$
	Bank	400			

Purchases

Date	Details	$	Date	Details	$
	Bank	200			
	S Stone	400			

Sales

Date	Details	$	Date	Details	$
				Bank	300
				K Long	250

Payable – S Stone

Date	Details	$	Date	Details	$
	Bank	200		Purchases	400

Receivable – K Long

Date	Details	$	Date	Details	$
	Sales	250		Bank	100

Drawings

Date	Details	$	Date	Details	$
	Bank	75			

Rent

Date	Details	$	Date	Details	$
	Bank	40			

Loan

Date	Details	$	Date	Details	$
				Bank	600

Insurance

Date	Details	$	Date	Details	$
	Bank	30			

Solution

Step 1 Balance each account and bring down the balances.

Bank

Date	Details	$	Date	Details	$
	Capital	1,000		Motor car	400
	Sales	300		Purchases	200
	K Long	100		S Stone	200
	Loan	600		Drawings	75
				Rent	40
				Insurance	30
				Balance c/d	1,055
		2,000			2,000
	Balance b/d	1,055			

Capital

Date	Details	$	Date	Details	$
				Bank	1,000

Motor car

Date	Details	$	Date	Details	$
	Bank	400			

Purchases

Date	Details	$	Date	Details	$
	Bank	200			
	S Stone	400		Balance c/d	600
		600			600
	Balance b/d	600			

Sales

Date	Details	$	Date	Details	$
				Bank	300
	Balance c/d	550		K Long	250
		550			550
				Balance b/d	550

Payable – S Stone

Date	Details	$	Date	Details	$
	Bank	200		Purchases	400
	Balance c/d	200			
		400			400
				Balance b/d	200

Receivable – K Long

Date	Details	$	Date	Details	$
	Sales	250		Bank	100
				Balance c/d	150
		250			250
	Balance b/d	150			

Drawings

Date	Details	$	Date	Details	$
	Bank	75			

Rent

Date	Details	$	Date	Details	$
	Bank	40			

Loan

Date	Details	$	Date	Details	$
				Bank	600

Insurance

Date	Details	$	Date	Details	$
	Bank	30			

Tutorial note: Accounts with only a single entry in them do not need to be balanced off as this one entry is the balance on the account.

Step 2 Prepare the trial balance showing each of the balances in the ledger accounts.

Avylon
Trial balance as at 31 December 20X4

Account	Debit $	Credit $
Bank	1,055	
Capital		1,000
Motor car	400	
Purchases	600	
Sales		550
Payable – S Stone		200
Receivable – K Long	150	
Drawings	75	
Rent	40	
Loan		600
Insurance	30	
	2,350	2,350

The total debit balances and the total credit balances are the same, $2,350. It therefore appears that the double entry accounting has been consistently carried out.

ACTIVITY 1

The following are the ledger accounts of a business for an accounting period.

Tasks

1. Balance each of the accounts.
2. Then draw up a trial balance.

Bank

Date	Details	$	Date	Details	$
	Capital	10,000		Van	2,400
	Loan	5,000		Purchases	700
	Sales	600		Expenses	200
	A Singh	1,200		K James	400
				Drawings	400

Capital

Date	Details	$	Date	Details	$
				Bank	10,000

Loan

Date	Details	$	Date	Details	$
				Bank	5,000

Van

Date	Details	$	Date	Details	$
	Bank	2,400			

Purchases

Date	Details	$	Date	Details	$
	Bank	700			
	K James	400			
	K James	1,600			

K James

Date	Details	$	Date	Details	$
	Bank	400		Purchases	400
				Purchases	1,600

Sales

Date	Details	$	Date	Details	$
				Bank	600
				A Singh	1,200
				T Edwards	1,400
				A Singh	650

A Singh

Date	Details	$	Date	Details	$
	Sales	1,200		Bank	1,200
	Sales	650			

T Edwards

Date	Details	$	Date	Details	$
	Sales	1,400			

Expenses

Date	Details	$	Date	Details	$
	Bank	200			

Drawings account

Date	Details	$	Date	Details	$
	Bank	400			

For a suggested answer, see the 'Answers' section at the end of the book.

2 IDENTIFICATION OF ERRORS

From time to time in a manual accounting system, the total debits and total credits in a trial balance may be different. Whenever this happens, there must be an error, or possibly several errors, causing the imbalance.

The error could be caused by:

- A mistake in balancing off the ledger accounts, and calculating a closing balance incorrectly.

- A mistake in drafting the trial balance. An account balance could have been omitted from the list of accounts in the trial balance, or an account could have been included twice. Another type of mistake is to put a balance in the wrong column, showing a debit balance as a credit or a credit balance as a debit.

- A mistake in recording transactions in the ledger accounts. These are the errors that an initial trial balance is used to identify.

2.1 ERRORS IN THE ACCOUNT BALANCES OR PREPARING THE TRIAL BALANCE

Before starting to look for errors in the ledger accounting records, a check should be carried out to make sure that the account balances have been calculated correctly and that the trial balance has been prepared correctly.

ACTIVITY 2

The trial balance below does not balance.

Trial balance as at [date]

Account	Debit $	Credit $
Motor vehicles		25,800
Bank	16,600	
L Hamilton – receivable	45,100	
K Jackson – payable		23,200
Capital		47,000
Loans		8,000
Sales	41,100	
Purchases	21,400	
Expenses	4,300	
Drawings		5,000
Petty cash		200
	128,500	109,200

You have been asked to check for errors in the calculation of account balances and in the preparation of the trial balance itself. On checking the ledger account balances, you find that the bank account and the payable account for K Jackson have been balanced off as follows:

Bank

Date	Details	$	Date	Details	$
	Opening balance b/d	5,700		K Jackson	1,200
	L Hamilton	14,200		Motor car	14,700
	Sales	800		Purchases	300
	T Brown	20,100		K Jackson	12,500
	Loan	3,000		Drawings	5,000
	F Abdul	11,800		Expenses	4,300
				Balance c/d	16,600
		55,600			55,600
	Balance b/d	16,600			

K Jackson

Date	Details	$	Date	Details	$
	Bank	1,200		Opening balance b/d	15,600
	Bank	12,500		Purchases	8,950
	Closing balance c/d	23,200		Purchases	12,450
		36,900			36,900
				Opening balance b/d	23,200

Tasks

1   Check the account balances for bank and K Jackson and make any necessary corrections.

2   Prepare a correct trial balance.

For a suggested answer, see the 'Answers' section at the end of the book.

2.2 ERRORS IDENTIFIED BY THE TRIAL BALANCE

If the failure of a trial balance to 'balance' is not the result of errors in calculating account balances or preparing the trial balance itself, the error or errors must be somewhere in the accounting records in the ledger accounts.

Somehow, transactions must have been recorded in such a way that the debit entry for the transaction was not matched by a credit entry. One option is for only one part of the double entry to be posted, say Dr $100 but not the other part. This is called an **error of single entry**.

The following are examples of errors which could be revealed by a trial balance.

Example

Transactions are recorded incorrectly, with different amounts on the debit side and the credit side of the ledger accounts.

For example, total purchases in the purchases day book are $30,760, and this total is posted as $30,760 to the purchases account but as $37,060 in total to the payables ledger control account. (Sales tax is ignored here, for simplicity.)

When this type of error happens, total debits and total credits are different, and there will be an imbalance in the trial balance.

Example

A transaction is recorded twice as a debit entry or twice as a credit entry, instead of being recorded as a debit in one account and a credit in another.

For example, sales returns from customers are recorded by mistake with a credit entry in the sales returns account. As a result, the returns would be recorded as:

Credit: Receivables ledger control account

Credit: Sales returns account

FA1: RECORDING FINANCIAL TRANSACTIONS

Similarly, purchases returns to suppliers are recorded by mistake with a debit entry in sales returns, so that instead of:

Debit: Payables ledger control account

Credit: Purchases returns

We have instead:

Debit: Payables ledger control *account*

Debit: Sales returns

Here, there is an incorrect entry in the wrong account.

These errors cause an imbalance between total debits and total credits, and so the trial balance will not balance.

ACTIVITY 3

1   Which of the following items would appear on opposite sides of a trial balance?

   A   Capital and sales

   B   Purchases and discounts received

   C   Inventory and expenses

   D   Motor vehicles and cash

2   Which of the following would be identified as an error by a trial balance?

   A   Overstating the balance on the receivables ledger control account and the payables ledger control account by $100

   B   Omitting an invoice which had fallen behind a filing cabinet from the books of accounts

   C   Recording a cash purchase in cash and inventory accounts

   D   Recording $100 commission received as commission paid

For a suggested answer, see the 'Answers' section at the end of the book.

2.3 ERRORS NOT IDENTIFIED BY THE TRIAL BALANCE

The trial balance identifies errors involving differences in posting double entry transactions. There are errors, as identified in the last activity, which the trial balance does not show. The errors which are not disclosed by the trial balance are categorised as follows:

- **Error of commission**

    This is where the correct amount is entered in the right class of account but the wrong account. For example, a business pays $100 for stationery supplies and posts the following entry to the ledger:

    Dr   Motor expenses $100

    Cr   Bank $100

The debit entry has been made to an expense account. However it is the wrong expense ledger account. The entry should have been as follows:

Dr   Stationery $100

Cr   Bank $100

Although they are not part of the double entry system, errors of commission are commonly found in the memorandum accounts in the receivables and payables ledgers. Suppose a customer, Ken Lines, bought goods for $105 but the following transaction was posted to the accounts of the supplier:

Dr   Kat Lymes $105

Cr   Sales $105

This is an error of commission which needs to be corrected by the following journal entry:

Dr   Ken Lines $105

Cr   Kat Lymes $105

Kat Lymes debited in error for a sale to Ken Lines

- **Error of principle**

    Such an error occurs when an entry has been made in the incorrect 'class of accounts'.

    Example

    The cost of repairs to a van might have been recorded as:

    Dr Vans account

    Cr Bank account.

    It should be recorded as

    Dr Motor vehicles repairs account

    Cr Bank account.

    So there has been a debit to the motor vehicles repairs account (an expense account) and not to the vans account (an asset account). However, the error has not mixed up debits and credits, and so will not cause total debits and total credits to differ.

- **Error of omission**

    An example of this was given in the last activity in the case of the omitted invoice. Both sides of the double entry have been omitted. Again the trial balance does not show this.

    Example

    The purchase of a computer on credit is not recorded at all.

    If a transaction has been omitted entirely, there has been no debit entry and no credit entry in the ledger accounts. An omission of this kind will not cause an imbalance between debits and credits.

- **Transposition error**

  A transposition involves putting numbers in the wrong order, 142 instead of 124 for example. If this occurs on both debit and credit sides of the double entry then there is no impact on the trial balance. This is a difficult error to identify and is best avoiding initially by not recording the debit and credit aspect of a single transaction at one time. However, you will recognise that this is exactly what occurs in computerised accounting. Careful checking is needed when using computers to avoid this.

- **Compensating error**

  One error cancels out another. Rent is understated by $40. Heat and light is overstated by $40. Both are debits balances in the trial balance so cancel out.

- **Error of original entry**

  The original transaction is entered incorrectly in the books of account. For example, a handwritten invoice for $150.00 is received. It is difficult to read and it is recorded in the day book, the purchases account and the payable's account as $130.00. An error such as this may not come to light until the supplier asks why only $130.00 has been paid for a debt of $150.00.

- **Complete reversal of entries**

  A debit is entered as a credit. For example, a purchase is made and an invoice is received from the supplier. Because it has been issued by the supplier it says 'sales invoice' on the invoice. An inexperienced bookkeeper enters it as a sale and creates a receivable account for the supplier (who should be a payable).

ACTIVITY 4

1   A purchase of goods has been posted to motor vehicles account. What kind of error is this?

    A   Error of commission

    B   Compensating error

    C   Error of principle

    D   Transposition error

2   Which of the following indicates a complete reversal of entries?

    A   Dr Sales; Cr Bank

    B   Dr Purchases; Cr Cash

    C   An invoice for $50 has not been posted to the books of account

    D   Recording $100 discount in the cash book and discount received account but not the payables ledger control account

For a suggested answer, see the 'Answers' section at the end of the book.

Errors which are either revealed or not revealed by the trial balance need to be corrected and this takes place using the journal. Where one side of the trial balance does not equate with the other, a suspense account is commonly used too.

Note that it is good practice to extract a trial balance after any errors identified have been corrected.

3 SUSPENSE ACCOUNT

When there is an imbalance between total debits and total credits in the initial trial balance, the failure of the trial balance to 'balance' should be reported and there should be established procedures within the organisation for investigating and correcting the errors.

The first step is to open a special account in the ledger called a suspense account.

The account should be opened by entering a balance in the account, such that if the suspense account is added to the trial balance, total debits and total credits will be equal.

Example

A draft initial trial balance has been prepared, and total debits are $145,600 and total credits are $127,100.

The calculation of the account balances and the trial balance itself are checked, but no errors are found in the preparation of the trial balance. The error or errors are therefore somewhere in the ledger accounting entries.

A suspense account should therefore be opened. Total debits exceed total credits by $18,500 ($145,600 – $127,100). The opening balance in the suspense account should therefore be a **credit** balance of $18,500, to make total debits and total credits equal.

Suspense

Date	Details	$	Date	Details	$
				Opening balance	18,500

ACTIVITY 5

You have prepared a draft initial trial balance, with total debits of $267,109 and total credits of $295,133.

The calculation of the account balances and the trial balance itself are checked, but no errors were found in the preparation of the trial balance. The error or errors are therefore somewhere in the ledger accounting entries.

As the first step in the process of identifying and correcting the errors, open up a suspense account.

For a suggested answer, see the 'Answers' section at the end of the book.

3.1 INVESTIGATING THE ERRORS

The balance on a suspense account is the amount by which total debit balances and total credit balances on the ledger accounts are different. It therefore represents the effect of one or more errors where debit entries and credit entries have not matched each other.

The next step is to identify the reasons for the errors, and having identified the errors, put them right.

- The process of looking for the errors involves going back through all the records of accounting transactions posted to the ledger since the previous trial balance was prepared, looking for errors that have been made. This can be a very long and time-consuming process. This is why it is usually a good idea to prepare a trial balance regularly. If an imbalance occurs, there will not be so many transactions to check, since the error must have occurred since the previous trial balance was checked and verified.

- Although the search is for mistakes where the debit entry and the credit entry for a transaction have not matched each other, the checking process could reveal other errors too, that have not resulted in a mismatch between debits and credits. If any such errors are found, these should be corrected too, although the correction will not affect the suspense account.

3.2 CORRECTING ERRORS

Most errors, when found, are corrected by recording a double entry adjustment in the ledger accounts.

- When an error is a cause of an imbalance between total debits and total credits, the double entry adjustment to correct it will involve either a debit entry or a credit entry in the suspense account.

- When an error is found that has not caused an imbalance between total debits and total credits, the double entry adjustment to correct it will not involve an entry in the suspense account.

The procedures for correcting errors are as follows:

1 Having found an error, think about what has gone wrong.

   (a) Is there an error or omission in any of the ledger accounts? If not, correcting the error will not affect the ledger or the trial balance.

   (b) If the error means that one or more ledger accounts are incorrect, has it caused an imbalance between total debits and total credits? If it has not caused an imbalance, correcting the error will not affect the suspense account. If it has caused an imbalance, correcting the error will affect the suspense account.

2 If there is an error or omission in any ledger accounts which has not caused an imbalance between total debits and total credits, think about what needs to be done to correct it. The correction will involve a debit entry in one account and a credit entry in the other.

   (a) If there is an omission from the accounts, it can be corrected by entering a record of the transaction in the accounts, with an appropriate debit and credit entry.

(b) If a transaction has been debited to the wrong account, you should credit this account with the value of the transaction, and debit the transaction to the correct account.

(c) If a transaction has been credited to the wrong account, you should debit this account with the value of the transaction, and credit the transaction to the correct account.

3 If there is an error or omission in any ledger accounts that has caused an imbalance between total debits and total credits, think about what needs to be done to correct it.

(a) Which ledger account is incorrect? Is a debit entry or a credit entry needed to correct the balance on this account? What is the amount by which the account balance has to be corrected? Remember that when an error is due to a transaction having been recorded as a debit when it should have been a credit in the account, or as a credit when it should have been a debit, the adjustment to correct the error will be twice the size of the transaction.

(b) Having decided how the ledger accounts should be corrected, with a debit or a credit adjustment, the matching credit or debit should be made to the suspense account.

(c) All the errors have not been properly corrected until the balance on the suspense account is zero.

(d) Following correction of errors and clearance of the suspense account, a new trial balance should be extracted to ensure that the trial balance is in agreement before financial statements are prepared.

4 Before making any corrections in ledger accounts, the details of the correction should be recorded first of all in the journal, and then posted from the journal to the ledger. The journal entries will provide a record of the corrections that have been made, for future reference if required.

Example

A trial balance has been produced, but the total debits and total credits are unequal.

Trial balance as at 30 June

Account	Debit $	Credit $
Equipment	20,700	
Bank	540	
Receivables ledger control	8,820	
Payables ledger control		3,100
Capital		14,700
Sales		56,270
Purchases	29,200	
Expenses	14,500	
Sales returns	760	
	74,520	74,070

An investigation of the accounting records reveals the following errors:

(a) The business had purchased $2,400 of new equipment, paying by cheque. The payment has been correctly entered in the bank but has not been posted to any other ledger account.

(b) Purchases on credit of $800 have been debited to the payables ledger control account.

(c) Sales returns of $760 have been debited to the receivables ledger control account.

(d) Cash sales of $1,250 were posted from the cash book (bank account) to the sales account as $1,520.

1   Open up a suspense account and enter the balance.

2   Show how each of these errors should be corrected.

3   Make the correcting entries in the suspense account.

4   Prepare a corrected trial balance.

Solution

Task 1

Total debits exceed total credits by $450 ($74,520 − $74,070), so we open a suspense account and enter a credit balance of $450.

Suspense

Date	Details	$	Date	Details	$
			30/6	Opening balance	450

Task 2

Error (a)

This error has caused an imbalance between total debits and total credits, because the cash account has been correctly credited with a payment of $2,400, but there has been no matching debit entry in the equipment account.

To correct:

Journal entry

Dr Equipment $2,400

  Cr Suspense $2,400

Correction of error of single entry on cash purchase of equipment

THE TRIAL BALANCE : CHAPTER 14

Error (b)

Credit purchases should be credited to the payables ledger control account, not debited. This error has therefore caused an imbalance between total debits and total credits. To correct the error we need to credit the payables ledger control account with $800 to reverse the incorrect debit and then credit the account with another $800 to enter the transaction correctly.

To correct:

Journal entry

Dr Suspense $1,600

 Cr Payables ledger control account $1,600

Correction of error, purchases debited to C(P)LCA, now credited

Error (c)

Sales returns should be credited to the receivables ledger control account, not debited. This error has therefore caused an imbalance between total debits and total credits. To correct the error we need to credit the receivables ledger control account with $760 to reverse the incorrect debit and then credit the account with another $760 to enter the transaction correctly.

To correct:

Journal entry

Dr Suspense   Dr $1,520

 Cr Receivables ledger control account $1,520

Correction of error, sales returns incorrectly credited to RLCA, now credited

Error (d)

This error has caused an imbalance between total debits and total credits, because the sales account should have been credited with $1,250, not $1,520. The credit entry is therefore $270 too much. To correct this, we have to debit the sales account with $270.

To correct:

Journal entry

Dr Sales $270

 Cr Suspense $270

Transposition error, sales incorrectly credited with $1,520, corrected to $1,250.

FA1: RECORDING FINANCIAL TRANSACTIONS

Task 3

The correcting entries in the suspense account are as follows:

Suspense

Date	Details	$	Date	Details	$
	Payables ledger control	1,600	30/6	Opening balance	450
	Receivables ledger control	1,520		Equipment	2,400
				Sales	270
		3,120			3,120

There is no remaining balance so the error has been corrected.

Task 4

A revised trial balance can now be prepared. Remember that the corrections have adjusted the balances on other ledger accounts. Here, the equipment account, receivables ledger control account, payables ledger control account and sales account all have altered balances.

Check these amended balances in the trial balance below, to make sure that you agree with how they have been calculated.

- A debit entry to an account increases the debit balance or reduces the credit balance.

- A credit entry to an account increases the credit balance or reduces the debit balance.

Corrected trial balance as at 30 June

Account	Debit $	Credit $
Equipment (20,700 + 2,400)	23,100	
Bank	540	
Receivables ledger control (8,820 – 1,520)	7,300	
Payables ledger control (3,100 + 1,600)		4,700
Capital		14,700
Sales (56,270 – 270)		56,000
Purchases	29,200	
Expenses	14,500	
Sales returns	760	
	75,400	75,400

ACTIVITY 6

A trial balance has been prepared for a business as at 31 March, as follows:

Trial balance as at 31 March

Account	Debit $	Credit $
Capital		24,000
Equipment	25,000	
Bank	2,800	
Receivables	14,500	
Payables		9,300
Sales		35,600
Purchases	15,600	
Expenses	4,500	
	62,400	68,900

Investigation into why the trial balance does not balance uncovers the following errors:

Error 1. A payment of $2,000 for new equipment has been omitted from the accounts entirely, including the cash book (bank account).

Error 2. Total for sales on the sales day book was $15,970. This was correctly posted to the receivables account but was posted to the sales account as $19,570.

Error 3. Cash purchases of $700 were credited to the purchases account.

Error 4. Cash expenses of $1,500 were correctly entered in the cash book but were not posted to the expenses account.

Tasks

1. Open up a suspense account and enter the balance.

2. Show how each of these errors should be corrected. Prepare journal entries.

3. Make the correcting entries in the suspense account. Close off the suspense account by correcting the errors.

4. Prepare a corrected trial balance.

For a suggested answer, see the 'Answers' section at the end of the book.

CONCLUSION

This chapter looked at how to prepare an initial trial balance of all the ledger accounts in the ledger. These may need to be balanced manually, and the important reconciliations covered in the previous chapter need to be completed before the initial trial balance is drawn up. The trial balance proves that accounting entries have been completed with arithmetical accuracy. However, there are a number of errors which are not highlighted by the trial balance. These are errors within the accounts which do not lead to a difference between debit column and credit column totals in the trial balance. Any errors need to be investigated and resolved using the journal to record adjustments. If, initially, the trial balance columns do not equate, a temporary suspense account is used. When errors have been resolved the suspense account is closed.

KEY TERMS

Suspense account – Temporary account used to identify the difference between trial balance column totals. Once errors have been identified and corrected, the suspense account is closed.

Trial balance – A memorandum listing of all the nominal *(general)* ledger account balances.

SELF TEST QUESTIONS

		Paragraph
1	What is a trial balance?	1
2	Give two reasons for preparing a trial balance.	1
3	How is a trial balance prepared?	1
4	State two errors highlighted by a trial balance.	2
5	Name and explain three types of error not revealed by a trial balance.	2
6	Explain the purpose and use of a suspense account.	3

THE TRIAL BALANCE : **CHAPTER 14**

EXAM-STYLE QUESTIONS

1   The following are balances in Lim Soon's ledgers at the end of the year:

	$
Sales	21,500
Purchases	8,000
Motor van	11,000
Bank overdraft	4,000
Inventory	9,500
Capital	3,000

What is the total of each column in Lim Soon's trial balance?

A $22,500

B $28,500

C $31,500

D $57,000

2   The following are the year-end balances in the business ledgers:

	$
Fee income	58,900
Expenses	21,200
Receivables	?
Payables	3,300
Capital	20,000
Bank	24,500
Office equipment	7,500

Assuming the trial balance balances, what is the missing figure for receivables?

A $29,000

B $53,200

C $67,700

D $82,200

3   Which of the following errors is identified by a trial balance?

A   A complete reversal of entries

B   Error of principle

C   Error of single entry

D   Transposition error

4   Which of the following errors requires a suspense account to be opened?

   A   Error in addition of individual supplier account balances

   B   Error of commission

   C   Cash sale recorded as $50, not $55 in the sales account and cash book

   D   Cash purchases of $25 credited to the purchases account and credited in the cash book

For suggested answers, see the 'Answers' section at the end of the book.

ANSWERS TO ACTIVITIES AND EXAM-STYLE QUESTIONS

CHAPTER 1

ACTIVITY 1

1   **D**   The client has purchased the service of receiving a haircut.

2   **A**   The client has paid immediately by cash for the service 'sold' by the hairdresser.

ACTIVITY 2

1   **A**   Paying for electricity is for the provision of a service rather than a purchase of goods. C and D relate to income rather than payments.

2   **B**   This is a small payment made for convenience as it prevents the need for a full stationery order. The car repairs (A) is personal expenditure and is not a business payment. Petty cash expenditure is on cash terms so paying for goods supplied on credit cannot be correct. Wages and salaries are for larger amounts than would be paid by petty cash.

3   **C**   These are all payroll items although not all may apply in all countries.

ACTIVITY 3

1. It is important to keep records of receipts and payments in order to correctly account for the costs associated with the project. Also, it will assist in the evaluation of the project in terms of whether the money has been well spent.

2. A system of authorisation and control will help prevent the spending of money that is not within the terms of the project.

3. It is important to make any payments on time to avoid problems with suppliers. Any receipts should also be recorded and paid into the bank quickly to avoid risk of loss. Timely recording enables management to continuously review the up to date position. For example, if expenses are not included in the books of the business until after the project ends it may look as if the project was less expensive than it really was.

ANSWERS TO EXAM-STYLE QUESTIONS

1 **C** The business needs to keep track of the amounts due to credit suppliers. This means that they need to record all purchases on credit when goods are received and all payments to suppliers. A consignment of goods that has been purchased will not necessarily be sold in a single transaction and so the consumption of inventory will not be recorded in the manner described in the question.

2 **B** Because the Internet Service Provider gives its clients the service of access to internet facilities. A, the sale of goods is trading in goods. C, paying the employee is employing them for labour. It is a payroll payment. D is money invested by shareholders.

3 **A** Petty cash is available for small payments and is more convenient than obtaining cash from the bank each time it is needed. The other options are related to the bank account of the business.

4 **C** It is always important to maintain records in case of query. It is also important to ensure that the customer pays for the goods actually received. This is a credit transaction and not a cash transaction and it is not expenditure by the stationery business.

5 **B** The payroll department in an organisation has responsibility for paying salaries in most organisations. In the smallest businesses, it may be the business owner who pays wages and salaries.

CHAPTER 2

ACTIVITY 1

A sales order form is produced by the seller, and confirmed by a signature of the customer.

A purchase order is generated by the buyer and sent to the supplier.

ACTIVITY 2

The sales invoices of a business all have the same format, size and colour and have the name of the business clearly stated at the top. Sales invoices are sequentially numbered. The name of the customer will be different for each sales invoice.

Purchase invoices all look different, because they come from different suppliers. They could be printed on paper of different sizes and colours, they are laid out in different ways and they have different business names at the top. The invoice numbers vary and have little or no relevance to the purchaser.

ANSWERS TO ACTIVITIES AND EXAM-STYLE QUESTIONS

ACTIVITY 3

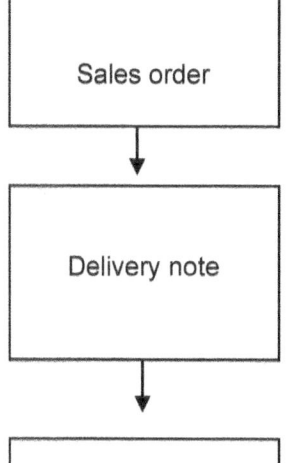

Sales order — In some cases, a business might take down the details of a customer's order on a sales order form. A sales order form is produced by the seller, and confirmed by a signature of the customer.

↓

Delivery note — When goods are delivered to the customer, the customer is normally asked to sign a delivery note, as evidence that the delivery has been made. In the same way, the provider of a service, such as a telephone engineer visiting a customer's premises, might ask the customer to sign a document as evidence that the work has been done.

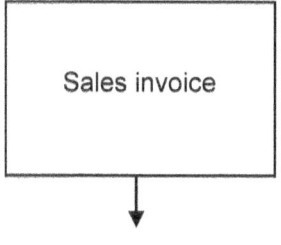

↓

Sales invoice — When the goods have been delivered, or the service provided, the seller sends an invoice to the customer. A sales invoice is a demand for payment, sent out by the business to its customer, giving details of the items sold and the amount owing. The invoice also includes a date, and the customer is then required to pay the invoice within the credit period that has been agreed.

↓

Remittance advice — Some businesses attach a tear-off payment skip to their invoices and ask the customer to return it with their payment. These tear-off payment slips are often called remittance advices. When a remittance advice is received with the payment, it is easier for the business to identify what the payment is for – in other words, it is easier to match the payment with the invoice.

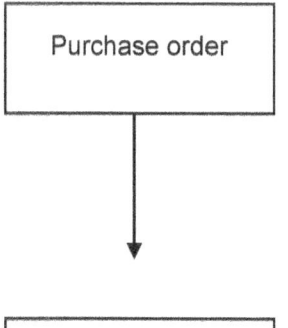

Purchase order — A business places an order to buy goods or a service with a supplier. Whereas a sales order is generated by the seller, a purchase order is generated by the buyer. The purchase order is sent to the supplier.

(Purchase orders are sometimes placed by word of mouth, for example by telephone. However, there has to be a high level of trust between the buyer and seller to rely on the word of mouth, so that the buyer will not later disagree with the supplier about the order details.)

↓

Goods received note — When the goods are delivered, the buyer will receive a delivery note from the supplier. The delivery note might be used to prepare a goods received note. A goods received note sets out the details of the delivery in a standard form for the buyer.

↓

Purchase invoice — The supplier will send an invoice to the buyer. Invoices received by a business from its suppliers are called purchase invoices.

The purchase invoice is checked against a copy of the purchase order and the goods received note, and is authorised by a manager in the buyer's organisation. At the appropriate time, the invoice is paid.

ACTIVITY 4

1 **A** Credit note, which serves to decrease the amount owed. A debit note would be raised by the customer and sent to the supplier to request that the amount owed is reduced because, for example, they have returned goods. The credit note is notification that the amount owing from the customer has been reduced.

2 **D** Statement of account. It includes details of invoices and amounts received. The cheque requisition is an internal document used within the customer's business. The advice note is issued before delivery.

ACTIVITY 5

Sales invoices are numbered sequentially, and it is probably best to file sales documents in invoice number order. As long as the invoice number is known, the documents can be easily retrieved.

Purchase orders are not necessarily numbered sequentially, so it might be appropriate to file documents relating to purchases in date order, probably purchase invoice date order rather than by purchase order due date.

However, you might find that in your own firm, documents are filed differently.

ACTIVITY 6

When a company holds personal data about an individual, the company must comply with the data protection principles. These include not disclosing personal data to others. Therefore, you cannot tell the bank manager any details. If you did, the customer will probably have the right to legal action against you.

ANSWERS TO EXAM-STYLE QUESTIONS

1 **B** As the manufacturer provides rather than asks for information. The quotation is accepted by the customer who is supplied with the goods after making a deposit. This is followed by the invoice from the manufacturer to indicate the amount outstanding.

2 **A** The delivery note lists the goods supplied. It does not include any costs. All of the other documents include prices or amounts paid/received.

3 **B** Follows the order of a purchase from a supplier. The other options are out of sequence.

4 **B** Which reduces the amount owing. The advice note is simply advice of forthcoming delivery.

5 **D** This omission would require an increase in the amount due from the customer, perhaps by raising a new invoice for postage and packaging charges. All other options require a reduction in the amount owed.

ANSWERS TO ACTIVITIES AND EXAM-STYLE QUESTIONS

6   **B**   Which provides a common document to be used within the business rather than dealing with a variety of different purchases invoices.

7   **C**   A quotation does not involve any transfers of funds or of obligations. The bookkeeping records will only be adjusted if the customer subsequently orders the goods that have been quoted.

CHAPTER 3

ACTIVITY 1

1   **A**   Assets and liabilities. The computer equipment is an asset and the overdraft a liability.

2   **A**   Dual aspect, which reflects that a transaction has two sides.

ACTIVITY 2

(a)

Cash

		$			$
1 June	Balance b/d	4,200	3 June	Purchases	1,600
3 June	Sales	3,700	8 June	Telephone expenses	850
10 June	Sales	6,100	15 June	Equipment	2,000
15 June	Sales	4,900	28 June	Purchases	3,700
26 June	Sales	8,800	29 June	Salaries payable	14,200
			30 June	Balance c/d	5,350
		27,700			27,700
1 July	Balance b/d	5,350			

(b)   A credit balance on the bank account would indicate that the business has an overdraft on its account with the bank, because payments out of the account have exceeded receipts into the account. A bank overdraft is a liability, because it represents money owed to the bank. As a liability, it is a credit balance in the account.

ACTIVITY 3

The figures in brackets are used here to indicate the transaction number in the activity. They can be used to match the debit entry for the transaction with the corresponding credit entry.

Capital

	$		$
		Cash at bank (1)	150,000

Property

	$		$
Cash at bank (2)	140,000		

Purchases

	$		$
Cash at bank (3)	5,000		
Cash at bank (5)	8,000		

Sales

	$		$
		Cash at bank (4)	7,000
		Cash at bank (7)	15,000

Sundry expenses

	$		$
Cash at bank (6)	100		

Wages payable

	$		$
Cash at bank (8)	2,000		

Postage costs

	$		$
Cash at bank (9)	100		

ANSWERS TO ACTIVITIES AND EXAM-STYLE QUESTIONS

Cash at bank

	$		$
Capital (1)	150,000	Property (2)	140,000
Sales (4)	7,000	Purchases (3)	5,000
Sales (7)	15,000	Purchases (5)	8,000
		Sundry expenses (6)	100
		Wages payable (8)	2,000
		Postage costs (9)	100
		Closing balance c/f	16,800
	172,000		172,000
Opening balance b/f	16,800		

ACTIVITY 4

Cash at bank account

		$			$
(a)	Capital a/c	5,000	(b)	Purchases a/c	600
(c)	Sales a/c	800	(d)	Purchases a/c	300
			(e)	Rent a/c	500
			(f)	Motor van a/c	2,000

Capital account

		$			$
			(a)	Cash at bank a/c	5,000

Purchases account

		$		$
(b)	Cash at bank a/c	600		
(d)	Cash at bank a/c	300		

Sales account

		$			$
			(c)	Cash at bank a/c	800

Rent account

		$			$
(e)	Cash at bank a/c	500			

Motor van account

		$			$
(f)	Cash at bank a/c	2,000			

ANSWERS TO EXAM-STYLE QUESTIONS

1 **B** Current assets are used on a day-to-day basis and not kept for the long-term. Capital is the name given to what the business owes the owner of the business, and the owner takes drawing from the business.

2 **C** Factory premises are kept for more than a year and are non-current assets. Inventory and receivables are current assets and a bank overdraft is a current liability.

3 **B** The loan is a liability which would be reduced. Cash is a current asset which would also be reduced by this transaction.

4 **D** The asset stationery is increased or debited and the bank balance is decreased and therefore this is represented by a credit to bank.

5 **C** All transactions are recorded initially in a book of prime entry whether they be sales and purchases on credit in the sales and purchase day books, cash transactions which would feature in the cash book or other transactions in the journal. The books of prime entry are not part of the double-entry system.

6 **D** The bank account is a ledger account. All the other options are separate books in which transactions are first recorded.

7 **C** Office equipment should be debited in the correct account initially. It would seem that it has been incorrectly recorded in purchases initially and this adjustment is now needed. The narrative in the journal would confirm that this is indeed what the transaction represents.

8	C	Office premises are not bought for resale but to provide space for the administration staff. It will be kept for more than a year.
9	A	A debit is used to record an expense, the purchase or increase of an asset.
10	C	Vulnerability because it can be subject to vandalism, attacks by viruses and so on.

CHAPTER 4

ACTIVITY 1

1	D	Customers must not be careless in handling their own money. The bank is merely looking after it for them.
2	A	Provides instances when a bank is entitled to return the cheque. If it is six months out of date it may be that the underlying contract has been resolved in another way and the cheque has been forgotten about. An unsigned cheque may indicate carelessness or a decision not to make payment. Banks agree to pay cheques up to the balance of the customer's account or an agreed credit facility but not beyond so if there are insufficient funds on the account it is entitled to return the cheque. A payee who pays in an 'account payee' cheque is following the instructions written on the cheque.
3	B	The endorsement 'account payee' is a restriction on who can pay the cheque into a bank account. In this case, it can only be done by the payee.

ACTIVITY 2

	Cheque no.	Amount $	Signed by:
(a)	11723	5,379.20	any two of the three directors
(b)	11724	1,406.29	T Tims and S Simon, the managers
(c)	11725	293.50	either T Tims or S Simon
(d)	11726	20,501.80	F Freud, the managing director and G Gammage, the finance director

ACTIVITY 3

1	D	A debit card provides an immediate form of payment and from the bank account of the customer rather than from a credit facility which would be typical of a credit card or a separate account as in the case of a charge card. Payment by cheque may have a delay between making payment to the seller and the cheque being presented for payment.
2	A	BACS is a medium for the electronic transfer of funds and is more appropriate for wages and salaries than a standing order or a credit transfer.
3	B	If the limit would be exceeded the customer will not be able to make payment so will need to provide cash, a cheque or some other form of payment. The other options are all valid.

ACTIVITY 4

Cash paid in

Note/coins	Number	Amount $
$50	1	50.00
$20	2	40.00
$10	17	170.00
$5	51	255.00
$2	40	80.00
$1	89	89.00
50c	258	129.00
20c	391	78.20
10c	307	30.70
5c	219	10.95
2c	381	7.62
1c	245	2.45

		$
Silver	10c	30.70
	5c	10.95
		41.65
Bronze	2c	7.62
	1c	2.45
		10.07

Cheques, POs, etc			Brought forward	712	20	Brought forward	972	11
Unifloss Ltd	279	30	North Bank					
A Armad	27	18	vouchers	259	91			
H Knight	55	19						
P Dilip	104	72						
N C Fishes	31	95						
L Lister	82	82						
Z Sgolai	131	04						
Total carried forward	712	20	Total carried forward	972	11			
Date			Account			Carried over $	972	11

ANSWERS TO ACTIVITIES AND EXAM-STYLE QUESTIONS

Bank Giro Credit				
Date:	16 July 20X5	$50	50	00
Code No.	16 39 64	$20	40	00
Bank	Aylesford Bank	$10	170	00
Branch	Brighton	$5	255	00
Account in the name of		$2	80	00
Account No.	1 7 2 3 4 5 5 2	$1	89	00
		50c	129	00
Number of cheques	7	20c	78	20
Fee	Paid in by / Ref:	Silver	41	65
		Bronze	10	07
		Total cash	942	92
	PLEASE DO NOT WRITE BELOW THIS LINE	Cheques POs, etc.	972	11
	C3 0D92157A C77	$	1,915	03

Tutorial note: The actual items that would accompany this paying-in slip to the bank would be:

- the notes and coins suitably packaged and bagged
- the cheques
- the copy card vouchers
- the copy card summary.

When these are actually paid into the bank the person paying them in would sign the paying-in slip.

ANSWERS TO EXAM-STYLE QUESTIONS

1 **B** This facilitates the payments and receipts between customers and suppliers between their different banks.

2 **A** Every bank customer an individual bank account number. Every cheque issued by a bank customer has a different number but each customer's cheques could run the same sequence. The drawee is the bank and branch and each branch has its own identifying sort code.

3 **D** The parent is making the payment direct from their bank account to the child's bank account and has control over it. If the child was claiming the amount it would be a direct debit. BACS is used by companies rather than individuals.

4 **B** The partnership has, in effect, not paid the amount due and is still liable to pay it. No-one else takes over liability without a separate agreement.

5 **C** Consistency causes potential difficulty. For example, if criminals become aware that the same person deals with the banking all the time they could apply pressure on that individual in some way.

CHAPTER 5

ACTIVITY 1

1 **D** Copies are needed to assist in communicating with the customer, as evidence for posting transactions to the accounts and as a record for possible future use.

2 **B** Indicates that this is the price 'at the factory gates'. Additional costs would be added for delivery.

3 **D** This links the credit note with the invoice and, therefore, the transaction in the strongest way. Credit notes are numbered sequentially so that number alone would not assist. The amount and reason for issue of the credit note may or may not be of some assistance depending on the number of returns between customer and supplier.

4 **C** 3 × $77 = $231

$231 − (10% × $231) = $207.90

5 **A** $500 × 0.95 = $475.00 after trade discount deducted

$475.00 × 0.96 = $456 after early settlement deducted as the customer is expected to pay promptly to take up the discount offer.

6 **C** $1,500 × 0.94 = $1,410.00 after trade discount deducted.

$1,410.00 × 0.97 = $1,367.70 after early settlement discount deducted as the customer is expected to pay promptly to take up the discount offer. The initial sale transaction is recorded as follows:

Debit Receivables $1,367.70   Credit Revenue $1.367.70

When the customer does not pay promptly, the full amount of $1,410.00 is due, and when the cash is received, it is accounted for as follows:

Debit Cash $1,410.00   Credit Revenue $42.30

                                        Credit Receivables $1,367.70

7 **B** $750.00 × 94% = $705.00 after trade discount deducted. Note that early settlement discount is not deducted as the customer is not expected to take advantage of the settlement discount offer.

ANSWERS TO ACTIVITIES AND EXAM-STYLE QUESTIONS

ACTIVITY 2

Step 1 Calculate the net amount (the sub total) less the discount.

	$
Net amount	443.00

Very important note: This amount is not shown on the invoice but is used to calculate the sales tax.

Step 2 Calculate the sales tax based on the net amount

Sales tax = $443.00 ×20/100

= $88.60

Remember to round down to the nearest 1c.

Step 3 The invoice will show:

	$
Sub-total	443.00
Sales tax at 20%	88.60
Amount payable	531.60

ACTIVITY 3

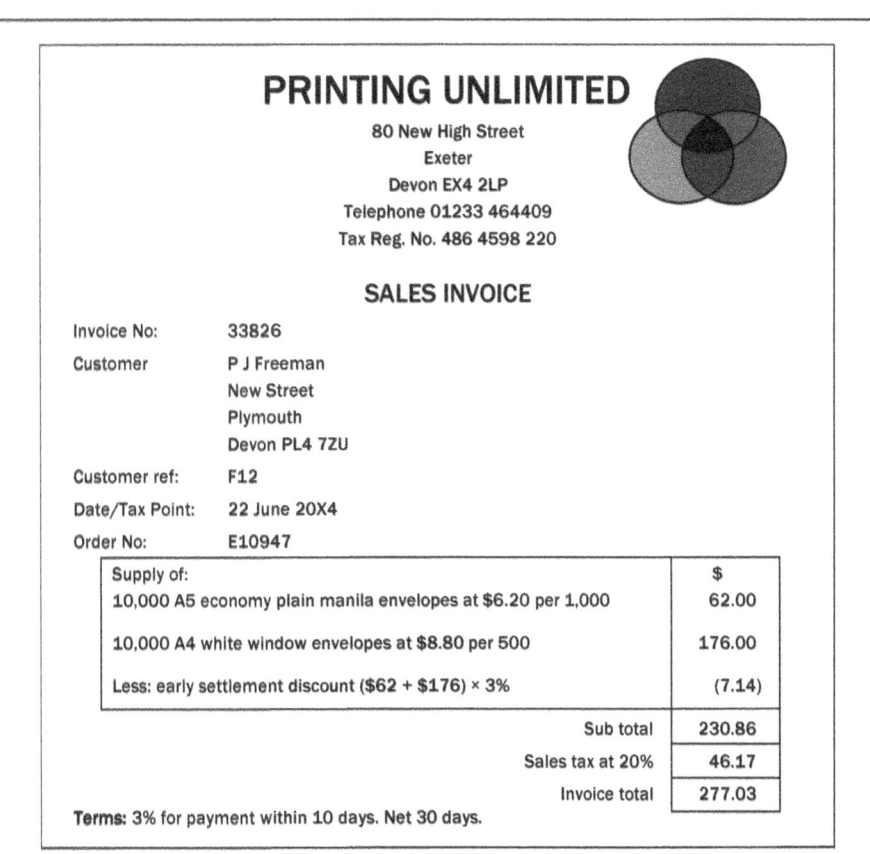

PRINTING UNLIMITED
80 New High Street
Exeter
Devon EX4 2LP
Telephone 01233 464409
Tax Reg. No. 486 4598 220

SALES INVOICE

Invoice No:	33826
Customer	P J Freeman
	New Street
	Plymouth
	Devon PL4 7ZU
Customer ref:	F12
Date/Tax Point:	22 June 20X4
Order No:	E10947

Supply of:	$
10,000 A5 economy plain manila envelopes at $6.20 per 1,000	62.00
10,000 A4 white window envelopes at $8.80 per 500	176.00
Less: early settlement discount ($62 + $176) × 3%	(7.14)
Sub total	230.86
Sales tax at 20%	46.17
Invoice total	277.03

Terms: 3% for payment within 10 days. Net 30 days.

Note that early settlement discount is deducted as the customer is expected to take up the early settlement discount offered.

KAPLAN PUBLISHING

PRINTING UNLIMITED

80 New High Street
Exeter
Devon EX4 2LP
Telephone 01233 464409
Tax Reg. No. 486 4598 220

SALES INVOICE

Invoice No: 33827
Customer   DU Enterprises
                 Finch Estate
                 Dartmouth
                 EX55 99R
Customer ref: D46
Date/Tax Point: 22 June 20X4
Order No: E10948

	$
200 Suspension files at $26.70 per 50	106.80
500 Document wallets (paper) at $4.21 per 50	42.10
400 Document wallets (plastic) at $15.80 per 100	63.20
Total for goods before discount	212.10
Less trade discount at 5%	(10.61)

Sub total	201.49
Sales tax at 20%	40.29
Invoice total	241.78

Terms: Net 30 days

PRINTING UNLIMITED

80 New High Street
Exeter
Devon EX4 2LP
Telephone 01233 464409
Tax Reg. No. 486 4598 220

SALES INVOICE

Invoice No: 33828
Customer   Tab Design
                 22 Fairmount Road
                 Tavistock
                 Devon TA4 8BB
Customer ref: T03
Date/Tax Point: 22 June 20X4
Order No: E10949

Supply of:	$
3 Whiteboard marker sets (10) at $8.30	24.90
1 Personal lockable file at $28.30	28.30
7 Accordian expanding files at $3.40	23.80
3,000 Plain self-seal envelopes at $7.99 per 500	47.94
	124.94
Less: 10% trade discount	(12.49)

Sub total	112.45
Sales tax at 20%	22.49
Invoice total	134.94

Terms: 4% for payment within 10 days
Net 30 days

Note that early settlement discount is not deducted as the customer is not expected to take up the early settlement discount offered.

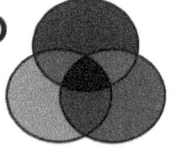

ACTIVITY 4

	$
Credit note sub-total	28.30
Sales tax at 20%	5.66
Credit note total	33.96

ACTIVITY 5

Sales day book

Date	Invoice number	Customer name	Sales ledger ref	Total $	Sales tax $	Net sales $
19 Jan	06254	Louch & Co	184	164.78	27.46	137.32
19 Jan	06255	Framells	221	71.14	11.85	59.29
20 Jan	06256	Position Co	002	537.60	89.60	448.00
21 Jan	06257	Reflon Bros	042	405.92	67.65	338.27
22 Jan	06258	Stonecast	114	175.52	32.58	142.94
23 Jan	06259	Piltdown Co	089	662.16	110.36	551.80

Sales returns day book

Date	Note number	Customer name	Sales returns ledger ref	Total $	Sales tax $	Net sales $
20 Jan	CN337	Piltdown Co	089	106.72	17.78	88.94
22 Jan	CN338	Worton & Co	143	61.52	10.25	51.27

ANSWERS TO EXAM-STYLE QUESTIONS

1 **B** ($2,000 − $400) − (20% ($2,000 − $400)) = $1,280. If half of the net balance is outstanding, that is $640.

2 **A** £364.20 × $\frac{20}{120}$ = $60.70

3 **D** Credit notes sent to customers reflect goods and services initially sold to customers which have been returned or on which a refund has been sought.

4 **C** $4,000 − (25% × $4,000) = $3,000. Sales tax is $3,000 × 20% = $600. The total is $3,600.

5 **B** The entitlement is to 1% discount. Therefore, invoice value and expected cash receipt would be: $520 × 1% = $5.20. $520.00 − $5.20 = $514.80.

6 **C** This indicates that the invoice has been posted.

7 **A** It is important only to charge customers when appropriate to maintain goodwill.

CHAPTER 6

ACTIVITY 1

The double entry record for this would be:

Dr	Forks Ltd (1001)	$24,000
Dr	BL Lorries (1002)	$4,800
Dr	MA Meters (1003)	$2,928
Cr	Sales tax account (2000)	$5,288
Cr	North sales (5000)	$22,440
Cr	South sales (5500)	$4,000

Forks Ltd 1001

Date	Details	Folio	$	Date	Details	Folio	$
9/X6	Sales	(SDB)	24,000				

BL Lorries 1002

Date	Details	Folio	$	Date	Details	Folio	$
9/X6	Sales	(SDB)	4,800				

MA Meters 1003

Date	Details	Folio	$	Date	Details	Folio	$
9/X6	Sales	(SDB)	2,928				

Sales tax 2000

Date	Details	Folio	$	Date	Details	Folio	$
				9/X6	Receivables	SDB	5,288

North sales 5000

Date	Details	Folio	$	Date	Details	Folio	$
				9/X6	Receivables	SDB	22,440

South sales 5500

Date	Details	Folio	$	Date	Details	Folio	$
				9/X6	Receivables	SDB	4,000

Note: How the 'details' column of these ledger accounts refer to the name of the account which contains the other side of the double entry, while the 'folio' column refers to the day book which lists out how the total figure is arrived at. This is best practice when posting accounting entries into ledger accounts.

ACTIVITY 2

Rollit Co 1004

Date	Details	Folio	$	Date	Details	Folio	$
				20/9	Sales returns	(SRDB)	38.61

Marcus Ltd 1005

Date	Details	Folio	$	Date	Details	Folio	$
				20/9	Sales returns	(SRDB)	71.88

Alans Ltd 1006

Date	Details	Folio	$	Date	Details	Folio	$
				20/9	Sales returns	(SRDB)	53.55

Sales tax 2410

Date	Details	Folio	$	Date	Details	Folio	$
20/9	Receivables	(SRDB)	27.33				

Sales returns 3000

Date	Details	Folio	$	Date	Details	Folio	$
20/9	Receivables	(SRDB)	136.71				

ACTIVITY 3

Viking Paper Limited
Viking House, 27 High Road, Sheffield S16 6HD

STATEMENT OF ACCOUNT

T Smith & Co
(Address)
Account 31702

Date	Transaction details	Amount	Balance
		$	$
01/03	Balance, start of March	90.11	90.11
02/03	Invoice – 15021	160.39	250.50
09/03	Invoice – 15100	115.73	366.23
15/03	Payment received	(250.50)	115.73
16/03	Invoice – 15183	66.25	181.98
23/03	Invoice – 15257	228.37	410.35
23/03	Payment received	(115.73)	294.62
25/03	Credit note – CN156	(14.56)	280.06
27/03	Invoice – 15302	14.56	294.62
30/03	Invoice – 15347	93.62	388.24
30/03	Payment received	(66.25)	321.99
	Amount due at statement date		**321.99**

ACTIVITY 4

1   **Arch Ltd – Aged receivables analysis as at 31 August**

Credit customer	Total owing	Outstanding for				
		Less than 30 days	30–60 days	60–90 days	90–180 days	More than 180 days
	$	$	$	$	$	$
P Casey	260.50	50.25	210.25			
H Smith	8.40					8.40
K Wild	74.30			74.30		
T Major	170.50	–	–	–	170.50	–
Total	513.70	50.25	210.25	74.30	170.50	8.40

ANSWERS TO ACTIVITIES AND EXAM-STYLE QUESTIONS

2   **Journal entry**

Entry number	Date	Account name	Folio ref	Debit	Credit
				$	$
	31 Aug	Irrecoverable debts expense		8.40	
		H Smith			8.40

Being the write-off of a bad debt owing from H Smith.

Nominal *(general)* ledger

Irrecoverable debts expense

Date		$	Date		$
31 Aug	H Smith	8.40			

Sales ledger

H Smith

Date		$	Date		$
28 Feb	Balance b/d	8.40	31 Aug	Irrecoverable debt	8.40

3   The amount due from T Major has been outstanding for four months and it is important that the account is reviewed to see what credit control measures have already been taken and what promises have been given, if any, by the customer. There may be a need for further communication to ensure the debt does not become an irrecoverable debt. Consideration could be given to creating an allowance for receivables for all or part of the amount due.

ANSWERS TO EXAM-STYLE QUESTIONS

1   **C**   A credit sale to a customer creates a receivable (a debit). The other part of the transaction is a credit to sales.

2   **A**   Sales and purchases are recorded either in the day books or the cash book. Expenses are generally first recorded in the cash book or petty cash book.

3   **B**   Higher discounts should encourage higher sales and increase the total of receivables.

4   **A**   The supplier sends a copy of the ledger account of the customer regularly to summarise the transactions in the last period, usually a month. The statement includes details of invoices and credit notes for sales and returns.

5   **D**   Careful monitoring of credit sales to receivables enables the supplier to operate an efficient credit control system.

CHAPTER 7

ACTIVITY 1

Calculation errors identified:	$
Item EE27 20,000 × $8.50 per 1,000 =	170.00
Less: 7% trade discount (7% × $170.00)	11.90
	158.10
Item RE20 30,000 × $11.50 per 1,000 =	345.00
Less: 8% trade discount (8% × $345.00)	27.60
	317.40

The net total should be:

$158.10 + $242.25 + $317.40 = $717.75

Sales tax is calculated before taking account of settlement discount offered, i.e.

$717.75 × 20% = $143.55

The corrected invoice is presented below for completeness:

MARCHANT PAPER LTD

74 High Road
Leeds LS14 0NY
Telephone: 0191 328 4813
Tax Reg. No. 947 4565 411

SALES INVOICE

Invoice No: 47914
Customer: J Forrester Wholesale Supplies Ltd
Unit 79b
Oakhampton Industrial Estate
Bristol BS27 4JW
Date/Tax Point: 2 March 20X3
Order No: E9471

Item No.	Description	Quantity	Item value	Discount	Total $
EE27	Envelopes A5	20,000	$8.50 per 1,000	7%	158.10
EE29	Envelopes A4	20,000	$12.75 per 1,000	5%	242.25
RE20	Recycled A4 envelopes	30,000	$11.50 per 1,000	8%	317.40
				Total before taxes	717.75
				Sales tax at 20%	143.55
				Total	861.30

Terms: 5% cash discount for payment within 30 days
Carriage paid
E&OE

ANSWERS TO ACTIVITIES AND EXAM-STYLE QUESTIONS

ACTIVITY 2

Invoice from Lighting Inventory Ltd

Brandish light fittings – 20 ordered and delivered but 27 invoiced. There is a problem to resolve.

Farell light fittings – 14 ordered, delivered and invoiced. This is OK.

Barnstable wall mounts – 20 ordered, 15 delivered but 19 invoiced. There is a problem resolve.

There are two problems with the invoice, both of which must be resolved before it is passed for payment.

Invoice from Summerhill Supplies

PC21 light fittings – 6 ordered, 4 delivered, 4 invoiced. This is OK.

TL15 wall fittings – 11 ordered, delivered and invoiced. This is OK.

MT06 lamp stands – 12 ordered, delivered and invoiced. This is OK.

This invoice can be passed for payment, but whether and when the remaining 2 PC21 light fittings will be delivered should be followed up.

Invoice from Stonewall Stationery

106924 2 Hole Files – 25 ordered, delivered and invoiced but 6 were damaged. There is a problem to sort out.

17240 Lever Arch Files – 40 ordered, delivered and invoiced. This is OK.

The damaged goods situation must be resolved; therefore this invoice cannot be passed for payment.

ACTIVITY 3

1   **A** $400 + [$400 \times 20] = $480.00

2   **B** $[$300 - (20\% \times $300)] = 240. This is the amount net of the trade discount. The cash discount does not appear on the face of the invoice.

3   **C**   Only by checking the basic documentation can you confirm that the transaction is valid.

ACTIVITY 4

Date	Supplier	Supplier account number	Total	Sales tax	Purchases	Motor	Rent	Telephone	Power
			$	$	$	$	$	$	$
03/05	G J Kite	K06	270.12	45.02	225.10				
	BT	BT01	322.09	53.68				268.41	
	Yelson Ltd	Y03	136.68	22.78	113.90				
	Henn Garage	H02	972.00	162.00		810.00			
	Dino & Co	D09	70.17	11.69	58.48				
	T Tortelli	T11	663.21	110.53	552.68				
	Lynn Prtnrs	LP02	960.00	160.00			800.00		
	Franco Bros	FB08	144.00	24.00	120.00				

ANSWERS TO EXAM-STYLE QUESTIONS

1   C   This is evidence of work done which is charged for the service. A written contract does not provide evidence that the work has been done, only that there is an agreement between two parties for work to be done.

2   C   First, determine total price of the goods 20 × $50 = $1,000, and then deduct 10% of that amount for trade discount ($1,000 – 10% = $900). Finally, increase this amount by 20% to arrive at the invoice total ($900 × 120% = $1,080.00.

3   C   Returns are recorded separately from purchases.

4   D $960 \times \dfrac{20}{120} = \$160.00$ input tax on purchases and ($400 × 20%) = $80 output tax on sales. Net input tax paid by the business $160 – $80 = $80 – it is reclaimable.

CHAPTER 8

ACTIVITY 1

Date	Supplier	Supplier account number	Total	Sales Tax	Purchases	Motor expenses	Rent	Telephone
			$	$	$	$	$	$
03/05	G J Kite	3011	270.12	45.02	225.10			
	Brit Telecom	3012	322.09	53.68				268.41
	Yelson Ltd	3013	136.68	22.78	113.90			
	Henn Garage	3014	972.00	162.00		810.00		
	Dino & Co	3015	70.17	11.69	58.48			
	T Tortelli	3016	663.21	110.53	552.68			
	Lynn Prtnrs	3017	960.00	160.00			800.00	
	Franco Bros	3018	144.00	24.00	120.00			
			3,538.27	589.70	1,070.16	810.00	800.00	268.41
	Ledger code			3050	5001	5002	5003	5004

G J Kite — 3011

Date	Details	Folio	$
03/05	Purchases	PDB35	270.12

Brit Telecom — 3012

Date	Details	Folio	$
03/05	Purchases	PDB35	322.09

Yelson Ltd — 3013

Date	Details	Folio	$
03/05	Purchases	PDB35	136.68

Henn Garage — 3014

Date	Details	Folio	$
03/05	Purchases	PDB35	972.00

Dino & Co — 3015

Date	Details	Folio	$
03/05	Purchases	PDB35	70.17

T Tortelli   3016

	Date	Details	Folio	$
	03/05	Purchases	PDB35	663.21

Lynn Prtnrs   3017

	Date	Details	Folio	$
	03/05	Purchases	PDB35	960.00

Franco Bros   3018

	Date	Details	Folio	$
	03/05	Purchases	PDB35	144.00

Sales tax   3050

Date	Details	Folio	$	
03/05	Payables	PDB35	589.70	

Purchases   5001

Date	Details	Folio	$				$
03/05	Payables	PDB35	1,070.16				

Motor expenses   5002

Date	Details	Folio	$				$
03/05	Payables	PDB35	810.00				

Rent   5003

Date	Details	Folio	$				$
03/05	Payables	PDB35	800.00				

Telephone   5004

Date	Details	Folio	$				$
03/05	Payables	PDB35	268.41				

Note: In posting these entries from the purchase day book to the ledger, the total value of debit entries equals the total value of credit entries.

ACTIVITY 2

Cutler Ltd 3050

Date	Details	Folio	$
21/04	Purchase returns	PRDB	56.80

Platter Bros 3051

Date	Details	Folio	$
21/04	Purchase returns	PRDB	27.46

Linden Ltd 3052

Date	Details	Folio	$
21/04	Purchase returns	PRDB	10.74

Sales Tax 3215

				Date	Details	Folio	$
				21/04	Payables	PRDB	15.82

Purchases returns 4406

				Date	Details	Folio	$
				21/04	Payables	PRDB	56.29

Stationery expenses 6322

				Date	Details	Folio	$
				21/04	Payables	PRDB	22.89

ANSWERS TO EXAM-STYLE QUESTIONS

1 **B** Trade payables and trade creditors are the same and both are credit balances. The day book is not part of the double entry.

2 **D** Trade discount appears on invoices, but not in the accounts. As statements are a reflection of ledger accounts, trade discount does not appear on statements.

3 **A** Aged payables' analysis is concerned with payables rather than receivables.

CHAPTER 9

ACTIVITY 1

Date	Reference	Account number	Total	Receivables	Cash sales	Sales tax
1 June			$	$	$	$
	A C Bhatt	1037	265.40	265.40		
	Flowers Limited	1002	319.64	319.64		
	E Murphy	1053	396.61	396.61		
	P Taylor	1025	236.98	236.98		
	F Willis	1129	326.89	326.89		
	Young Fashions	1042	115.79	115.79		
	Perry & Co	1079	163.26	163.26		
	L Connor Ltd	1023	115.37	115.37		
	O McGovern	1152	327.36	327.36		
	J Shepard	1116	372.45	372.45		
	Cole and Porter	1014	325.67	325.67		
	P Smith	1046	235.89	235.89		
	D Smith	1103	117.80	117.80		
	Cash sales		2,480.95	–	2,067.46	413.49
			5,800.06	3,319.11	2,067.46	413.49

ACTIVITY 2

Cash receipts book

Date	Description	Total	Receivable	Cash sales	Sales tax	
		$	$	$	$	
20 April	Cash sales	798.91	–	665.76	133.15	
20 April	D Middleton, a/c 5469	884.84	884.84			
	Totals	1,683.75	884.84	665.76	133.15	

Bank

Date	Details	Folio	$	Date	Details	Folio	$
20 April	Sales	CBR?	798.91				
20 April	D Middleton	CBR?	884.84				

D Middleton – receivable

Date	Details	Folio	$	Date	Details	Folio	$
				20 April	Bank	CBR?	884.84

Sales

Date	Details	Folio	$	Date	Details	Folio	$
				20 April	Bank	CBR?	665.76

Sales tax

Date	Details	Folio	$	Date	Details	Folio	$
				20 April	Bank	CBR?	133.15

ACTIVITY 3

Analysed cash payments book

Date	Cheque number	Payee/ account number	Total	Payables	Sales tax	Wages and salaries	Other	Discount received
			$	$	$	$	$	$
23/7/X4	1003	N Hudson, P4153	4,230	4,230				130
24/7/X4	1004	G Fazaal, P4778	2,350	2,350				
28/7/X4	1005	Purchases	960		160		800	
30/7/X4	1006	Salary	2,500			2,500		

Note: There is no entry for sales tax for payment of the credit invoices, because the sales tax on the invoices has already been accounted for in the purchases day book and ledger.

ACTIVITY 4

Date	Cheque number	Payee/ account number	Total $	Payables $	Sales tax $	Wages and salaries $	Other $	Discount received $
23/7/X4	1003	N Hudson, P4153	4,230	4,230				130
24/7/X4	1004	G Fazaal, P4778	2,350	2,350				
28/7/X4	1005	Purchases	960		160		800	
30/7/X4	1006	Salary	2,500			2,500		
			10,040	6,580	160	2,500	800	130

Arithmetic accuracy check:

	$
Other	800
Wages	2,500
Sales tax	160
Payables	6,580
Total column total	10,040

The **discounts received** column total is a memorandum only column and is not included in this total.

ACTIVITY 5

Date	Narrative	Cheque No	Folio Ref (PL)	Bank $		Purchase Ledger $		Sales Tax $		Non-current Assets $		Telephone & Postage $		Travel Expenses $		Sundry $		Discounts received $	
22/6	Step Wholesale Supplies	114321	PL56	200	00	200	00												
22/6	Northern telephone	114322	–	419	23			69	87			349	36						
22/6	Computer Supplies	114323	PL32	618	26	618	26											32	54
				1,237	49	818	26	69	87			349	36					32	54

ACTIVITY 6

1 **B** Receipts are recorded as debits in the cash book. This transaction is by cheque and so appears in the bank account.

2 **B** $25 less 20% = $20. Sales tax at 20% = $4.00.

ANSWERS TO EXAM-STYLE QUESTIONS

1 **C** As this is a cash transaction, there is no need to refer to Georgio Caterers.

2 **D** Discount is received from settling payables before their normal due date.

3 **C** Sales tax is recorded when the actual transaction takes place.

4 **A** Discount received and sales tax are memorandum columns.

5 **A** The transaction is a cash-based one.

CHAPTER 10

ACTIVITY 1

Net goods amount = $22.80 × (100/120) = $19.00. The sales tax amount is $19.00 × 20% = $3.80.

Petty Cash Voucher		No. 105	
Date 30/5/X7			
For what required		AMOUNT $	¢
Stationery		19	00
Sales tax @ 20%		3	80
Total		22	80
Supporting documentation			
Till receipt			
Signature T. Jones			
Authorised R. Smith			

ACTIVITY 2

The vouchers total $4.67 + $12.90 + $2.99 + $5.06 + $16.25 = $41.87. The amount required to top up petty cash to $100 is therefore $41.87.

There should be $58.13 ($100 – $41.87) in notes and coins left in petty cash before it is topped up. The cash should be totalled to check that this is indeed the amount in the tin.

ACTIVITY 3

Petty cash book – May

Date	Receipts $	Voucher/ Reference No	Details	Total payment $		Sales tax $		Travel expenses $		Office expenses $		Client entertaining $		Stationery $		Sundry $	
1/5	100.00		Bank														
1/5		832	Printing	31	50	5	25							26	25		
1/5		833	Taxi	7	40			7	40								
3/5		834	Tea, coffee	8	23					8	23						
4/5		835	Stationery	12	49	2	08							10	41		
5/5		836	Taxi	11	30	1	88	9	42								
5/5		837	Train fare	6	50			6	50								
8/5	77.42		Bank														
				77	42	9	21	23	32	8	23			36	66		

ACTIVITY 4

Step 1   Draw up a petty cash book.

Step 2   Record the transactions for the month.

Step 3   Total the columns.

Step 4   Calculate the imprest top up.

Step 5   Post the petty cash book totals to the ledger.

Date	Receipts $	Details	Total payment $		Sales tax $		Cleaning $		Repairs $		Sundry $	
1/9	50.00	Balance b/d										
2/9		Coffee	1	89							1	89
4/9		Light switch	12	00	2	00			10	00		
10/9		Taxi	5	00							5	00
15/9		Cleaner	15	00			15	00				
25/9		Repairs	5	88	0	98			4	90		
30/9	39.77	Imprest top up										
			39	77	2	98	15	00	14	90	6	89

Petty cash

Date	Details	Folio	$	Date	Details	Folio	$
1/9	Opening balance b/f		50.00	Sept		PCB	39.77
30/9	Bank	PCB	39.77	30/9	Closing balance c/f		50.00
			89.77				89.77
1/10	Opening balance b/f		50.00				

Bank

Date	Details	Folio	$	Date	Details	Folio	$
				30/9	Petty cash		39.77

Sales tax

Date	Details	Folio	$	Date	Details	Folio	$
30/9	Petty cash	PCB	2.98				

Cleaning

Date	Details	Folio	$	Date	Details	Folio	$
30/9	Petty cash	PCB	15.00				

Repairs

Date	Details	Folio	$	Date	Details	Folio	$
30/9	Petty cash	PCB	14.90				

Sundry office expenses

Date	Details	Folio	$	Date	Details	Folio	$
30/9	Petty cash	PCB	6.89				

ACTIVITY 5

Total cash:	$	Total of petty cash vouchers:	$
4 × $20 notes	80.00	731	15.90
2 × $10 notes	20.00	732	6.73
2 × $5 note	10.00	733	21.90
5 × $1 coins	5.00	734	35.60
3 × 50¢ coins	1.50		
7 × 20¢ coins	1.40		80.13
15 × 10¢ coins	1.50		
6 × 5¢ coins	0.30		$
4 × 2¢ coins	0.08	Cash	119.87
9 × 1¢ coins	0.09	Petty cash vouchers	80.13
	119.87		200.00

ACTIVITY 6

Total cash:	$	Petty cash vouchers:	$
1 × $5 note	5.00	1142	6.50
2 × $1 coins	2.00	1143	7.00
6 × 50p coins	3.00	1144	21.00
5 × 20¢ coins	1.00	1145	1.20
3 × 10¢ coins	0.30	1146	1.66
2 × 5¢ coins	0.10		
24¢ in small denomination coins	0.24		37.36
	11.64		

	$
Cash	11.64
Vouchers	37.36
	49.00

The petty cash box is short by $1. Although this amount may seem insignificant it is important that the reason for the difference is discovered. Possible reasons could be:

(a) $1 too much cash has been paid out on one of the petty cash claims

(b) One of the petty cash vouchers has been made out for $1 too little although the correct amount was paid out in cash

(c) $1 has been lent to an employee by the petty cashier but no voucher or IOU has been filled out, or

(d) $1 has been stolen from the petty cash box.

ANSWERS TO EXAM-STYLE QUESTIONS

1   **D**   The imprest amount equals cash in the petty cash tin plus the vouchers which indicate how much has been spent.

2   **A**   Total of vouchers is $35.22. Net amount is $35.22 \times \dfrac{100}{120} = \$29.35$.

      Sales tax = $29.35 × 20% = $5.87

3   **A**   It is the amount spent, represented by the petty cash vouchers.

CHAPTER 11

ACTIVITY 1

1   **D**   Wages and salaries plus employer's pension contributions.

2   **A**   Wages and salaries less deductions paid by employees.

ACTIVITY 2

1   **D**   Pension details are provided separately.

2   **A**   BACS provides for transfer of funds from the employer's bank account to those of the employees.

ACTIVITY 3

C   (100 × $3) + (9 × $4) = $336

ACTIVITY 4

The bonuses they will receive will be:

Employee B

	$
Scheme 1: Sales exceed $100 million by $2m.	
Bonus 2 × $10	20
Scheme 2: Less than 1,000 boxes	—
Scheme 3: Department's output exceeded 10,000 boxes 10% × $120	12
Total bonus	32

Employee C

	$
Scheme 1: Sales exceed $100 million by $2m.	
Bonus 2 × $10	20
Scheme 2: 30 excess boxes @ $5 for 10 boxes	15
Scheme 3: Department's output exceeded 10,000 boxes 10% × $130	13
Total bonus	48

ACTIVITY 5

Employee K earns commission of:

	$
Total sales	35,000
Less: cancellations $(1,500 + 2,500)	(4,000)
Commissionable sales	31,000
Commissionable payable	
First $20,000 @ 5%	1,000
Next $11,000 @ 7.5%	825
Total commission	1,825

ANSWERS TO ACTIVITIES AND EXAM-STYLE QUESTIONS

ACTIVITY 6

Wages and salaries control account

	$		$
Bank	4,697.04	Wages and salaries expense	
Tax authority	1,963.36	Gross pay	6,172.20
(488.20 + 1,029.96 + 445.20)		Employer's state benefit	488.20
	6,660.40		6,660.40

Wages and salaries expense account

	$		$
Wages and salaries control account:			
Gross wages and salaries	6,172.20		
Employer's state benefit	488.20		

Tax authority account

	$		$
		Wages and salaries control account:	
		Income tax and state benefit	1,963.36

Bank account

	$		$
		Wages and salaries control account:	
		Net wages and salaries	4,697.04

ACTIVITY 7

Wages and salaries control account

	$		$
Bank	569.38	Wages and salaries expense	
Tax authority		Gross pay	801.25
(122.69 + 72.18 + 80.53)	275.40	Employer's state benefit	80.53
Pension payable	67.00	Employer's pension contribution	30.00
(37.00 + 30.00)			
	911.78		911.78

KAPLAN PUBLISHING

Wages and salaries expense account

	$		$
Wages and salaries control account:			
Gross wages and salaries	801.25		
Employer's state benefit	80.53		
Employer's pension contributions	30.00		

Tax authority account

	$		$
		Wages and salaries control account:	
		Income tax and state benefit	275.40

Pension payable account

	$		$
		Wages and salaries control account:	
		Pension contributions	67.00

Bank account

	$		$
		Wages and salaries control account:	569.38
		Net wages and salaries	

If you add up all the debits and credits made in these accounts, you will find that they add up to the same total. This shows that the double entry is complete.

ANSWERS TO EXAM-STYLE QUESTIONS

1   C   Each item completed counts towards pay.

2   D $2,000 + $100 bonus less $350 income tax less $180 contributions.

3   C   (35 × $5) + (8 × $5 × 1.5) = $235.

4   A   Like all other payments they are made from either cash or bank accounts ultimately.

CHAPTER 12

ACTIVITY 1

1 **C** The bank statement offers an external check on the business records of the cash book, bank account. Reconciliation enables the cash book to be updated and any omissions or errors in the business or bank records to be identified.

2 **B** A positive balance is a credit in the bank and debit in the business bank account records. The standing order payment is a credit in the cash book and so reduces the debit balance.

ACTIVITY 2

The cash book would require amendment for these additional receipts. They would be posted to the bank account. The corresponding double entry in the ledger is also shown.

Dr	Bank	$200
Cr	Dividends received	$200
Dr	Bank	$100
Cr	Interest received	$100

ACTIVITY 3

Tasks 1, 2, 3 and 4

The difference between the two opening balances is explained by cheque 144680, which appears on the bank statement and so can be ticked off.

When you match the transactions on the bank statement with those in the cash book, you should find three discrepancies (unticked items) on the bank statement.

- A credit transfer of $150.00 shown as a receipt on the bank statement. This receipt should be investigated and the payer identified. The cash book and the individual customer's account should be amended to reflect this receipt.

- Bank interest of $3.40 should be entered into the cash book as a receipt (debit) and credited to the bank interest received account in the ledger.

- Bank charges of $27.50 should be entered into the cash book as a payment (credit) and also debited to the bank charges account in the ledger.

Statement of Account

Larry Bank
5 High Cross
Edinburgh EH1 2WS

Sheet number 247

Account number 34267115

Date	Details	Payments	Receipts	Balance
20X7				
1 April	Balance b/f			65.60
2 April	BGC: 47619		✓ 110.29	175.89
3 April	SO: Tartan Water	✓ 98.20		77.69
4 April	144684	✓ 171.93		
	144682	✓ 41.28		
	144680	✓ 100.00		235.52 O/D
7 April	144683	✓ 25.67		
	BGC: 47620		✓ 338.97	77.78
8 April	BGC: 47621		✓ 10.15	
	144685	✓ 231.71		143.78 O/D
13 April	144686	✓ 319.06		462.84 O/D
24 April	BGC: 47622		✓ 430.06	
	144687	✓ 86.21		118.99 O/D
25 April	BGC: 47623		150.00	
	BGC: 47624		✓ 341.36	372.37
30 April	Bank interest		3.40	
	Bank charges	27.50		
	Balance c/f			348.27

SO standing order DD direct debit
BGC bank giro credit O/D Overdrawn

ANSWERS TO ACTIVITIES AND EXAM-STYLE QUESTIONS

Cash book – Bank

Date 20X7	Details	Reference/ Cheque number	Receipts Debit	Payments Credit	Balance
April			$	$	$
1	Opening balance			34.40	34.40 Cr
1	Turner Ltd		✓ 110.29		75.89
1	Collins & Co	144682		✓ 41.28	34.61
1	Long Ltd	144683		✓ 25.67	8.94
1	Jimmy Dino	144684		✓ 171.93	162.99 Cr
2	Danton & Co	144685		✓ 231.71	394.70 Cr
3	Water rates	SO		✓ 98.20	492.90 Cr
4	Simone Ltd		✓ 338.97		153.93 Cr
5	M Smith		✓ 10.15		143.78 Cr
10	Grossman	144686		✓ 319.06	462.84 Cr
19	Butch Ltd	144687		✓ 86.21	549.05 Cr
21	Grape & Co		✓ 430.06		118.99 Cr
22	Mothball Ltd		✓ 341.36		222.37
25	Betty Ltd	144688		89.24	133.13
28	South Ltd	144689		303.13	170.00 Cr
29	Oak & Sons	144690		475.00	645.00 Cr
30	ABC & Co		549.19		95.81 Cr
30	P D Plant	144691		61.35	157.16 Cr
30	[Detail to be added]		150.00		7.16 Cr
30	**Interest received**		3.40		**3.76 Cr**
30	**Bank charges**			27.50	**31.26 Cr**

Note: Here there is an overdraft closing balance.

Task 5

Bank reconciliation statement as at 30 April 20X7

	$	$
Balance as per bank statement		348.27
Unpresented cheques:		
144688	89.24	
144689	303.13	
144690	475.00	
144691	61.35	
		(928.72)
Outstanding lodgements		
ABC & Co		549.19
Balance as per cash book		(31.26)

FA1: RECORDING FINANCIAL TRANSACTIONS

ANSWERS TO EXAM-STYLE QUESTIONS

1   **A**   Each item listed appears in the bank statement but not the cash book. The cashbook must therefore be updated.

2   **C** $269.36 – $40.00 + $15.20

3   **A** $12,500 – $2,300 + $2,000

4   **C**   The cheques have been recorded in the cash book but not yet in the bank. When they are presented it will increase the overdraft in the bank.

CHAPTER 13

ACTIVITY 1

Step 1   Find the balances on each of the accounts.

Receivables ledger control account

		$			$
1 Jan	Bal b/d	2,508.24	5 Jan	Bank	936.02
5 Jan	Sales	883.26	5 Jan	Bal c/d	2,455.48
		3,391.50			3,391.50
5 Jan	Bal b/d	2,455.48			

Receivables ledger

Gunn & Co

			$			$
1 Jan	Bal b/d		114.50	5 Jan	Bank	114.50
5 Jan	Sales	SDB	77.40	5 Jan	Bal c/d	77.40
			191.90			191.90
5 Jan	Bal b/d		77.40			

Jane & Sons

			$			$
1 Jan	Bal b/d		624.76	5 Jan	Bank	517.03
5 Jan	Sales	SDB	337.49	5 Jan	Bal c/d	445.22
			962.25			962.25
5 Jan	Bal b/d		445.22			

Lees Ltd

			$			$
1 Jan	Bal b/d		253.91	5 Jan	Bank	150.00
5 Jan	Sales	SDB	271.76	5 Jan	Bal c/d	375.67
			525.67			525.67
5 Jan	Bal b/d		375.67			

Rupert Ltd

			$			$
1 Jan	Bal b/d		95.60	5 Jan	Bank	64.50
5 Jan	Sales	SDB	47.40	5 Jan	Bal c/d	78.50
			143.00			143.00
5 Jan	Bal b/d		78.50			

J T Mumby

			$			$
1 Jan	Bal b/d		1,419.47	5 Jan	Bank	89.99
5 Jan	Sales	SDB	149.21	5 Jan	Bal c/d	1,478.69
			1,568.68			1,568.68
5 Jan	Bal b/d		1,478.69			

FA1: RECORDING FINANCIAL TRANSACTIONS

Step 2 Reconcile the total of the receivables ledger control account to the totals of the individual customers' accounts.

	$
Sales ledger control account balance	2,455.48
Individual customers' balances	
Gunn & Co	77.40
Jane & Sons	445.22
Lees Ltd	375.67
Rupert Ltd	78.50
J T Mumby	1,478.69
	2,455.48

The balance on the receivables ledger control account agrees with the total of the individual customer balances in the receivables ledger. This indicates that, on the face of it, the entries from the sales day book and cash (receipts) book have been correctly recorded in both the control account and in the receivables ledger.

ACTIVITY 2

The closing balances on the payables ledger control account and individual supplier accounts in the payables ledger are also shown below.

Payables ledger control account

Ref		$	Ref		$
PRDB8	Purchase returns/ Sales tax	648.00	PDB50	Purchases Sales tax	5,976.72
CB65	Bank	2,849.32			
CB65	Discounts rec'd	32.00			
	Balance c/d	2,447.40			
		5,976.72			5,976.72
				Balance b/d	2,447.40

Purchases account

Ref		$	Ref	$
PDB50	Sundry purchases	4,980.60		

Sales tax account

Ref		$	Ref		$
PDB50	Sundry purchases	996.12	PRDB8	Sundry purchase returns	108.00

Purchase returns account

Ref		$	Ref		$
			PRDB8	Sundry purchase returns	540.00

Bank account

Ref		$	Ref		$
			CB65	Sundry payables	2,849.32

Discounts received account

Ref		$	Ref		$
			CB65	Sundry payables	32.00

Piper account

Ref		$	Ref		$
PRDB8	Purchase returns Credit note C66	288.00	PDB50	Purchases Inv 780	675.60
CB65	Bank Cheque 257454	387.60			
		675.60			675.60

Romeo account

Ref		$	Ref		$
CB65	Bank Cheque 257455	225.60	PDB50	Purchases Inv 781	741.60
	Balance c/d	741.60	PDB50	Purchases Inv 786	225.60
		967.20			967.20
				Balance b/d	741.60

Sierra account

Ref		$	Ref		$
PRDB8	Purchase returns Credit note C67	360.00	PDB50	Purchases Inv 782	517.20
	Balance c/d	646.80	PDB50	Purchases Inv 789	489.60
		1,006.80			1,006.80
				Balance b/d	646.80

Tango account

Ref		$	Ref		$
CB65	Bank Cheque 257453	2,008.00	PDB50	Purchases Inv 783	1,080.00
CB65	Disc received	32.00	PDB50	Purchases Inv 787	960.00
		2,040.00			2,040.00

Victor account

Ref		$	Ref		$
			PDB50	Purchases Inv 785	428.40
	Balance c/d	1,062.00	PDB50	Purchases Inv 788	633.60
		1,062.00			1,062.00
				Balance b/d	1,062.00

North Electric account

Ref		$	Ref		$
CB65	Bank Cheque 257456	228.12	PDB50	Purchases Inv 784	225.12
				Balance c/d	3.00
		228.12			228.12
	Balance b/d	3.00			

There is a debit balance on this account because the payment to North Electric was $3 more than it should have been. This was probably an error writing the cheque. The detail in the above accounts is more than the necessary double entry narrative to illustrate the 'big picture'.

ANSWERS TO ACTIVITIES AND EXAM-STYLE QUESTIONS

Reconciliation statement

Individual payables ledger account balances	$
Piper	0.00
Romeo	741.60
Sierra	646.80
Tango	0.00
Victor	1,062.00
North Electric (minus value, because debit balance)	(3.00)
Total of individual account balances	2,447.40
Balance on control account	2,447.40

ACTIVITY 3

Step 1 Deal with each of the errors.

- As the Sales Day Book was undercast, the total sales figure needs to be increased by $300. Therefore an extra $300 must be posted to both the receivables ledger control account and sales account in the nominal *(general)* ledger.

- The credit note for $97.50 was wrongly posted from the sales returns day book into the nominal (general) ledger as $79.50. Therefore the receivables ledger control account balance needs to be reduced by a further $18.00.

- There has been a transposition error with one of the receivables ledger balances as it was included in the list of customer account balances. This means that the total of receivables ledger balances is $90 too high.

Step 2 Amend the control account.

Receivables ledger control account

	$		$
30 April Balance b/d	3,765.20	Credit note adjustment	18.00
Sales	300.00	(should be $97.50, not $79.50)	
(Sales day book undercast)			
		Amended balance c/d	4,047.20
	4,065.20		4,065.20
Amended balance b/d	4,047.20		

KAPLAN PUBLISHING 375

FA1: RECORDING FINANCIAL TRANSACTIONS

Step 3 Produce a reconciliation.

Reconciliation of receivables ledger control account and list of receivables ledger balances at 30 April

	$
Original receivables ledger balances total	4,137.20
Less: transposition error ($764.90 – $674.90)	(90.00)
Amended total and control account balance	4,047.20

ACTIVITY 4

Step 1 Deal with each of the errors individually..

- The cash (payments) book total that has not been posted must be entered in the nominal *(general)* ledger by debiting the payables ledger control account and crediting cash/bank account.

- The discounts received must be entered into the nominal *(general)* ledger as follows.

Debit	Payables ledger control account	$853.20
Credit	Discounts received	$853.20

- The omitted balance should simply be added to the list of balances to reconcile with the amended control account total.

Step 2 Amend the control account – when this is done the balance will be $22,208.35.

Payables ledger control account

Date		$	Date		$
31 Mar	Cash	1,400.37	31 Mar	Balance b/d	24,461.92
31 Mar	Discounts received	853.20			
31 Mar	Amended balance c/d	22,208.35			
		24,461.92			24,461.92
			31 Mar	Amended balance b/d	22,208.35

ANSWERS TO ACTIVITIES AND EXAM-STYLE QUESTIONS

Step 3 Produce a reconciliation statement.

Reconciliation of payables control account and list of payables ledger balances at 31 March 20X4

	$
Total of balances originally extracted from payables ledger	21,836.27
Errors:	
Add: Account omitted from the list	372.08
Adjusted total of payable ledger balances and control account balance	22,208.35

ANSWERS TO EXAM-STYLE QUESTIONS

1	A	$3,172 + $30. Discount received is associated with purchases, not sales.
2	A	The items listed all offset the figure for sales made on credit.
3	B	The suppliers' balances represent the outstanding amount owed as does the balance of the payables ledger control account.

CHAPTER 14

ACTIVITY 1

Step 1 Balance each of the ledger accounts.

Bank

Date	Details	$	Date	Details	$
	Capital	10,000		Van	2,400
	Loan	5,000		Purchases	700
	Sales	600		Expenses	200
	A Singh	1,200		K James	400
				Drawings	400
				Balance c/d	12,700
		16,800			16,800
	Balance b/d	12,700			

Capital

Date	Details	$	Date	Details	$
				Bank	10,000

KAPLAN PUBLISHING

Loan

Date	Details	$	Date	Details	$
				Bank	5,000

Van

Date	Details	$	Date	Details	$
	Bank	2,400			

Purchases

Date	Details	$	Date	Details	$
	Bank	700			
	K James	400			
	K James	1,600		Balance c/d	2,700
		2,700			2,700
	Balance b/d	2,700			

K James

Date	Details	$	Date	Details	$
	Bank	400		Purchases	400
	Balance c/d	1,600		Purchases	1,600
		2,000			2,000
				Balance b/d	1,600

Sales

Date	Details	$	Date	Details	$
				Bank	600
				A Singh	1,200
				T Edwards	1,400
	Balance c/d	3,850		A Singh	650
		3,850			3,850
				Balance b/d	3,850

A Singh

Date	Details	$	Date	Details	$
	Sales	1,200		Bank	1,200
	Sales	650		Balance c/d	650
		1,850			1,850
	Balance b/d	650			

T Edwards

Date	Details	$	Date	Details	$
	Sales	1,400			

Expenses

Date	Details	$	Date	Details	$
	Bank	200			

Drawings

Date	Details	$	Date	Details	$
	Bank	400			

Step 2   List each account name and balance then total up the debits and the credits.

Trial balance as at [date]

Account	Debit $	Credit $
Bank	12,700	
Capital		10,000
Loan		5,000
Van	2,400	
Purchases	2,700	
Payable – K James		1,600
Sales		3,850
Receivable – A Singh	650	
Receivable – T Edwards	1,400	
Expenses	200	
Drawings	400	
	20,450	20,450

ACTIVITY 2

Task 1

The account balances should be calculated as follows:

Bank

Date	Details	$	Date	Details	$
	Opening balance b/d	5,700		K Jackson	1,200
	L Hamilton	14,200		Motor car	14,700
	Sales	800		Purchases	300
	T Brown	20,100		K Jackson	12,500
	Loan	3,000		Drawings	5,000
	F Abdul	11,800		Expenses	4,300
				Balance c/d	**17,600**
		55,600			55,600
	Balance b/d	**17,600**			

K Jackson

Date	Details	$	Date	Details	$
	Bank	1,200		Opening balance b/d	15,600
	Bank	12,500		Purchases	8,950
	Closing balance c/d	**23,300**		Purchases	12,450
		37,000			37,000
				Opening balance b/d	**23,300**

ANSWERS TO ACTIVITIES AND EXAM-STYLE QUESTIONS

Task 2

The trial balance has been prepared with a few balances in the wrong column. The correct trial balance should be prepared as follows, with the corrected account balances included.

Trial balance as at [date]

Account	Debit $	Credit $
Motor vehicles	25,800	
Bank	17,600	
L Hamilton – receivable	45,100	
K Jackson – payable		23,300
Capital		47,000
Loans		8,000
Sales		41,100
Purchases	21,400	
Expenses	4,300	
Drawings	5,000	
Petty cash	200	
	119,400	119,400

ACTIVITY 3

1 **B** Purchases is a debit and discounts received (a benefit for paying early) is a credit.

2 **D** Commission received should be a credit, but commission paid is a debit balance so this incorrect posting will be revealed by the trial balance. The two ledger control accounts are overstated by $100 – one is a debt balance and the other is a credit balance. This will not be identified by a trial balance. Omitting the invoice involves omitting both the debit and credit sides of the transaction. Both purchases and inventory are accounts with debit balances so although the wrong accounts are used, the error will not affect the arithmetical agreement between columns.

ACTIVITY 4

1 **C** The transaction has been posted to the incorrect class of account.

2 **A** Income from sales is debited to the bank account.

ACTIVITY 5

Total credits exceed total debits by $28,024 ($295,133 – $267,109). The opening balance in the suspense account should therefore be a **debit** balance of $28,024, to make total debits and total credits equal.

Suspense

Date	Details	$	Date	Details	$
	Opening balance	28,024			

ACTIVITY 6

Task 1

Total credits exceed total debits by $6,500 ($68,900 – $62,400), so we open a suspense account and enter a debit balance of $6,500.

Suspense

Date	Details	$	Date	Details	$
31/3	Opening balance	6,500			

Task 2

Error 1. This transaction has been omitted entirely from the accounts, and should be entered. The double entry required is:

Journal entry

Dr Equipment $2,000

    Cr Bank $2,000

Omitted entry. Cash purchase of equipment.

Error 2. This error has caused an imbalance between total debits and total credits, because the sales account should have been credited with $15,970 but was credited with $19,750, which is $3,600 too much. To correct this error, we need to reduce sales by debiting the sales account with $3,600. The correction is:

Journal entry

Dr Sales $3,600

    Cr Suspense $3,600

Correction of transposition error, sales posted as $19,570, now corrected to $15,970.

Error 3. This error has caused an imbalance between total debits and total credits, because purchases should be debited to the purchases account, not credited. To correct the error, we need to debit the purchases account with $700 to reverse the error, and debit the account with a further $700 to record the purchases properly. The correction is:

Journal entry

Dr Purchases $1,400

    Cr Suspense $1,400

Correction of purchases of $700, incorrectly credited.

Error 4. This error has caused an imbalance between total debits and total credits, because the cash book has been correctly credited with the payment of $1,500, but the expenses account has not been debited. To make the correction:

Journal entry

Dr Expenses $1,500

    Cr Suspense $1,500

Correction of single entry of cash expenses

Task 3

The suspense account entries are as follows. The letters in brackets refer to the errors and their correction.

Suspense

Date	Details	$	Date	Details	$
31/3	Opening balance	6,500		Sales (error 2)	3,600
				Purchases (error 3)	1,400
				Expenses (error 4)	1,500
		6,500			6,500

Task 4

A corrected trial balance can now be prepared. Remember to change the balances on all the ledger accounts for which adjustments have been made.

- A debit entry adds to a debit balance or reduces a credit balance.

- A credit entry adds to a credit balance or reduces a debit balance.

Trial balance as at 31 March

Account	Debit $	Credit $
Capital		24,000
Equipment (+ 2,000, error 1)	27,000	
Bank (– 2,000, error 1)	800	
Receivables	14,500	
Payables		9,300
Sales (– 3,600, error 2)		32,000
Purchases (+ 1,400, error 3)	17,000	
Expenses (+ 1,500, error 4)	6,000	
	65,300	65,300

ANSWERS TO EXAM-STYLE QUESTIONS

1   B   Total of $57,000 divided by two.

2   A   Total payables $82,200 – total receivables $53,200 = $29,000.

3   C   Of the options, this is the one which leads to a difference between debit and credit columns in a trial balance.

4   D   The entry to the purchases account should be debited.

INDEX

A
Account(s), 6, 47
    codes, 64, 124
Accounting
    equation, 42
    system, 6
Advice note, 14
Aged creditors analysis, 188
Aged payables analysis, 188
Asset(s), 40
    account codes, 170

B
BACS
    payments, 86, 201
    receipts, 264
Bank
    charges, 265
    customer relationship, 74
    obligations, 74
    reconciliation(S), 263, 266
    reconciliation statement, 266
    statement, 265
Banking, 73
Batch processing, 174
Batching processing, 194
Block codes, 66
Bonuses, 249
Book-keeping system, 6
Books of prime entry, 60, 125
Bought ledger, 184
Business transactions, 1

C
Capital, 41
    expenditure, 59, 170
Cash, 76
    discount(s), 113, 127, 176
    handling procedures, 96, 100
    payments book, 202
    receipts book, 194
    transaction(s), 2, 15
Cash book, 61, 126, 194, 202
    computerised, 208
    errors, 275
    omissions, 275
Charge cards, 84, 85
Chart of accounts, 66

Cheque(s), 76, 264
    crossed, 77
    dishonoured, 76, 264
    drawer, 77
    endorsed, 78
    payee, 77
    preparation, 80
    requisition, 17
    signatories, 82
Clearing
    banks, 75
    system, 75, 264
Clock cards, 240
Code number, 64
Coding systems, 65
    features, 67
Commission, 252
Computerised accounting, 61
    advantages, 62
    disadvantages, 63
Computerised ledgers, 140, 184
Computerised records, 208
Contract, 159
Control accounts, 282
Correcting errors, 300
Credit card vouchers, 94
Credit cards, 83, 84, 85
Credit facilities, 147
Credit(s), 47
    limit, 18, 148
    note(s), 26, 110, 111, 118, 169
    purchase, 20
    sale, 18, 106
    terms, 18
    transaction, 2
    transaction procedures, 18
    transfer, 79, 80, 264
Creditor, 74
Creditors control account, 289
    reconciliation, 290, 301
Creditors ledger, 184, 185
Current assets, 59
Customer(s), 2
    obligations, 75

D

Data Protection, 30
Data Protection Act 1998, 31
Day book(s), 125, 131
Debit(s), 47
    cards, 84
    note, 27
Debt collection policy, 145
Debtors control account, 282
    reconciliation, 286, 296
Delivery note, 14, 16, 18, 22, 159
Department codes, 254
Direct debit(s), 79, 201, 264
Discount(s), 112, 176
    cash, 113, 127, 176
    settlement, 113, 127, 176
    trade, 112, 176
Dispatch note, 16
Document retention policies, 29
Double entry
    accounting system, 47
    bookkeeping, 48
    bookkeeping system, 47

E

Electronic
    payments, 265
    receipts, 265
Equity, 41
Error
    compensating, 320
    of commission, 318
    of omission, 319
    of original entry, 320
    of principle, 319
    reversal of entries, 320
    transposition, 320
Estimate, 15
Expenditure, 3
Expense(s), 3, 43
    account codes, 170
    claims, 89

F

Faceted codes, 65
Fixed assets, 59
Flexitime, 247

G

General ledger, 47, 197
Goods received note, 22, 159
Goods returned note, 123
Grid box stamp, 124
Gross pay, 234, 239

H

Hierarchical codes, 66

I

Imprest system, 222
Income, 3, 43
Integrated accounting packages, 63
Internet order, 16
Inventory, 43, 44
Invoice, 14, 15
Irrecoverable debts, 149, 151

J

Job cards, 241
Journal, 61, 126
    entry, 300

L

Ledger, 47
    accounts, 6
Liabilities, 40

M

Main ledger, 47, 198
Memorandum accounts, 130, 182
Mnemonic codes, 65

N

Net pay, 234
Nominal ledger, 47, 197

O

Order form, 16
Overdue payments, 145, 149, 150, 151
    letter to customer, 146
Over-the-counter sale, 15
Overtime, 247
    pay, 248

P

Payables ledger, 185
Payables ledger control account, 289
    account reconciliation, 290
    reconciliation, 301
Paying-in slips, 90
Payment(s), 3, 76
    automated, 86
    electronic, 265

Payroll, 4, 234
  accounting, 256
  authorisation, 253
  basic pay, 245
  calculations, 239
  confidential information, 255
  department codes, 254
  gross pay, 239
  job codes, 254
  non-statutory deductions, 235
  other deductions, 235
  security, 255
Payslip, 236, 237
Personal data, 30
Personnel department, 255
Petty cash, 4, 28, 214
  book, 61, 126
  imprest system, 222
  non-imprest system, 222
  reconciliation, 226
  vouchers, 214
Posting, 131
Profit, 45
Purchase(s), 3
  day book, 61, 125, 173, 182
  invoice(s), 22, 160, 170
  order, 16, 18, 20, 158
  requisition, 20, 158
  returns day, 183
  returns day book, 125, 174, 177
  ledger, 184, 185
Purchase ledger control account, 289
  reconciliation, 290, 301

Q

Quotation, 15

R

Receipt(s), 3, 14, 15, 16, 76, 192
  BACS, 265
  banking, 90
  cash sales, 192, 194
  credit sales, 192, 194
  electronic, 265
Receivables ledger, 197
  control account, 282
  control account reconciliation, 286, 296
Reimbursement – expenses, 89
Remittance
  advice, 19, 23
  list, 192
Revenue expenditure, 59
Ruling off accounts, 56

S

Sales, 3
  day book, 61, 125, 126, 136
  invoice(s), 19, 106, 118
  ledger, 198
  ledger account code, 127
  ledger control account reconciliation, 286, 296
  order, 14
  order form, 15, 16
  returns, 26
  returns day book, 125, 128, 139
  tax, 117
Separate entity concept, 41
Sequential codes, 65
Settlement
  discount(s), 113, 127
  terms, 109, 110
Significant digit codes, 65
'Smart' cards, 240
Standing order(s), 79, 201, 264, 265
Statement(s), 185
  of account, 25, 140
  supplier, 186
Statutory deductions, 234
Stores requisition, 20
Supplier(s), 2
  account, 185
  account codes, 170
Suspense account, 321

T

Tax point, 109, 131
Telephone order, 16
Timesheet(s), 159, 240
Trade discounts, 109
Transfer journal, 61, 300
Trial balance, 308
  errors, 315

V

VAT
  invoice, 117
  petty cash, 215
  registration number, 109
  tax point, 117
Verbal order, 15

W

Wages and Salaries
  control account, 257
  payable account, 257
Written order, 16